THE PROCUREMENT AND SUPPLY MANAGER'S DESK REFERENCE

CUSTOM UPDATE EDITION

Fred B. Sollish, C.P.M.
John Semanik, C.P.M.

To order books or for customer service, please call 1(800)-CALL-WILEY (225-5945).

. Printed in the United States of America.

ISBN 978-1-118-34003-5

Printed and bound by Bind-Rite.

10 9 8 7 6 5 4 3 2 1

THE PROCUREMENT AND SUPPLY MANAGER'S DESK REFERENCE

FRED B. SOLLISH, C.P.M.

JOHN SEMANIK, C.P.M.

JOHN WILEY & SONS, INC.

Published by John Wiley & Sons, Inc., Hoboken, New Jersey.
Published simultaneously in Canada.

Wiley Bicentennial Logo: Richard J. Pacifico

For general information on our other products and services please contact our Customer Care Department within the U.S. at 877-762-2974, outside the U.S. at 317-572-3993 or fax 317-572-4002.

Wiley also publishes its books in a variety of electronic formats. Some content that appears in print, however, may not be available in electronic format.

For more information about Wiley products, visit our Web site at http://www.wiley.com.

Library of Congress Cataloging-in-Publication Data:

Sollish, Fred.
   The procurement and supply manager's desk reference / Fred B. Sollish, John Semanik.
      p. cm.
   Includes bibliographical references and index.
   ISBN: 978-0-471-79043-3 (cloth)
   1.   Industrial procurement–Handbooks, manuals, etc. 2.   Purchasing–Handbooks,
manuals, etc. 3.   Materials management–Handbooks, manuals, etc. I. Semanik, John. II. Title.
   HD39.5.S66 2007
   658.7'2—dc22

                                                                                    2006034362

Printed in the United States of America.

10 9 8 7 6 5 4 3 2 1

CONTENTS

APPENDIX G   Request for Quotation Example   **446**

APPENDIX H   Outline of Uniform Commercial Code and
                Article 2   **447**

APPENDIX I   Important U.S. Import/Export Regulations   **452**

APPENDIX J   Sample Terms and Conditions   **453**

APPENDIX K   Links to Related Professional Organizations   **460**

                Bibliography   **465**
                Index   **470**

PREFACE

This book is written for the procurement and supply chain management professional needing reference to the working methods available today for use on the job. It also has in mind the newly appointed executive or the staff member with only a cursory knowledge of the workings of procurement and supply management. It provides, we trust, a complete compendium of the information that is required to effectively carry out the responsibilities incumbent in the procurement and supply management area.

In today's business environment, leading edge business enterprises constantly look for ways to remain competitive. The procurement and supply chain management processes outlined in this book are just some of the ways business supply managers can make key contributions to their company's bottom line. The modern world of outsourcing requires proficient expertise in procurement and supply chain management that has not been seen in any other period during our lifetimes. The future is bound to rely even more on the expertise of effective leverage and the management of supply resources.

Change is inevitable. And our profession is changing now even more rapidly than it has in the past. Therefore, we also hope this book will enable you to assess the value of new concepts and processes in our field, and assist you in keeping up with these changes. To be successful in this field you must stay well ahead of the curve yet ever mindful of the responsibility that rests with your choices. Make the right choices and you *will* succeed.

Fred Sollish, MS, C.P.M.
San Francisco, California

John Semanik, MBA, C.P.M.
San Jose, California

ACKNOWLEDGEMENTS

The authors wish to acknowledge the support received over many years from the members and Board of Directors of ISM Silicon Valley. Without their participation in our training programs, the knowledge put forward here would never have had an opportunity to be assembled. We would also like to thank Mr. James D. Reeds for his drafts of the Project Management and Logistics chapters, and his general support of our efforts throughout the community.

PROCUREMENT AND BEST BUSINESS PRACTICES

LEARNING OBJECTIVES

1.   Describe the role of procurement and the supply management professional in today's business environment.
2.   Define the common elements in the process of submitting orders to the Procurement Department.
3.   List the conditions which are necessary to ensure that competitive bidding will result in the lowest market price for a given purchase.
4.   Build a pie chart for the "total cost of ownership" for a hypothetical product or service.

The role of the procurement and *supply management* professional is rapidly changing. While in the past the procurement professional's area of responsibility was clearly relegated to efficient "processing" of purchase orders, the pace of today's business environment has expanded that role to control of the entire sourcing and acquisition process. To be successful in this rapidly changing, dynamic marketplace requires not only the traditionally disciplined approach to managing critical business relationships but also the ability to quickly understand and employ strategic new methods and technology. Procurement professionals today must have the ability to assess and respond effectively to current market conditions and the foresight to envision the future needs of the organization, setting into motion plans that will respond to the changing dynamics of the continually reinvented organization. Indeed, today's procurement management professional must be a master of change. And to facilitate that dynamic of change, the procurement professional must also be a master of best practices—methods shown to provide outstanding results—to continually ensure that change drives improvement in the *business process* and does not simply replace one poorly functioning system with another poorly functioning system. That is why we begin this Desktop Reference by reviewing the key elements of those processes and best practices that are fundamental to excellence in procurement.

1.1   UNDERSTANDING PROCUREMENT

Effective *procurement* requires the utilization of sound business practices that maximize value to the organization through the acquisition of goods and services. This follows the old adage that the Procurement Department's role is to deliver the right material (or service) in the right amount to the right place at the right time and at the right price. You can do this by employing well-conceived strategies—a plan to enhance competitive bidding, for example—that leverage clearly defined

what is project management?
- *procurement*
- *why contracts and contracting*
- *Project procurement management*

- *we always have to fill out contracts*

1.2 Understanding and Conveying Requirements   **3**

processes to manage the supply base. As a procurement professional, you will be expected to conceive and implement strategies that employ best practices.

Employing best practices in procurement ensures that the organization and ultimately the procurement professional make correct decisions. This means that an organization must develop plans that are in alignment with its goals and best interests. Frequently, these plans evolve from well-defined sourcing strategies developed to help the organization achieve its overall objectives. In turn, sourcing strategies rely on a clear set of tactical procedures to ensure their implementation. At the root of these tactical procedures are the day-to-day methods the organization employs to convey its requirements to the supplier. Many organizations refer to these processes as *standard operating procedures (SOPs)* and maintain them in formalized document libraries.

1.2 UNDERSTANDING AND CONVEYING REQUIREMENTS

Sound business practice requires that you understand and can clearly describe to a prospective supplier the requirement of your purchase. Unless you can describe to a supplier exactly what you need, the procurement process will not be successful. As we will detail below, this description often takes the form of a *specification* for materials or a *statement of work (SOW)* for services. Most commonly, it is the internal user who generates this information—often called a *requirement*—and it is the procurement professional's responsibility to ensure that it is properly conveyed to the supplier in the procurement document (such as the purchase order or contract). In the case where a purchase is particularly complex, the process of stating organizational needs is so critical that you may find a face-to-face meeting with your supplier is in order. That way, you can ensure that there are no misunderstandings or faulty interpretations of the requirement. A well-developed and well-stated requirement describing exactly what it is you expect to receive is the key to successful procurement. For this reason, you must ensure that there are systems in place that accurately convey the needs of your customers to you so that you can formalize them into a contract or purchase order. At the minimum, you should include the following elements in your procurement documents when stating requirements:

(a) MATERIAL OR SERVICE.   This describes what it is you expect to receive from the supplier. This description can be provided in the form of a specification, an SOW, a drawing, a part number, or the nomenclature of an *off-the-shelf* or brand-name part. Along with the stated quantity and the quality of the purchase, this can be the basis for approving payment and must be easy for third parties such as receiving personnel, finance, and auditors to understand the transaction after it is completed.

(b) SPECIFICATION.   A specification contains a technical description of the material being purchased. In its simplest terms, it can be a reference to a supplier's stock number or a brand name. It can also refer to an engineering drawing (or a set of drawings) provided by the user that shows the part or assembly with call-outs for the type of materials required and all necessary dimensions to produce the part. Or, in the case of chemicals and other formulated and processed materials, the specification can be tendered as a recipe or in compositional format.

(c) STATEMENT OF WORK (SOW).   Unlike a specification, the SOW describes the requirements for a service. It may be stated in detailed and prescriptive format, describing not only what needs to be done but the method to be used and how often the service must be done as well. Or it may simply be stated in terms of expected outcomes. Frequently, the SOW also contains a set of metrics describing the level of performance required. These are called **key performance indicators (KPIs)** and are often used to determine the level of performance requiring corrective action or, conversely, when an incentive bonus may be due.

NOTE

> We'll discuss the SOW in greater detail in Chapter 2, "Sourcing Management."

(d) TIME OF PERFORMANCE.   This indicates the date when you expect to receive the product or service you're procuring in the procurement document. The document must clearly state delivery or work completion dates so that the supplier understands precisely what is required.

TIPS AND TECHNIQUES

> Expressions such as "Rush" or "ASAP" are inappropriate because they can be open to a variety of interpretations. It requires only a little more effort to specify an exact date. Consider calling the supplier to determine the earliest possible date and pass that along to your internal customer. If the proposed date is acceptable, it should then be included in your procurement document.

(e) PRICE AND PAYMENT TERMS.   You'll need to include exactly how much your organization has agreed to pay for the specified product or service in the requirement so that you avoid misunderstandings and can clearly determine your organization's financial obligation.

The procurement document should also specify when payment is due. This is usually expressed as a net number of days, such as Net 30 or Net 45. A discount period may be included where the supplier specifies the amount of the discount as well as the number of days the buyer can make payments and still earn the discount. The discount period is often expressed as a formula:

2/10 Net 45

This means that if payment is made within 10 days, a 2 percent discount can be taken, but the total balance is nevertheless due in 45 days. The annualized discount savings for a 2 percent discount for 10 days (in this example) actually equals 73 percent! $(2 \times 365 \div 10)$

(f) SHIPPING DESTINATION, METHOD, AND TERMS.   If you're procuring materials and intend to use a specific carrier to transport the purchased material, you should include this in your requirement as well. You'll need to specify the level of service—overnight air, second-day air, ground, and so on—and indicate if the supplier is to bill your account, pay for it, and then bill your organization or absorb the freight cost outright. In your instructions, include the exact destination of the shipment and the point at which the ownership of the goods, or title, transfers from the seller to the buyer. Fortunately, there are standard expressions for these terms, which we will introduce in Chapter 3 when we outline transportation terms.

1.3 CREATING STRATEGIC PLANS AND TACTICS

Virtually all organizations develop a set of key goals and objectives to guide their operations and, typically, formulate a broad plan to achieve them. This plan is usually referred to as a *strategic plan*. It focuses activities to achieve the organization's overall mission. So, as each segment of the organization pursues individual commitments to achieve its goals, it generates the need for materials and services from the supply community. The Procurement Department, as the interface between internal departments and their suppliers, then formulates its plans based on meeting these needs and commitments in alignment with the various conditions that drive its supply base.

As you look closely at the various missions within the organization based on their functional roles, specific sets of strategies that determine how and when goods or services must be purchased become apparent:

(a) FINANCE.   Strategies involving finance are critical to the organization's success. Cash position relative to the overall economy often determines when new technology can be acquired or when additional product lines can be launched. In a period of declining prices, organizations may want to postpone major purchases for a period of time in the anticipation of lower pricing in the near future. Business organizations with strong cash positions during weak economic times frequently find acquisitions of other companies an attractive way to expand market position. Obviously, these strategies generate procurement requirements that must be dovetailed with overall procurement strategies so that they are properly met with appropriate action when it is needed.

(b) MANUFACTURING AND OPERATIONS.   Manufacturing and operational strategies develop from the need to meet customer demand. The influx of orders and the development of new product lines generate procurement requirements that are critically time phased to meet current market demands. At various phases of the product life cycle, significantly different requirements must be met, so it is imperative that the Procurement Department develop its strategy accordingly. For example, early involvement in the development phase of a new product can be critical since that is when much of the sourcing, supplier qualification, and contracting activity will take place.

Other strategies developed in conjunction with procurement can similarly support operational strategies. These include *just-in-time (JIT)* delivery, *supplier-managed inventory (SMI)*, and a variety of other programs developed to enhance well-run operations and eliminate non-value-added costs.

(c) SALES AND MARKETING. Sales and marketing drive product or service adoption and develop strategies that are critical to the organization's revenue stream. Accurately forecasting anticipated volumes provides critical data to operations and can be the basis for developing supply management strategies. The timing of a new product launch typically generates requirements for additional capital equipment and marketing material, so it is important that strategic plans be coordinated with the Procurement Department to the extent that its involvement will be required.

(d) SUPPLY MANAGEMENT. While procurement strategies are generally created to respond to the needs of other internal organizations, it is important for Procurement to develop plans that anticipate changing conditions in the marketplace as well. As a result, you often find strategies for procurement formulated along commodity lines to allow for specific trends that may be affecting one industry more than another. Changes in supply or demand can trigger decisions to hold procurement plans for later or to accelerate them in the face of temporary opportunity. Prices are rarely in equilibrium, so commodity-specific strategies must be developed to react quickly to changing supply-and-demand conditions.

Typically, supply management strategies focus on key areas of spending and technology, seeking formularies to balance various needs at any given time. Thus, it is important to have well-conceived decision-making strategies for favoring one aspect over another. For example, it must be clear to the individual buyer whether the acquisition of advanced technology overrides the need to reduce costs when the organization's strategy seeks to gain greater market penetration of its products or services based on price competition. You can easily see how the interpretation of this strategy can affect supplier selection, favoring a supplier with superior technology over a supplier with best pricing (or vice versa). Supplier selection, therefore, becomes one of the key elements in the Procurement Department's strategic plan.

The purchaser must understand that strategic planning has a dual aspect: internal strategies that drive procurement decisions in response to market conditions. In the final analysis, the key to effective strategy for procurement is the proper alignment of procurement activity with the strategic plans of its internal customers and conditions in the supply base. This will be manifest in both long-term and short-term commodity plans that relate procurement decisions to individual market conditions and specific internal needs.

1.4 FINDING INNOVATIVE METHODS AND EXPLORING ALTERNATIVES

Closely linked to the development and implementation of procurement strategy is the traditional role of the Purchasing Department as a strategic tool itself. In most organizations, policy requires the implementation of business processes through procurement activities that reduce cost and increase life-cycle value. Later in this chapter, we explore some of these methods in more detail, but for now it would be valuable to point out that the strategies just outlined require specific tactics to ensure favorable results. A program to reduce the purchase prices of a specific set of materials may best be implemented through a competitive bidding process— as a tactical tool—whereas the codevelopment of new technology that requires prodigious engineering costs from a potential supplier might be more easily gained through negotiation.

To be effective, the procurement professional must continually explore new methods and seek out alternatives that will improve existing processes. In turn, these improvements will spawn new strategies. Tactics and strategies thus feed one another in a cycle of *continuous improvement*.

1.5 PROVIDING PROCUREMENT SERVICES

The decision to initiate a particular purchase develops in a variety of ways and from a variety of circumstances. Usually, purchases are initiated by an internal user based on some planned and budgeted need that can be justified by a specific operational purpose. For example, new technology may require the purchase of new manufacturing equipment, or the development of a new product line may require building models or ordering special tools. In a manufacturing environment, raw material needs are generated through a formal planning process based on incoming customer orders and forecasts of anticipated production needs.

For the purchaser, it is important to understand the overall needs and responsibilities of the internal customer so that when requirements are generated, they can be fulfilled in the most expeditious manner possible. Often, this requires the development of close relationships with those staff members responsible for generating the procurement requirements you will be handling. It also involves understanding the supplier community and its marketplace, including an in-depth knowledge of industry standards and methodologies, so that you can best advise your internal users on which supplier may be best able to handle a specific requirement or how to develop a requirements statement using language common to the industry. While you are rarely expected to provide technical expertise, your customers should be able to rely on you and your team to find new suppliers, assist in the selection of an existing supplier for a specific job, and advise them on which supplier provides the best business solution in any given situation.

Your customers will frequently have specific goals that relate to how and where purchases are made, such as the development and use of a new source for advanced technology or the use of a supplier who is willing to undertake the codevelopment of new engineering processes, that will enable your organization to develop a better position in the marketplace for its products or services. Occasionally, the need will arise to use *minority business enterprises (MBEs)* suppliers, which are classified as minority or disadvantaged businesses or sources within a certain geographical region or national boundary, to enhance your organization's own competitive position in these areas. Your sensitivity to such issues and ability to enhance these positions will help build strong relationships within your customer base that will open further opportunities for your involvement in their business processes.

You and your team will also be responsible for evaluating overall supplier performance and developing ways to work with suppliers to improve that performance. If you can do this effectively, you will add measurable value to your internal customers' mission.

1.6 ACCEPTING ORDERS

Requests to purchase or contract for materials and services can be submitted to the Procurement Department in a number of ways. However, regardless of the method of submission, a number of common elements define the process and requirements in most organizations:

1. The procurement staff must have documented evidence that the order has been duly authorized in accordance with prescribed organizational policy prior to processing it for placement.
2. The information outlined in the "Understanding and Conveying Requirements" section that originates with the requestor must be present, along with any required accounting data, user information, and known supplier sources. Briefly summarized, this information includes:
   a. The user's name and department
   b. The cost code, general ledger (GL) account, or budgeting center being charged
   c. A description of the purchase in terms that can be understood by the supplier
   d. The quantity needed (and the amount of acceptable overage or underage, if applicable)
   e. The date required
   f. Estimated cost (if not exactly known)
   g. Suggested suppliers (and justification if a specific *sole source* is required)
   h. The shipping address or location where the materials are to be delivered or where the work is to be performed
3. The order must not have been placed previously without proper procedural due diligence by the Procurement Department. In most organizations, the Procurement Department is the only authorized buying entity, and purchases made outside the authority of the Procurement Department are considered unauthorized and are frequently referred to as *maverick purchases*.

(a) ORDER APPROVAL AND AUTHORITY. Most organizations designate individuals or job positions within each department that are authorized to approve requests for purchases. Often, this authority is hierarchical, requiring increasingly higher approval according to an existing chain of command and depending on the spending amount represented by the request.

In most organizations, all but a few specialized spending requirements must be placed by the Procurement Department. Buying through other channels is usually considered unauthorized spending and is strongly discouraged. There are a number of important considerations for this. First of all, spending outside of the recognized procurement channels cannot benefit from negotiated discounts accorded the larger volumes that are placed within the system, and the volume of these purchases do not count toward further discounts since they are often purchased from noncontractual sources. Second, these purchases do not benefit from the trained due diligence performed by the professional buyer and can result in liability for the organization. Third, they are not likely to be properly captured in the budget and so cannot provide visibility for future requirements and expense allocations. And, finally, they are not likely to be placed with the most qualified supplier because the maverick buyer will have few resources or incentives to perform more than the most perfunctory competitive analysis.

(b) TYPES OF PURCHASE REQUESTS. Purchase requests can be generated in a number of different ways depending on the organization's level of automation and the nature of the purchase. We'll discuss some of the more commonly used processes, such as requisitions, catalog ordering, material requirements planning (MRP), and system-generated orders.

(i) Requisitions. **Requisitions** are documents generated by the user or user department containing the specific information outlined in the preceding paragraphs. They may be submitted as a paper form through standard internal distribution channels or as an electronic document through an existing computerized system, often linked to the organization's primary data system. Sometimes organizations use e-mail to transmit them.

NOTE

Paper requisitions usually contain the written signatures of the approving professionals, whereas electronic requisitions are signed digitally. In general, today's electronic systems automatically route user requests to the approval authority based on an existing work-flow hierarchy. Approval dates and times are maintained in a work-flow database within the system and kept for future audit reference. Appendix A contains a sample material requisition.

(ii) Catalog Ordering. The *electronic catalog* is another automated method for ordering standard products. Here, the user accesses a listing of products available for ordering within the organization's electronic requisitioning system (usually

available as a distinct section on the organization's internal network or *intranet*). By using a search engine that returns data stored by key words or product categories, users can find products they are authorized to purchase and in some systems perform side-by-side comparisons of pricing, features, and functions from competing suppliers in order to make the appropriate selection.

There are numerous ways to generate and store electronic catalog data, depending on the system being used. However, the Procurement Department (or a cross-functional team led by Procurement) generally selects the suppliers in advance; negotiates the prices, terms, and conditions; and processes whatever contractual documents are needed. In many systems, the supplier actually maintains the data, either outside or inside the organization's firewall, depending on security requirements. Changes to the data can be made in real time (that is, immediately) or at periodic intervals and typically require the designated buyer's approval.

Systems are available today that enable users to "punch out" of the existing electronic catalog and access a supplier's Web site catalog (or a group of catalogs) directly, often through the common tools such as a Web browser. Once accessed, items can be captured and moved directly into the user's system and then processed as a normal catalog order. This can be as simple as dragging a desired item into the user's requisitioning system. As convenient as this sounds, there is a catch: The supplier must be prequalified since significant work is required in advance to ensure compatibility between the systems of each party.

NOTE

Appendix C contains a sample electronic catalog page.

(iii) Electronic Data Interchange (EDI).   *Electronic Data Interchange (EDI)* and its European counterpart maintained by the United Nations *(EDIFACT)* is a process widely used by large organizations and government entities and their trading partners. Its primary function is to exchange data related to procurement between computers. EDI, along with other procurement standards and processes such as ebxml, Rosettanet, OASIS, and OAG, is covered in Chapter 7.

(iv) MRP and System-Generated Orders.   *Material Requirements Planning (MRP)* systems, typically used in manufacturing operations, generate automated requisitions or special electronic listings of current and planned requirements that can be transmitted directly to a supplier. Overall requirements are based on a combination of incoming customer orders and forecasts of customer orders and can be time phased so that material reaches the organization at a specific time. (We will review this in more detail in Chapter 10.) Each product (or line of products) has a distinct *bill of materials (BOM)*, a formulary of the parts that constitute the final product, from which detailed requirements can be quantified and summarized by the supplier. These summaries are usually transmitted electronically.

Level	Part Number	Revision	Quantity	Unit of Measure	Description	Supplier
1	15400–10000	A	Parent	Each	Lamp assembly	Make
2	24001–30010	A	1	Each	Lamp switch	Delta
2	25950–40010	B	1	Each	Lamp switch housing	Delta
2	34009–40023	A	2	Each	10–32 hex nut	Omni
2	35010–45098	B	2	Each	10–32 bolt	Omni
3	40900–10000	C	1	Each	Light socket assembly	Delta
4	60902–29845	B	1	Each	40-watt light bulb	Consolidated
4	48098–60090	B	1	Each	Lamp cone assembly	Delta
5	89009–34896	D	1	Each	Swing arm assembly	Marsten
5	34009–40023	A	10	Each	10–32 hex nut	Omni
5	35010–45098	B	10	Each	10–32 bolt	Omni

TABLE 1.1   BILL OF MATERIAL: SWING ARM TASK LAMP ASSEMBLY (LISTING)

Table 1.1 contains an exploded BOM, with a brief summary of the combined requirements by the supplier in typical printed format. As you can see in Table 1.1, in a simple listing, parts are grouped by level. In most production environments, the final product is composed of a number of *subassemblies*, sections that must be assembled or manufactured separately before being built into the product being sold, so the order in which they are assembled is designated by a level number. Thus, Level 5 parts in a subassembly are put together before Level 4 parts, and so on. This table lists the parts by their order of assembly but does not show their relationship to one another. A listing such as this shows the number of common parts being used and their specific order of assembly. Note that Part Number 34009-40023, a hex nut, is listed on both Level 2 and Level 5. Another type of listing would list the BOM by specific part number so that total requirements for the product could be determined.

Table 1.1 shows the format used for a simple listing of a BOM. It shows the assigned part number, the engineering revision number, the quantity (and the unit of measurement), along with their nomenclature and the supplier.

Figure 1.1 shows where the parts from the Table 1.1 BOM are actually used in relation to one another. This view of the lamp assembly BOM shows the relationships between individual parts in their subassemblies and how they roll up into the final product.

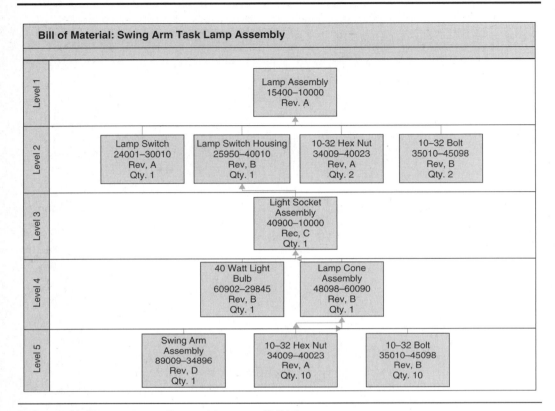

FIGURE 1.1   Diagrammatic Bill of Materials (BOM)

1.7 PLACING ORDERS

There are two key considerations that must be addressed in any system for placing orders with suppliers: first, the format used to convey the order to the supplier, and second, the priority of placement. We'll discuss these issues in this section.

(a) ORDERING FORMATS.   A number of different formats can be used to convey purchase orders (POs) to the supplier, depending on the circumstances and the nature of the requirement. Each method has its own specific requirements, as you can see from the following: POs, blanket POs, contracts, credit cards, and system-generated orders.

(i) Standard Purchase Orders.   The *purchase order* is likely the most commonly used form of procurement document. As a contractual document, the PO contains all of the information outlined in the requirements section, along with the organization's standard *Terms and Conditions* boilerplate. POs are numbered for unique identification and audit control and, in paper format, usually contain a number of copies for distribution to the supplier, the Accounting Department, the original

requestor, and the files. POs can be transmitted by any common form of mail, by fax, or by a variety of other electronic processes, including e-mail.

(ii) Blanket Purchase Orders.   The *blanket purchase order* covers a procurement commitment to a supplier for specific products or services at an agreed-upon price for a set period of time or for a limited quantity or spending amount. Commonly used to eliminate many smaller orders so as to minimize the amount of paperwork processed, the blanket PO, once placed by the Procurement Department, can be used by other groups within the organization to set releases as frequently as needed and when needed.

(iii) Contracts.   A *contract* generally covers services or other complex purchases that require special legal language or terms and conditions beyond the scope of a typical PO. A contract is also used when requirements extend over periods of time longer than a year or when automatic renewal may be required to ensure continuing operations.

Under the broader heading of contracts, we can include a number of similar documents used in the normal course of business, such as the *memorandum of understanding (MOU)* and the *letter of intent (LOI).* Many organizations also have specialized agreements used for particular purposes, such as an *agreement for consignment* or a *master supply agreement.* We discuss these in more detail in Chapter 3.

(iv) Procurement Cards or Credit Cards.   Issued to specific users within the organization whose duties require making frequent small purchases, the *procurement card (P-card)* or credit card can effectively reduce the clutter of low-value requisitions and purchases processed by the Procurement Department that can interfere with efficient supply management. Used mainly for incidental purchases associated with nonproduction or *maintenance, repair, and operations (MRO)* products, P-card purchases can be controlled through limits placed by the organization for specific products or services (or classes of products and services), or even through limits on the industry type or individual supplier.

The card also reduces the time it takes to place an order as well as the cycle time for payment to the supplier, reducing (or eliminating) the typical cost associated with the buying and payment of POs.

Estimates of the transactional cost of the PO and payment process vary widely, often ranging from $50 to $250. According to the National Association of Purchasing Card Professionals (NAPCP, www.napcp.org), purchasing card efficiencies result in savings ranging from 55 to 90 percent of this transactional cost. NAPCP adds that additional savings can accrue through:

- Supply base consolidation.
- Reinforcement of general purchasing best practices.
- A significant source of spend information.

- Streamlining payees in the accounts payable system.
- An opportunity for suppliers to streamline their processes.

Of course, one of the major drawbacks to use of the P-card is the limited amount of control over where purchases are made. When an organization is attempting to consolidate suppliers for better pricing, Procurement has no way to ensure that existing suppliers under contract get used.

(v) System-Generated Orders.   There are a variety of orders that are generated internally through various planning and scheduling systems such as MRP or other automated inventory replenishment systems. For the most part, organizations using these systems issue documentation electronically as agreed upon with the supplier in advance (and usually according to a contract). MRP and system-generated orders have already been described in this chapter.

Externally managed inventory through a formal SMI program is a relative of system-generated orders, insofar as replenishment signals are controlled by the supplier based on a negotiated level of inventory or the receipt of incoming orders.

(b) PLACEMENT PRIORITY.   Electronic catalog and system-generated orders are most commonly transmitted in real time directly to the supplier through some electronic media. A manually generated order, however, requires buyer intervention to accomplish several tasks. With a manually generated order, the buyer must determine proper authorization, establish the source of supply, and review requirements for legality and conformance to applicable regulations such as those related to the *Environmental Protection Agency (EPA)* or the *Occupational Safety and Health Administration (OSHA)*. A manually generated order also requires that the buyer convert the requisition to a PO or contract. Because buyers typically have backlogs of multiple orders to place, some process for determining the order and timing of their placement must be implemented.

(i) First In, First Out (FIFO).   Using the *first in, first out (FIFO)* method, orders received in the buyers' queues are prioritized by order of receipt so that the oldest one becomes the next to be placed. While this sounds fair, it could adversely affect operations if applied too blindly because it ignores the need for urgency in the case of emergencies or critical outages.

(ii) Priority System.   Using a *priority system* method, priorities are established within the department to address specific needs. For example, conditions that could create a work stoppage in a manufacturing operation or situations that may immediately jeopardize employee health require immediate attention, and buyers are required to put other work aside to address them. Separate priority is often assigned to orders with specific lead times so that user needs can be uniformly accommodated. Items with the longest lead time may be placed soonest.

(iii) Cycle Time.   In some organizations, buyers' performance metrics include the *cycle time* for orders based on the date and time received and the date and time placed with the supplier. Buyers are measured on how long it takes, on average, for a particular buyer to place orders during a specific time period. Obviously, if this becomes the key consideration, it will provide incentives to the buyers to place the easy orders first—the ones requiring the least amount of sourcing or negotiation— to reduce the average turnaround time in the queue. However, as a measure of internal service, cycle time and customer satisfaction with the procurement process go hand-in-glove.

1.8 MASTERING PROCUREMENT AND BUSINESS TACTICS

Procurement tactics naturally follow the course established by organizational and departmental strategies. Indeed, you might well consider that tactics are the methods and processes through which we implement effective strategies. A buyer may develop the most appropriate and innovative strategies, but unless they can be effectively executed through practical measures, the organization may never realize their benefits.

In this section, we explore how business and procurement strategies are generally applied.

1.9 BUDGETS AND EXPENSE ALLOCATION

Most organizations implement critical strategies through some form of spending. Typically, this spending comes in the form of the purchase of capital equipment or the hiring of additional staff and their accompanying support materials and services. It may also be reflected in larger spending on new product development or through additional marketing and advertising. All of these are strategic efforts that are usually implemented through Procurement.

A budget can be viewed as an organization's spending plan. Usually, budgets get allocated (or funded) to specific departments or functional areas, cost centers, or projects, and incoming goods and services are charged against those accounts. To a large extent, an approved budget may be the final authorization to proceed with expenditures.

Because adherence to an established budget can mean the difference between profit and loss in a business organization or the continuation of operations in a nonprofit, management takes the budget seriously and pays close attention to individual areas of conformance. This may explain the sensitivity that internal users often manifest when ensuring that expenses are charged to the correct cost code.

The Finance Department usually manages the control and allocation of expenses and is responsible for categorizing and reporting actual expenditures. Finance is also responsible for paying suppliers and requires that specific criteria are met prior to disbursing the organization's funds. For materials, accounting practice typically requires that a duly authorized PO and a Receiving Document, along with the supplier's invoice, are in place prior to payment. (In the case of services, usually a sign-off on the supplier's invoice by the budgeting manager or department head indicating satisfactory completion of the service is required in lieu of a receiving document.) This is commonly referred to as a *three-way match*.

Finance, along with internal and external auditors, verifies that purchases are made in accordance with approved policies and procedures. To the extent that Procurement implements (or at least touches in some significant manner) most of these procedures in its dealing with suppliers, it becomes an instrument of the organization's financial apparatus and undergoes periodic audits to ensure proper conformance. Public companies must meet regulatory audit requirements under the *Sarbanes-Oxley Act of 2002 (SOX)*. SOX determines that corporate management is responsible for establishing and maintaining adequate controls and procedures for financial reporting. Maintenance of procurement policies, procedures, and records is included among these responsibilities.

SOX was passed to ensure that senior corporate executives would be held responsible for any financial misconduct within the organization. It also requires that organizations develop and implement reporting processes that safeguard financial integrity. A summary of the act can be found at www.aicpa.org/info/sarbanes_oxley_summary.htm.

1.10 INTERNAL CONTROL SYSTEMS

An effective internal control system enables you to manage significant risks and monitor the reliability and integrity of financial and operating information. It also ensures that the audit committee acts as a powerful and proactive agent for corporate self-regulation. The Committee of Sponsoring Organizations of the Treadway Commission (COSO, www.coso.org) developed a list of internal control questions to help senior executives and directors gain a better understanding of their organizations' control systems.

The COSO framework is summarized as follows:

In an "effective" internal control system, the following five components work to support the achievement of an entity's mission, strategies and related business objectives.

CONTROL ENVIRONMENT

- Integrity and Ethical Values
- Commitment to Competence
- Board of Directors and Audit Committee
- Management's Philosophy and Operating Style
- Organizational Structure
- Assignment of Authority and Responsibility
- Human Resource Policies and Procedures

RISK ASSESSMENT
- Company-wide Objectives
- Process-Level Objectives
- Risk Identification and Analysis
- Managing Change

CONTROL ACTIVITIES
- Policies and Procedures
- Security (Application and Network)
- Application Change Management
- Business Continuity/Backups
- Outsourcing

INFORMATION AND COMMUNICATION
- Quality of Information
- Effectiveness of Communication

MONITORING
- Ongoing Monitoring
- Separate Evaluations
- Reporting Deficiencies

Source: www.knowledgeleader.com/iafreewebsite.nsf/content/
COSOFrameworkDescription!OpenDocument

1.11 ESTABLISHING PROCUREMENT METHODS

Many systematized processes exist for placing POs, as outlined earlier in this chapter. But far more important than simply determining the appropriate document or format for a particular purchase, the Procurement Department also has responsibility for actually driving the deal. By this we mean that the procurement professional has a fiduciary obligation to ensure that goods and services are acquired in accordance with the best interests of the organization. This can be accomplished either through negotiations (bargaining) or through some form of competitive bidding process.

(a) PROCUREMENT NEGOTIATIONS.   Negotiation, in its simplest form, can be a way of striking a deal through a process of give and take. Buyer and seller each have specific objectives in developing the bargain, and generally accepted best practice indicates that, in a successful negotiation, each party achieves an equal measure of satisfaction. Techniques and methods for accomplishing this, so critical to maintaining a competitive, motivated supply base, will be discussed in Chapter 6.

(b) COMPETITIVE BIDDING.   Another common way to strike a procurement agreement with a supplier is through the competitive bidding process. The typical objective of competitive bidding is to ensure that the buying organization receives the lowest market pricing for a given purchase, with all other terms and conditions remaining equal. To do this, the buyer needs to ensure that a number of conditions are present:

- **Competition.** The marketplace contains a reasonable number of qualified or qualifiable suppliers who are willing to compete. The more suppliers available (within manageable degrees), the greater the competition will be. Competition is the buyer's best friend.
- **Value.** The goods or services have significant enough value to make the bidding process worthwhile.
- **Savings.** The bidding has the potential to result in lower prices.
- **Requirements.** A clear specification or SOW (or industry standard) is available to all bidders.
- **Contract.** The suppliers have the capability and are willing to commit to furnishing the goods or services at the price bid and under.
- **Time.** There is sufficient time to conduct a fair and impartial process.
- **Corrections and clarifications.** A process exists to provide suppliers with answers to questions or corrections to specifications. Answers to questions asked by one supplier must be shared with all others.

TIPS AND TECHNIQUES

Unscrupulous suppliers have developed an onerous repertoire of dirty tricks to circumvent the competitive bidding process. We refer to these as traps.

One competitive bidding trap occurs when a supplier intentionally bids for a new product without including associated tooling or startup costs, thus providing a price that the more forthright competition cannot possibly meet. However, the price offered is usually somewhat above the normal cost associated with production. In this way, the supplier can gradually recover the tooling costs over a period of several years, while at the same time always excluding competitors who will be unable to match the price without absorbing the tooling or startup costs that are continually rising due to inflation. As the years go on, the supplier not only recovers the full cost of the tooling, but can also charge a significantly higher price for the materials as long as it stays just below the next lowest bid (which includes tooling).

Another competitive bidding trap occurs when the supplier realizes that the specifications will require further change after the bid is awarded. This is often the result of improperly designed products or an ill-conceived SOW, although it sometimes results from a simple mistake made by the buyer. The supplier makes the original quote at below cost and reasonable market prices. However, the inevitable changes are then quoted on a substantially higher basis than would ordinarily be justified (since there will be no other bidders at that point) and thus the supplier can recover the difference and earn a handsome premium as well.

NOTE

We'll discuss competitive bidding in more detail in Chapter 2.

(c) REVERSE AUCTION.   A recently popularized automated process known as the **reverse auction (RA)** has enabled the acceleration of bidding from what formerly took months to a mere few days. It is called a "reverse" auction because the roles of buyer and seller are reversed, requiring the **suppliers** to bid down the price, and the **lowest** price, rather than the highest price, wins the bid. (In a more typical auction, the seller puts an item up for sale, multiple buyers bid for the item, and depending on the nature of the auction—English or Dutch—one or more of the highest bidders buy the goods at a price determined by the bidding.)

NOTE

Auction types are described in Appendix D.

The RA provides an electronic marketplace where prequalified suppliers can bid on a buyer's requirements in real time instead of through a delayed process and, most importantly, can determine their position in the overall bidding process so that they can improve their bids as they deem appropriate. An auction serves the additional benefit of ensuring to the buyer that a fair and reasonable price has been established.

1.12 INTERNAL COST-RELATED ANALYSIS TOOLS

A number of tools and methods are used internally to track the performance of the Procurement Department relative to the nature of the organization's *costs*. For the procurement professional to effectively manage this critical area requires a detailed knowledge of the various aspects of costs and how they are calculated.

Costs are categorized and defined both in terms of their method of calculation and their relationship to the organization's balance sheet. Following are some of the more common ways accountants characterize them.

(a) DIRECT COSTS.   *Direct costs* are those expenditures directly incorporated into the product or service being delivered to the end customer. Typically, these costs are generated only when there is a product or service being sold, or when *finished goods* inventory is being built in the anticipation of future demand. This implies that without sales there will be no direct costs.

In most manufacturing operations, it is common to account for and distribute the total company *overhead* (see the next section) as a percentage *burden* added to each separate product or product line. That way, the total cost of producing a specific product can be calculated on a stand-alone basis.

(b) INDIRECT COSTS.   The elements of cost that are associated with the organization's operation but not directly with a specific product or service are classified as *indirect costs*. These costs can be further subdivided into three other categories: fixed, variable, and semivariable.

(i) Fixed Costs.   Costs that remain relatively constant within a specific range of operations, regardless of changes in production or service volumes, are considered *fixed costs*. When calculated on a per-unit-produced basis, they increase and decrease with corresponding variations in volumes. Examples of such expenses include rent, facilities maintenance, nonproduction-related service contracts, and administrative support from information technology providers. They are usually expenses committed by management as part of the general planning process and are often reallocated to various departments based on a standard financial formula.

(ii) Variable Costs.   *Variable costs* are costs that increase or decrease in relation to production or service volumes. When calculated on a per-unit-produced basis they remain relatively constant regardless of the organization's output. Examples of these expenses include consumable materials and spare parts used in manufacturing. Variable costs are typically incurred in relation to some specific reaction to a change in demand and so are accountable at the consuming departmental level.

(iii) Semivariable Costs.   *Semivariable costs* are costs that change in response to changes in operational levels but not necessarily on a uniform basis. They exhibit qualities of both fixed and variable costs, having elements of both. Managerial bonuses might be considered an example.

(c) OVERHEAD.   *Overhead costs*, usually called *general and administrative expenses (G&A)* on the *profit-and-loss statement (P&L)*, are those costs generally connected with the operation of the organization as a whole and cannot be directly connected with any specific operational activity. Examples include equipment depreciation, utilities, interest expense, outside auditing, and legal fees. Commonly, overhead and indirect costs are kept separate.

Overhead expenses are usually allocated back to the various operational units or product lines on a percentage basis. Some organizations use direct labor for the method of calculation, while others may use direct materials or even machine hours.

(d) TOTAL COST OF OWNERSHIP.   The total cost of acquiring and using a material or service is sometimes called the *total cost of ownership (TCO)*. Total cost methods typically track all the additional costs beyond the purchase price that are associated with the life cycle of the materials or services purchased by an organization. This can include the cost of transportation and customs duties—called the *landed price*—to acquire the product; installation and maintenance (in the case of equipment); training; rework; inventory carrying and storage costs; handling; and, finally, disposal at the end of life, as illustrated in Figure 1.2. As you might surmise, the typical life-cycle costs far outweigh the simple purchase

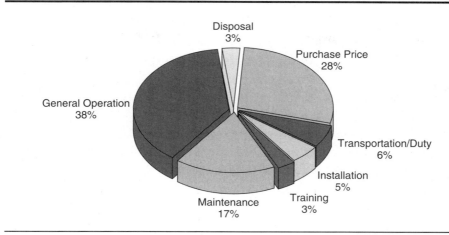

FIGURE 1.2   TOTAL COST OF OWNERSHIP BUILD-UP

price. Figure 1.2 illustrates what a typical breakdown might look like for capital equipment. Notice that the actual purchase price accounts for just over one-fourth of the total life-cycle costs.

The TCO calculation can be used to assess direct and indirect costs as well as benefits related to a particular purchase covering not only the cost of the initial purchase, but all aspects in the further use and maintenance of the equipment. Typically, this includes installation, ongoing maintenance, and training of support personnel and the users of the system, as well as end-of-life disposal.

TCO can be a useful tool when evaluating various alternative solutions to a particular acquisition requirement and when demonstrating or comparing return-on-investment alternatives. Figure 1.2 illustrates how the TCO build-up takes place.

Standard costs are the planned costs to manufacture specific products or to provide a unit of service, as defined for a specific time, either at the present time or for some specific date in the future. In the case of a newly introduced product or service, they are often based on engineering estimates. Standard costs typically determine the selling price of an item or operating budgets and projected cash flow. They are also used as benchmarks and to set goals for cost reduction efforts.

The *purchase price variance (PPV)* is the reported difference between the actual price paid by the organization and the standard cost shown in the Bill of Materials. Despite the fact that it is widely used to measure procurement performance, there are numerous, often indeterminate reasons for a typical PPV, many of which are the result of market conditions or engineering changes that are beyond the control of the procurement professional.

(e) HARD AND SOFT COSTS.   Internal savings are frequently calculated on the basis of reduced labor requirements or the elimination of certain building space.

Unless these savings actually result in the elimination of cost—that is, reduced head count or lower rent—they are considered *soft costs*. Soft costs may or may not result in a benefit to the organization. Savings that are actually reflected in a lower price paid for an item or the elimination of specific head count are considered *hard costs*. In the calculation of a savings contribution to the organization, the procurement professional must consider the relevancy of the cost.

(f) ACCOUNTING SYSTEMS.   Virtually all organizations use an accounting system to maintain their financial records. The system usually incorporates a *chart of accounts* to classify expenditures and determine how to allocate individual purchases. The chart of accounts simply lists the names and numerical designations of the various expense codes such as office supplies, telephone, travel, or equipment. When combined with a specific *cost center* (the designation for a section or department within the organization), the expenses can be clearly categorized and allocated to a specific department or individual.

Budgets are ordinarily created along these lines and so actual expenses can be rolled up into the same categories for comparison. Individual accounts are then rolled up into the P&L statement on the same basis. This method enables organizations to control spending and to evaluate performance to original budgets.

One method for allocation in common use today is *activity-based costing (ABC)*. This method allocates expenses from a company-wide cost center—Utilities, for example—to the actual project or operation using it. Often, these allocations are based on a business unit so that management can determine the profitability of one unit compared to another.

(g) UTILIZING FINANCIAL TOOLS.   When we refer to financial tools, we typically mean the methods used to analyze the financial performance of the organization or a particular activity within the organization. These methods are often expressed in terms of a specific ratio. Here are some common examples you should understand:

(i) Return on Investment (ROI).   *Return on investment (ROI)* describes the effectiveness of a particular investment in terms of how long it takes to recover (or earn back) the initial funding. ROI can be calculated as the *net present value (NPV)* of the revenue created divided by the initial investment:

$$ROI = (Savings \times Time) - (Discount\ Rate \times Time)$$

(ii) Return on Total Assets (ROTA)/Return on Net Assets (RONA).   *Return on total assets (ROTA)* and *return on net assets (RONA)* are measures used to determine how effectively capital is deployed within the organization. Here, net income (that is, revenue less expenses) is divided by the value of assets in operation to determine effectiveness:

$$ROTA = Net\ Income / Total\ Assets$$

(iii) Net Operating Margin (NOM).   *Net operating margin* (NOM) reflects the profitability of the organization by calculating the percentage of its *total operating income* (sales less direct costs) to its overall sales:

$$NOM = Net\ Operating\ Income / Revenue$$

(iv) Current Ratio.   The current ratio is calculated by dividing current assets by current liabilities and is used to measure a company's liquidity. A higher current ratio indicates a greater cushion between current obligations and a company's ability to pay them.

(v) Quick Ratio.   The quick ratio is a measure of a company's financial strength (or weakness); it is also known as the "acid test." It is calculated by taking liquid assets (which are current assets less inventories), divided by current liabilities. By excluding inventory, this key liquidity ratio focuses on the company's more liquid assets and indicates the firm's ability to pay off short-term obligations without relying on sale of inventories. This ratio is also used to determine creditworthiness.

   The procurement professional uses these measures both internally for gauging the organization's performance and externally for assessing the performance of suppliers. Often, these measures help select or qualify suppliers on the basis of their financial strength and leverage.

NOTE

A description of commonly used ratios can be found in Appendix E.

1.13 KEEPING SUPPLIER INFORMATION

One of the key responsibilities of the Procurement Department is the maintenance of ethical and sound business relationships with the organization's suppliers. In this pursuit, it is especially important to note the adage that "perception is everything." In ordinary dealings with suppliers, the procurement professional must always ensure that there is not the least compromise of integrity or even the perception of impropriety. (We cover this topic more in the section covering ethical principles in Chapter 3.)

(a) CONFIDENTIALITY.   Confidentiality is a mutual responsibility and a critical obligation, both legal and ethical, that buyer and supplier owe one another. Maintaining confidentiality becomes especially important when the information one has received or is divulging can affect the organization's competitive position and result in financial loss. Typically, organizations sign a contractual document—called a *nondisclosure agreement (NDA)*—legally binding them to maintaining one another's intellectual property.

The procurement professional must ensure that no one in the organization discloses information about one supplier to another, such as bids, pricing, manufacturing methods, designs, plans, formulas, nonpublic measures of performance, or any other form of intellectual property. Both Procurement and Legal have an obligation to instruct and inform all personnel in the organization who come into contact with suppliers or the general public about these obligations and to conscientiously protect supplier information from compromise through special care and diligence.

(b) BUSINESS REPORTS.   The Procurement Department maintains a variety of reports covering supplier performance, such as cost profiles, quality records, and on-time delivery performance. It is important that the department uses this information properly and confidentially. Internal users with access to this information should be similarly informed.

(c) SAMPLES AND RETURNS.   Samples should be accepted from suppliers only when there is a specific need for evaluation, and following evaluation, they should be returned. If there is no immediate need or internal request for the particular sample, it should not be accepted in the first place. The organization should pay for any samples that it keeps.

It is also good business practice and the Procurement Department's responsibility to ensure that rejected or excess goods for which credits have been issued by the supplier are properly returned. Many times credits are taken by Procurement and sent to Accounts Payable before the supplier has authorized returns. This practice simply messes up the books of the respective organizations and creates a great deal of ill will. For continued good business relations, it is important that organizations keep their financial accounts in proper order.

1.14 SUMMARY

In procurement, best practices generally cover the creation of strategic and tactical plans for the acquisition of goods and services that align with the organization's mission, as well as implementing those plans in a manner that provides added value. Best practices in procurement also cover the processing of user requests to purchase goods and services.

In order to meet their responsibilities effectively, the procurement professional must be an enabler capable of matching the needs of internal customers with what is available to purchase in the marketplace. The Procurement Department requires effective and efficient operation through its interface with suppliers, to ensure that critical requirements are conveyed properly and in a timely manner.

The procurement professional should also demonstrate the ability to use the tools available to obtain the best value for organizations in dealings with suppliers. These tools include methods for financial analysis and determining total cost of ownership, as well as processes to develop competition that results in greater purchased value to the organization. The procurement professional also needs to have a strong understanding of accounting methods and techniques so as to add further value to internal customers and to make sound judgments in the application of fiduciary responsibilities.

In addition, the procurement professional must ensure that all personnel in the organization honor the dictates of good ethical practices and that information furnished by suppliers is maintained in confidence.

KEY TERMS

Supply management
Business process
Procurement
Standard operating process (SOP)
Statement of work requirement (SOW)
Off-the-shelf
Key performance indicators (KPI)
Strategic plan
Just-in-time (JIT)
Supplier-managed-inventory (SMI)
Continuous improvement
Minority business enterprises (MBEs)
Maverick purchases
Requisitions
Electronic catalog
Intranet
Electronic Data Interchange (EDI)
Bill of materials (BOM)
Subassemblies
Memorandum of understanding
    (MOU)
Letter of intent (LOI)
Procurement card (P-card)
Maintenance, repair and operations
    (MRO)
Environmental Protection Agency
    (EPA)
Occupational Health & Safety
    Administration (OSHA)

First in, first out (FIFO)
Priority system
Cycle time
Three-way match
Sarbanes-Oxley Act of 2002 (SOX)
Reverse auction (RA)
Direct costs
Indirect costs
Fixed and variable costs
Semivariable costs
Overhead costs
General & administrative expenses
    (G&A)
Profit-and-Loss statement (P&L)
Total cost of ownership (TCO)
Purchase price variance (PPV)
Soft costs
Hard costs
Cost center
Activity-based costing (ABC)
Return-on-investment (ROI)
Return on total assets (ROTA)
Return on net assets (RONA)
Net operating margin (NOM)
Net present value (NPV)
Current ratio
Quick Ratio
Nondisclosure agreement
    (NDA)

SOURCING MANAGEMENT

LEARNING OBJECTIVES

1. Describe the elements of the requirements needed for effective procurement.
2. Create a hypothetical specification document, emphasizing technical, functional and performance specifications.
3. Describe the differences between the various categories of supplier listings: *approved supplier list; certified suppliers; qualified suppliers list; preferred suppliers.*
4. List the five historical legislative acts which determined the current US "anti-trust" provisions.
5. Name the common sections in a Statement of Work (SOW).

In this chapter, we introduce you to some of the most valuable tasks performed by the Procurement Department: developing bids and proposals, evaluating suppliers' responses, and selecting the supplier that provides the greatest value to your organization. The procurement professional is expected to ensure that this process results in fair and consistent supplier selection that is fully aligned with organizational objectives.

    To manage this effectively, you will also need to know how specifications, statements of work, and performance criteria are commonly developed, along with your role in properly conveying them to the supplier. Since you will also have responsibility for ensuring compliance to laws and regulations throughout this process, you will be required to have a working knowledge of how they affect the selection and contracting process. Additionally, we will review the various supplier classifications and their general requirements and how this information is maintained for internal use.

2.1 ESTABLISHING REQUIREMENTS

As noted in Chapter 1, a description of the organization's detailed needs for any purchase consists of a number of elements, including terms and conditions, lead time, and technical requirements. In order for the organization's procurement team to select the most appropriate source for any specific purchase or for any potential supplier to submit an accurate bid or proposal, these elements must be available for documentation. In this section, we explore how to generate and document requirements, convey them to suppliers, and use them in your supplier selection process.

2.2 CREATING AND ORGANIZING REQUIREMENTS

In most organizations, new requirements are developed by the **using department** (the department that will actually receive the goods or services) in conjunction with other interested parties. Similarly, existing specifications are periodically reviewed by the using group, and any changes generated are conveyed to the Procurement Department prior to any subsequent purchases. Specifications and subsequent changes for standard products and services are usually documented and filed by the **Document Control** section responsible for physically maintaining the organization's specifications. However, when there are no formal processes within the organization for developing specifications, it is the responsibility of the **requisitioner**—the individual initiating the request—to supply sufficient information to the Procurement Department so that the correct product or service gets procured.

(a) ROLES AND RESPONSIBILITIES.   The responsibility for creating and maintaining specifications generally resides with the user or the using department. For direct materials used in a manufacturing organization, that usually means an engineering group or research and development group closely associated with making the product being shipped to the organization's final customer. In other cases, the department responsible for the budget is also responsible for the specifications. When a statement of work (SOW) for a service used by the entire organization is being purchased (e.g., travel, consulting services, or telecommunications), most commonly an administrative department, such as Finance, Human Resources, or Information Technology, will take responsibility.

(b) PROJECT TEAM.   The development of complex requirements often takes on a project-oriented nature, and a cross-functional team is chartered with the responsibility to define and document the organization's specific need in that particular situation. This team is composed of technical experts, users, and, of course, the Procurement Department. On occasion, outside information sources may be required, and consultants may be engaged to assist the project team. Frequently, it is this team that actually makes the final supplier selection.

(c) CUSTOMER INPUTS.   In situations where the components or service being performed are critical to the operations of the organization, customers may play an important role in the development of specifications. It is not uncommon in high-tech industries, for example, where speed of product development and time to market introduction can be critical for success, to have representatives of the organization's final customer participating in the development of specifications. Occasionally, customers will actually determine the specifications themselves if they are felt to be critical.

(d) OTHER INPUTS.   Besides the internal user or engineer, the most common additional information detailing the specification or SOW comes from existing or potential supplier(s) of the item to be purchased. Based on the degree of collaboration, it is common to find suppliers participating actively in the development of specifications. While this may sound like a conflict of interest, the supplier is usually in the best position to help formulate requirements, especially where there is no internal core competency in a particular commodity area. This collaboration often leads to a more complete understanding of the user's requirement on the part of the supplier and substantially lowers the risk of the user receiving inadequate product or service quality.

It is also not uncommon, as noted previously, for organizations to engage third-party consultants who are experts in a particular industry or commodity to assist with the development of requirements and the writing of the specification due to their unique domain knowledge, especially when there is insufficient expertise within the organization and where cost or overall risk is substantially high.

In addition, there are many third-party organizations that provide industry standards for products or services in common use. Such standards exist for a large number of commodities—fasteners, lubricants, and grades of ore, to name a few—and can be used to speed the development process or align specifications with commonly employed definitions. Standards are often in place for an entire industry, making the specification process fairly straightforward.

2.3 DEVELOPING SPECIFICATIONS AND FORMATS

Detailed requirements are typically described by a written specification (in the case of materials) or a statement of work (for services). These describe the precise parameters or standards that a supplier must meet in order for the purchase to be accepted by the buyer. Having a "tight" specification, that is, one that clearly and completely defines the organization's intended purchase, helps prevent problems later on. First of all, it creates the need to fully develop and define the purchase requirements internally so that they can be clearly documented by the Procurement

Department on orders or contracts. Second, it enables the supplier to have a full understanding of what your organization expects to receive so that the supplier can properly meet your requirements. In both cases, documentation is important in avoiding future conflict because a clear, unambiguous description is difficult to dispute after the receipt of the goods or services.

Specific formats vary from organization to organization and can range from a variety of written descriptions to detailed drawings or even actual samples. The key is to convey your requirements so that they cannot be misunderstood by the supplier. The old carpenter's adage, "Measure twice, cut once," also applies to the value of well-developed specifications. It is far less costly to develop a clear description of your requirements in the first place than to have to go through the return and repair process because they were not specific enough or presented clearly.

(a) SPECIFICATIONS.   There are two elements to consider when developing a specification. First, there is the actual description of the product or material in terms of its physical characteristics, what it looks like, or how it functions. Second, there is an element of quantification that evaluates the level of performance. Certain measures of quality, such as the frequency or **mean time between failure (MTBF)** for equipment and the allowable number of rejected **parts per million (PPM)** for purchased parts, are typically systematized into an inspection process for determining acceptance at delivery and subsequent payment.

Specifications are typically created using one of three approaches, depending on the organization's objectives:

(i) Technical Specifications.   **Technical specifications** describe the physical characteristics of the material or product being purchased, such as dimensions, grade of materials, physical properties, color, finish, and any other data that defines an acceptable product. Written technical specifications may be supplemented by drawings or samples. Table 2.1 demonstrates an example of a technical specification.

(ii) Functional Specifications.   The function of a product can be defined in terms of its actual role and what it is intended to do. **Functional specifications** define the job to be done rather than the method by which it is to be accomplished. Typically, functional specifications do not limit the supplier to providing a specific solution, as in the case of a technical specification, thus enabling the supplier to create the best possible solution. For example, a functional specification may require "the safe and efficient movement of passengers from Zone A to Zone B" at an airport.

Functional specifications are typically used to solicit suppliers' proposals for further evaluation by the procurement organization when a specific solution is not known. They are often combined with **performance specifications**, outlined next, to create a more detailed requirement.

ITEM	SPECIFICATION
Display area (mm)	170.9(H) x 128.2 (V) (4.5-inch diagonal)
Number of dots	640 × 3 (H) x 480 (V)
Pixel pitch (mm)	0.267 (H) x 0.267 (V)
Color pixel arrangement	RGB vertical stripe
Display mode	Normally white
Number of colors	262,144
Contrast ratio	450
Optimum viewing angle (contrast ratio)	6 o'clock
Brightness (cd/m^2)	450
Module size (mm)	199.5 (W) x 149.0 (H) x 11.5 (D)
Module mass (g)	360 (Typ)
Backlight unit	CCFL, 2 tubes, edge-light, replaceable
Surface treatment	Antiglare and hard-coating 3H

TABLE 2.1   SAMPLE TECHNICAL SPECIFICATIONS

(iii) Performance Specifications.   While technical specifications define the product's physical characteristics, and functional specifications describe what role the product plays, neither describes just how well the product must perform. This is the purpose of a performance specification, which describes the parameters of actual performance the item or service must meet. With a performance specification, you are primarily interested in results rather than in method.

In the example just given of passenger movement at an airport, a performance specification might call out just how many passengers must be moved in any particular time period, or it may state the number of hours the device must be operational in any specific period.

Performance specifications can be described by a virtually unlimited choice of criteria. However, they must be capable of some clearly stated measurement. Some of the more common parameters include:

- **Speed.** Product must travel at 20 miles per hour.
- **Output.** Product must produce 400 acceptable parts per hour.
- **Quality.** Product must be capable of 2,000 operational hours before failure.
- **Efficacy.** Product must reduce rejected parts by 20 percent.

TIPS AND TECHNIQUES

Be sure to keep the specification types clear in your mind. There are subtle differences that may be confusing. For example, performance characteristics *can* be included in a technical specification, and technical data *can* be included in a performance spec. The purpose of the specification must be made clear.

(iv) Standards.   Using preestablished standards is another way of describing specifications or supplementing the description when that is appropriate. Literally dozens of organizations provide published standards available for general use, including the **American National Standards Institute (ANSI)**, the **National Institute of Standards and Technology (NIST)**, and the Society of Automotive Engineers (SAE), to name just a few. A detailed listing of Military and Industry Standards and Specifications has been assembled by the Los Angeles Public Library and can be found on the Internet at www.lapl.org/resources/guides/standards. html.

(v) Benchmarking.   In its simplest form, a **benchmark** provides a measurement as a guide for establishing a specific requirement. However, benchmarking can also be a detailed process for determining how one organization is performing in relation to other organizations. For example, your organization's cost for packaging a particular product is 12 percent of its total cost. Are you overspecifying your packaging requirements? Obtaining data or finding a benchmark from other organizations in your business sector might indicate an opportunity to save cost by reducing specifications to less expensive alternatives. The organized use of methodologies that focus on the function of a material, process, or service in providing value to the customer is also called value analysis.

(vi) Quality Control.   Most people readily agree that quality is less costly when controlled within the initial process itself rather than through some form of inspection at a stage following manufacture or shipping. Prevention is less expensive than finding a full-blown cure.

Methods of **quality control** typically include automated controls to measure compliance to specification and site inspection at the point of manufacture where corrections can be made. It also includes control of the process through a continual sampling and measurement discipline known as **statistical process control (SPC)**. This process relies on a variety of data collection and measurement systems, reports using run data and flow charts, and diagrams showing the actual distribution of measures in relation to process control limits. Figure 2.1 shows the actual time taken to process a work package in relation to the **upper control limit (UCL)** (the highest point of measurement at which performance is acceptable) of 17.5 days and the **lower control limit (LCL)** (the lowest point of measurement at which performance is acceptable) of 1.5 days. The average for the period shown is described by a line at 9.4 days. Whenever a statistically significant number of occurrences fall outside this range—1.5 to 17.5 days—the process being used is out of control and will need to be reengineered.

One of the more commonly used tools in SPC is the measurement of *process capability* (C_{pK}). This compares the actual process range of the supplier's manufacturing capability with the buyer's acceptable range of variation. A C_{pK} of 1.00 means that the supplier's actual variation range and the buyer's allowable variation

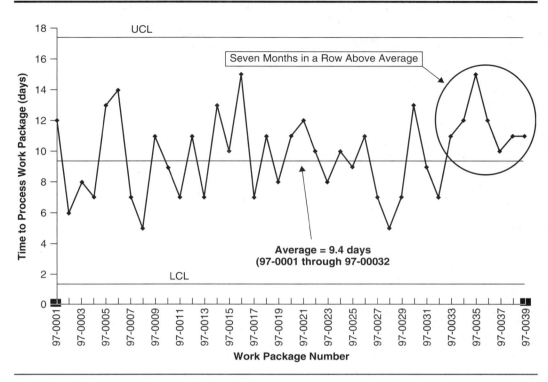

FIGURE 2.1   STATISTICAL PROCESS CONTROL CHART

range are the same. A C_{pK} of more than 1.00 indicates that the supplier's process is in better control than the buyer requires, while a C_{pK} of less than 1.00 indicates that the supplier will produce greater variation than the buyer will allow. Ideally, the process yields a C_{pK} of 1.33.

(b) STATEMENT OF WORK.   A *statement of work (SOW)* outlines the requirements for a purchase of services rather than a product. Nevertheless, like a specification, it defines exactly what is needed in enough detail so that disputes will be avoided when it comes time for payment for the services performed.

All SOWs, whether simple or highly complex, usually contain a number of common elements. They often include:

(i) Description of the Work to Be Performed.   This is often task oriented and provided in sequential terms following some logical, defined process of workflow. For example:

- Generate a detailed design for the lab work area.
- List all work to be performed by the nature of the subcontract required.
- Submit work specification to at least three applicable subcontractors for each major trade.

(ii) Timeline.   Each section of the work must be completed within a specific time. The timeline details the expected completion times of each element in the workflow and ensures that the project finishes on time. Often, the timeline specifies the points at which approval is required before proceeding further to ensure that requirements for one section are met before proceeding on to another. Timeline approval points may also trigger payment to the suppler for acceptable work performed.

(iii) Performance.   The SOW must clearly define the parameters for acceptable quality and performance and the metrics by which they will be determined. Subjective terms such as "good" or "best" should be avoided whenever possible and replaced with more objective measurements such as "100 percent" or "within two hours of notification" so that it is clear to both parties if (or when) the requirements have been met.

TIPS AND TECHNIQUES

Statement of work and scope of work are interchangeable terms. You might notice the use of both in other books and materials about procurement.

(c) TERMS AND CONDITIONS.   As an adjunct to both specifications and statements of work, terms and conditions, which was discussed at length in Chapter 1, define the contractual obligations of the supplier and the procurement organization. To the extent that your organization's standard terms and conditions will be included in all solicitations for quotations, they should be considered an integral part of the specifications.

While terms and conditions naturally vary from organization to organization, each generally uses a set of standard terms and conditions for purchase requirements, modified from time to time by terms and conditions tailored specifically for a given purchase. Typically, these are included in the boilerplate on the reverse side of a purchase order or in the standard library of contracts prepared by the Legal Department.

Standard terms and conditions usually include sections covering warranties, liability, indemnity, payment terms, legal jurisdiction, contingencies, cancellation, shipping requirements, and inspection. For a more complete picture, you may want to look at the back of one of your organization's purchase orders or one sent in by a customer. Terms that are customized for a particular purchase and tend to apply uniquely to that specific purpose may include such provisions as installation, acceptance criteria, training, and timelines. These are typically added as amendments to the standard contract or in the wording on the face of the PO.

On the face of a PO, special terms and conditions are usually included as a subset of the item's description. For example, you might have a description in the

PO such as "Valve, pneumatic as described in the attached specification." And then following that description, you might see a list like this in the PO:

The following additional terms and conditions apply:

- Approval by Robert Johnson required prior to payment.
- Delivery no later than July 23.
- Call 24 hours before delivery: (234) 555–1212

2.4 SPECIFICATION TRAPS

There are a number of traps that purchasers unknowingly build into their specifications. Some increase cost unnecessarily while others unwittingly ensure that the best solutions are not accepted. We discuss these traps in this section.

This trap arises from the mistaken assumption that the product being purchased must be customized to conform to user requirements. *Customization* typically adds cost, so the purchaser is well advised to investigate if this is truly required. An internal change in process with little or no resulting cost can often eliminate the need for customization. The term *standardization* also refers to the methods used to reduce or eliminate custom, one-time, and seldom-used components and processes that introduce variability and can potentially create added cost and quality problems.

(i) Disregarding Performance Requirements. Specifications unnecessarily stricter than actual performance would require simply add cost without adding benefits. They may also eliminate potential suppliers who are unable to perform to the higher requirements and thus eliminate price-reducing competition.

Conversely, specifications that are too open or loose, or with important details missing, tend to invite unacceptable quality and can create costly mistakes. The supplier can provide a product or material that meets specification precisely but will not perform in its intended function. Often, a supplier will "low-ball" an initial bid, purposely bidding well below market price to buy the business knowing that a **change order** request will follow. Having already received the contract, the supplier is then relatively free to charge any amount it wishes and thus recover its loss on the initial bid.

(ii) Brand Name. Specifying a brand name limits competition and thus increases the likelihood of higher prices. Brand names may or may not improve the chances of receiving better quality; nevertheless, they typically cost more as a result of higher advertising costs to create the brand name in the first place and because of the perception that users have that substitutes will not perform as well. One way to avoid this trap is to specify the brand name and include the verbiage "or equivalent" to allow for greater competition. This means that any product meeting the same specifications as the brand name will be acceptable to the purchaser.

The Hidden Cost of Using Brand-Name Products

Companies spend a great deal of effort and money creating a brand name that is indistinguishable from the actual process being performed. A case in point is Xerox. So common has this name become that we use it as though it were a verb: "Please xerox five copies forme."

We once received an order for several testers that were called out by brand name. Checking with the user, we discovered that he was simply using shorthand for the function and that there were many brands that would perform as well and be equally acceptable. Subsequent bids from competitors produced a savings of $70,000 on an original request for $300,000.

2.5 LOCATING AND DEVELOPING SOURCES OF SUPPLY

In its traditional sense, **sourcing**, the identification, evaluation, and development of potential suppliers, has been the fundamental strategic role of the procurement activity. Today, this role has expanded to a broader level and includes the understanding and analysis of the specific marketplace from which the purchase is being made, as well as developing and employing various processes to enhance competition. In this section, we examine the basic elements of finding potential sources.

The nature of the source from which the purchase is made can vary widely and be dependent on the nature of the purchase, the nature of the industry in which the purchase is being made, and the size of the purchase. The procurement professional must develop an understanding of how various supplier types can affect sourcing decisions.

For instance, a buyer needs to know whether to use a local source as supplier or whether location is irrelevant. The buyer should also be concerned with the size of the supplier; perhaps the organization would receive better service from a smaller supplier, where the volume of business might be more significant for the supplier and the buying organization would have more leverage. The buyer should also determine whether the organization should use a distributor or a manufacturer.

(a) LOCAL, DOMESTIC, OR INTERNATIONAL.   Sourcing decisions based on the suppliers' location can often provide distinct advantages in specific situations. A local supplier, for example, may feel a greater obligation to maintain higher levels of service because it shares the same community as the buyer. And buying organizations may have the same preference for supporting other members of the immediate community. Local suppliers, too, can frequently provide faster response time as well as lower freight costs.

The buying organization can develop greater competition simply by expanding the geographical range of its sourcing to national sources that may provide better pricing and wider choices.

Similarly, there are numerous trade-offs to consider when making a decision to source domestically or internationally. Typically, communications and delivery are more reliable with domestic sources, whereas international sources can usually provide lower prices due to reduced labor costs.

There are also payment methods to consider when evaluating offshore or domestic sources. Commonly, sellers will want overseas buyers to guarantee payment through some form of bank document, such as a **letter of credit (LC)**. An LC usually contains provisions triggering an automatic payment from the buyer's bank upon documented proof of shipment or at some specific predetermined time intervals. This can be a relatively costly process and can tie up cash or credit lines for an inordinate period of time.

In addition, considerations regarding additional risks due to fluctuations in currency exchange rates must also be taken into account when purchasing internationally, and long-term contracts often contain a clause that adjusts the selling price based on any significant change in the exchange rate at the time of delivery.

Finally, you should also take into account logistical issues such as customs duties, taxes, **tariffs**, and added shipping costs.

(i) Duties.   Most governments, including the United States, charge taxes for the import and export of certain types of goods. There are three major types of duties in common use:

- **Ad valorem** duties are duties charged as a percentage of the shipment's value (e.g., 10 percent). Ad valorem is the most commonly assessed form of tariff.
- **Specific duties** are duties imposed as a flat rate for some specified measure of goods, for example $6 per ton.
- **Compound duties** combine both ad valorem and specific duties, such as $6 per ton *and* 10 percent of the total value of the shipment.

(ii) Shipping.   The procurement professional has to consider the additional costs of shipping as well as the potential delays and risks of conducting business along an extended supply chain when making a decision to source overseas. Goods that are sensitive to environmental conditions or are needed in a reliable and timely manner are often shipped by air since the alternative, ocean freight, can be very slow. This can add significantly to shipping costs.

(iii) Inventory.   Longer supply chains typically require higher levels of inventory to buffer the long lead times and potential fluctuations in demand. The longer pipeline may also contain several weeks of inventory in various stages of manufacture or shipment if it is a regularly used product. Because most products are paid for at the time of shipment, this can tie up significant amounts of the organization's cash and can result in increased costs for carrying the inventory.

(iv) Documentation.   Goods traveling across international borders often require special documentation and licenses or must comply with certain restrictions. The most common of these include export and import licenses, commercial invoices, certificates of origin, insurance certificates, and international bills of lading. The **Convention on Contracts for the International Sale of Goods (CISG)** establishes uniform regulations in an attempt to standardize the rules governing international commerce but has not yet found universal acceptance. The **United Nations Commission on International Trade Law (UNCITRAL)** publishes an updated list of countries that have adopted the CISG at www.uncitral.org.

(b) SIZE.   As a procurement professional, you should consider the size of the organizations you are sourcing from before making a final decision to choose a specific source. Smaller-sized organizations often have a greater incentive to provide more customized and personalized service than larger ones since they rely more heavily on individual accounts. Larger organizations, however, may have greater technical resources and may be better able to respond to wide swings in demand.

(c) ORIGINAL MANUFACTURER OR DISTRIBUTOR.   Distributors frequently service the spot buying market and typically maintain substantial inventories in order to better service their clientele. As a result, they must often charge somewhat higher prices than the original manufacturing sources. Consequently, the procurement professional's decision should take into consideration the volume of the purchase. The greater the volume, the more likely you are to obtain lower prices directly from the manufacturer. However, if you need small quantities of many different products (such as hardware), your advantage may lie with a local stocking distributor.

2.6 TYPES OF COMPETITION

Supplier selection is also determined to a large extent by the nature of competition, whether that competition is established directly by the buyer as an offshoot of an organizational policy or as a result of conditions prevailing in the industry. In the following section, we will define the various competitive conditions that you may encounter.

(a) OPEN COMPETITION.   **Open competition** is said to exist when there are multiple suppliers available to fill your specific requirements and they are willing to vie for your business. When strong competitive factors exist in the marketplace, the buyer's negotiating position is stronger, and there are greater opportunities for gaining concessions in price as well as in payment terms, service, and support. To continue to foster robust competition, the buyer will want to avoid customization so that as many companies as possible can easily supply the product or service and maintain the widest possible area of source selection to keep the number of competitors high.

(b) SOLE SOURCE.   What if only one source is capable of meeting the buyer's needs? Then, you have a **sole-source** situation—the exact opposite of open competition. Sole-source situations are often the result of a government-created monopoly, such as a local utility, and there is little the buyer can do to gain concessions. Typically, in this kind of situation there is formal oversight by some governing body to ensure customers get fair treatment, but beyond such public regulation, there is sometimes little incentive on the part of the sole source to negotiate.

(c) SINGLE SOURCE.   A **single-source** situation is similar to the sole source but is a condition created by the buying organization, either through product customization where only one supplier is capable of producing the product, or through some predefined collaborative relationship that by its nature excludes competition. In this case, the benefits of the relationship itself provides a competitive advantage—such as a supplier-managed inventory program or joint development of new technology—that outweighs the benefits of open competition.

(d) TECHNICAL OR LIMITED COMPETITION.   Technical competition (also known as **limited competition**) is created when only a limited number of suppliers are available for a particular product due to patents or limited production capability. Competition in a particular industry can also be limited to only a few suppliers within a geographical area, commonly due to the existence of franchises or large initial investments required to enter the business, and the buyer can find it financially impractical to extend procurement beyond the limited area.

(e) PARTNERSHIP/JOINT VENTURE.   On occasion, organizations will form a joint venture to create a source of supply when none exists or to jointly share the expenses of developing new technology. While not specifically limiting competition, the investing organizations have little or no incentive to purchase outside the bounds of this partnership because the costs of development have already been invested and there are no other ways to recover the investment.

(f) CO-SOURCES.   Multiple sources are sometimes used by the same organization, either to foster competition or because no single supplier is capable of fulfilling 100 percent of the requirements. Frequently, multiple sources will be maintained to reduce the risk of interrupted supply, and there are also situations where some percentage of the business may be set aside for small or minority enterprise.

(g) REQUIREMENTS INTEGRATION.   Sometimes organizations will choose to combine the requirements of a class of products or services—maintenance, repair, and operations (MRO), for example—and source them through one supplier. Doing so can consolidate and leverage spending in many commodity areas that would ordinarily produce little discount and marginal service. By integrating supply, buyers can often provide service benefits, such as desktop delivery for office supplies or online procurement.

2.7 LOCATING SUITABLE SUPPLIERS

There are so many ways to locate potential suppliers; it is hardly possible to list them all. Our methods have ranged from using online search engines and business directories to calling colleagues and attending networking activities at our local **Institute of Supply Management (ISM)** affiliate. There may also be sources of information available to you through the technical staff within your own organization, and that is often the best place to begin your supplier sourcing activity.

In this section, we'll discuss some of the more common methods of locating sources.

(a) DIRECTORIES AND INDUSTRIAL GUIDES.   The most traditional means of locating potential suppliers is through industry-focused directories and buyers' guides. These are typically published in conjunction with a trade magazine or an industry association and contain listings of suppliers grouped by specialty or geographical location. These directories also often contain information about the supplier's products or services, capabilities, and size and market segment, along with contact names and telephone numbers.

One of the most commonly used directories is the *Thomas Register*, a general directory covering several hundred industries and hundreds of thousands of suppliers. Other directories are focused more specifically on one particular industry, such as those published by *Ceramic Industry* magazine directed at the ceramic manufacturing industry and the Buyers' Guide published by *Electronics Weekly* magazine.

There are also the ever-popular telephone directories such as the local Yellow Pages. These provide listings of businesses for a local calling area by category but typically provide no specific information beyond the advertising paid for by the organization. Regional business directories published by local newspapers to promote business in the readership area are also popular.

(b) INTERNET SEARCH TOOLS.   Today, it is common to use the Internet to search for suppliers. Using easily accessed search engines such as Google, you can locate multiple suppliers for any product or service simply by entering product key words in the search. The problem, as you may have already experienced, is that there is so much information available on the Internet that it can be impractical to search through it all. For example, a Google search for the phrase "paper cup manufacturer" returned 130,000 entries in less than one second.

(c) TRADE ASSOCIATIONS/TRADE SHOWS.   Trade organizations typically sponsor magazines and online directories that help the buyer find sources. More importantly perhaps, these organizations sponsor local or national trade shows that bring together all of the significant suppliers within a specific industry for several days of workshops and exhibits where buyers can effortlessly contact a significant number of suppliers in one location. An example is WESCON, an annual exhibit held on the West Coast for electronic component suppliers. This is a trade show that brings together hundreds of established and newly organized companies that supply the electronics OEM (original equipment manufacturer) marketplace and is cosponsored by several professional organizations, including the **Institute of Electrical and Electronic Engineers (IEEE).**

(d) GOVERNMENTAL AGENCIES.   Many governmental agencies provide information and directories that can be used for sourcing. The most commonly available are those published by the U.S. Department of Commerce and the U.S. General Services Administration's Federal Supply Service.

(e) MINORITY SUPPLIER DIRECTORIES.   For those seeking minority suppliers, there are literally dozens of minority business directories available, many through local minority business councils. One of the most useful directories is released by the U.S. *Small Business Administration (SBA)* online at www.sba8a.com.

(f) CONSULTANTS.   When a significant or critical need arises and there are no internal resources to provide adequate sourcing activities, procurement professionals often reach outside the organization for proven expertise. Engaging consultants who are industry experts can save the time it takes to find and prepare detailed studies and comparisons of sources since they already have substantial knowledge of suppliers and can leverage their expertise to shorten the time it takes to develop the best supplier fit. While this might appear to be an expensive approach, in the long run it can save valuable time and expense.

2.8 DETERMINING CHANGING MARKETPLACE FACTORS

One of the most significant determinants of sourcing decisions generates from the nature of changes in the marketplace. Supply and demand continually interact to produce varying pricing profiles. When product is in short supply or production resources come under threat (e.g., oil and the Middle East), prices can rise dramatically and capacity limits may, in addition, create supply *allocations*. Organizations wishing to continually work with the most price-competitive suppliers who stay up to date on the latest technological advances and business methods must maintain an aggressive review process that periodically surveys the market as conditions change.

(a) ECONOMIC CONDITIONS.   Supply and demand continually drive prices up and down. As economic conditions change, demand increases or declines, generating shortages or excesses in supply at any given time. As previously noted, increased supply or decreased demand (or combinations of both) generally lead to reduced prices. What drives these fluctuations can be a mystery. However, the astute procurement professional can take advantage of these conditions by seeking increased competition during periods of abundant supply and declining prices when suppliers are more anxious to seek new business or, conversely, by locking in prices through contracts when facing periods of shortage or inflationary pricing.

(i) Market Complexity.　The extent to which an organization's economic strategy can be employed—for example, when to lock in prices through extended contracts or when to pay more for higher quality levels—depends somewhat significantly on the complexity of the market. Markets with few suppliers and little potential for product substitution tend to offer only limited opportunities for the buyer to use competition to advantage. However, markets in which widely competitive forces exist and shortages in one product can be easily offset by substituting another—that is, markets with greater complexity—provide the buyer with a great deal of leverage to gain improvements. Cost reduction efforts can produce the greatest results in industries with broadly diverse alternatives, so the buyer's sourcing effort should always begin by determining the nature of the marketplace.

(ii) Nature of Competition.　The nature of competition in any particular market varies. Are there many technical solutions available or only one or two? Is the market characterized by geographical limitations with very high transportation costs? If, for example, the product being purchased is covered by a patent or controlled by patented manufacturing technology, competition will be unlikely. Similarly, when startup costs are high, such as those that occur in the development of proprietary tooling, competition tends to become constricted once the initial sourcing decision is made. It is always wise to understand the nature of competition in this regard before committing to generating short-term cost reductions since the sourcing effort will likely require major engineering efforts.

　　When dealing with sources of critical supplies or services, the buyer needs to maintain continual vigilance for potential traps that will unknowingly limit the nature of the competition for that particular product or service. The buyer must also develop strategies for dealing with them in the future.

(b) TECHNOLOGY.　When technological change drives conditions in the marketplace, new sources of supply must always be under consideration. New technology frequently generates new opportunities for capital investment, and emerging businesses tend to spring up everywhere. The buyer should be sensitive to these opportunities but be able to balance them with the need for maintaining long-term relationships that produce value beyond price or the latest fad in technology.

　　With critical supplies and services, one should always monitor the supply base to ensure that existing sources are keeping abreast of technology and adding improvements as necessary. Suppliers that do not constantly upgrade their processes to take advantage of new technology could easily become obsolete. The buyer should consider ways to continually monitor existing suppliers and their technological position relative to their competitor so that ongoing changes do not adversely affect their organization's own competitive position.

(c) PERFORMANCE.   As economic conditions change, so can supplier performance. Suppliers under continual pricing pressures due to emerging global markets, for example, may tend to sacrifice some of the quality that qualified them for your business in the first place. Delivery delays, cuts in services, and quality failures are often the early signs of declining performance due to economic hardship. Companies providing critical supplies and services need to be continually measured against industry performance standards. Initial signs of deteriorating performance should be met with clear improvement projects and, depending upon the rapidity of decline, additional sourcing activities.

2.9 OBTAINING BIDS AND PROPOSALS

Bids and proposals are integral elements in the procurement process. When a clear specification or SOW exists, the buyer will typically solicit a competitive bid or a **request for quotation (RFQ)**. When specific information does not exist or when there are a number of potential ways to meet the user's requirements, proposals are often requested, often through a formal **request for proposal (RFP)** process. How the buyer structures the bidding or proposal strategy depends on a number of factors outlined in the next section.

2.10 BIDDING GUIDELINES

Bidding is a competitive process that enables the buyer to leverage several potential sources of supply through a single activity to obtain the most favorable business terms. In order for this process to be successful, a number of conditions, such as those outlined here, must be met.

(a) PROVIDE CLEAR CONTENT.   A solicitation for bid should provide sufficient information about the requirement so that a supplier will be able to offer exact pricing and provide whatever other detailed information is required to successfully obtain the purchase order. Typically, this will include facts such as the exact specification of the required goods or an SOW for a service, the quantity required, payment terms, the expected time of performance, necessary quality levels, and shipping or performance location. The solicitation must also include the deadline for submission.

(b) DETERMINE COMPRESSIBLE SPENDING.   Before engaging in the solicitation process, the buyer is responsible for determining if market conditions will support a reduction in price or an improvement in terms. Unless favorable market conditions are present, competitive bidding will not be worthwhile. While there is no precise way to ensure this under all conditions, benchmarking industry trends, whenever possible, might provide some guidance.

(c) ENSURE RESPONSIVE, RESPONSIBLE COMPETITION. When selecting potential suppliers or candidates to which bids will be sent, it is important that the buyer prequalify them to ensure that the bids returned will be responsive to the organization's needs. This means that the supplier has the means to fully understand the buyer's needs and can, under normal business conditions, fulfill the requirements.

The buyer should ensure that the suppliers are in a position to meet any procurement requirements; that, for example, they have the necessary financial means to produce the product being specified or that they have the equipment needed to meet the requirement in a timely manner. If tooling is required, the buyer must be careful to ensure that the supplier is not applying the bidding trap by absorbing the cost of the tooling as a way of buying the business.

(d) ENABLE FAIR AND ETHICAL BIDDING PROCESSES. As a buyer, your job is to properly ensure ethical conduct in the solicitation and acceptance of bids, making sure that all suppliers are provided with exactly the same information and have an equal amount of time to respond. Answers to questions submitted by one supplier need to be distributed to all suppliers bidding to further enhance the competitive process.

Suppliers should also be made aware of the process for awarding the business by the buying organization, whether it is the lowest price or some combination of terms, as well as the criteria for making the final selection. Many organizations use a weighted-average scoring process developed by a cross-functional internal team to select suppliers for complex services, since it can be extremely difficult to unilaterally evaluate and select the best supplier.

(e) HOLD AN OPEN PREBID CONFERENCE. A prebid conference, where all potential suppliers have the opportunity to receive a briefing on the bid package from the organization's staff, may be used when the requirement is relatively complex. Usually, this is held for all potential suppliers at one time and provides an opportunity to review the specification, time frames, drawings or blueprints, and to meet the staff. The prebid conference also provides an opportunity for suppliers to become familiar with the organization's policies and procedures, payment practices, and code of conduct, as well as any special requirements that relate to the particular procurement.

Although this practice in the bidding process can enhance competition through personal contact and expedite the process through real-time resolution of questions, it can also be time consuming for both parties. For this reason, it is important to schedule the conference far enough in advance so that all parties may attend and so that you can have the right personnel available to provide answers. This is especially relevant when the prebid conference is mandatory or when the requirements are particularly complex.

2.11 FORMULATING THE BID OR PROPOSAL TYPE

There are a number of procedures that can be used in the solicitation of bids and proposals, depending on the nature of the requirements and the objectives of the bidding process. Some widely used solicitation types include sealed bids, offers to buy, RFPs, and RFQs. Each of these have a variety of potential applications, so choosing the optimal method for obtaining a specific bid requires a clear understanding of its advantages and limitations. The section that follows provides the background for making the best selections.

(a) SEALED BID.   Typically used in government-related contracting, the *sealed bid* is an offer submitted in a sealed envelope that is opened with other bids at a previously designated time and place. This method is used when the buyer does not wish to publicly reveal any of the bids prior to a specific deadline to prevent others from leveraging it to unfair advantage. There are two types of sealed bids that are used frequently in procurement: **open bidding** and **restricted bidding**.

The bidding process may be open to any qualified supplier that wishes to enter a bid. In most cases, qualification takes place at an earlier date, and the supplier must be approved by the time the bids are sent out. Or the bidding process may be open only to a specific group of suppliers due to the requirements of a regulatory process (e.g., minority or small business set asides) or to ensure that sensitive information does not get into the wrong hands.

(b) POSTED OFFER TO BUY.   Government contracting requirements are often posted in a public bidding document or online. This ensures that the general public

---

BUREAU OF FINANCIAL MANAGEMENT

Current Invitations to Bid

May 17, 2004
Invitations to Bid

The website is first to post new bid invitations and we hope that you will stop by occasionally to learn about new opportunities as they are made available. Questions regarding any bid may be directed to the numbers below.

Home Improvement Program/Lead IV **(Rehabilitation of Properties Located in the City of Harrisburg)**	**No 2107–04**
Sealed proposals will be received by the city of Harrisburg, Office of Purchasing, 10 North Second Street, Suite 302C, Harrisburg, Pennsylvania, 17101 until **3.00 p.m., Tuesday, June 8, 2004** at which time they will be publicly opened and read in Suite 304B of the same building, immediately thereafter.	
Bid security in the amount of ten percent of the total bid amount is required with each bid submitted in the form of a certified check, cashier's check, treasurer's check, an irrevocable letter of credit drawn on a bank acceptable to the City or a bid bond. Copies of the Project Documents, including specifications, may be seen at and obtained from the Office of Purchasing, 10 North Second Street, Suite 302C, Harrisburg, PA 17101, 717.255.6472	
The City reserves the right to reject any or all bids and also reserves the right to waive irregularities in any bids or proposals.	
The City of Harrisburg is commited to providing employment opportunity in all aspects of employment, without regard to race, color, religion, gender, sexual preference/orientation, national origin, citizenship, age or physical/mental disability.	

FIGURE 2.2 A   SAMPLE INVITATION TO BID

has open access to the process. In common usage, this notice is referred to as a **posted offer to buy**. This process is not used by commercial organizations much, although notices on Procurement Department Web sites open to the supplier community are now becoming more common. Figure 2.2 illustrates a typical online posting as an invitation to bid from the Bureau of Financial Management at the City of Harrisburg, Pennsylvania. Notice that some of the business requirements, such as the due date and required format, are posted outside of the actual specifications as a way of calling particular attention to them.

(c) AUTOMATED BIDDING.   It is common today to generate automated bids using a number of computer-based processes. In addition to submitting and receiving bids and proposals directly through the Internet, many organizations are turning to the *reverse auction* process to enhance competition.

A reverse auction is typically an event that enables prequalified suppliers to submit many bids in sequence with the objective of outbidding their competitors and thereby winning the business. Outbidding in this case means submitting real-time offers that go below the prices submitted by their competition. The bidding process ends at a specific time, and usually the lowest bidder obtains the order. On occasion, the business may be divided among several bidders on a percentage basis, with the lowest bidder receiving the largest allotment.

(d) REQUEST FOR INFORMATION (RFI).   The **request for information (RFI)** is used by organizations seeking to develop a bid list or prequalify potential suppliers. Generally, the RFI asks suppliers to submit general information about their companies, such as size, financial performance, years in business, market position, product lines, and a variety of other information that can determine the supplier's suitability for participating in some future competitive event. Of the three requests we discuss in this section, the RFI is used the least because of the advent of the Internet and how easy it is to gather information now.

(e) REQUEST FOR PROPOSAL (RFP).   The RFP is used when a specification or SOW has not yet been developed, or when the buyer has a general requirement and wants to solicit various ideas on how that requirement can best be met. Included in the RFP are typical objectives of the future contract and as much of the background behind the requirement as is already known. The language of the RFP usually allows the supplier some freedom in determining the most effective solution and often enables the supplier to actually establish the specifications. Sometimes prices are requested along with the proposal, and sometimes suppliers are specifically requested not to submit price quotations.

TWO-STEP BIDDING

When RFPs are not used to solicit price quotations, the buyer may use a two-step process. In this procedure, the buying organization generally assembles a specification or SOW based on the collective responses of the suppliers (or a modification of the most agreeable solution) and then submits the requirement back to the suppliers for a price quotation.

The time required to fully implement this process is often a factor limiting its use. In a complex RFP, it is not uncommon to allow suppliers three to four weeks to respond, so it is easy to see that the overall time to progress through a two-step process can take several months, considering the time it takes to formulate the initial proposal, then work it into a specification and resubmit it for quotes.

(f) REQUEST FOR QUOTATION (RFQ).   The RFQ is virtually no different than the second part of the two-step bidding process just described. It is used when a specification or SOW has already been formulated and the buyer needs only to obtain price, delivery, and other specific terms from the suppliers in order to select the most appropriate source. The specifications are sent to prequalified suppliers soliciting price and other terms and conditions.

2.12 MANAGING SOURCING DATA

Most organizations maintain listings of suppliers with whom they have established some form of business relationship. These listings provide other users with both the current status of a particular supplier and whatever historical data may be available. Historical data is particularly useful as a method of avoiding duplication of effort, since the organization's prior records can tell a buyer if the supplier is qualified for a particular purpose. This prevents having to gather the usual information needed to qualify that supplier.

There are numerous ways to designate and list suppliers. Outlined next are a few of the more common ways.

2.13 TYPES OF SOURCING

To enhance their usefulness, supplier listings are usually developed according to some form of commodity categorization—in addition to the product or service they supply—indicating their current supplier status. Some of the more common listings in use include the commonly used **approved supplier list (ASL)**, along with listings of certified, qualified, preferred, and disqualified suppliers. These lists are usually developed and maintained by the Procurement Department but are considered an integral part of the quality control process. Let's describe these in more detail.

(a) APPROVED SUPPLIER LIST.   One type of list the buyer keeps is an ASL, which contains a listing of suppliers who have met the organization's compliance criteria and are qualified to provide specific **direct materials**, **controlled materials**, or manufacturing-related services to the organization. ASLs are usually used in manufacturing environments where technical and quality control requirements are necessary. Suppliers are often expected to pass on-site inspections and to maintain preestablished levels of quality, service, and on-time delivery. Suppliers listed on the buyer's ASL are considered first-tier suppliers.

(b) CERTIFIED SUPPLIERS.   When the need to integrate the quality standards and systems of multiple organizations exists so that inspection and training costs can be held to a minimum, procurement departments often establish a listing of suppliers that have met these particular requirements. **Certified suppliers** are suppliers that do not furnish direct materials and are, therefore, not appropriate for inclusion on the ASL. They might apply to suppliers removing hazardous waste or specially licensed consultants, as well as companies supplying certain types of telecommunications or network hardware.

(c) QUALIFIED SUPPLIERS.   **Qualified suppliers** are those that have successfully completed a formal screening process but may not yet have been qualified for the ASL or that may be supplying a product or service that does not require the stringent supplier site inspection criteria used to establish eligibility for the ASL. These are usually suppliers who meet all of the business requirements of the organization and are approved by the Procurement Department for future business as may arise.

(d) PREFERRED SUPPLIERS.   A **preferred supplier** listing generally includes suppliers who have proven capabilities that make them especially valuable to the buying organization. Often, they are suppliers who provide exceptional service or favorable pricing. They may be suppliers already under contract to provide particular products or services, so the Procurement Department will encourage their use.

Preferred supplier listings may also include minority- or female-owned and disadvantaged businesses, and companies that are engaged in contractual (or similarly formalized) partnerships, as well as good customers or clients of the buying organization.

TIPS AND TECHNIQUES

Watch out. Subtle differences in terminology usage regarding the supplier's actual status may confuse you. Remember that the approved supplier list is used in audit-controlled environments.

(e) DISQUALIFIED SUPPLIERS.   On occasion, a supplier will be unable to meet the organization's requirements, have a contract terminated for violations, or consistently fail to maintain acceptable performance or quality levels. Under these circumstances, suppliers will often be banned from conducting further business and will be added to a listing of **disqualified suppliers**. This listing may be further reinforced by a reference stating "Do Not Use" following the supplier's name in the buying organization's computer system.

2.14 MAINTAINING SOURCING LISTS

To take full advantage of the value inherent in maintaining sourcing lists, the buyers must take special efforts to keep them up to date. Fortunately, computerization and **enterprise resource planning (ERP)** software has greatly aided this process. Keep in mind that some listings, such as the ASL, are auditable for compliance with ISO (International Organization for Standardization) certification. Some of the other considerations you may want to keep in mind include:

(a) ELECTRONIC TOOLS. Most computer-based procurement systems in use today enable the buyer to include special status in the **supplier master record**, the database that maintains information about the supplier such as their address, key contact personnel, and payment terms. Reports can then be run listing suppliers by specific sourcing list status. This can be extremely useful when sourcing requirements dictate using suppliers from one of these categories.

(b) CONTRACTS DATABASE. Organizations that do a substantial portion of their business through contracts often maintain a database where they are centrally stored. This is useful not only in providing historical guidance to the buyer but in assisting with future sourcing decisions and avoiding duplication of effort.

2.15 REGULATORY FACTORS GOVERNING PROCUREMENT

As you may imagine, numerous laws and governmental regulations—federal, state, and local—affect procurement activities to one degree or another in the United States. Many of these play key roles in the way business organizations can function, while others establish the legal framework for buying and selling.

In your role as procurement professional, you will not only need to understand how laws and regulations affect business conducted domestically, but you will also need a thorough understanding of how the laws governing businesses in other countries vary widely from those in the United States. What is taken for common business practice in one country may be unheard of in another.

In this section we've outlined the laws and regulations that you might stumble across frequently as procurement professional.

(a) UNIFORM COMMERCIAL CODE. The *Uniform Commercial Code (UCC)*, especially Article 2, the section governing sales, is perhaps the regulation most commonly used by procurement departments in conducting day-to-day business. The UCC was developed by the legal community early in the last century as trade between the states began to accelerate and the need for uniform laws became evident. It has subsequently been adopted and ratified by 49 U.S. states and the District of Columbia.

TIPS AND TECHNIQUES

UCC applies in every state except Louisiana. Louisiana operates under a legal system more closely tied to French law than the English legal system that formed the foundation of law in the other states.

The UCC governs a variety of commercial areas, most importantly the sale and purchase of goods. It does not generally apply to services except in the case of combined purchases of goods and services and only if the product represents more than 50 percent of the total transaction value.

Section 2.2, governing sales, is the most applicable section of the UCC to procurement. Its scope is extremely broad and covers virtually every area related to the sale and purchase of goods between merchants. The section is divided into parts dealing with specific elements of the commercial relationship within the scope of business-to-business activities. For example, Part 2 covers the broader aspects of contract formation while Part 3 details specific aspects of contracts such as delivery, warranty, and shipping; Part 5 deals with the important aspects of performance; Part 6 covers contract breach and repudiation; and Part 7, the final segment, covers remedies.

NOTE

Appendix H contains an index listing each of the Parts of Section 2.2 and the subsections they cover.

You can find out more about the UCC and obtain the full text by visiting: www.law.cornell.edu/ucc/ucc.table.html.

(b) ANTITRUST LEGISLATION. While the system of conducting business in the United States requires open and fair competition to ensure economic justice, many individual assaults have been made on this system in an attempt to gain personal advantage. These have typically been met with appropriate legislation by the U.S. Congress. For instance, you might recall from U.S. history what happened when railroad monopolies began selective pricing of freight to favor businesses in which they held an interest. They were able to effectively reduce competition by charging exorbitant freight rates to competing companies, resulting in higher prices for their products compared to those in which the railroad owners had an interest. The result of these unethical business practices is government regulation, which we discuss in depth in this section.

(i) Sherman Antitrust Act (1890). In response to increasing public concern over the formation of monopolies in the United States and their negative impact on commercial trade, Congress passed the Sherman Antitrust Act in 1890. The act banned business contracts made in the form of a trust, or those created under unethical circumstances such as through bribes, graft, or coercion. The act restricts "every contract and combination in the form of trust or otherwise, or conspiracy, in restraint of trade or commerce." The law was accompanied by sharp teeth in the form of criminal penalties and treble damages for violations. Included in the outlawed practices were conspiracies to fix pricing and to require reciprocal buying.

The Sherman Act has seen several amendments over the years designed to further refine its prohibitions, most significantly the Clayton Antitrust Act of 1914.

(ii) Clayton Antitrust Act (1914).   The Clayton Antitrust Act of 1914 was designed to bolster the provisions of the Sherman Act and further reduce monopolistic practices. It made certain corporate practices illegal, including price cutting to freeze out competitors, exclusive pricing arrangements, and tying contracts (where the purchase of specific goods and services by the buyer is contingent upon the purchase of other goods or services as a package). It also outlawed the holding of stock by one company so that it could gain control over another, thus reducing or eliminating competition, and the practice of interlocking directorates where a few influential individuals controlled an industry by sitting on the boards of related companies.

(iii) Robinson-Patman Act (1958).   The key element of the Robinson-Patman Act of 1958 is that it barred direct or indirect price discrimination that would substantially reduce competition. This federal legislation prohibits suppliers from exclusively charging lower prices to certain customers simply because they purchase in larger quantities than other customers. While some specific exceptions apply, quantity discounts for exactly the same quality of like material (or services related to the purchase of the material) are basically illegal under this law unless all competing buyers are eligible for the same discount.

In addition, the provisions of Robinson-Patman prohibit the *purchaser* from knowingly receiving a discriminatory price or forcing the supplier to provide one. It also forbids the seller from providing and the buyer from accepting any commission related to the sale.

The law, however, does allow the seller to match the prices of its competitors and to lower prices when there is a valid justification—for example, when there are differences in distribution costs or when perishable goods have reached the end of their shelf life.

For the act to be enforced (which, by the way, it rarely is), it must be proven that the alleged price discrimination produced an adverse effect by limiting competition and at least one of the alleged discriminatory sales crossed state lines. In addition, the act applies only to goods and materials of a predominantly physical nature rather than intangibles such as services (unless related and subordinate to the goods being purchased), and the goods in question must be of "like grade and quality." Altogether, there are some 10 provisions that must be violated concurrently for enforcement to take place.

(iv) Federal Trade Commission (FTC) Act (1914).   The FTC Act, also created in 1914 along with the Clayton Act, established the FTC as the watchdog agency for restraint of trade activities and to investigate any alleged improprieties between buyers and sellers. The agency is empowered to root out and prosecute instances of illegal, unfair, or deceptive business practices. However, buyers rarely have dealings with the FTC, so it's unlikely that as a procurement professional you'll have much to worry about in this regard.

(v) OFPP (Office of Federal Procurement Policy) Act (1974).   Though it's been through several amendments, the OFPP Act of 1974 established the official *Federal Acquisitions Regulations (FAR)*, the U.S. government's procurement policies, which are overseen by the OFPP.

OFPP oversees several statutes related to acquisitions for such government organizations as the Department of Defense, the General Services Administration, and the National Aeronautics and Space Administration.

(c) OTHER GOVERNMENTAL LEGISLATION.   Most governmental regulation affecting commercial business dealings is focused on eliminating collusion and conspiracy to fix pricing. However, a procurement professional should be aware of a number of other laws enacted by Congress that impact the conduct of routine procurement activities, such as the Small Business Act, the Davis-Bacon Act, the Walsh-Healey Public Contracts Act, the Service Contract Act, the Prompt Payment Act, the False Claims Act, and the Buy American Act.

(i) Small Business Act (1953).   The Small Business Act represents an effort by Congress to foster the participation of small, disadvantaged, and female-owned businesses in federal contracting. It requires federal purchasers to assign a designated volume of procurement to small businesses (called "set asides") and to allow some contracts to be split between large and small businesses, where the small business has the opportunity to share part of the contract providing it can match the bid terms.

(ii) Davis-Bacon Act (1931).   The Davis-Bacon Act and its amendments require that federal construction projects over $2,000 contain a clause establishing the minimum wages to be paid to various classes of workers employed under the contract. Under the provisions, contractors and subcontractors are required to pay workers employed under the contract wages at least equal to the locally prevailing rates and fringe benefits for similar projects.

(iii) Walsh-Healey Public Contracts Act (1936).   Closely related to the Davis-Bacon Act, the Walsh-Healey Act applies to government purchase and contracts exceeding $10,000. Going beyond requiring minimum wage, the act limits the work week to 40 hours and attempts to ensure safe and sanitary working conditions.

There is also a provision that, in effect, blackballs violators by making them ineligible for further government contracts for three years and distributing a list of their names to federal contracting agencies.

(iv) Service Contract Act (1965).   The Service Contract Act empowers the Employment Standards Administration to predetermine the prevailing wage and benefit rates to be paid for federal service contracts that are over $2,500. It also provides the enforcement mechanisms for the Davis-Bacon and Walsh-Healey that include safety standards and record-keeping requirements.

(v) Prompt Payment Act (1982).   The Prompt Payment Act ensures that federal agencies pay suppliers and contractors in a timely manner and even allows for the assessment of late-payment penalties and interest.

(vi) False Claims Act (1863).   Under the False Claims Act, those who knowingly submit, or cause another person or entity to submit, false or fraudulent claims for payment of government funds can be held liable for treble damages plus civil penalties.

(vii) Buy American Act (1933).   The Buy American Act of 1933 was passed to ensure that the federal government supports domestic companies and domestic workers by buying goods manufactured in the United States that are made from materials mined or produced in the United States. The law provides exceptions for items not commercially available in the United States or if the price is more than 6 percent higher than comparable foreign products. It also allows exceptions for purchases under $100,000 or by department head waiver.

TIPS AND TECHNIQUES

SHOULD THE U.S. WAIVE THE BUY AMERICAN ACT?

How important is it to ensure that the U.S. government support U.S. businesses during poor economic times and in a time of military activity? You'd assume it was very important, especially during the Iraq conflict. But the State Department decided to waive requirements that the military purchase U.S.-made cars and trucks for the war effort. This led to a strong complaint to the Secretary of State from a leading minority congressman stating that if U.S.-produced cars were good enough to win the war, they should be good enough to win the peace.

Do you agree? Is a law passed in the Depression of the 1930s to protect U.S. jobs still appropriate for the United States to follow today?

(d) FOREIGN TRADE REGULATIONS.   In addition to numerous domestic laws governing trade, Congress has enacted several key pieces of legislation affecting foreign trade, and the U.S. government has been signatory to a number of others that were negotiated internationally. Some of the more significant of those include:

(i) General Agreement on Tariffs and Trade (GATT).   This international agreement, first signed in 1947, has now become a significant element of the World Trade Organization (WTO). Affecting trade in goods only, the agreement was designed to help reduce restrictive tariffs and encourage international trade. Approximately 110 countries now participate.

(ii) North American Free Trade Agreement (NAFTA).   This treaty was designed to enhance trade between the United States, Mexico, and Canada, offering favorable tariffs and removing import and export barriers for goods that primarily originate in one of the three countries.

(iii) United Nations Convention on Contracts for the International Sale of Goods (CISG).   Ratified by Congress in 1986, this treaty was initiated to provide uniformity to global sales and automatically applies to commercial sales between the signatory countries. It does not apply to trade for services only. The full text of the agreement can be found on the Internet at www.uncitral.org/english/texts/sales/CISG.htm.

(iv) Trade Agreements Act of 1979.   One of the stated purposes of this act is "to foster the growth and maintenance of an open world trading system." It was also enacted to expand opportunities for U.S. international commerce and to support and enforce the rules of international trade.

(v) Foreign Corrupt Practices Act.   This law is primarily known for its anti-bribery provisions that make it illegal for any U.S. citizen to bribe a foreign official in order to obtain or sustain business. It is somewhat confusing because it applies only to officials and does not include payments made to facilitate routine duties (sometimes called "grease").

2.16 IMPORT/EXPORT ISSUES

While international trade creates a wide array of financial benefits, those benefits are not without major obstacles. Regulatory initiatives such as Customs-Trade Partnership Against Terrorism (C-TPAT), CSI, Antidumping and Countervailing Duties (ADCVD), and Sarbanes-Oxley (SOX) have had significant impact on global trade by requiring more information from importers and new processes to meet the regulatory demand of such policies.

Regulations today have become more stringent and evolving, covering not only the shipment of goods but also the flow of funds. Exporting organizations are under greater scrutiny than ever before regarding their global trade practices and face multiple challenges that affect the entire company from sales to finance. The challenges facing export management businesses include:

- Restrictions on those with whom business is conducted, including financial and services providers, as well as buyers and consumers
- Stiff fines and loss of ability to export goods for noncompliance with regulations
- Increased regulatory requirements, such as mandatory Automated Export System (AES) filing requirements
- New free trade agreements
- Maintaining and increasing shipment tracking with little added cost
- Compliance with multiple regulatory bodies, such as the Department of Commerce's Bureau of Industry and Security (BIS) and the State Department's Office of Defense Trade Controls (ODTC)
- Updating of supply chain information
- Continually changing duty classifications
- Maintaining accurate audit trails and ensuring the security and integrity of data

NOTE

Appendix I contains details on recent import and export legislation.

2.17 SUMMARY

Sourcing is one of the most important functions performed by the Procurement Department. The procurement professional with a thorough knowledge of how to effectively find, develop, and manage sources of supply will truly add value to the organization.

A key activity in sourcing is to ensure that your internal users establish and effectively communicate their requirements to the suppliers. When obtaining quotations or proposals, it will be your task to objectively analyze supplier responses so that when a decision is made to use a particular source, the organization can be assured it will obtain optimal value in the procurement. This often involves gaining a thorough understanding of the marketplace and the economic factors that prevail. It also requires that you fully understand the various methods for obtaining information and competitive bids from suppliers and when to use them.

The procurement professional is also responsible for ensuring the development and maintenance of sourcing lists so that others within the organization will have access to up-to-date information about which suppliers are qualified for any particular purchase.

Closely related to sourcing activities are regulations and laws governing the conduct of business, such as the Uniform Commercial Code and the various antitrust acts. It is important that you understand how these laws affect the sourcing decisions you make and how they may impact ongoing relationships with suppliers so that you are able to minimize the risk of the negative impact a violation would have on your organization.

KEY TERMS

Using department

Document Control

Requisitioner

Mean time between failure (MTBF)

Parts per million (PPM)

Convention on Contracts for the
   International Sale of Goods
   (CCISG)

Compound duties

Tariffs

Ad valorem

Specific duties

Technical specifications

Functional specifications

Performance specifications

American National Standards Institute
   (ANSI)

National Institute of Standards and
   Technology (NIST)

Benchmark

Quality control (QC)

Statistical process control (SPC)

Upper control limit (UCL)

Lower control limit (LCL)

Change order

Sourcing

Letter of credit (LC)

United Nations Commission on International Trade Law (UNCITRAL)

Open competition

Sole-source

Single-source

Technical, or limited competition

Institute for Supply Management
   (ISM)

Institute of Electrical and Electronic
   Engineers (IEEE)

Request for quotation (RFQ)

Request for proposal (RFP)

Posted offer to buy

Open bidding

Restricted bidding

Request for Information (RFI)

Approved supplier list (ASL)

Direct materials ditto

Controlled materials

Certified suppliers

Preferred supplier

Disqualified supplier

Qualified supplier

Enterprise resource planning (ERP)

Supplier master record

CHAPTER 3

SELECTING SUPPLIERS AND MEASURING PERFORMANCE

LEARNING OBJECTIVES

1. Describe the processes available to qualify suppliers.
2. Name the three specific quantitative statements used to understand a company's financial well-being.
3. List the three criteria a buyer uses in reviewing a supplier.
4. Describe the "supplier evaluation scorecard," the technique recommended for analyzing suppliers.

The Procurement Department is expected to lead the process of evaluating competitive offers and selecting the supplier for any particular contract. The methods used for selection are some of the most important elements of the procurement professional's skill set. Indeed, effective supplier management, one of Procurement's most vital functions, truly begins with establishing the proper initial selection criteria and ensuring that the right supplier gets chosen. Too often, inadequate preparation and effort goes into this process with predictably disastrous results: the wrong supplier chosen or disappointing supplier performance. Even worse, in too many organizations a weak and poorly trained buyer staff has virtually no input into supplier selection and contract awards in the first place, yet is expected to manage ongoing supplier performance. That is why it is critical that you clearly understand the methods available in supplier selection and employ them professionally.

This chapter introduces you to evaluating and selecting suppliers for specific contracts and some of the methods available to measure and manage a supplier's ongoing performance.

3.1 SELECTING THE SUPPLIER AND AWARDING THE CONTRACT

You cannot make a silk purse out of a sow's ear. To produce a specific result, you must choose the correct mechanism. The supplier is the fundamental resource employed by your organization to meet its requirements, and if you do not select correctly, you will never achieve satisfactory results.

Proper supplier selection, despite requiring a strong measure of distinctly human intuition, must be performed systematically and to the most objective criteria you are capable of developing. As you read the steps to selecting the right supplier outlined in this section, think about how your organization might benefit from a more rigorous approach to this discipline.

(a) EVALUATING OFFERS. Before selecting an offer, every buyer should employ some process of evaluation to ensure adequate consideration that all aspects of the organization's needs are being optimized. Evaluating a supplier's offer means not only evaluating its bid or proposal from a cost perspective, but it also means evaluating the supplier's ability to perform to the required level of speed and quality. You need to evaluate offers in terms of potential risk as well as potential benefits. In providing incentives to obtain the contract by reducing the **price**, for example, will the supplier continue to maintain the level of quality the organization requires? Issues such as this will be merely one among the many you will have to consider during the supplier selection process.

TIPS AND TECHNIQUES

In contract law, the term "offer" has a specific legal meaning. We discuss some of the legal aspects of contracts in Chapter 4. For our purposes here, we are using the term more loosely to mean any valid bid or proposal submitted by a supplier.

In performing proper **due diligence**, the buyer reviewing a supplier offer evaluates three key criteria before reaching a decision to award the contract to a specific supplier: responsiveness, capability, and **competitive value**. Because of the inherent subjectivity of much of evaluating suppliers, there is strong evidence to show that a thorough review process produces the most reliable results when it involves several individuals from a cross section of functional departments. In fact, we generally find that the evaluation process can be best performed in a cross-functional team environment where individuals perform separate evaluations but come together to develop a consensus opinion.

Here, then, are the guidelines for determining responsiveness, capability, and competitive value that you will want to consider when awarding a supplier contract.

(b) RESPONSIVENESS. Most obviously, the basic criteria for receiving the award will be the supplier's ability to perform to the specification or scope of work contained in your **request for proposal (RFP)**. In high-value or high-profile contracts, it is wise to actually visit the supplier's facility and physically inspect the facility (we'll discuss qualifying when we discuss site visits later in this chapter) to qualify the supplier and determine its ability to meet your requirements.

In many situations, however, site visits may be physically or financially impractical, so other methods to confirm the supplier's ability to respond should be used. For instance, you might consider contacting a supplier's references to ask about similar work performed in the past. This is frequently an effective way of determining overall supplier competency. You may also want to review the response document to ensure that the supplier has answered all the questions in your bid proposal and successfully addressed any mandatory requirements you may have set forth. While oversights sometimes occur, it is not a good sign to discover that some of the key elements of your requirement remain unaddressed. Offers that do not answer your specific questions should be considered **nonconforming** and rejected.

The thoroughness of the supplier's response and the level of detail the supplier provides generally signifies the supplier's level of understanding of your requirements and its expertise in providing workable solutions, services, or conforming parts.

You should also determine the extent to which the supplier's proposal conforms to your organizational business and environmental and ethical policies and procedures. Does the offer appropriately address warranty and replacement issues? Does it conform to your organization's policy regarding commercial liability and *damages*? Is it signed by the proper authority? Are the correct documents, such as evidence of insurance certificates and copies of applicable licenses, attached?

Perhaps even more significantly, how closely do the supplier's terms and conditions match those of your organization? You may want to keep in mind that reconciling conflicts in terms and conditions can require a great deal of negotiation effort and typically requires participation by your risk management and legal organizations.

(c) CAPABILITY. While many capable suppliers may respond to your proposal, your task will be to determine which supplier is the most qualified for this particular contract award. In your evaluation, you should consider several critical factors, which we'll discuss in this section.

(i) Operational Capacity.   One of the key considerations in award determination will be the supplier's physical capacity to meet your needs as promised. You do not want to select a supplier that could have difficulty meeting the required volume due to capacity constraints or conflicts with the scheduling of other jobs. A simple ratio of current output to capacity can provide a valuable indication of this ability. Your risk of on-time delivery failure increases when a supplier's loading for your products or service exceeds 90 percent of capacity, especially in industries where skilled labor or production capacity can be difficult to obtain.

You will also need to ensure that the supplier has the ability and systems to properly schedule orders and keep track of current production operations to meet its customers' commitments. With little or no technology to assist in the scheduling process, the supplier may have difficulty keeping track of its customer order obligations and may prove unreliable in meeting delivery promises. You should be able to benchmark this through the customer references the supplier provides.

Past performance, while not necessarily a clear predictor of future performance, can provide some further insight into the supplier's operational capability. You may be able to develop data on this from your own organization's internal records such as supplier delivery efficiencies or your own production lead times, if applicable. If not, you may need to perform some benchmarking activities and, certainly, check with as many referenced accounts as possible.

TIPS AND TECHNIQUES

AVOIDING THE OBVIOUS

We recall a situation when our contract award team prepared a recommendation to select a particular supplier for a molded plastic part. High quality was critical since this particular part held a key function in the assembly, and its failure in the field could create enormous problems. This supplier produced far and away the best quality we could find for this particular material. Pricing was competitive, and the company agreed to all our terms and conditions.

It was just prior to issuing the purchase order that one of our team members discovered a startling fact. Our annual volume for this part was approximately $3 million. The company chosen had sales in the prior year of just over $7 million, putting in question the supplier's capacity to handle this award in an orderly manner. Upon further questioning, we learned it was the supplier's intent to subcontract a good deal of the work to another shop, one we had previously declined to qualify for this particular project since it did not have the ability to meet the exceptional quality requirements needed for this part.

We decided to award the entire contract to the runner-up, although there was much discussion about using the first supplier we selected for part of the contract so that we could include them on our list of approved suppliers. However, we chose not to do so since we did not want to dilute the volume by awarding business to two suppliers and thus potentially increase the price.

From this exercise, we learned to include a clause in future RFPs indicating that subcontracting would not be allowed without our express written permission.

(ii) Technical Capability.   Another key capability to be evaluated is the supplier's technology and technical ability. Does it have the necessary equipment, tools, and talent to meet your requirements? This can be determined not only through site visits but also through historical performance records and active participation in industry events. How many patents does the company hold in comparison to its competition? How often does it lead the market with the introduction of new products? To what extent is it funding its research and development efforts?

You might also consider supplier certification as an adjunct to technical enablement. Does the supplier have the necessary licenses, insurance, and certifications required to ensure regulatory compliance? This not only reduces the supplier's liability, but in many cases it may reduce the liability of your own organization, too, because lawsuits directed at your supplier while it is performing your contract will potentially bring your organization into potential litigation as well.

(iii) Financial Ability.   A key indication of the supplier's ability to service your needs is its history of profitability and cash flow management. When a company's profit trend spirals downward at a faster rate than its competitors, it is usually an indication that it will soon begin to experience financial strain. This may also affect its ability to meet current schedules, to effectively invest in new equipment, to employ new technologies for future efficiency, or to hire the best talent available.

Refer to the section on Utilizing Financial Tools in Chapter 1 and to Appendix E for many of the commonly used financial ratios and their definitions.

(d) COMPETITIVE VALUE.   Most of all, buyers should expect to gain the greatest value possible through the award of business. Value, as illustrated in Figure 3.1, can be considered the optimal combination of a number of factors. Most importantly, these factors include price, service, technology, and quality.

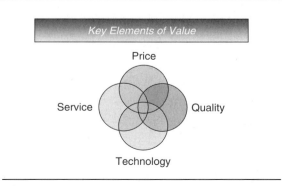

FIGURE 3.1   ELEMENTS OF VALUE

(i) Price.   Price is driven by a number of factors, not the least of which is the current supply-and-demand ratio situation in the particular marketplace. While there is in general an identified tendency for supply and demand to seek an equilibrium, the condition where one exactly matches the other, it is rarely the case that markets ever reach this condition for long. More often, the two factors are in continual flux.

When supply of available goods or services exceeds the demand generated by willing buyers, prices usually drop. Conversely, when demand exceeds supply, that is, when many buyers are chasing fewer available products, prices traditionally rise. However, faced with declining prices, suppliers usually move away from marketing the product or service and on to other, more profitable, offerings. Similarly, faced with rising prices, consumers tend to move to less costly alternatives. Keep in mind, though, in today's economy, conditions are rarely uniform from industry to industry or cycle to cycle. In addition, in the more complex industries, such as electronics, numerous factors beyond supply and demand come into play. This makes price trend predictions virtually impossible.

Price, of course, is relative to other considerations as well. As buyers analyze price, they should consider two factors: competition and return on investment (ROI). First, how does the price offered by the supplier compare to prices commonly found in the open market for other products or services of a similar nature? A buyer, negotiating price, wants to achieve at the very least a **fair and reasonable price**. Second, does the price paid provide a reasonable ROI? That is, does the price paid reduce costs substantially enough to justify the initial expenditure? Organizations typically look for an ROI that returns the value of the investment in less than one year or adds profit at a rate above what is traditionally earned.

When considering price, the buyer may also want to consider overall life-cycle costs, which include all of the costs associated with procurement and using the product for the duration of its useful life. This consideration is also known as total cost of ownership (TCO) and includes various other costs, such as maintenance or storage, that might affect the comparison of suppliers' offers. At the very minimum, an analysis of the cost of materials should include the expense of transportation. The cost of goods, which include transportation, is known as landed price.

(ii) Service.   When you evaluate service, you will look at a number of factors:

- Full support for just-in-time delivery
- The flexibility to accommodate rush orders
- Strong engineering and design support
- An accommodating credit policy or a guarantee of satisfaction

Buyers also evaluate how well the supplier responds to unexpected situations, such as accepting return of slow-moving or obsolete parts. From the customers' perspective, service is the element that bonds the organization to the supplier.

In developing relationships with customers, the supplying sales team generally strives to develop a perception of responsiveness to problems and issues. But in your evaluation, you should evaluate the selling organization's proactive efforts in avoiding problems in the first place.

(iii) Technology.   In any consideration of value, two questions regarding the use of technology are important: first, how effectively does the proposed technology meet current requirements? Second, how long into the future will the technology continue to be viable? In answering these questions, your evaluation should rely heavily on input from engineering and other user groups familiar with the technical qualities in the requirements.

Always keep in mind, though, that technological innovation can provide your organization with a competitive advantage. So your evaluation will also want to take into account the reputation of the supplier as a technical leader in the market.

(iv) Quality.   The evaluation of quality involves both the supplier's ability to conform to specifications and the perceived satisfaction of the user. This concept parallels the argument that a Ford or Nissan is as functional as any of the luxury automobiles, yet buyers are willing to pay substantial premiums to own the latter. Clearly, variations in such intangibles as comfort and appearance can be hard to evaluate mathematically, yet consumers continue to value and pay for them.

Key to any supplier evaluation will be an analysis of the systems the supplier has in place to control the quality of its output, such as statistical process control (SPC), which was discussed in Chapter 2, and the programs it utilizes to maintain continuous improvement. Effective application of process improvement programs such as **Six Sigma** or **Total Quality Management (TQM)** can have a tremendous impact on the long-term quality of a supplier's product or service and should be regarded as a form of insurance. Certifications, such as those issued in accordance with the standards of the **International Organization for Standardization (ISO)**, also provide assurances that the supplier has programs in place that will reasonably ensure continued levels of quality.

NOTE

For more information on Six Sigma, visit www.isssp.com.
For more information on Total Quality Management, visit www.asqc.org.
Finally, for more information on the International Organization for Standardization, check out www.iso.org

3.2 APPLYING SELECTION CRITERIA

Qualifying a supplier requires the disciplined application of an objective process. This typically includes a set of criteria appropriate for that particular supply segment to which some form of measurement can be added. Evaluation is most commonly performed by a cross-functional team with members chosen from the various departments or **stakeholder** groups affected by the choice of supplier. It is the team's job to develop the final supplier selection through some method of achieving consensus. Commonly, consensus is generated through the application of a scoring evaluation matrix that averages the inputs from each of the team members. We'll discuss consensus matrices and other methods for supplier selection in this section.

(a) SITE VISIT.   The site visit is one of the more common tools used to develop an evaluation of a supplier. While not every member of the team will attend the site visit, it is important that, at the least, representatives of the user group, the quality group, and supply management attend.

In addition to performing an inspection to audit the supplier's facilities (and perhaps records), the site visit provides an opportunity to establish or further develop working relationships with staff that you may not get to know under arm's-length circumstances. If you use this tool effectively, it may save time in the future when you need a problem solved quickly.

(b) QUALIFYING THE SUPPLIER.   Clearly, the site visit is conducted to qualify or continue the qualification status of a particular supplier. It is a formal process and should be well prepared for in advance. And since it can be somewhat costly considering travel expenses, the team should develop a process that will enable it to come away with as much information as possible.

By way of a checklist, here are several key areas you should cover during the site visit, which we will discuss here in this section.

(i) Order Processing and Fulfillment.   Order processing and fulfillment covers the methods by which the supplier receives, processes, and schedules incoming customer orders. It includes shipping and tracking records. Some of the specifics you should cover include the efficiency and effectiveness of:

- Systems employed for entering and verifying customer orders, level of automation, and reliability.
- Methods used to prioritize orders.
- Processes used to schedule orders and monitor delays.
- Comparative length of backlog.
- Cycle times.
- Flexibility in meeting spikes and valleys of incoming orders.
- Training and expertise of the staff.

(ii) Operations.   The areas of operations you should consider reviewing for a supplier audit include manufacturing, technical document control, engineering, facilities management, and procurement. Specifically, you should be concerned with:

- Capacity (the current level of operation as a percentage of the maximum level of operation).
- Degree of automation and technological enablement.
- Complexity of the product line.
- Flexibility to fulfill additional requirements.
- **Work-in-process (WIP)** tracking and lot tracking ability.
- Inventory management.
- Preventative maintenance.
- Record keeping including technical specification control.
- Production flexibility.
- Reliability of suppliers and methods used to improve performance.
- Training and expertise of the staff.

(iii) Quality Systems.   Quality systems generally consist of the methods used to ensure current quality and the processes employed for longer-term improvement. A buyer performing a supplier audit should review the following in regard to quality systems:

- Systems used to evaluate and control quality (including testing).
- Management commitment to quality improvement.
- Processes employed for continuous improvement.
- Record keeping.
- Compliance control.
- Internal and external audit procedures.
- Measures and methods used to determine customer satisfaction.
- Supplier quality engineering.
- Communications programs.
- Training and expertise of the staff.
- Training programs for employees.

(iv) Cost Control.   The method used for controlling costs is one of the key elements that should be covered in a site visit, largely because the supplier's ability to manage cost will indicate its future viability as a partner. To a large extent, your organization's ability to compete with others in your market depends on the effectiveness of your suppliers and their ability to keep pace with market pricing. Some of the most important areas you should review include:

- Ability to properly account for cost by job.
- Systems used to allocate costs by task.
- Effectiveness of cost control initiatives.
- Process documentation.
- Engineering support.
- Performance of value analysis.
- Adherence to accepted standards of cost accounting.

- Establishment of aggressive company-wide goals.
- Ability to manage cost variances to limit margin loss.

(v) Finance.   How an organization manages its finances generally determines how long it will stay in business. Today, the U.S. government sets strict rules for financial accountability, and site inspections can effectively determine the efficacy of government regulations. Look for evidence of:

- Effective profitability management.
- Strong balance sheet.
- Excellent credit ratings.
- Sarbanes-Oxley compliance (for public companies).

For publicly held companies, you can use a number of reports (some of which are available online) to determine an organization's financial condition, including:

- **Annual statements and reports,** some of which are available for free online at www.prars.com.
- **10-K reports** filed with the **Securities and Exchange Commission (SEC)** are available online at www.sec.gov/edgar.shtml.
- **Ratio of current liabilities to current assets** (also called **current ratio**) are available online through any financial report search engine, such as finance.yahoo.com—just enter the ticker or company name.
- **Earnings per share of stock.** Found on any financial report search engine, such as finance.yahoo.com—just enter the ticker or company name.
- **Return on net assets (RONA).** Found on any financial report search engine, such as finance.yahoo.com—just enter the ticker or company name.
- **Ratio of debt to assets.** Found on any financial report search engine, such as finance.yahoo.com—just enter the ticker or company name.

Other generalized ratio categories include:

- **Leverage ratios.** Show the extent that debt is used in a company's capital structure.
- **Liquidity ratio.** Present a company's short-term financial situation or solvency.
- **Operational ratios.** Use turnover measures to show how efficient a company is in its operations and use of assets.
- **Profitability ratios.** Employ margin analysis to show the return on sales and capital employed.
- **Solvency ratios.** Provide analysis of a company's ability to generate cash flow and pay its financial obligations.

(vi) Financial Reporting Mechanisms.   All U.S. publicly held corporations are required to file certain financial reports with the SEC. Although specific line items may differ from company to company, these reports follow a roughly standardized format that allows for relatively easy comparison.

You will likely need to examine three specific items in order to get a full picture of an organization's financial health: the balance sheet, the **income statement**, and the **cash flow statement**. Examples are on subsequent pages in Figures 3.2 and 3.3.

- **Balance sheet.** Provides a snapshot of an organization's financial position in terms of its liabilities, assets, and equity on a specific date.
- **Income statement.** Also known as a profit-and-loss statement or statement of operations; shows an organization's income and expenses for a given period, along with the associated net profit or loss. Most of the ratios noted previously are drawn from this information.
- **Cash flow statement.** A report showing the organization's movement of money. It presents cash receipts and cash expenditures for a particular period, detailing any changes in the cash position from the previous statement. It appears in the format shown in Figure 3.4.

(vii) Management.   You should evaluate the management team and its style of management to determine an organization's compatibility with that of your organization. Some things to consider in relation to management include:

- Management policies, for instance, whether they reflect honest dealing and strong adherence to an ethical code of conduct.
- Management's commitments to other customers and to suppliers.
- Management's maintenance of long-term and short-term needs.
- Management's commitment to sound environmental practices and adherence to a code of ethics and social responsibility.

QUANTITATIVE ANALYSIS

There's an old adage: "If it's worth doing, it's worth measuring." (Or sometimes alternatively expressed: "Nothing that can't be measured is worth doing.") This measurement process is called **quantitative analysis** to indicate that the analysis is provided in mathematical terms. With quantitative analysis you will use statistics and analytical matrices to suppliers.

Well in advance of any site visit, the team should establish the criteria it will use to evaluate and select a supplier. To the extent possible, you should conduct this evaluation using objective, quantitative methods so that you can easily present data that requires a minimum amount of interpretation.

BALANCED SCORECARD

Robert Kaplan (of Harvard Business School) and David Norton introduced the "balanced scorecard" in the early 1990s, and it has gained widespread recognition as a key management tool. Essentially an analysis technique, it was designed

Consolidated Balance Sheets
(in thousands, expect par values)

	December 31, 2004	December 31, 2003
ASSETS		
Current assets:		
Cash and cash equivalents	$ 713,182	$ 365,606
Short-term investments	404,659	215,906
Accounts receivable, net of allowances for doubtful accounts of $10,184 in 2004 and $9,206 in 2003	187,306	77,964
Prepaid expenses and other current assets	108,586	31,333
Total current assets	1,413,733	690,809
Property and equipment, net	275,612	244,491
Long-term investments	595,234	394,297
Restricted cash	31,226	30,837
Goodwill	4,427,930	983,397
Purchased intangible assets, net and other long-term assets	255,979	67,266
Total assets	$ 6,999,714	$ 2,411,097
LIABILITIES AND STOCKHOLDERS' EQUITY		
Current liabilities:		
Accounts payable	$ 113,890	$ 61,237
Accrued compensation	82,946	42,650
Accrued warranty	38,921	35,324
Other accrued liabilities	107,330	66,743
Deferred revenue	159,750	59,434
Total current liabilities	502,837	265,388
Deferred revenue, net of current portion	22,700	15,878
Other long-term liabilities, net of current portion	81,440	25,312
Long-term debt	400,000	542,076
Commitments and contingencies		
Stocksholders' equity:		
Convertible preferred stock, $0.00001 par value, 10,000 shares authorized; none issued and outstanding	—	—
Common stock, $0.00001 par value, 1,000,000 shares authorized; 540,526 and 390,272 shares issued and outstanding at December 31, 2004 and 2003, respectively	5	4
Additional paid-in capital	5,888,215	1,557,372
Deferred stock compensation	(32,394)	(1,228)
Accumulated other comprehensive (loss) income	(716)	4,414
Retained earnings	137,627	1,881
Total stockholders' equity	5,992,737	1,562,443
Total liabilites and stockholders' equity	$ 6,999,714	$ 2,411,097

FIGURE 3.2 BALANCE SHEET

Consolidated Balance Sheets
(in thousands, expect par values)

	December 31, 2004	December 31, 2003
ASSETS		
Current assets:		
Cash and cash equivalents	$ 713,182	$ 365,606
Short-term investments	404,659	215,906
Accounts receivable, net of allowances for doubtful accounts of $10,184 in 2004 and $9,206 in 2003	187,306	77,964
Prepaid expenses and other current assests	108,586	31,333
Total current assets	1,413,733	690,809
Property and equipment, net	275,612	244,491
Long-term investments	595,234	394,297
Restricted cash	31,226	30,837
Goodwill	4,427,930	983,397
Purchased intangible assets, net and other long-term assets	255,979	67,266
Total assets	$ 6,999,714	$ 2,411,097
LIABILITIES AND STOCKHOLDERS' EQUITY		
Current liabilities:		
Accounts payable	$ 113,890	$ 61,237
Accrued compensation	82,946	42,650
Accrued warranty	38,921	35,324
Other accrued liabilities	107,330	66,743
Deferred revenue	159,750	59,434
Total current liabilities	502,837	265,388
Deferred revenue, net of current portion	22,700	15,878
Other long-term liabilities, net of current portion	81,440	25,312
Long-term debt	400,000	542,076
Commitments and contingencies		
Stockholders' equity:		
Convertible preferred stock, $0.00001 par value, 10,000 shares authorized; none issued and outstanding	—	—
Common stock, $0.00001 par value, 1,000,000 shares authorized; 540,526 and 390,272 shares issued and outstanding at December 31, 2004 and 2003, respectively	5	4
Additional paid-in capital	5,888,215	1,557,372
Deferred stock compensation	(32,394)	(1,228)
Accumulated other comprehensive (loss) income	(716)	4,414
Retained earnings	137,627	1,881
Total stockholders' equity	5,992,737	1,562,443
Total liabililites and stockholders' equity	$ 6,999,714	$ 2,411,097

FIGURE 3.3 INCOME STATEMENT

Consolidated Statements of Cash Flows
(in thousands)

	Year Ended December 31		
	2004	2003	2002
OPERATING ACTIVITIES:			
Net income (loss)	$ 135,746	$ 39,199	$ (119,650)
Adjustments to reconcile net income (loss) to net cash from operating activities			
Depreciation	40,843	43,998	41,570
Amorization of purchased intangibles, deferred stock compensation and debt issuance costs	104,831	26,042	21,477
Restructuring and other	321	3,621	1,701
In-process research and development	27,600	—	83,479
Write-down of investements	2,939	—	50,451
(Gain) loss on redemption of convertible subordinated notes	4,107	1,085	(62,856)
Gain on sale of investments	—	(8,739)	—
Tax benefit of employee, stock option plans	65,968	10,813	—
Changes in operating assets and liabilities			
Accounts receivable, net	(81,398)	537	39,362
Prepaid expenses, other current assets and other long-term assets	(56,253)	(3,092)	13,278
Accounts payable	29,390	12,963	9,093
Accrued compensation	40,296	17,528	(3,183)
Accrued warranty	3,597	2,966	(6,388)
Other accrued liabilities	27,893	2,467	(61,263)
Deferred revenue	93,648	29,166	(4,661)
Net cash provided by operating activities	439,448	178,554	2,410
INVESTING ACTIVITIES:			
Purchases or property and equipment, net	(63,185)	(19,388)	(36,127)
Purchases of available-for-sale investements	(739,437)	(734,679)	(977,926)
Maturities and sales of available-for-sale investments	704,740	1,085,929	1,095,541
Increase in restricted cash	(249)	(30,837)	—
Minority equity investments	(1,225)	(900)	(1,150)
Acquisition of businesses, net of cash and cash equivalents acquired	40,889	—	(375,803)
Net cash (used in) provided by investing activities	(58,467)	300,125	(295,486)
FINANCING ACTIVITIES:			
Proceeds from issuance of common stock	175,172	91,755	26,620
Redemption of convertible subordinated notes	(144,967)	(762,013)	(145,975)
Retirement of common stock	(63,610)	—	—
Proceeds from issuance of convertible senior notes	—	392,750	—
Net cash used in financing activities	(33,405)	(307,508)	(119,355)
Net increase (decrease) in cash and cash equivalents	347,576	171,171	(412,410)
Cash and cash equivalents at beginning of period	365,606	194,435	606,845
Cash and cash equivalents at end of period	$ 713,182	$ 365,606	$ 194,435
Supplemental Disclosures of Cash Flow Information			
Cash paid for interest	$ 4,424	$ 45,864	$ 53,787
Cash paid for taxes	$ 7,340	$ 3,156	3,621
Supplemental Schedule of Non-Cash Investing and Financing Activities			
Common stock issued in connection with business combinations	$ 3,651,226	$ —	$ 376,416
Deferred stock compensation	$ 93,558	$ —	$ 499
Common stock issued in correction with the retirement of convertible subordinated notes	$ —	$ 2	$ —

FIGURE 3.4 CASH FLOW STATEMENT

70

to translate an organization's mission statement and overall business strategy into specific, quantifiable goals and to monitor the organization's performance in terms of achieving these goals. The balanced scorecard outlines what organizations need to measure from a financial perspective so that they can work toward achieving a "balanced" operation. It is a means to translate strategic planning from an academic exercise into a fully functional operational process.

The balanced scorecard method suggests that we consider and manage the organization from four perspectives, and that we develop metrics and collect and analyze data relative to each of them:

1. The learning and growth perspective
2. The business process perspective
3. The customer perspective
4. The financial perspective

The authors outline the scorecard's intended approach as follows:

> The balanced scorecard retains traditional financial measures. But financial measures tell the story of past events, an adequate story for industrial age companies for which investments in long-term capabilities and customer relationships were not critical for success. These financial measures are inadequate, however, for guiding and evaluating the journey that information age companies must make to create future value through investment in customers, suppliers, employees, processes, technology, and innovation.[1]

(viii) Weighted Average Scorecard.   When evaluating a supplier, you may often use a rating matrix called a **weighted average**. A weighted average defines critical areas and attempts to develop an objective, average score based on the opinions of the various team members. Table 3.1 shows you an example of a typical weighted-average evaluation chart. Although the category titles and values will vary widely depending on what is being evaluated, the format will likely always look similar.

During the initial development of the weighted-average matrix, the team assigns percentages to each of the major sections. In the example shown in Table 3.1, these major categories are cost, quality, technology, and service. The categories are then broken down into subsets composed of each of the individual elements being scored. Each is assigned a portion of the total percentage allocated to the broader category. In a simple analysis, there may be only two or three subsets, while in a complex analysis there may be dozens.

Each member of the team, represented by letters A–E on the table, prepares a separate rating, evaluating any of the categories they are qualified to assess. Assessment is made on a sliding scale and scored accordingly. Some scales use a 1–3 rating system; others use 1–5. Occasionally, you see scales of 1–10, but that

---

1.   Kaplan, Robert S., and David P. Norton. *The Balanced Scorecard: Translating Strategy into Action.* Boston: Harvard Business School Press, 1996.

Category	Value	A*	B*	C*	D*	E*	Average Score	Weighted Average
Cost	**35%**							
Relative bid	15%	4	4	3	4	5	4.0	.60
Containment tools	8%							
Tracking system	4%							
Market leadership	8%							
Quality	**30%**							
Historical defect levels	10%							
Incoming insp.	08%							
Six Sigma	06%							
SPC	06%	5	3	3	4	2	3.4	.204
Technology	**15%**							
Road map alignment	7%							
Market leadership	4%							
R&D budget	4%							
Service	**20%**							
24x7 Customer service	4%							
Scheduling flexibility	8%							
Design assistance	5%							
Automatic status updates	3%							
TOTAL	100%							

TABLE 3.1   SUPPLIER EVALUATION MATRIX EXAMPLE
*Rating Scale: 1 = Poor 3 = Average 5 = Excellent

gets far more complex than necessary. Some users prefer scales with even numbers (such as 1–6) so that individuals are forced onto one side or another and cannot select a midrange score to remain neutral. All relate the numbers to some measure of judgment, for example, 5 = excellent and 1 = inadequate.

Individual scores are then tallied into a master score sheet, averaged by subset, and then weighted by the percentage allocated to it. As an example, let's say that the team decides quality should be given an overall value of 25 percent and one of its subsets, SPC measurement systems, should be given 6 percent. The five individuals (A–E) rate the subset on a scale of 1–5, as follows: A. 5, B. 3, C. 3, D. 4, and E. 2. The average of the five ratings comes to 3.4 (17/5). This average is then multiplied by 6 percent (.06), the amount allocated to the subset, to determine its total value: $3.4 \times .06 = .204$.

The sum of the subsets equals the total percentage score for each category. The total scores for each category then add up to the supplier's total rating. However, a word of caution is in order: Regardless of the number of team members used to develop the rating, it will still be a subjective rating. As a result, you should consider a wide margin of error when evaluating scores, and only when the order of magnitude clearly separates one supplier from the rest should you consider using this as an absolute selection criterion. If, for example, your team evaluates six suppliers, five of which score in the 50–60-point range and one that scores 87 points, you have a clear mandate. On the other hand, if three score in the 50–60-point range and three score in the 75–85-point range, you may simply have developed a short list of suppliers in the top range for further evaluation.

(ix) Weighted Bid Analysis. Another method for comparatively evaluating suppliers' offers can be implemented through the use of a **weighted bid analysis**, or **cost-ratio analysis**. This method is also known as **transformational bidding** because it weighs one supplier's bid in comparison to others by transforming the value of their offer to some equivalent percentage based on their demonstrated performance or added value.

In simple terms, let's say you know from past experience that Supplier A's billing process results in more errors than Supplier B's. You have been able to measure the additional cost and found it adds about 1 percent to the cost of all the products you purchase from Supplier A. You also know that it costs 2 percent more for shipping from Supplier A than from Supplier B. Therefore, you transform their bids to equivalency by adding 3 percent to Supplier A's bid.

Here's the math for this example:

$$\text{Supplier A's total bid} = \$142{,}000$$

$$\text{Supplier B's total bid} = \$144{,}000$$

$$\text{Supplier A's transformed bid (adding 3\%)} = \$146{,}260$$

Supplier A's bid is actually higher than Supplier B's using this method.

(c) REVIEWING, APPROVING, AND ISSUING THE CONTRACT. Once the scoring or other method for determining supplier selection has been completed and approved by the team, the contract may need to be reviewed and approved by other internal groups or individuals according to company policy. If the contract is for tangible goods covered by the UCC, chances are good that the organization's standard purchase order (PO) terms and conditions will apply and the issuance of a PO will be all that is required. In this case, any further approvals needed depend on the PO value. Some organizations require a Procurement professional's approval prior to the issuance of a PO if it exceeds a certain value. Since the budgeting manager has already approved the expenditure, the Procurement professional reviews the PO for its conformance to organizational policy and good business practices.

In the case of contracts for services not covered by the organization's standard terms and conditions, the buyer may have to write up a special contract. Typically, organizations rely on a previously developed set of contracts for each particular category of service—construction or consulting, for example. These contracts will have already had legal review. However, should the supplier wish to change any of the clauses in the contract that may impact its legal value, a further legal review will be required.

Depending on company policy and procedure, most POs can be signed by an authorized buyer. Contracts, however, are usually signed by an officer of the company or a senior manager as a means of ensuring one last sanity review. A PO often must be issued even with a contract in place, so that it can be recorded on the organization's financial system for payment.

3.3 ADMINISTERING THE CONTRACT

Once the contract has been approved and implemented, the procurement professional is in charge of providing continuous supplier evaluation and performance improvement in relation to the contract. Your objective is not only to measure current performance, but also to identify areas for improvement and collaboratively develop programs to implement improvement. Let's discuss some of the ways in which you will do this.

(a) IMPLEMENTING PERFORMANCE STANDARDS AND RATING SYSTEMS. Managing supplier performance is one of the most valuable functions performed by the Procurement Department. While this responsibility by its nature must be shared with technical and quality groups, it is generally expected that the Procurement professional will assume overall responsibility for the relationship with a supplier. This especially applies to ensuring that key suppliers receive timely input regarding their performance from the customer's perspective.

While there are many ways to evaluate a supplier's performance, two of the more common methods, tracking performance and customer surveys, are outlined in this section.

(i) Tracking Performance.   Many organizations monitor supplier performance using a weighted-average matrix similar to the one used for the initial selection (see Table 3.1, earlier in the chapter). Some of the specific criteria will change, of course, but it lends the credibility that comes with consistency to continue to use the same or closely related evaluation data.

As an alternative, you may consider using a matrix with similar criteria but have it relate to agreed-upon levels of service. To do this requires that you attach a **service-level agreement (SLA)** to the original contract that outlines the expected level of performance in quantitative terms. Incorporated into the contract, these metrics then become the agreed-upon guide for evaluating performance.

As an example, under Cost in the matrix, you might include a target price that produces a 4 percent decrease in each quarter. A supplier that achieves only a 3 percent decrease in cost will receive a score of 75 percent since only three-fourths

Category	Target Score	Actual	Value	Actual Weighted Score
Pricing	40	30	15%	
Inventory reduction	30	20	8%	
Packaging	20	20	4%	
Competitive benchmark	10	8	8%	
TOTAL SCORE/COST	100	78	35%	27.3%

TABLE 3.2   QUARTERLY PERFORMANCE EVALUATION EXAMPLE

of the goal was reached. Similarly, a quality metric might establish the number of lots rejected in a particular period, and a supplier would be rated according to actual performance. Be certain to have the individual subsets rated only by qualified individuals who are members of the team, and average the scores if there is more than one person performing the rating for any subset.

In the example of a quarterly performance evaluation shown in Table 3.2, we've included only the cost data for illustration purposes. While the four major categories remain the same as in the original selection matrix from Table 3.1, and their total percentage is the same, the corresponding subsets have changed to more objective criteria, which are based on the signed SLA. In this example the supplier achieved a score of 26.5 of a possible 35, something just above a 75 percent score. Accordingly, this leaves much room for improvement.

The formula for calculating the actual weighted score is a little bit tricky, so we're providing it here for you. Simply put, you take the amount under Actual divided by the amount under Target Score and multiply that number by the % Value. In the example shown in Table 3.2, the actual weighted score is:

$$\% \text{Value} \times (\text{Actual/Target}) = 35\% \times (78/100) = 35\% \times .78 = 27.3\%$$

(ii) Customer Survey.   In situations where uniform metrics may be difficult to establish, it is possible to use a customer evaluation instead. This is typically conducted in the form of a periodic survey, as shown in Figure 3.2 The results of this survey then provide the data for an element (or perhaps all elements) of the evaluation. Surveys are more commonly used for service providers.

(b) FOLLOWING UP AND EXPEDITING.   In addition to ongoing evaluation of standard contract terms, a Procurement professional must carry out a number of other internal duties when problems occur during the performance of the contract. These typically include such activities as expediting delayed orders, tracking lost shipments, resolving accounting discrepancies, and returning defective product. To the extent that these problems recur, you should establish uniform processes to ensure that they are eliminated so that the internal customer perceives a well-managed supplier. If these problems become issues (rather than isolated occurrences) through nonperformance, they should be included in the evaluation matrix and reviewed with the supplier on a regular basis.

(c) DEVELOPING GOOD PRACTICES.   Compliance with good business practices goes a long way to cementing the relationship between two organizations. To that end, the buyer must be continually aware of how well the supplier sticks to its stated policies and how conscientiously its management values ethical principles and strict adherence to legally responsible behavior. Let's discuss policy, law, and principles for a moment.

(i) Conformance to Policy.   Many organizations develop policy statements regarding ethical and legal conduct. They do this so that there can be no misunderstanding by employees, customers, and suppliers of their intentions to manage in accordance with community-accepted principles.

These policies need to be aligned with the actual practices of the supply base and compliance enforced to the extent possible. While it would be useless for you to expect every supplier to adopt the precise wording of your organization's policy, you should obtain copies and review the actual policies of your suppliers and, at the same time, ensure they have read copies of yours.

(ii) Conformance to Law.   In Chapter 2 we reviewed applicable laws and regulations that would likely apply to supplier relationships. This is by no means an exhaustive list. There are literally thousands of additional laws governing environmental regulations, working conditions, health and safety, equal opportunity, and financial practices. If your organization is global, it is likely there are local variations for all of them. No individual can possibly be knowledgeable about all of them.

For this reason, and for a variety of other practical reasons, you should rely on both the spirit of the supplier's desire to conform and its actual history of doing so. You can audit the former by reviewing documents and questioning their staff; you can audit conformance history through public records.

This is important, believe us. You never want to see the CEO of one of the suppliers *you* have chosen appearing on the evening news being led away to prison in handcuffs. If you have any doubts whatsoever about the supplier's compliance, you should contact your legal counsel immediately.

(iii) Ethical Principles.   Would you recommend doing business with an organization that utilizes child labor? Would you recommend doing business with a supplier that evades taxes by hiding revenues in another country? Would you approve a supplier that pays substandard wages? Some of these actions may not actually violate a law, but they may violate the law of your conscience.

So how do you regulate conformance to a set of moral expectations that may or may not violate any laws? You can do so by establishing a set of ethical principles

Sample Supplier Performance Evaluation			
Supplier Name:		Date:	

Summary Supplier Evaluation	Excellent	Average	Poor
CORPORATES/SALES	☐	☐	☐
COST MANAGEMENT	☐	☐	☐
QUALITY	☐	☐	☐
DELIVERY	☐	☐	☐
RESPONSIVENESS	☐	☐	☐
TECHNOLOGY	☐	☐	☐

Supplier Performance Factors	Excellent	Average	Poor
CORPORATE			
Billing processes	☐	☐	☐
Sales support	☐	☐	☐
Personnel turnover	☐	☐	☐
Timely response to inquiries	☐	☐	☐
Employee knowledge	☐	☐	☐
Employee courtesy	☐	☐	☐
COST MANAGEMENT			
Price reductions	☐	☐	☐
Peripheral costs	☐	☐	☐
Warranty administration	☐	☐	☐
QUALITY			
Quality & process control	☐	☐	☐
Continuous improvement	☐	☐	☐
Errors and emissions	☐	☐	☐
Corrective measures	☐	☐	☐
Incoming inspection requirements	☐	☐	☐
DELIVERY			
Meets customer requests	☐	☐	☐
Accurancy	☐	☐	☐
Documentation	☐	☐	☐
Advance delay notification	☐	☐	☐
RESPONSIVENESS			
Timely implementation of spec changes	☐	☐	☐
Manages complaints expeditiously	☐	☐	☐
Customer-focused attitude	☐	☐	☐
Continuous improvement processes	☐	☐	☐
TECHNOLOGY			
Provides timely technical assistance	☐	☐	☐
Engineering support	☐	☐	☐
Maintains roadmap	☐	☐	☐
Communicates changes	☐	☐	☐
IT systems	☐	☐	☐

FIGURE 3.5   CUSTOMER EVALUATION SURVEY

governing your expectation of how suppliers will behave. These, if you like, are the rules *buyers* expect suppliers to meet.

Ethical principles are usually issued in the form of a document, such as an *ethical code of conduct*, outlining the organization's expectations for employees and suppliers. Sometimes this document is the same for both groups; sometimes organizations will write them separately.

The ethical code of conduct is usually organized by specific subject matter such as legal compliance, working conditions, financial accounting practices, and so on. There is no clear formula, and different organizations emphasize different elements.

NOTE

Here are URLs for two examples of organizations with ethical codes of conduct that you might find useful:

HSBC is a globally positioned bank headquartered in the United Kingdom: www.hsbc.com/hsbc/purchasing/ethical-code-of-conduct.

Hewlett-Packard is a well-known global supplier of computers: www.hp.com/hpinfo/globalcitizenship/environment

(iv) Environmental Standards Requirements. Since the publication in 1962 of Rachel Carson's *Silent Spring*, governments and business entities worldwide have come under scrutiny for the manner in which they handle their relationship with the environment. A number of significant governmental initiatives have begun to address the issues and regulate both how environmentally sensitive resources are to be used and how materials that could harm the environment are to be handled. Of major significance are the following:

- **ISO 14000.** In 1996, the International Organization for Standardization issued standards for management, measurement, evaluation, and auditing of the impact of organizations' activities that affect the environment.
- **U.S. Environmental Protection Agency (EPA) Regulations.** Established in 1970, the EPA is charged with protecting human health and the environment in the United States. The EPA is chartered to develop and enforce regulations that implement environmental laws enacted by Congress. Where national standards are not met, the EPA can issue sanctions and take other steps to assist the states and tribes in reaching the desired levels of environmental quality.
- **Waste Electrical and Electronic Equipment (WEEE).** WEEE is the European Community directive on waste electrical and electronic equipment, which became European law in February 2003, setting collection, recycling, and recovery targets for all types of electrical goods.

- **Restriction of Hazardous Substances (RoHS).** RoHS became European law in February 2003. It is part of a legislative initiative to solve the problem of huge amounts of toxic e-waste.
- **Kyoto Protocol.** In 1997, the United Nations sponsored an agreement to prevent global warming. It was signed by 38 developed nations who agreed to reduce their emission of greenhouse gases by 2012.

(d) MANAGING RECORDS AND DATA.   Most organizations have policies regarding the management and retention of records. Some of these policies are based on legal requirements (e.g., the Internal Revenue Service requires documents relating to taxes be stored for seven years), and others are based on good business practices, such as keeping journals of engineering activity to limit future liability and to prove the development history of a particular patent.

Those policies notwithstanding, it is important that you maintain historical data indicating supplier performance so that there can be no misinterpretations and disputes in the conduct of the evaluation process.

3.4 SUMMARY

Supplier evaluation and selection is one of the key organizational functions led by the Procurement Department. It is critical, therefore, that the Procurement professional develop and implement effective processes for qualifying suppliers and determining the award of business. We have explored how supplier responsiveness and capability can be evaluated and how these attributes need to be combined with the elements of value to ensure that your organization receives the best return for its expenditure.

There are many ways to evaluate supplier performance, but we strongly recommend using a quantitative approach. This approach generally requires team input to gain appropriate objectivity and, in the case of key suppliers, data should be gathered from physical visits as well as from the evaluation of written offers. Most commonly, supplier selection data is put into a weighted-average matrix as a means of comparing various suppliers and their offers.

Ongoing contract administration requires the use of continuous improvement methods to generate greater value for your organization. Here, too, the use of a weighted-average method for evaluating performance is strongly recommended. You will also find that customer surveys can provide important feedback when measurement is not altogether practical.

Organizations must strive to develop sound business practices that conform to applicable law as well as fundamental ethical principles. It is a key function of the Procurement professional to ensure that there is alignment between the requirements of their organization and that of the supplier.

In the next chapter, we will look at how these methods are best applied in day-to-day operations.

KEY TERMS

Due diligence
Request for proposal (RFP)
Nonconforming
Operational capacity
Technical capability
Financial ability
Competitive value
Price
Service
Fair and reasonable price
Six Sigma
Total quality management (TQM)
International Organization for
    Standardization (ISO)
Stakeholder

Work-in-progress (WIP)
Securities and Exchange Commission
    (SEC)
Current ratio
Balance sheet
Income statement
Cash flow statement
Quantitative analysis
"Supplier evaluation scorecard"
Weighted average
Weighted bid analysis
Cost-ratio analysis
Transformational bidding
Service-level agreement (SLA)
Environmental standards requirements

CONTRACT ADMINISTRATION

LEARNING OBJECTIVES

1. Name the four key elements needed to make a contract legally enforceable and explain their meaning.
2. List five types of procurement contracts and describe a situation in which each would be applicable.
3. List the 12 elements of a Letter of Intent described in the chapter.
4. Define *intellectual property rights* and provide an example of a possible infringement.

In this chapter, we focus on reviewing key aspects of creating and managing various types of procurement contracts and documents. As a Procurement professional, you are required to understand the nature and purpose of contracts and what constitutes a legally binding obligation. You will also need to become familiar with a variety of standard elements that are required for contracts and what types of contracts should be used in any particular procurement transaction.

As you probably know by this time, forming and administering contracts covers a broad range of the department's responsibilities and constitutes a major investment of required talent. Problems with document verbiage, issues regarding unclear specifications, lack of supplier performance, and unseen financial obligations plague many organizations. The vast majority of these contractual problems, however, can be reduced or even eliminated by establishing clear process requirements for developing them and ensuring they receive appropriate approval and legal review.

Properly administering **purchase orders (POs)** and contracts also requires close attention to detail so that the supplier's compliance with the terms and conditions adds the full measure of value that was originally intended by the organization. This often involves resolving discrepancies and expediting deliveries, as well as handling disputes and contractual violations. Establishing procurement policies and practices that conform to ethical behavior and enhance the organization's integrity are keys to the Procurement Department's effectiveness in performing these obligations.

4.1 CONTRACT ESSENTIALS

The Procurement Department is responsible for the issuance and management of a variety of procurement contracts and documents. Since they generate both legal and financial obligations for the organization, the buyer needs to apply due diligence to their formation and management.

TIPS AND TECHNIQUES

In its basic form, a contract represents a legally binding agreement made by two or more parties to complete a specified action at a specific point in time. It represents a *bargain* that is valid in a court. Contracts may be generated to cover the purchase of either goods or services.

In this section, we will review the basis for forming contractual obligations and the key elements that provide their validity.

(a) CONTRACT ESSENTIALS. Contracts cover the purchase of both goods and services. Services are generally covered by state laws (known as common law or case law), which establish precedents that can help resolve disputes. Goods are considered personal property and are covered by Article 2 of the Uniform

Commercial Code (UCC). You will recall from Chapter 2 that the UCC was developed to provide a measure of standardization in the laws of commerce between the states and has been adopted by 49 U.S. states (all states except Louisiana) and the District of Columbia. One other body of law, known as **statutory law**, covers acts and regulations enacted by the U.S. Congress and state legislatures.

(i) Written Contracts.   In broad terms, contracts can use either written or oral formats. While from a procurement point of view, written contracts pose the least amount of risk, it is important to understand that oral contracts can be equally enforceable if they meet a common set of conditions. However, the **Statute of Frauds**—laws designed to prevent fraud—requires certain types of contracts to be validated in written form:

- Contracts for goods sold under the UCC exceeding $500 that are not specifically manufactured for the user. (This amount will likely increase to $5,000 under pending proposals.)
- Contracts for the sale or transfer of real estate.
- Contracts to assume the debt or duty of another.
- Contracts that cannot be completed within one year, either by their own terms or because they are objectively impossible to complete.

Agreements required to be evidenced in writing (such as those just listed) do not have to take a specific contractual form. However, at the least, the writing must contain:

- Identification of the other party as the individual responsible for the contract.
- Some form of signature of the above.
- A clearly identified subject of the contract.
- Specific terms and conditions.
- Identification of the **consideration** (as an exchange of value).

There are a number of exceptions to the written requirements of the Statute of Frauds under which an oral contract will be enforced, including the partial completion of an oral contract up to the point of performance. If, for example, a contract to buy $10,000 worth of parts has not yet been committed to writing and is canceled by the buyer after $2,000 worth of parts has been received and accepted, will the seller be able to force the buyer to honor the entire contract? The answer is no. Since the value of the remaining portion of the contract exceeds $500 and there is no evidence in writing of any contract, the buyer is under no obligation to honor the original agreement. Similarly, the seller would not be responsible for delivering any more than that already shipped.

(ii) Oral Contracts.   The **principle of detrimental reliance** applies when it can be shown that reliance on the oral promise will produce substantial or unconscionable

injury to the promisee or will unjustly enrich the promisor. The fact that the promisee relies on the oral promise to its detriment is generally not considered sufficient reason to entitle it to enforce an oral contract. However, when customized products are made for a buying organization under an oral agreement and cannot be sold to any others, the contract is enforceable by the seller.

If an oral contract not required to be in writing (e.g., for goods under $500) is modified to the extent that it falls within the statute of fraud, then the contract must be in writing to be enforceable. For example, if $200 worth of goods is added to an oral contract already totaling $450, it's required that the entire contract be put in writing since the total amount ($650) exceeds the limit of $500 for an oral contract.

Also considered in the formation of a contract is the law of promissory estoppel. An oral contract unenforceable under the Statute of Frauds may be enforced under the doctrine of promissory estoppel if one party made an oral promise and the other party relied on that promise and performed part of or its entire obligation. Under these conditions, the oral promise cannot be rescinded simply because it is not evidenced in writing.

TIPS AND TECHNIQUES

THE TROUBLE WITH ELECTRONIC PROCUREMENT

Electronic procurement is a relatively new process that has yet to be fully recognized under the UCC or the Statute of Frauds. The primary issue concerns the ability of one party to fraudulently alter a document after agreement has been reached. While faxed signatures and documents, along with electronic data interchange (EDI) transactions, are generally considered reliable evidence of contractual obligations, other forms such as e-mail have yet to be fully accepted as legal. Parties using electronic transmission for business are usually counseled to initiate some contractual documentation, such as a formal trading partner agreement, outlining the processes and obligations that will govern them.

(b) CONTRACT REQUIREMENTS.   In order for a contract to be legally enforceable, it is commonly agreed that four key elements need to be demonstrated: mutual agreement, legality, consideration, and capacity. Let's discuss each of these in more detail.

1. **Mutual agreement.** As evidence of a "meeting of the minds," **mutual agreement** includes an **offer** and its **acceptance**. When a buyer places a PO, for example, it is considered an offer to buy, and the seller's acknowledgment is generally considered an acceptance. An acceptance can also be demonstrated by actual performance, such as a shipment of materials or some constructive action of service that indicates such acceptance. This is called a **unilateral contract**, whereas a contract containing both an offer to sell and an agreement to buy is considered a **bilateral contract**.

If a seller extends an offer in the form of a quotation but the buyer requests modification to some of the terms, it is considered a **counteroffer** rather than an acceptance. By requesting modification, the buyer, in effect, rejects the original offer and proposes a new one.

If a buyer issues a solicitation for a certain quantity of materials and a seller provides a quotation, does it signify a contract exists? No, because a solicitation is not necessarily an offer to buy.

2. **Legality.** A contract requires a legal purpose. Contracts that violate a legal statute or are against public policy are invalid.

3. **Consideration.** Consideration means an exchange of anything of value. To be valid, a contract has to show evidence that an exchange of some value for a promise is part of the agreement. Consideration does not necessarily have to be exchanged in the form of money. It can also be in the form of various types of services rendered.

TIPS AND TECHNIQUES

One way to think of consideration is by referring to the Latin term **quid pro quo**. Translated literally, quid pro quo means "this for that" or "something for something." While we generally consider this to mean something of equal value, it is also generally considered that value is subjective and must be determined by the parties to the exchange.

4. **Capacity.** Parties to a contract need to be legally **competent** to enter into it and perform its **obligations**. Minors, for example, are not considered legally competent. A person who is legally insane cannot be a valid party to a contract.

(c) CONTRACT TYPES. Typically, a Procurement Department will use a wide variety of contractual documents during the normal course of business. The exact document you choose will largely depend on the business needs of your organization and the type of purchase being made. Outlined in this section are the contracts that are most commonly used.

(i) Purchase Orders (POs). In almost all environments, the PO is the most common procurement document available and is, in effect, a contract. As a standard form, it is the easiest way to order purchased materials and services and provides the most commonly required audit trail. A standard PO can be used for recurring or repetitive purchases as well as one-time purchases. In addition to stating the specific requirements for the purchase, the PO usually conveys your organization's standard terms and conditions, sometimes termed a "boilerplate."

The PO can be both an offer and a means of acceptance, depending on the existing circumstances. When issued in response to a solicitation for bids, it can be considered evidence of contract formation. However, when sent to a supplier without having previously received a quote or proposal, it may be considered simply an offer to buy.

In addition to standard terms and conditions covering remedies, warranties, liabilities, rights of inspection and rejection, ability to cancel, and other typical clauses (usually transmitted by the fine print on the reverse side of the PO), the PO will generally describe on its face what is being purchased, the price being paid, the terms of delivery, and any other instructions needed to describe the specific requirements of that particular order.

Blanket POs, also known as indefinite delivery contracts, are used when the buyer wishes to establish set pricing and terms but does not yet wish to place orders for specific quantities or delivery times.

(ii) Requirements or Indefinite Delivery Contracts.   **Requirements contracts** or **indefinite delivery contracts** are used when the buyer wishes to lock in pricing or lead time in exchange for a commitment to purchase all of the organization's requirements (or at least some described minimum and/or maximum amount) but specific quantities and delivery dates are not yet known. Sometimes, the requirements contract will be used to make commitments to a supplier for a certain line of products (e.g., office supplies) in exchange for a specified discount level or for some other consideration such as setting up an automated, online ordering program.

(iii) Definite Quantity Contracts.   A *definite quantity contract* specifies the amount being purchased during a given time frame but not the specific delivery dates. This type of contract is also known as a **take-or-pay** contract because the buying organization cannot cancel it and must pay for it at the end of the contractual period even if it is not used.

(iv) Fixed-Price Contracts.   **Fixed-price contracts** are the most commonly used contracts in typical business environments. Most fixed-price contract types are defined in the Federal Acquisitions Regulations (FAR) as they apply to government purchases; however, they are commonly adapted for commercial use by procurement departments. Essentially, they are contracts where prices are agreed to in advance of performance. There are five types of fixed-price contracts that we will discuss in more detail here.

FIRM FIXED PRICE
A **firm-fixed-price contract** is exactly what its title states: The price is not subject to adjustment. The buyer and seller agree to performance at the stated price, and the risk of profit and loss passes solely to the supplier.

FIXED PRICE WITH INCENTIVE
For the **fixed-price-with-incentive contract**, a profit formula is established based on target cost and target profit within an agreed-upon maximum price. The final price is established by adjusting the actual profit the supplier receives based on the

difference between the final cost agreed to by the parties and the original target cost. Typically, the amount saved by reducing the cost is shared by both parties. In other words, this contract type provides an incentive to the supplier to hold down the costs and thereby increase its profit.

FIXED PRICE WITH ECONOMIC PRICE ADJUSTMENT

The *fixed-price-with-economic-price-adjustment contract* allows pricing to be adjusted upward or downward based on established contingencies such as escalating labor and material rates. Changes in actual costs beyond the supplier's control or reasonable ability to foresee, above or below the contract's baseline, can lead to an adjustment reflected in the supplier's pricing. This method is frequently used for multiyear contracts or when economic conditions are unstable. Often, this is a standard contract with the inclusion of a clause allowing *escalation* or *deescalation* of prices under agreed-upon conditions. When it is difficult to calculate actual prices, adjustments are sometimes based on some readily available business or financial index.

FIXED PRICE WITH PRICE REDETERMINATION

Similar to the economic price adjustment contract, the *fixed-price-with-price-redetermination contract* is used when prices are anticipated to change over time but the extent of those changes cannot be predicted, such as during startup operations. Generally, the specific time for redetermination will be included.

FIXED PRICE, LEVEL OF EFFORT

The **fixed-price, level-of-effort** method of pricing, although relatively uncommon, is usually used in situations when the precise amount of labor or materials is unknown but the parties can agree on a standard level of effort (such as the type and quantity of tools to be used or the rated proficiency of the employees) and a given price. Thus the fixed-price, level-of-effort contract is similar to the concept in the time and materials contract, which will be discussed shortly.

(v) Cost-Reimbursable Contracts. **Cost-reimbursable contracts** are primarily used by government organizations and large corporations as an inducement for supplier participation in situations where the initial research and development engineering or capital investment may be very high and the financial risk great. These contracts assure the supplier that the buyer will cover, at a minimum, agreed-upon costs up to an agreed-upon monetary ceiling. The supplier may not exceed that amount without prior approval, unless it wishes to go forward at its own risk. Cost-reimbursable contracts are used in a variety of ways, as you will see in this section.

(vi) Cost Plus Fixed Fee. The **cost-plus-fixed-fee contract** is a cost-reimbursement contract that allows the supplier to recover actual costs plus a fee negotiated prior to the contract's inception. The fee is considered fixed because it does not vary from the amount of the cost, although further negotiation of the fee based on changed conditions can be considered.

(vii) Cost Plus Incentive Fee.   The **cost-plus-incentive-fee contract** is another reimbursable contract that, like the fixed-price-plus-incentive contract outlined previously, provides an initially negotiated fee with a formula-based adjustment that reflects the relationship of total allowable cost to total target cost.

(viii) Cost Plus Award Fee.   The **cost-plus-award-fee contract** provides additional incentive for the supplier to produce excellent results by enabling the buyer to make a financial award in addition to the cost and negotiated fee. It is designed to provide the supplier with a financial incentive for excellent performance.

TIPS AND TECHNIQUES

At one time, the federal government used a **cost-plus-percentage-of-cost** contract. For obvious reasons, this provided the supplier no incentive whatsoever to hold down costs. The **Government Accounting Office (GAO)**, the federal watchdog agency, caught on and banned this practice with legislation as of November 14, 2002. For more information, go to this site: www.fcw.com/fcw/articles/2003/0224/pol-legal-02-24-03.asp; you can also see what the GAO does and get more information at www.gao.gov. and www.fcw.com.

(ix) Cost Sharing.   A **cost-sharing contract** is generally used in a partnering relationship where all parties share the cost and the accruing benefits according to a negotiated formula. The costs are typically limited to a specific amount or an *in-kind exchange* that is defined at the contract's formation. In many ways, this type of contract is similar to a *joint venture*, where all parties own a portion of the operation.

(x) Cost Only.   Used primarily between universities and other nonprofit and research organizations, the *cost-only contract*, as its name implies, covers reimbursement only for actual costs, without including a fee. This contract typically supplements one organization's capabilities and enables full utilization of the other's resources that might otherwise remain idle.

TIPS AND TECHNIQUES

INCENTIVE CONTRACTS

We have outlined two commonly used incentive contracts in this section, the fixed-fee-plus-incentive and the cost-reimbursable-plus-incentive contracts. These are based primarily on cost reduction. However, there are often other reasons to provide incentives to the supplier, such as when accelerated delivery may be highly valuable (such as in development work) or when specific elements of performance (e.g., quality) are needed. Typically, such contracts fall into the fixed-price or cost-plus categories but contain clauses calling for additional payments for improvements in the negotiated level of performance.

(xi) Time and Materials Contracts.   **Time and materials (T&M) contracts** are used when there are no acceptable ways to determine what a fair and reasonable price may be for a particular project, such as a well-digging contract where the exact depth of the water and the composition of the soil may be unknown. With this type of contract, the rates for labor and the markup for materials are initially negotiated with a cap, or **not-to-exceed (NTE)** amount, specified as a limit. In most ways, T&M contracts are similar to cost-reimbursable contracts.

(d) LETTERS OF INTENT.   A **letter of intent (LOI)** can be useful when parties are seriously working toward a final contract and wish to proceed with some of their preliminary efforts under a formal agreement. Letters of intent can outline the broad intent of the contract regarding some terms that have not yet been specified or agreed upon. Depending on how complete LOIs are, they can be a legally binding contract between buyer and supplier. They can also induce the supplier to perform some specific action such as reserving production scheduling time or ordering materials in advance of an actual contract. Some of the most common elements of an LOI include:

- **Price and terms.** May include projected costs and how they will be determined. It may also broadly outline the terms and conditions that will apply under a given set of assumptions. In some instances, the LOI may specify the accrual of payment to the supplier for work performed in the development of the contract, such as research needed to validate a statement of work. It may also include payment terms.
- **Obligations.** A section covering obligations is also typically included. This section generally outlines what each party must do prior to proceeding with a contract and which party will pay for what activities.
- **Confidentiality.** Generally, an LOI binds the parties to the same level of confidentiality as a standard contract. This enables the free exchange of proprietary information so that certain elements of the contract can be predefined.
- **Exclusivity.** This section outlines the length of time the parties are bound to an exclusive relationship. Following this period, the parties may enter into agreements with others under preestablished confidentiality conditions and protection of any **intellectual property** developed.
- **Structure.** Often, the nature of the relationship needs to be stated prior to beginning even basic aspects of the work. This includes defining the nature of the final agreement—for example, the type of contract or the disposition of **intellectual property (IP)**—and what the nature of the relationship will be subsequent to a contract.
- **Time and conditions.** The elements related to time and specific conditions express the parties' intent to form a final agreement by a specific date and under described conditions. These reflect the known conditions that must

be present at that time in order to proceed and without which either of the parties are not obligated to form a further contract.

- **Binding or nonbinding clauses.** Included in most LOI documents are statements indicating which portions of the agreement shall be binding and which shall not. For example, the parties may agree to be bound by an IP clause granting the rights to any IP developed to one or the other of the parties.

- **Licensing agreements.** When another party has secured ownership rights to specific IP—such as an invention or a software program—through a **patent** or **copyright**, your organization will need to obtain permission to use it. Usually, this permission is given in the form of a **licensing agreement**, a contract for which the licensee will pay either a fixed fee or a *royalty* based on usage. A royalty is similar to a commission insofar as it is generally calculated as a percentage of gross sales. There are a number of different formats you may encounter, but the more common ones you will likely come in contact with include:

- **Exclusive license.** Grants usage rights to only one party so that no others may be so licensed.

- **Nonexclusive license.** Grants usage rights to a party but does not limit the number of others that may be similarly licensed by the owner.

- **Partially exclusive license.** Grants exclusive rights to use the patent within a geographical area or for specific products.

- **End-user license agreement (EULA).** A three-way contract among the manufacturer, the author, and the *end user* written to cover proprietary software. It is often attached to a program that requires you to check a box indicating acceptance of the terms prior to being able to use it.

TIPS AND TECHNIQUES

INTELLECTUAL PROPERTY
In general, IP is protected in the United States by specific law and a number of registration processes. The more common of the registration processes are outlined below:

PATENTS
A patent is generally considered a set of exclusive rights granted by a government to an inventor for a specified period of time. In the United States, this is usually for 20 years. For the period of time covered by the patent, the patent holder owns a monopoly, and others wishing to use it must obtain a license. **Patents** are granted for inventions and processes, as opposed to **copyrights**, which are granted to written documents, designs, and software; or trademarks, which identify products.

COPYRIGHTS
Copyrights grant ownership of various forms of expression such as works of art, literature, software programs, or audiovisual material (and similar forms of expression). Ownership enables the exclusive right to publish, sell, or license it.

TRADEMARKS

A **trademark** is a word or symbol that identifies a particular brand, product, or business. Like a patent, it can also be registered with the U.S. Patent and Trademark Office so that exclusive ownership can be reserved.

(i) Consigned Goods Contracts.   It is becoming increasingly common for organizations to require suppliers to stock inventory at the buyers' sites in order to support rapid delivery. These arrangements are called supplier-managed inventory (SMI) and are included in a contract covering specific conditions, such as when and under what conditions the transfer of ownership from the supplier to the buyer takes place, which party bears the financial liability of loss during storage or potential obsolescence, and the general payment terms.

(ii) Other Contract Types.   A wide variety of contracts are employed in special circumstances that broadly outline the terms and conditions of ongoing relationships outside of any specific statement of work. There are so many types that it would be impossible (and beyond our scope) to list them all. For reference, here are just a few:

- **Master purchase agreement.** Covers special terms and conditions for the purchase of critical materials. You may also find this listed under *master supply agreement* in directories of legal agreements.
- **Master services agreement.** Addresses terms and conditions related to the purchase of nontangible goods. Since the UCC does not cover services directly—except when the major portion (greater than 50 percent) of the contract is actually for goods—it is always a good idea to have an overriding contract in place for each significant service purchased by your organization.
- **Construction contract.** Used for significant building and facilities improvement contracts where special risks of performance and liability exist.
- **Nondisclosure agreement (NDA).** An NDA or **confidentiality agreement** protects sensitive information from disclosure to third parties or the general public. An NDA can be unilateral, that is, binding on only one party, or mutual and binding on both parties.
- **Commercial lease agreement.** Forms a contract for equipment owned by one party and used by another for a fee. Leases are essentially rental agreements that outline the responsibilities and liabilities assumed by each of the parties. Terms generally state which party is responsible for maintenance and upkeep as well as the conditions for use and warranties.

(e) METHODS OF EXCHANGE.   As discussed earlier in this chapter, a contract requires both an offer and acceptance in order to be legally enforceable. Questions often arise regarding how to handle disparities between the form of the contract and the form of its acceptance, one issued by the supplier and the other by the buyer. If the terms of the two differ, which should prevail? This brings up the topic referred to as the "battle of the forms."

(i) Battle of the Forms.   Typically, for low-value goods orders, the buyer will issue a simple PO containing the organization's standard terms and conditions in the form of a boilerplate on the reverse side. The supplier acknowledges the order, issuing its own form with a corresponding boilerplate on its side. In common practice, neither party reads the other's boilerplate. But what happens when the two sets differ?

The answer to this gets rather complicated and has created some confusion. Section 2-207 of the UCC looks at this from three different perspectives:

1. Do the conflicting forms establish a contract?
2. If a contract does exist, what terms are then enforceable?
3. If a contract does not exist, but the parties have performed anyway, what are the terms of the contract established by their performance?

While many courts have ruled on these questions, there seems to be no uniform conclusion. For material goods, what appears to emerge is the concept that if one party *says* it accepts an offer, a contract exists even though the terms may be different or additional terms are included in the acceptance. But how are the additional terms or conflicting terms handled?

To complicate the answer to this question, Section 2-207 indicates that additional terms included by the seller in its acknowledgment become part of the contract unless the buyer's contract expressly prohibits such additions or if they materially alter the original contract. If not, the added terms become part of the contract unless the buyer specifically objects within a reasonable time frame. Thus, the additional terms are added to the buyer's contract.

Conflicting terms, however, are generally considered self-canceling, that is, they do not apply. Instead, standard terms contained in the UCC become the default provisions.

(ii) Mirror Image Rule.   Because the UCC does not expressly apply to services, the battle of the forms does not arise when services are contracted. Instead, the **mirror image rule** applies under the Statute of Frauds. This requires that offer and acceptance match exactly, that is, be mirror images of each other, before a contract can be enforced. If the acceptance differs from the offer, it is considered a counteroffer. However, if either of the parties initiates performance following such counteroffer, it is considered an acceptance.

TIPS AND TECHNIQUES

Careful: Actions speak louder than words. Initiating any act that indicates the existence of a contract can be tantamount to accepting the other parties' terms.

(iii) Acceptance of an Oral Agreement.   Under the terms of the UCC, oral agreements require written confirmation if they are for material goods with values greater than $500. If they are and the confirmation has been offered, the party receiving the written confirmation has 10 days from the receipt of such confirmation to object. Otherwise, the contract is considered accepted.

(f) OTHER CONTRACT ELEMENTS.   As you may imagine, numerous important legal elements are included in every contract. Each of these varies with the nature of the particular situation for which the contract is being written. Let's discuss some of the more common ones.

(i) Revocation.   In most cases, an offer may be revoked by the party making it any time before it is accepted. The **revocation** can take any form that expressly or implicitly indicates that the party making the offer is no longer willing or able to enter into a contract. A clear example of this would be the incapacity of the seller to perform as a result of a fire that destroys its facility or the sale of the item being offered to another party.

An action inconsistent with the offer is also considered a revocation if notice of the action is provided to the other party prior to acceptance. If, for example, we offer to perform a service for your organization next week and, before you can accept, leave you a voice mail that we have gone on vacation, we have then revoked the offer.

(ii) Change Orders.   Common in construction projects and other services, **change orders** present another issue. Having established a contract with your organization, is the supplier required to accept changes to the SOW? Most service contracts include appropriate criteria for making unilateral changes, including the method of pricing them. Without such protection, the supplier is under little obligation to accept changes or to price them in relation to its initial contract pricing. Change orders are subject to the same requirements of writing as the original contract.

(iii) Dispute Resolution.   Most contracts, including POs, contain legal remedies should a dispute arise. Many contain mediation or arbitration clauses or some other method for resolving them, such as a formal appeals process. In commercial transactions, disputes may ultimately come to a court for resolution.

NOTE

Section 2-207 of the UCC can be a handy reference for more detail regarding contract modification, rescission, and waiver.

(g) LEGAL AUTHORITY AND THE BUYERS' RESPONSIBILITIES.   In dealing with contracts, there are some specific principles you will need to keep in mind so that you fully understand your role and responsibilities, as well as the limits of your authority. Consider agency, authority, and financial responsibility, discussed in this section.

(i) Agency.   An *agent* is an individual with the authority to act on behalf of a principal, in most cases an employer. This means that your organization may be legally bound by the terms of any contract you have signed. The law of agency covers the legal principles governing this relationship and the buyer's relationship to the supplier. As an agent, however, *you* will not be held *personally* liable for such acts, providing you have not violated the law or your organization's express business and/or ethics policies.

(ii) Authority.   As an agent, the buyer is required to perform certain duties. Within the scope of these duties the buyer is given certain authority, both by role and by specific designation.

APPARENT AUTHORITY

Apparent authority comes with the role of buyer. It differs from *actual authority* insofar as no specific charter is given to perform designated duties other than those typically associated with buyers' duties through common business practice. In effect, it is an implied authority but one on which third parties may legally rely. The title of buyer (or any similar association) will generally be taken to mean that authority has been granted to contract and buy goods and services for the organization. The buyer's spending limit is technically controlled only by internal policy, meaning that a supplier may rely on the buyer's authority even if it exceeds the amount allowed by the organization.

TIPS AND TECHNIQUES

> If you place or authorize an order in an amount that exceeds your authority, your organization will likely be bound by the amount since, in your role, you have apparent authority. However, your organization may hold you personally responsible for any amount exceeding your designated authority should any liability arise.

LIMITED AUTHORITY

Limited authority means that the agency may be limited within the scope of an individual's responsibility. Most commonly, in commercial environments, the agency of a salesperson is specifically limited. Sales representatives are hired to solicit business and coordinate activities between the respective organizations and thus have limited authority. They are not empowered through the agency to commit their company to any specific obligations. For this, you will need to find an individual who is at least designated as a manager.

(iii) Ratification.   When an agent acts beyond the designated scope of its responsibility, the contracting organization may nevertheless choose to ratify the action.

This ratification thus binds the obligations created by the contract and releases the agent from personal liability.

(iv) Financial Responsibility. At all times, the buyer, as an agent, holds a position of *fiduciary* trust, as well as business responsibility, toward the principal. Thus, the buyer is expected to act prudently and in the best interest of the organization, especially in carrying out financial duties. This responsibility covers conformance to legal, as well as ethical, principles. Needless to say, the exercise of good judgment and integrity are paramount to meeting this responsibility.

Sarbanes-Oxley

Corporate financial malfeasance has resulted in several scandals in recent years and, as a reaction, Congress enacted the Sarbanes-Oxley Act (or SOX, as it is called). This law, passed in 2002, affects only publicly traded corporations for now but will likely expand to include all corporate entities that have dealings with them, whether public or private. Section 404 of the act requires, among other things, that corporate policies and procedures are documented and that key accounting and finance processes are clearly stated. More importantly, the act requires that CEOs and CFOs attest to the veracity of the financial statement in a written statement. The firm's financial reports must include disclosure of all financial obligations, including procurement contracts that could create a liability for the shareholders. Penalties for violation include very stiff prison sentences.

The impact that this will have on procurement activities is still being sorted out, but it is clear that all risks associated with any significant supply agreement will need to be disclosed and steps taken to mitigate the risk included in reporting documents. For example, any high-dollar "take or pay" contract requiring payment regardless of whether or not the products or services are needed (often used as an inducement to the supplier to invest in capital equipment or engineering) will need to be disclosed, along with the rationale for entering into such agreement and the steps that can be taken to minimize the loss to shareholders should the need for cancellation arise.

4.2 REVIEWING CONTRACTS FOR LEGAL REQUIREMENTS

Legal decisions are typically based on historical precedent—how prior cases regarding the same circumstances have been resolved by the courts. Unfortunately, as a Procurement professional you are not always aware of the most recent decisions and how they might affect your contract since you are primarily focused on the business issues. Before issuing a contract, therefore, you should ensure that it conforms to appropriate legal requirements in addition to the business needs of your organization. To this end, it is best to obtain legal input prior to its writing. In fact, many organizations have policies requiring that only their Legal Department can draft contracts.

In some organizations, standard contracts drafted by legal counsel are available for your use when needed. Whenever possible, you should use these rather than the contracts submitted by the supplier since they likely offer more specific protection in your circumstances. It is never a good idea to simply sign a contract presented by the supplier.

Legal counsel provides assurance that the contract conforms to applicable law and regulations and that your organization's liability is minimized. In addition to this, you may also want to employ counsel for a number of specific circumstances, such as those listed following:

- **Intellectual property rights.** As just discussed, you need to be certain that your organization does not infringe on any IP rights legally granted to others and that you have properly protected its own IP rights through proper disclosure processes.
- **Legal venue.** Your legal counsel will require language in the contract to determine which state's laws will be considered and in which state's court action will be taken should litigation be required.

   This can be quite difficult when dealing with international suppliers. Some countries recognize the rules established by the United Nations Convention on Contracts for the International Sale of Goods (CISG) as discussed in Chapter 3, but others do not. Your counsel may wish to obtain advice from a local attorney in the country in which you are conducting business.
- **Assignability.** Legal review may also be required to ensure that the contract will be transferable to any future business interests your organization may acquire (such as through acquisition, merger, or the creation of a subsidiary) and, at the same time, limit the supplier's ability to transfer the contract without prior approval.
- **Insurance.** For some contracts, you will want to be certain that the supplier carries the proper insurance, such as workmen's compensation, so that additional liability does not accrue to your organization. Legal counsel will often require that you obtain copies of the supplier's certificate of insurance as evidence that it is in place. In some cases, in addition to insurance, a performance bond may be required. These bonds are usually purchased to insure against the buyer's loss should the supplier default in providing the agreed-upon services.
- **Reviews and claims.** Under certain circumstances, you may wish to include a process for review should there be a dispute regarding the contract. This benefits both parties. Reviews are generally a form of mediation and often simply refer questions and decisions to more senior management or to corresponding company counsel. In government environments, however, the process is generally more formal and will often involve an actual review board convened for the express purpose of reviewing supplier protests and claims.

- **Parol evidence.** The rule of *parol evidence* prevents the use of oral testimony to alter a written contract. This means that any oral promises made by the supplier during the contracting process must be put in writing or they will not apply. Only the written contract can be used as evidence of an agreement. As a result, it is extremely important to review the deliverables with legal counsel to ensure that all commitments are accurately reflected in the document.

  Keep in mind that the parol evidence rule also requires any amendments or changes to an existing written contract to also be in writing and be certain that this is clearly written into your contract to avoid disputes when field personnel become involved and begin to make *ad hoc* changes.

- **Reservation of rights.** Your legal counsel will also want to similarly review any clauses that specifically limit your organization's rights to the full performance of the contract. This will include a requirement that no changes can be made in the contract without the express consent of the buyer.

- **Liability limitations.** Suppliers typically want to limit liability to replacement of a product or service under the terms of the warranty. Depending on the circumstances, however, this may limit your organization's rights to claim *incidental damages* such as transportation or special handling costs. In some cases, *consequential damages*—including lost revenue or profit, damage to property, or injury to persons—may be in order. Clauses covering these conditions are often contentious and best left in the hands of your attorney.

- **Liquidated damages.** It will often be impossible to calculate the actual monetary damage or loss suffered under certain circumstances. In such situations, the parties will agree to a predetermined amount—known as liquidated damages—to be paid in the event of default. This is also a contentious process and so requires input from legal counsel. It is important to determine a reasonable amount for damages in any particular case so that it will be upheld if the argument goes to court.

- **Regulated materials.** Laws governing the transportation, use, and disposal of regulated and hazardous materials, such as the Toxic Substances Control Act (1976) and the Resource Conservation and Recovery Act (1976), require special attention since these substances can create exceptional liability for your organization. Special legal and technical expertise is definitely required when dealing contractually with any material that might fall under these regulations. These are high risk areas and, at the minimum, require that the roles and responsibilities of the parties be clearly defined.

- **Force majeure.** *Force majeure* identifies acts or events that are outside the control of human beings, such as wars, natural disasters, fires, floods and the like. Typically, either or both parties to a contract are relieved of performance when such uncontrollable actions occur and are not held liable for damages. It is important, however, to be certain proper legal language is included in your contract since there are no automatic provisions covering this topic.

4.3 ALIGNING CONTRACTS AND PRACTICES WITH POLICY

Most organizations maintain a set of documents governing the practices conducted by the Procurement Department. These usually take the form of written policies or operating procedures. They are designed to provide effective guidance in the conduct of activities so that employees understand their obligations to the organization. In scope, these policies and procedures vary, but they typically cover elements such as procurement authority, supplier management, quality standards, record retention, conformance to law, and good business and ethical practices.

The Procurement professional is expected to bring to the job sufficient expertise to interpret and enforce these policies and may expect to be called upon for input when they are being created or revised. In some organizations, the Procurement professional will have the additional responsibility of actually writing and maintaining the procurement portion of organizational policy.

(a) CONFORMANCE TO LAW.   At the minimum, organizations are required to conform to antitrust, environmental, and health and safety laws. As you will recall, antitrust regulations were covered in Chapter 3, and some of the laws covering environmental and health and safety processes were outlined earlier. In addition, there are numerous laws governing intellectual property (which we discussed earlier in this chapter), and there are rules governing confidentiality such as the *Uniform Trade Secrets Act (UTSA)* that define rights for particular trade secrets. As a Procurement professional, you will be required to have a working knowledge of all of these laws and regulations.

In addition, you should become familiar with the activities and regulations of certain governmental agencies that are empowered to protect the rights and welfare of the general population. One of these organizations, the Environmental Protection Agency (EPA), is charged with enforcing federal laws relating to hazardous materials, clean air, and water and waste disposal. Many of the regulations and laws enforced by this agency carry criminal charges if violated, so you should become very familiar with their overall requirements.

The Occupational Safety and Health Act gives rise to a variety of rules and regulations governing safety in the workplace. Under certain circumstances, your organization will want to include a clause in its contracts that essentially shifts the burden of compliance to the supplier. A clause in the contract requiring compliance with applicable laws is generally sufficient protection, but it must be crafted by legal counsel since regulations are quite formal in this area.

(b) ETHICAL PRINCIPLES.   The Institute for Supply Management (ISM) maintains a set of ethical standards for the supply management profession entitled "Principles and Standards of Ethical Supply Management Conduct." These are excellent guidelines to use as a basis for your organization's business ethics policy and as individual guidelines for the staff. In light of continuing scandals involving the questionable integrity of corporate officers and the subsequent U.S. requirements for reporting imposed by SOX, we cannot emphasize enough the importance that you understand, adopt, and strictly adhere to the covenants of viable code of ethics.

Following are some areas that should be of particular concern:

- **Conflict of interest.** Occurs when Procurement employees conduct the organization's business in such manner as to further their own personal gain or that of their families and friends. This includes providing insider tips on activities that would affect the price of stock, or buying and selling from relatives. It also includes owning a share of any organization that conducts business with the organization that employs you.
- **Bribes.** It is illegal to accept *bribes* and *gratuities* in the form of money or any other valuable goods or services with the intent to influence decisions. You probably understand this. However, it is important to also understand that even the perception of unethical conduct must always be avoided. This includes accepting frequent meals and entertainment from suppliers or any gifts that could be considered to have even nominal value. In a position of financial trust, one must exercise impeccable judgment.

  Similarly, it is also illegal for the buyer to offer bribes to others. Although in some countries, gratuities are customary for work performed in the normal course of duties, it is clearly a violation of U.S. law to offer a bribe to any government or business official to influence a decision, regardless of the country in which it takes place.
- **Personal purchases.** Be certain that any purchase you make for your personal use from a supplier conforms to the organization's policy and that it is fair to the supplier and others in your organization. Some organizations encourage this as a means of supporting valued suppliers and gaining benefit for their employees; others look upon it as a conflict of interest.
- **Proprietary information.** You will be expected to maintain confidentiality at all times and to protect the *proprietary information* in the possession of your organization, regardless of its ultimate ownership. This includes maintaining the confidentiality of plans and intentions. If you must disclose information to a supplier or other third party in the normal course of your business, be certain that you obtain a signed confidentiality agreement or nondisclosure agreement before so doing.

NOTE

Institute for Supply Management (ISM) provides excellent references for codes of ethics in their "Principles of Social Responsibility and Principles and Standards of Ethical Supply Management Conduct." You can find these documents on the ISM Web site at www.ism.ws/ISMMembership/PrincipleStandards.cfm.

4.4 MAINTAINING PROCUREMENT DOCUMENTS AND RECORDS

To comply with standard records retention programs and legal processes, you are required to know how to maintain certain documents and for what specific period of time they must be retained. Some of the requirements are mandated by law (such as those outlined by the Internal Revenue Service [IRS]), while others are based on organizational policy and sound business practices. Keep in mind it is equally important to know when *not* to keep documents as it is to know when they should be kept. There is no inherent value to storing records that will never require access if it is not a legal or regulatory requirement. You must ask if the records are worth the cost and space of storage and if you want to keep them on-site or at a third-party storage facility. You must also determine if they should be kept in printed format or in electronic media.

Not all documents related to contracts and POs will be maintained by the Procurement Department. In some organizations, it is common for the Legal Department to hold all documents related to written contracts. Also, equipment records and related drawings are often kept by the using department. However, it is more typical to find that most of these are stored by the Procurement Department if they are related to procurement activities.

Examples of the kind of records generated and maintained by the Procurement Department include:

- **POs and contracts.** Includes quotes and acknowledgment history. POs and contracts are typically filed by *open orders* (those that are still active) and *closed orders* (those that have been fully received or have expired). Today, of course, many of these records are being maintained electronically and require no filing space.

    POs are kept for a six-year period (following their expiration) as required by most taxing authorities, including the IRS. The UCC, it should be noted, requires that POs for goods be kept for only a four-year period.
- **Supplier qualification records and periodic reviews.** Historical records containing the original qualification data and supplier ratings and reviews. They are typically maintained as long as the supplier is active. Also included here might be the records of previous negotiations. All of these records are retained in accordance with organizational policy.
- **Catalogs.** Generally maintained in a central library, although it is becoming less common for organizations to keep printed catalogs because so many are available online or in electronic format. This media certainly reduces the storage and filing requirements and is preferred since it is typically more up to date. Electronic catalogs also do not vanish, as do some of their more popular paper counterparts.
- **Inventory records.** These records, such as traveling requisitions and historical ordering data by part, are also likely to be found in many procurement

departments. Commonly, today, these records are maintained on computer systems. These are kept for a relatively short period of time and only as required by organizational policy.

- **Project files.** Kept when appropriate and when they are for projects led by the Procurement Department, such as cost reduction or quality improvement programs. These are also kept for a relatively short period of time and only as required by organizational policy.

It may be worth mentioning that records are stored in a variety of formats, including paper and electronic media such as tape, floppy disks, and compact discs (CDs). In some environments, they are also stored on microfilm (or microfiche). From a record retention and legal perspective, the media should make little or no difference to the storage policy.

4.5 SUMMARY

One of the primary responsibilities of the Procurement Department involves creating and issuing purchase orders. Since contracts (and, of course, POs) are considered legally binding documents, the Procurement professional must become familiar with the basic principles of contract formation. These principles are founded on the basic requirements that are needed in order for a contract to be legally binding: mutual agreement, legal purpose, consideration, and the capacity to enter into a contract.

There are numerous types of standard procurement contract types available based primarily on payment schema. Contracts generally fall into two major categories: fixed price and cost reimbursable. To a large extent, the payment method selected determines the way that risk is shared between the contracting parties. In addition to these major categories, agreements are commonly developed for licensing intellectual property, maintaining confidentiality, leasing buildings and equipment, and consigning goods.

Buyers, as agents, are granted certain legal authority to commit the organization to a contract, but this authority also generates a measure of fiduciary responsibility to the employer. It is important, therefore, that in complex situations you seek legal review and proper approval prior to signature. It is also important that you align your contracts to conform to applicable law and organization policy. Today, ethical behavior is one of the key issues in business, and it is critical that you understand your obligations. A good reference point is the "Principles and Standards of Ethical Supply Management Conduct," a set of ethical standards published by the Institute for Supply Management (ISM).

Finally, the Procurement Department is also responsible for maintaining and retaining files and records commonly associated with procurement activities. You should become familiar with your organization's policy regarding records retention.

KEY TERMS

Statutory law

Statute of Frauds

Principle of detrimental reliance

Electronic procurement

Mutual agreement

Offer

Acceptance

Unilateral contract

Bilateral contract

Counteroffer

Consideration

Quid Pro Quo

Competent

Obligations

Purchase orders (POs)

Blanket POs

Requirements contracts/Indefinite
     delivery/Indefinite quantity (IDIQ)
     contracts

Take-or-pay

Fixed-price contracts

Firm-fixed-price contracts

Fixed-price-with-incentive contract

Fixed-price, level-of-effort pricing

Cost-reimbursable pricing

Cost-plus-fixed-fee contract

Cost-plus-incentive-fee contract

Cost-plus-award-fee contract

Cost-plus-percentage of cost

Government Accounting Office
     (GAO)

Cost-sharing contract

Time and materials contract
     (T&M)

Not-to-exceed (NTE)

Letter of intent (LOI)

Intellectual property (lP)

Patent and copyright

Licensing agreement

Trademark

Intellectual Property

Patents

Copyrights

Nondisclosure agreement (NDA)

Confidentiality agreement

Mirror image rule

Revocation

Change orders

CHAPTER 5

ADMINISTERING CONTRACTS FOR OPTIMUM SUPPLIER PERFORMANCE

LEARNING OBJECTIVES

1. Create a *Gantt chart* demonstrating the key steps in a hypothetical project.
2. Explain the difference between *express warranties* and *implied warranties*.
3. List and explain the five options for resolving supplier contracts.

Administering contracts to ensure supplier compliance is a very important responsibility of the Procurement Department.

    The central focal point for contract compliance is meeting the requirements of the internal customer. The Procurement Department does not usually have the resources to closely manage the hundreds of suppliers to the organization, nor would it make sense for its staff to even try to do so, since rarely will the Procurement Department be staffed with the same level of expertise as the using or customer department. Instead, you can be best served by relying on your internal customers, those employees and departments directly responsible for the supplier's performance, for day-to-day operational information such as quality evaluations and on-time delivery reports. Using this information enables you to conduct periodic business reviews with key suppliers to help them understand areas for improvement and how they can best achieve stronger performance. This is the essence of **supplier relationship management (SRM)**, a term recently coined to describe the activities related to monitoring and improving supplier performance. Integrated with the broader picture will be the Procurement Department's daily tactical activities that revolve around tracking and expediting deliveries as well as responding to supplier-related discrepancies.

This chapter summarizes the broader concepts of contract administration, including how the Procurement professional can establish proactive measures to ensure supplier compliance and internal customer satisfaction within the framework of existing contracts. In doing so, the chapter also reviews how to deal with problems relating to supplier payments and how change orders can affect contract terms and conditions.

5.1 MANAGING CONTRACT COMPLIANCE

The Procurement manager routinely oversees the management of contract administration and supplier relations. Part of this responsibility is to ensure that the terms and conditions of the contract are followed, especially where they may diminish the value of the contract to the organization. Another part involves the continuing effort to improve supplier performance and to maintain strong business relationships. While no Procurement professional can be an expert in all areas of the profession, you should constantly strive to provide solid advisement and procurement authority to your organization's suppliers. Handling potential problems early and in a proactive mode will go a long way toward defusing problems before they become major issues.

(a) POST PURCHASE ORDER ADMINISTRATION. Much of the Procurement Department's responsibility lies in the ongoing management of the purchase order (PO) or contract after it has been negotiated and placed with the supplier. This is very much of an organic process that takes on a life of its own, which often involves lots of routine work that generally fills much of the tactical buyer's day. To be successful, the Procurement professional must set a firm, proactive approach to monitoring day-to-day activities within the context of continuing fiduciary due diligence, ensuring that internal users receive the benefit of the bargain in good faith. Success will also depend in large part on the effective involvement of the using department and those most familiar with the specific requirements of the contract.

The following section reviews many of the routine duties associated with the activities of managing supplier performance to ensure that their contractual obligations are being met.

(i) Ensuring Supplier Performance.   Administering any contract can be a complex, dynamic process requiring skillful attention to detail and thorough familiarity with its objectives and terms and conditions. Therefore, it is important for your internal customers to understand that it is their responsibility to inform you or your staff of any discrepancies or areas of supplier dissatisfaction. You may be able to help them understand this process by reviewing some key contract administration principles with them prior to the contract's actual implementation:

- Clearly define roles and responsibilities in advance so that you can work as a coordinated team.
- Read and understand the contract's requirements. Be certain that the actions you take are in line with its terms and conditions.
- Develop a checklist of areas for periodic review to avert potential problems early.
- Maintain a sound, business-like relationship with the supplier, instituting clear lines of communication and conflict resolution and avoiding reactive positions.
- Anticipate areas that may require change, and develop an understanding of potential cost implications.
- Resolve problems quickly before they escalate or create major issues.

During the course of the contract, and for supplier performance in general, you and core members of the cross-functional supplier management team will likely want to monitor a number of key deliverables for specific performance. Some of the elements critical to successful contract fulfillment include compliance with cost objectives, on-time delivery performance, adherence to quality requirements, and accurate reporting. Specifics on how these elements can be controlled and periodically reviewed by the affected groups are covered in the section on Supplier Relationship Management later in this chapter.

Often, a project management approach to contract compliance can establish a framework and timetable to monitor performance, providing a useful reporting mechanism as well. Project management is the application of knowledge, skills, tools, and techniques to a set of activities in order to meet the detailed requirements of the project.

Figure 5.1 shows a simple timeline approach using a **Gantt chart** that graphically tracks the progress of the project by illustrating on a calendar when events are scheduled to take place, how long they will take, and when they are expected to be complete. The Gantt chart also shows the relationship between events, especially which events must complete first before others that are dependent upon them can start. You may also find this method useful for monitoring project management improvement programs.

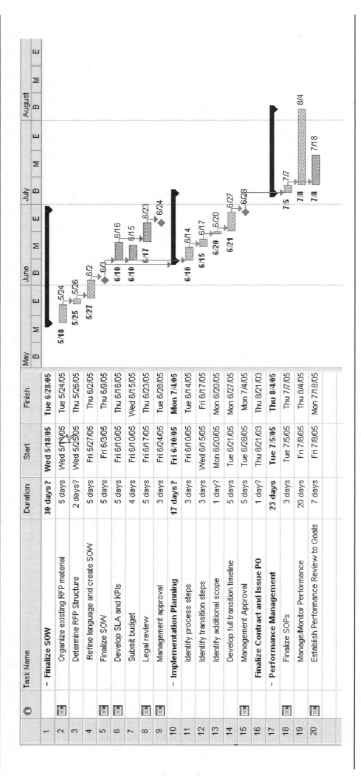

Figure 5.1 Timeline for Contract Development

Maintaining a complete file of reports and correspondence covering actual supplier performance will be useful for conducting subsequent business reviews and for resolving any disputes should they arise. Include in these files progress reports, notes from important meetings, change and amendment history, a log of corrective action issues, and customer feedback. In the case of ongoing supplier monitoring, records will include the history and details of periodic business reviews and documentation of ongoing improvements.

(ii) Processing Change Orders.   Having to process change orders is a typical event during the course of any contract. Formal change orders involving revised specifications or additional requirements are monitored and documented through processes known by a number of names, such as **engineering change order (ECO)** or **specification change order (SCO)**. Usually, these changes are tracked and recorded by the Document Control Department or through the quality engineering group. However, your responsibility will likely include negotiating the cost implications and effect on the delivery timetable with the supplier.

In addition to engineering-generated changes, amendments to the contract are sometimes required to reflect an additional scope of work, such as adding new areas of responsibility to the supplier's duties or redefining a completion timeline or milestone.

A seasoned procurement practitioner is aware of the likelihood of ongoing changes to the contract and negotiates the process in advance, maintaining an awareness of the competitive bidding trap (discussed in Chapter 3) where the supplier underprices the initial contract with an expectation of added profit margin from the inevitable change orders once the contract has been agreed to by the parties. Generally, the mechanics of implementing changes, including allocating their financial impact, can be outlined in the initial contract so that the delivery process works smoothly. To a large extent, this is the responsibility of the Procurement Department representative leading the contract negotiation team and is well facilitated when following the guidelines for internal customer review just provided.

(iii) Price Adjustments.   Firm-fixed-price contracts require pricing adjustments only when changes in the specifications or scope of work occur. However, many contracts—especially those developed in government procurement—require price adjustments and fee payments based upon a wide range of conditions and the nature of the contract. (We outlined contract types in Chapter 4.) The most common of these are the economic price adjustments required by escalation contracts or changes in the rates determining baselines in the cost-plus contracts. You will have already defined how and when such changes can be applied in the initial contract and will have linked them to a change in a specific index or a predetermined cost factor.

In most circumstances, escalation changes will be documented by changes in predetermined pricing such as the cost of labor (in union environments) or materials. Often, fluctuations in these prices cannot be known in advance and so a contract clause will allow for increases (rarely decreases) to the cost basis beyond a preset trigger threshold. Similarly, when procurement is through international sources, contracts may allow for cost fluctuations based on a predetermined currency exchange rate.

Sometimes the cost basis will be adjusted by increases or decreases in specific published indices governing labor or materials. Transportation rates, for example, are often based on fuel pricing from a published index and passed through to the buyer as a fuel surcharge.

(iv) Warranty Claims.   A **warranty** is a seller's guarantee to the buyer that if the product or materials being sold does not perform as specified, the seller will take a particular remedial action. Most frequently, the remedy will be to replace the products at the seller's expense. The buyer should be aware of the contractual rights granted by a warranty and practice diligence in exercising those rights.

Warranties and limitations of liability are generally the source of much negotiation during the contract formation process. To reduce their unknown financial exposure, suppliers will generally want to limit their warranties to a specific (and narrow) set of conditions and for a limited time. Often, warranty clauses are taken for granted and not specifically negotiated, becoming additional grist for the battle of the order acknowledgement forms.

The **Uniform Commercial Code (UCC)** specifically allows a seller to disclaim any or all warranties, but it does not provide any specific rules or guidelines as to how the warranty should be disclaimed. Because of this, the buyer must be aware of the actual language being used to reference or convey the warranty in any particular case. Generally, the seller is required to include a statement specifically disclaiming an actual warranty, such as all goods are sold "as is." Terms such as "no warranties, express or implied" are generally insufficient to disclaim a specific warranty.

Sections 2–312 through 2–318 of the UCC cover commercial warranties for goods and products. Under the UCC, warranties fall into two classifications: express warranties and implied warranties. Let's discuss the more important aspects of each of these in more detail:

1. **Express warranties** provide specific assurances regarding the performance of a product or service. Typically, they are explicitly spelled out within the framework of the contract or purchase order. Created by the words or actions of a seller, an express warranty can be provided either through a specific promise or the description of the product. An affirmative statement or a sample of the product can be considered as the basis for a warranty.
2. An **implied warranty** is provided by rule under the UCC simply by offering goods or products for sale, even when there is no mention of how the product will be expected to perform. As its title suggests, the warranty need not be stated; rather, it is implicit in the offer or acceptance by the seller. The intent of this warranty is to allow buyers to purchase goods and

products with reasonable assurance that they will meet certain inherent and basic requirements.

The UCC creates two distinct types of implied warranties: merchantability and fitness for a particular purpose:

a. **Merchantability** means that the seller implicitly warrants that the product is fit and suited to be used for the ordinary purposes for which it would be purchased. It also implies that it is of average quality and performs the basic functions that may be stated by the manufacturer.

   The UCC does not intend for a seller to create an implied warranty for goods not normally sold in its regular course of business. For example, a manufacturer of molded plastic parts does not create an implied warranty when it sells one of its obsolete molding machines to another business.

b. **Fitness for a particular purpose** means that if the seller knows (or has reason to know) the intended use by the buyer for the goods being sold, the seller then warrants that the goods will be suitable for that purpose. A seller, therefore, may not knowingly sell a product that will not do the job and then refute responsibility. In effect, this means that the buyer may rely upon the seller's expertise in selecting a suitable product and seek remedy should the product not perform as intended.

   As in the case of merchantability, the seller need only warrant goods that it would convey during the usual course of its business.

(v) Disclaimers. As noted earlier, sellers may disclaim warranties in writing if the writing is specific enough to describe the conditions not being warranted. In addition, the disclaimer needs to be conspicuous and stand out from other portions of the contract. That is why you will often see **disclaimers** written in bold or capital lettering. However, the UCC indicates that a buyer must have some recourse if the goods received are defective or unusable, and so the seller cannot enforce a clause that takes all the rights away from the buyer.

Figure 5.2 illustrates a liability disclaimer from the State of California's Department of Consumer Affair's Web page. Under the area titled Disclaimer of Warranties/Accuracy, you'll notice it disclaims express and implied warranties by specific reference. This disclaimer also uses capital letters that stand out conspicuously to state the legal requirements of the warranty.

(b) SUPPLIER RELATIONSHIP MANAGEMENT (SRM). Contract management also requires the use of SRM methodology, as well. SRM is the broad process of aligning the goals of your buying organization and the supplier community, one supplier at a time. Often, this is a process of tactically aligning the typical variation in processes between several organizations using analysis, collaboration, and jointly developed action plans.

SRM refers to both business practices and software. Its key objective is to improve the processes between an enterprise and its suppliers and enable them to

---

Disclaimer of Warranties/Accuracy and Use of Data/Computer Viruses
Although the data found using the Department of Consumer Affairs' Home Page access systems have been produced and processed from sources believed to be reliable, no warranty expressed or implied is made regarding accuracy, adequacy, completeness, legality, reliability or usefulness of any information. This disclaimer applies to both isolated and aggregate uses of the information. The Department of Consumer Affairs and the Department of Consumer Affairs' Home Page provide this information on an "AS IS" basis. All warranties of any kind, express or implied, including but not limited to the IMPLIED WARRANTIES OF MERCHANTABILITY, FITNESS FOR A PARTICULAR PURPOSE, freedom from contamination by computer viruses and non-infringement of proprietary rights ARE DISCLAIMED. Changes may be periodically added to the information herein; these changes may or may not be incorporated in any new version of the publication. If the user has obtained information from The Department of Consumer Affairs' Home Page from a source other than The Department of Consumer Affairs' Home Page, the user must be aware that electronic data can be altered subsequent to original distribution. Data can also quickly become out-of-date. It is recommended that the user pay careful attention to the contents of any metadata associated with a file, and that the originator of the data or information be contacted with any questions regarding appropriate use. If the user finds any errors or omissions, we encourage the user to report them to the Department of Consumer Affairs' Home Page.

©2004 State of California

FIGURE 5.2   SAMPLE DISCLAIMER OF WARRANTY AND LANGUAGE

operate more effectively. For example, consider the benefits of aligning the planning horizons of buying and supplying organizations so that their forecasts and operational plans coincide.

SRM practices intend to create a common frame of reference that supports effective communication between the organization and its suppliers who are using different business practices and terminology. As a result, SRM increases the efficiency of processes associated with acquiring goods and services, managing inventory, and processing materials.

In its automated format, SRM can be seen as a way of gathering information from multiple procurement systems in order to develop metrics that measure and evaluate supplier performance. Inherent in the measurement process, however, is the discipline of continuous improvement, the methodology for developing and implementing ongoing improvements in business and operational processes to achieve a specific goal. Let's discuss the elements of SRM in more detail.

(i) Monitoring Performance.   Expected supplier performance levels are generally included in the general terms and conditions, product specifications (in the case of goods), or in the statement of work (in the case of services) for any given purchase. Often referred to as service levels, they can also be included in a separate addendum to the contract known as a **service-level agreement (SLA)**. Within the SLA, **metrics** (sometimes referred to as **key performance indicators**, or **KPI**s, as we discussed in Chapter 1) are included to define the expected performance of the supplier.

Performance measures by themselves have little intrinsic value, so they are generally reviewed in terms of actual progress toward a specific goal or compared with a stated baseline standard. For example, if you are measuring cost reduction, you might indicate a KPI in terms of dollars per part or dollars per hour. Your goal would likely be stated in these same terms or perhaps as a percentage reduction. In this way, data and assessments can help reduce spending and risk and improve operations in quality, delivery, and service—the key goals of the supply management process.

In many organizations, supplier performance monitoring is automated through the use of some software system. Organizational procedures generally define what types of monitoring techniques are to be used and the frequency of reporting. The procurement and quality teams then implement a supplier review process through regular meetings, site visits, product testing, and customer surveys to determine where gaps exist in reaching the desired objective. Once gaps are identified, the next phase of enhancing supplier performance is the execution of corrective action plans.

(ii) Managing Supplier Activities.   In general, a fairly wide variation exists within the scope of typical supplier activities, and you may find that in your organization only the key elements of their duties are actually being measured on a routine basis. Yet, as a procurement professional, the responsibility for ensuring that all supplier commitments are met will be yours. With hundreds of suppliers and thousands of events taking place daily, how can you possibly manage them all?

There are several ways you might consider for managing a broad scope of activities such as the following:

- **Management by Exception.** One method of managing supplier activities relies on an automated reporting system and alerts you only when exceptions to the required standard occur. This is called **management by exception**. You receive notification only when events occur outside of the expected range of possibilities. For example, if you use a computer-based system for documenting receipts, you may be able to get notification of late deliveries whenever shipment is overdue by a specific amount of time.
- **Input from Internal Users.** You might solicit regular input from your internal users, either through surveys or through direct reporting methods. Or you might consider spending time with the users of the materials and services you purchase. This way, you observe the problems when they actually occur and from the perspective of your customer. It helps you understand the impact of actual failures (or successes) and enables you to better communicate them to your supplier.
- **Site Visits.** It is not uncommon to find buyers monitoring activities directly in the supplier's facility so that they can become more actively involved in resolving issues. As Yogi Berra, the retired coach of the New York Yankee baseball team, once said, "You can observe a lot just by watching."

(iii) Reviewing Performance.   Performance reviews are generally presented in a report format, outlining the supplier's actual performance to goal or standard for a

specific period of time. Often, these are conducted in a formal meeting environment and within the framework of a standard predefined agenda. Since extensive reviews are typically very time consuming, it is common to them and to critical suppliers to hold them on a quarterly basis, especially when the supplier's team must travel a long distance to visit your facility. Use of your organization's business review process, in fact, is probably one of the most widely accepted formats. Often, these are supplemented with an annual **executive review** where senior managers come together to exchange forthcoming **business plans** and **technology road maps**.

The use of a **performance scorecard** is a popular communication method for delivering supplier reviews. The scorecard is a compilation or summary of the supplier's performance to the preestablished metrics called for in the SLA. It is common to generalize performance into categories such as quality, cost, on-time delivery, and service on the scorecard, touching on the high points and low points of actual results.

It is important that you also allow time to obtain supplier feedback on problems from the supplier's perspective and to garner ideas on how your organization can better align their processes. While you want to avoid reducing the process to a sales presentation, you should also consider asking for feedback on how the supplier feels it can better serve you.

(iv) Developing Performance Improvements.   While many variations of continuous improvement exist, the basic steps are fairly well defined:

1. Analyze existing conditions.
2. Determine the gaps that exist between the actual conditions and the desired state.
3. Develop plans to eliminate (or reduce) the gaps.
4. Implement the plan.
5. Measure improvements.
6. Repeat the cycle.

These steps are generally conducted within the framework of a **commodity management** team that is sponsored by the **business unit leader**. We've found it useful to manage improvement initiatives as projects, using Gantt charts and assigning specific actions and timelines to individual team members. This creates both accountability and a sense of understanding of all the elements that are required to make the project successful.

NOTE

The identification of business process gaps that have a financial ramification to an organization, along with the identification of a plan to remedy the gaps, is a key element of the Sarbanes-Oxley Act of 2002, Section 404, which was discussed in Chapter 1.

5.2 TRACKING AND EXPEDITING DELIVERIES

In the normal course of daily routine, supplier shipments will not always meet their required delivery dates. Sometimes this is due to errors or damages in shipments; other times it is due to factors such as production delays, miscommunication of requirements, or just Murphy's Law. In any event, as a supplier manager you will be required to assist in resolving them and to handle the communications between the supplier and your internal customers. Two of the most frequent situations that will require your intervention, dealing with shipments and expediting orders, are described in this section.

(a) TRACKING AND MONITORING SHIPMENTS. Fortunately, today, most shipping agencies have automated tracking tools that can immediately report the status and whereabouts of virtually any worldwide shipment. Many of these tools can even be accessed through the Web, and likely many of you have already used the FedEx or UPS tracking systems to locate parcels.

Lost and damaged shipments require the submission of a claim in order to obtain reimbursement. You will likely find this process takes several weeks, so it is best to reorder immediately, keeping in mind that unless you specifically requested shipping terms that require the supplier to maintain ownership title of the goods until actual delivery, your organization will take ownership of the goods at the time of shipment and it will be your organization's responsibility to file the actual claim with the carrier. In most organizations, however, it will be the Traffic or Receiving Department's responsibility to handle the paperwork, and you will only become involved to the extent that corrective action or expediting is required.

(b) EXPEDITING ORDERS.   **Expediting** refers to the process of following up with suppliers (through some form of direct contact) to accelerate the shipment of orders or to determine the current status of a particular order and when it will be ready for shipment. It may be counterintuitive, but expediting provides no additional value whatsoever to the product or service and simply increases the associated overhead cost.

Expediting, however, can be required as the result of numerous circumstances and is fairly commonly used. In case you are wondering why it is necessary, some of the typical reasons for expediting include:

- **Late production**. You will expect your supplier to communicate with you in situations where your order has not been shipped (or delivered) as expected. You will need to reestablish a delivery date with the supplier, communicate with your internal customer, and determine if there is any way to mitigate the potential damage to your operations. Some situations may require you to follow up further on subsequent shipments to avoid the situation in the future.

- **Rush orders**. There are times and circumstances that will require you to request shipment in less than the normal lead-time cycle. You may be required to negotiate this with the supplier—offering some future value or additional fees as compensation. We once called a supplier to request a rush status be placed on an existing order. When we made the request to the supplier's customer service representative, she broke out in laughter. We asked what was so funny, and she replied, "Which of these six rush orders I have for you would you like me to do first?"
- **Back orders**. There are occasions when a supplier is only able to ship part of the order by the requested time. This is called a **split order**, and the remaining balance is called a **back order**. While your contract or purchase order may prohibit such practice, you may be willing to bend the rules when you need something urgently rather than see the entire shipment arrive late. You will likely want to flag the order so that you can follow up with the supplier prior to the promised date for shipping the balance to be sure you avoid any further delays.

TIPS AND TECHNIQUES

WHO'S RESPONSIBLE FOR EXPEDITING ORDERS?

Although it is most typical for the Procurement Department to handle expediting as part of the supplier management process, you may want to keep in mind that it is not always the responsibility of the Procurement Department to handle every circumstance that requires expediting. In some organizations, it is up to the using department to manage this, while in others it may be handled by the inventory planners or the Production Control Department, depending on their level of involvement. However, the stand-alone job function and title of expeditor is rapidly disappearing from contemporary organizations, since we are coming to recognize that prevention is more effective than cure.

You may want to consider the methods your organization uses to perform the expediting to ensure you are using the least costly and most effective method. *Status checks*, for example, may be performed today through some form of electronic media, such as e-mail, that will use fewer personnel resources, reserving personal contact for the more critical conditions. When expediting seems to become a way of life, it is important to develop a continuous improvement program to reduce or perhaps eliminate it altogether.

5.3 HANDLING SUPPLIER-RELATED DEVIATIONS

There are many circumstances—serious and minor—when you will find suppliers are unable to perform adequately or are creating errors that require corrective action. In some cases, issues can be resolved amicably with little lasting effect on the relationship; in others, legal recourse and a permanent parting of the ways may be in order.

In this section, you will find a review of some of the most common situations involving deviations and the typical ways of handling them.

Inadequate performance stems from a wide variety of conditions, some easily remedied while others are more critically serious. The simpler issues can be dealt with by the Procurement Department; the more complex ones may require the intervention of legal counsel. Most performance issues encountered are a result of a lack of clarity in the contract language and expectations that are not incorporated into the contract writing.

(a) CONTRACT BREACH.   Typically, a supplier's **breach of contract** will occur when it is unable or unwilling to perform to the terms and conditions required by the contract within the agreed-upon time frame. In the case of a shipment of nonconforming goods, however, the supplier has the right to **cure or remedy** any failure in a reasonable amount of time.

The UCC gives the buyer the right to ask the supplier of goods for adequate assurance that it can perform to the contract, should the buyer have reason to suppose that it will be unable to do so. If the supplier does not respond within 30 days, the buyer may then cancel the contract under the principle of **anticipatory breach**.

Similarly, *anticipatory repudiation* occurs in situations where, prior to the time the performance is required, the supplier informs the buyer that it will be unable to perform. This gives the buyer the right to consider the contract breached and act accordingly.

(i) Purchasers' Remedies.   When a supplier breaches the contract, it is quite likely that the buyer will suffer some form of damage. Under the UCC, the buyer has the right to be "made whole" for its loss. Several common categories of damages may be appropriately claimed by the buying organization as a result of loss:

- **Actual damages**. Cover compensation for the real losses that have been incurred in specific circumstances covered by the contract. However, to be recoverable (and enforceable) they must be capable of precise measurement. Actual damages might cover, for instance, the loss of an injection molding tool owned by your organization but stored at the supplier's facility.
- **Consequential damages**. The legal definition of consequential damages refers to those losses that arise not from the immediate act of the party but in consequence of such act.
- **Liquidated damages**. Provide for a predetermined fixed payment amount in the event of a breach of contract. They typically apply only when the actual damages would have been very difficult or impractical to determine and when the amount of the liquidated damages is reasonable. Courts have

generally not enforced a liquidated damages clause when it is intended to be punitive or when it is significantly in excess of a reasonable amount of damages that may have been incurred.

- **Incidental damages**. Cover the reasonable expenses or costs that result from loss or harm, such as the cost of transportation for replacement products.
- **Cover damages**. May be claimed when a contract is breached (e.g., in the case of late delivery) and the buyer must purchase replacement goods at a price higher than that contracted with the supplier. In this case, the buying organization may claim the difference between what it would have paid under the contract and what it actually paid.

(ii) Purchaser's Breach.   In addition to the supplier's breach, the UCC also covers the purchaser's breach. The procurement organization can breach the contract in a number of ways. For example, breach may occur if the buyer wrongfully rejects a conforming shipment upon receipt or later rejects the shipment having first accepted it. In the case of **latent defects** that do not show up on original inspection, the buyer is obligated to provide adequate time for the supplier to fix the problem once it has been discovered. The buyer may also establish anticipatory repudiation when it informs the supplier that it will be unable to accept the goods.

In the case of a purchaser's breach, the seller may also apply for remedies. Typical remedies available to the seller include:

- **Contract recovery.** The supplier may claim the entire contract value should the buying organization breach, providing that it makes a reasonable and diligent effort to sell the goods to another buyer. Whatever value the supplier may obtain through scrap is discounted from the total amount claimed.
- **Market value.** The seller may claim the difference between the sale at current market value and the sale to the purchaser.
- **Recovery of lost profits.** The supplier may include lost profit in any legal action to recover damages as a result of the purchaser's breach.
- **Costs.** The seller may recover the cost of selling or disposing of the goods to another party in the event of a purchaser's breach.

(b) LIABILITY ISSUES.   **Liability** in a commercial environment generally refers to the legal responsibility for the cost of damages. It is the Procurement Department's responsibility to reduce the risk to the organization whenever potential liability exists.

Potential financial liability can be a significant factor for the purchaser when evaluating risk and should be carefully considered during the contract formation process. It is always advisable, when there appears to be potential for significant liability to arise from a contract, to defer to legal counsel for review and the crafting of proper contract language. Similarly, when issues surrounding liability or potential liability actually do arise, it is always advisable to obtain legal advice.

Actual liability can generate from a number of conditions, including, for example, damage to goods during transit, damage from faulty equipment or workmanship, loss of revenue due to associated production delays, loss or damage due to field failure, loss due to the cessation of the supplier's operation or inability to perform, and legal responsibility for violation of public laws and regulations—to list just a few.

(c) MITIGATING LOSS.   The intent of legal language and the UCC is generally to provide for the recovery of actual losses from transactions involving goods and to compensate the party bearing the loss to the extent that it can be made whole again, or restored to its original position. However, documentation becomes critical in order to prove the value of the damages and to ensure adequate recovery.

This section highlights some specific factors you should be aware of regarding mitigation of loss.

(i) Limitations.   The supplier has the right to limit liability for consequential damages and incidental damages in the contract. You need to be certain that the **limitations** specified are favorable to your organization.

(ii) Hold Harmless.   A common clause in contracts is designed to protect the parties from the responsibilities for damages incurred through the violation of any laws or regulations. The term **hold harmless** refers to the language that places the liability for damages on the other party. Supplier contracts will often require that the buyer hold them harmless from any third-party suits arising from the performance of its obligations. This is especially contentious in cases where product liability due to loss or injury is involved and where each party has an obligation to indemnify the others when they do not contribute to the liability. It is not uncommon for parties to determine in advance the extent of each party's responsibility and subsequent liability.

Manufactured goods are also subject to the **Consumer Product Safety Act**, which requires reporting of any hazards to the public and to the Consumer Product Safety Commission. It also requires the recall of potentially unsafe products, so the buyer needs to be sure that there is adequate financial compensation when any recall is necessitated by a supplier's defective parts or material.

The supplier should also be required to hold the buyer harmless from any liability arising out of its violation of patent or copyright laws. Since this is an area of great complexity and potentially great financial liability, it is critical that the buying organization obtain maximum indemnification, including the requirement that the supplier defend it from any infringement suits.

(iii) Indemnification, Insurance, and Bonds.   Another way to limit liability is by requiring suppliers to carry and show proof of adequate insurance when the

potential for loss is very high so that your organization receives proper **indemnification** should a loss occur. Most important, of course, is the coverage for worker's compensation, and it is common for buyers to require suppliers that work on site to maintain certain levels of coverage.

Chances are good that your company carries insurance coverage for its property in the event of fire, theft, or loss due to certain natural disasters. You should determine if this coverage applies to property owned by your organization but stored at a supplier's facility (e.g., tooling) and if not, you should require that the property be insured in your organization's favor in the event of loss or damage.

Numerous forms of bonds (a form of insurance) are also available to ensure against contract performance failure, such as when the supplier fails to pay its subcontractors for labor or materials or when the supplier fails to meet the terms of the contract altogether.

(iv) Transportation and Title.   Risk of loss often depends on when the title to goods passes from the supplier to the buyer. The general rules covering ownership are specified in Incoterms, the widely accepted criteria for defining the passage of title in international trade. Procurement departments are generally aware of these terms and designate them on the face of their purchase orders. The Incoterms Web site provides a graphic view of how these terms affect title and thus risk of loss. For more detailed information, you may want to visit the **International Chamber of Commerce** (ICC) Web site at www.iccwbo.org.

(d) RESOLVING ERRORS AND OMISSIONS.   There are a myriad of problems that arise during the life of a typical PO or contract, generating a significant amount of supplier management duties for the Procurement Department. Here are some of the more routine problems you will encounter and be required to resolve.

(i) Mistakes.   Most errors in order fulfillment come as a result of inaccurate, incomplete, or erroneous descriptions on the PO. When you consider the sheer volume of manual transactions performed by the Procurement Department, this should come as no surprise. How to eliminate these errors has plagued procurement professionals around the world. Seemingly, the only cure will arrive when all routine transactions are automated through computer-based systems. While mistakes are part of human nature, the UCC does not recognize the concept of an honest mistake. Case law dealing with court decisions regarding mistakes does not appear to provide a unanimous and clear set of guidelines. However, there a few principles that might be useful to understand:

- For the most part, the courts do not seem inclined to review mistakes that are not considered material to the purchase.
- When a supplier acts in reliance of a purchase order that is erroneous, by manufacturing the wrong item, for example, the buyer will likely not be granted any relief. This is called a **unilateral mistake**.

- If a mistake made by the buyer is so obvious that it reasonably should have been discovered by the supplier, relief will usually be granted.

(ii) Shipment. Losses due to shipment errors or damages are so common in most organizations that it is often considered a standard element of cost. Indeed, in some organizations thefts during shipment can create a major problem. Despite the efforts of the best minds in logistics, it appears that this issue will continue.

However, there are some specific ways that you can minimize the risk of loss or damage in shipment. They include:

- Use a third-party logistics provider to leverage greater volumes for improved service and faster delivery.
- Specify terms that pass title to your organization only upon delivery to your facility. Keep in mind that the passage of title and who pays the freight are two separate specifications.
- Specify your own packaging requirements.
- Require shipment of the entire order prior to payment.

(iii) Pricing and Payment Issues. It has been said that the best way to maintain good supplier relations is to pay them on time. It has also been said that the more an organization owes to another, the greater the importance of servicing it becomes. Clearly, we are dealing with a double-edged sword.

It is equally important to pay suppliers in accordance with the contract as it is to refuse unwarranted and unjustified advance payments. Payments should always be made in accordance with some clearly defined event, such as receipt of goods or achievement of a specific milestone. Keep in mind that it is typical practice to invoice buyers upon shipment. If the shipment takes ten days to arrive and you are on payment terms of Net 30 Days, you can improve your organization's cash position by as much as 33 percent through payment terms predicated on the receipt of the goods and not just the invoice.

In many organizations, the rework generated by inaccurate or incomplete invoices can result in horrendous added costs. Eliminating these problems should be a key focus for continuous improvement. One company we know of rejects about 30 percent of the incoming invoices due to errors in pricing or in simply failing to include the PO number so that payment can be tied to a specific order. With volumes in excess of 5,000 invoices per month, you can imagine the additional cost this generates.

TIPS AND TECHNIQUES

It is standard practice in most organizations to pay suppliers for returned materials and then wait until a credit memo is issued to the buyer. Unfortunately, many organizations fail to recognize who needs to do the follow-up to ensure that the credit is actually issued. If you are in a position to write procurement procedures, be sure to include this step; otherwise, you may have no assurance that the credit has actually been issued.

Overages can also present billing problems. Does your organization have a clearly defined policy for the percentage or value of overruns that are acceptable? Is it prominently displayed on the face of your PO? If not, you are an easy target for cost overruns due to an overly aggressive sales agent.

Here are some of the other issues with payments you will likely encounter:

- **Late payments that generate credit holds**. Payments are often delayed by a manual sign-off process or invoices are incorrectly entered into the accounts payable system or, worse, lost.
- **PO and receiving documents cannot be matched**. Often, the supplier uses one nomenclature or part number while your organization uses another. Aligning the two systems can pay off for both.
- **Invoices and POs do not match due to price variations**. This can be avoided through the use of automated catalogs and through buyer diligence in obtaining quotes prior to placing the order.

(e) RESOLVING SUPPLIER CONFLICTS.   Conflicts are normal in any relationship. How you resolve your conflicts, however, can determine the quality of your relationship with suppliers. Through the judicious use of continuous improvement processes, you may be able to significantly reduce them and so foster even better relationships with your suppliers.

Best practices in contract compliance require a highly evolved, proactive approach to conflict resolution. To accomplish this, you must have precise and legally compliant documentation of your processes. You should review a number of key areas regularly to determine how well actual processes conform to standard operating procedures and legal requirements. Some specific areas for your attention such as contract modifications, rejection of nonconforming goods, termination, and dispute resolution are outlined in the following section.

(i) Contract Modifications.   Modifications and changes to a contract will likely occur throughout its life to fit changing requirements and market conditions. A modification, under the UCC, is typically treated differently from the original contract formation and does not require the presence of some of the key factors, such as consideration, that must be evident during the initial formation phase.

In the event that both parties are at general odds regarding the terms and conditions of a particular contract, they may simply decide to rescind it and renegotiate a new one. If it is discovered that a mutual mistake or fraud has occurred, the court may decide that reforming the contract is in the best interest of both parties.

(ii) Evaluation and Acceptance or Rejection of Goods.   The buyer typically reserves the right to inspect all goods and to accept or reject them in accordance

with the terms of the contract. Once the buying organization accepts the goods, however, it is generally not allowed to later reject them for quality or for quantity. Payment for goods does not evidence acceptance, though, so the buyer that subsequently rejects material in accordance with the contract has the right to recover payment.

Goods that are received and subsequently rejected may be returned. However, once accepted by word or deed (e.g., actual usage), then the goods cannot be subsequently rejected. As noted earlier in the chapter, a supplier generally has the right to remedy (through rework or replacement) nonconforming goods within a reasonable period of time and at its own cost. The buyer also has a duty to help mitigate the loss if there is a reasonable way of using the goods in another application or at a downgraded price.

The UCC requires that the buying organization provide the seller with timely notice of its intention to reject nonconforming goods and, if the seller does not act within a reasonable period of time, gives the buyer the right to return the goods freight collect or to store the goods in a public warehouse and charge for storage fees.

(iii) Contract Termination.   Typically, contracts are terminated when both parties have fulfilled their obligations. However, contracts can also be terminated for the convenience of the buying organization (if such rights exist in the contract) but usually require that all reasonable costs incurred by the seller up to the cancellation point are borne by the buyer.

Contracts can also be terminated for cause and canceled as a result of breach. An inexcusable delay can result in contract termination, unless the delay was caused by uncontrollable events (force majeure). There are also occasions when one party can be excused from a contract because performance becomes commercially impracticable, such as when raw material supplies are unavailable. To be so excused requires some relatively stringent conditions, and these are probably best reviewed by legal counsel. However, the simple fact that a supplier is losing money is not sufficient cause to terminate a contract.

Often, a buyer will discover that a particular supplier is having deep-rooted financial problems. If these problems continue, they are quite likely to result in service cuts and diminished quality. It is possible that the buying organization may be willing to assist by offering progress payments based on the level of completion of the products or services or even to pay for and take ownership of the material prior to their completion.

Federal bankruptcy laws do not allow for a buying organization to cancel its contract simply on the basis of the bankruptcy filing, so the rules covering anticipatory repudiation do not apply. The law, however, does allow the supplier to choose which contracts it intends to complete and which ones it will cancel.

It is also not unusual for a contract to be terminated by mutual agreement or suspended for specific periods of time. As long as both parties agree, it is perfectly acceptable to do so.

(iv) Dispute Mediation and Arbitration.   When parties are unable to reach agreement on how to administer a particular aspect of their contract, they often turn to third-party sources for resolution. Many of these avenues are outside the formal court system:

Mediation is the most commonly used method outside of the court system for reaching settlement in a dispute. Contracts often contain a clause requiring mediation when the two parties cannot agree on a solution. Generally, the mediation is conducted by a facilitator selected with the approval of both parties. Keep in mind, however, that mediation is not legally binding on the parties.

Arbitration is a similar process but one that does render a binding judgment that can be later enforced in court. Typically, arbitrators have either a legal background or a strong technical and business background in the matter being submitted. Arbitration tends to be less expensive than court systems since the same rules of evidence will not apply.

(v) Choice of Law.   When a dispute requires resolution, the question of jurisdiction becomes important: What law or rules should apply? What specific court and location should hear the case? Obviously, this could have a significant impact on the outcome or decision, so **choice of law** or legal venue is typically cited as part of the terms and conditions. The clause states the jurisdiction (in the United States, it is typically a state) that governs and in which disputes must be resolved. *Warning*: Since only a small fraction of purchases actually end in court litigation, you may think including this clause is unimportant. But be careful—if you use the supplier's terms and you *do* encounter a dispute requiring third-party resolution, you may be traveling to the supplier's location.

5.4 SUMMARY

Forming and administering contracts is one of the key competencies of the procurement professional. In this chapter we reviewed how you can best manage contract compliance and what potential value this brings to the organization. Post-purchase-order monitoring goes a step beyond the simple administration of the contract and includes ensuring compliance by working to achieve continuous improvement and an atmosphere of collaboration with your suppliers.

There is, of course, much routine work to be dealt with, as well. In administering contracts, the Procurement Department is also responsible for processing change orders and the daunting task of negotiating the additional pricing for those changes when the supplier already has been awarded the business. In addition, the Procurement Department is responsible for administering price adjustments on cost-plus contracts and reviewing claims for additional fees or increases in percentages.

Monitoring warranties, filing claims, and processing returns is another of the Procurement Department's routine tasks, which, under common circumstances, adds a great deal of value and support to the internal customer. Along with this, the Procurement Department handles the tracking and monitoring of the ongoing processes for expediting deliveries and maintaining on-time delivery performance.

There are a number of circumstances in which suppliers will be likely to create contract breaches, and the Procurement Department is charged with resolving them. Along with this goes the task of resolving conflicts through a variety of avenues such as arbitration and mediation.

KEY TERMS

Gantt chart

Engineering change order (ECO)

Specification change order (SCO)

Warranty

Uniform Commercial Code (UCC)

Express warranties

Implied warranties

Merchantability

Fitness for a particular purpose

Disclaimers

Supplier Relationship Management (SRM)

Service Level Agreement (SLA)

Metrics

Key Performance Indicator (KPI)

Management by exception

Executive review

Business plans

Technology road maps

Performance scorecard

Commodity management

Business unit leader

Expediting

Split order

Back order

Breach of contract

Cure or remedy

Anticipatory breach

Actual damages

Consequential damages

Liquidated damages

Incidental damages

Cover damages

Latent defects

Liability

Limitations

Hold harmless

Consumer Product Safety Act

Indemnification

International Chamber of Commerce

Material mistakes

Unilateral mistakes

Evaluation and Acceptance or Rejection of Goods

Dispute mediation

Arbitration

Choice of law

PROJECT MANAGEMENT

LEARNING OBJECTIVES

1. List the five basic process groups recognized by the PMBOK.
2. List the seven basic steps in effective project planning.
3. Name four steps to creating optimal project quality control.
4. Describe the budget-related characteristics the project manager should evaluate regularly.

Project management is the discipline of defining and achieving targets while optimizing the use of resources (time, money, people, materials, energy, space, etc.) over the course of a project (a set of activities of finite duration). Project management is quite often the responsibility of an individual project manager. This individual seldom participates directly in the activities that produce the end result, but rather strives to maintain the progress and productive mutual interaction of various parties in such a way that overall risk of failure is reduced or eliminated. Many projects characterized as complex span both functions, and processes within and between business enterprises, and are managed by cross-functional project teams.

6.1 THE FIVE PROJECT MANAGEMENT PROCESSES

The **project management body of knowledge (PMBOK)** is a collection of processes and knowledge areas generally accepted as best practice within the project management discipline. The organization that maintains and advances project management education and the body of knowledge is the **Project Management Institute**.[1]

The PMBOK recognizes five basic process groups and nine knowledge areas typical of almost all projects. The basic concepts are applicable to projects, programs, and operations. The five basic process groups are:

1. Project initiation
2. Project planning
3. Project execution
4. Project controlling
5. Project closeout

The project leader should understand that many of these processes overlap and interact throughout a project or phase. "Neat" boundaries between these processes do not, in reality, exist. Nonetheless, project management processes are typically described in these terms:

Inputs: Documents, plans, designs
Tools and techniques: Mechanisms applied to inputs
Outputs: Documents, products

PMI provides a knowledge framework for the cross-functional and process management skills required to deliver a successful project and has organized nine broad project management knowledge areas[2]:

1. Project integration management
2. Project scope management
3. Project time management
4. Project cost management
5. Project quality management
6. Project human resource management
7. Project communications management
8. Project risk management
9. Project procurement management

---

1. See www.pmi.org/info/default.asp.
2. Project Management Institute. *A Guide to the Project Management Body of Knowledge (PMBOK)*, 4th ed. Newtown Square, PA: Author, 2010.

(a) THE UNIQUE CHARACTER OF PROJECTS.   Projects differ from typical organizational operations activities in that projects are characterized as goal oriented; they are of finite duration, employ precision coordination of a set of interrelated activities, and are—in the end—unique. Operations activities and events on the other hand, are characterized as ongoing, or repetitive (see Figure 6.1).

Managing projects requires great skill and knowledge not only of the many technical aspects of project management, but also a keen awareness of individual and organizational behavior. The competencies required of project managers as well as members of a project team make project management a challenging endeavor. These competencies are outlined in Figure 6.2. Running a successful project has often been likened to leading and playing in an orchestra.

Projects are a means of organizing activities that cannot be addressed within an organization's normal operational limits. Projects are often utilized as a means of achieving an organization's strategic plan, whether the project team is employed by the organization or is a contracted service provider.

The five project management processes identified by the Project Management Institute (and shown in Figure 6.3) serve as the foundation for an understanding of the elements that help define a successful project and project management. These processes follow the span of the **project life cycle**.

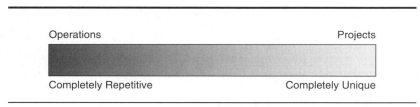

FIGURE 6.1   OPERATIONS VERSUS PROJECT MANAGEMENT CHARACTERISTICS

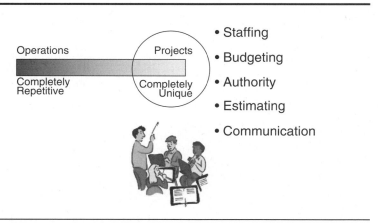

FIGURE 6.2   THE CHALLENGING PROJECT MANAGEMENT ENVIRONMENT

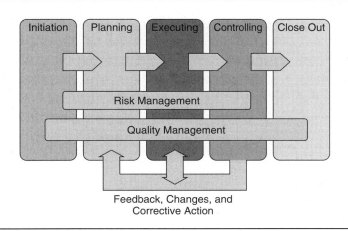

FIGURE 6.3   THE INTERRELATIONSHIP AMONG ELEMENTS OF THE PROJECT MANAGEMENT PROCESSPROJECT

The project management processes may be viewed as a closed-loop system, with process spanning activities focused on ongoing project risk assessment and mitigation, as well as continuous quality process improvement.

6.2 STAGE ONE: INITIATING A PROJECT

The purpose of project initiation is to begin to define the overall parameters of a project and establish the appropriate project management and quality environment required to complete the project.

Development of the project charter is a pivotal starting point for the project, establishing the project definition statement that will serve as the foundation for all future efforts. The completion of this process is marked by the project kick-off meeting, in which the project manager presents the project charter. Successful projects begin with a detailed project definition that is understood and accepted by stakeholders. Putting everything down in writing helps ensure a commitment among project team members and between the team and the customers or stakeholders.

As part of project initiation, an initial project plan is developed, which consists of the **project charter**, cost, scope, schedule, and quality documents, and preliminary risk identification list. These documents, once approved, ensure a consistent understanding of the project, help to set expectations, and identify resources necessary to move the project to the next level of detailed planning. Potential problems are identified and ranked in importance so that they can be addressed early in the project.

Also during project initiation, a high-level project schedule is developed as the road map to more detailed project planning and project execution and control. This high-level schedule will be refined over time, and will serve as the primary source of information regarding project status and progress. An accurate, realistic, and complete milestone schedule, rigorously maintained, is essential to the success of a project.

Sponsorship by management of the project must be confirmed or gained during project initiation. Having a project sponsor, and securing approval early in the project management life cycle, helps ensure a commitment to the project.

This phase consists of the following processes:

- Prepare for the project, where the project sponsor and initial project team are identified and work with the project manager to create the project charter.
- Define **cost/scope/schedule/quality (CSSQ)**, where the project manager, along with the project team, define the scope of the project and identify the preliminary budget, high-level schedule, and quality standards to complete the project.
- Perform risk identification, where the project manager and project team begin to identify and document any risks or critical path constraints associated with the project.
- Develop initial project plan, where the project manager and project team identify all stakeholders and document their involvement in the project, develop means of communicating with them, and compile all documentation created during project initiation to produce the initial project plan.
- Confirm approval to proceed to next phase, where the project manager reviews and refines the business case, secures resources required for project planning, and prepares the formal acceptance criteria package for review and approval by the project sponsor.

(a) THE PROJECT CHARTER.   The project charter is a tool to obtain commitment from all affected groups and individuals associated with a specific project. It is a communication vehicle that can be referenced throughout all phases of the project. It provides a quick reference and overview of the project and lays the foundation for the project structure and how the project will be managed.

> "The Project Charter can be described as the agreement between the organization providing the product or service, and the customer organization requesting and receiving the project deliverable"[3]

The project charter provides a consolidated and summary-level overview of the project. It allows all parties involved in the project (stakeholders) to document the agreed-upon scope and objectives, approach, and deliverables of the project. It also, at the outset of the project, documents the agreed-upon communications plans, control mechanisms, and responsibilities of team members. In other words,

---

3.   James D. Reeds. Project Management Course. *Masters in Supply Chain Management Program*. University of San Diego: Supply Chain Management Institute. June 2003.

PMI PMBOK PROCESS AREAS	LOCATION IN PROJECT *CHARTER*
Initiating	Project Purpose, Project Scope, Project Objectives
Planning	All sections
Executing	Project Deliverables and Quality Objectives, Stages, Project Schedule, Project Effort
Controlling	Project Control
Closing	Stages, Project Control

TABLE 6.1   RELATIONSHIP OF PROJECT MANAGEMENT PROCESSES TO THE PROJECT CHARTER[4]

the project charter is a first-step communications tool within the project planning environment. It is an agreement that defines: partners and external stakeholders; the project management framework to be used on the project; roles, responsibilities, accountabilities, and activities of the team members; management commitments (specifically in terms of communications and control); and, the empowerment framework.

The project charter is the first step of project planning, following completion of the project initiation stage. The project charter does not change throughout the project life cycle, but rather is developed at the beginning of the project (immediately following project initiation approval, and in the earliest stages of project planning). Further, the project charter can effectively serve to integrate all five stages of the project management process. See Table 6.1.

6.3 STAGE TWO: PROJECT PLANNING

The basic steps in effective project planning require that a project team[5]:

Define the project scope. The project manager and the project team develop the statement of work, which identifies the purpose, scope (boundaries), and deliverables for the project and establishes the responsibilities of the project team.

Develop a risk management strategy. The project team evaluates the likely obstacles and creates a risk mitigation strategy for balancing costs, schedule, and quality.

Build a work breakdown structure. The team identifies all the tasks required to build the specified deliverables. The scope statement and project purpose help define the boundaries of the project.

Identify task relationships. The detailed tasks, known as work packages, are placed in the proper time sequence.

---

4.   Ibid.
5.   Eric Verzuh. *The Fast Forward MBA in Project Management.* New York: John Wiley & Sons. 1999, pp.101–119.

Estimate work packages. Each of these detailed tasks is assigned an estimate for the amount of labor hours and equipment needed, and for the duration of the task.

Calculate initial schedule. After estimating the duration of each work package and figuring in the sequence of tasks, the team calculates the total duration of the project. (This initial schedule, while useful for planning, may need to be revised further down the line.)

Assign and level resources. The team adjusts the schedule to account for resource constraints. Tasks are rescheduled in order to optimize the use of people and equipment used on the project.

(a) THE IMPORTANCE OF THE WORK BREAKDOWN STRUCTURE (WBS). Once the project's scope has been determined, risk assessment has been performed, and the project has received approval from the firm's project sponsors, project planning may be initiated. A proven approach to effective project planning is the development of a project **work breakdown structure (WBS)**. The work breakdown structure identifies all the tasks in a project; in fact, a WBS is sometimes referred to simply as a task list. It turns one large, unique, perhaps mystifying, piece of work—the project—into many small, manageable tasks. The WBS uses outputs from project definition and risk management and identifies the tasks that are the foundation for all subsequent planning. Work breakdown structures can be set up in either graphic or outline form. Either way, they list the various tasks involved.

The graphic WBS gives a picture that makes it easy to understand all the parts of a project, but the indented (list) WBS is more practical because you can list hundreds of tasks (compare Figures 6.4 and 6.5). The WBS clarifies and provides necessary details for a number of project management activities. Firms that standardize project management quickly identify similar types of projects and build WBS templates as a tool for their project managers. Building a WBS helps to:

- Provide a detailed illustration of project scope.
- Monitor progress.
- Create accurate cost and schedule estimates.
- Build project teams.

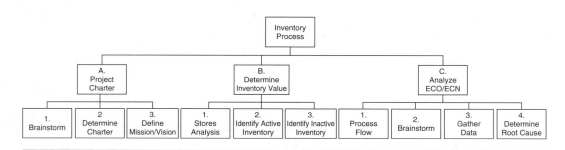

FIGURE 6.4   EXAMPLE OF A GRAPHIC WORK BREAKDOWN STRUCTURE (WBS)

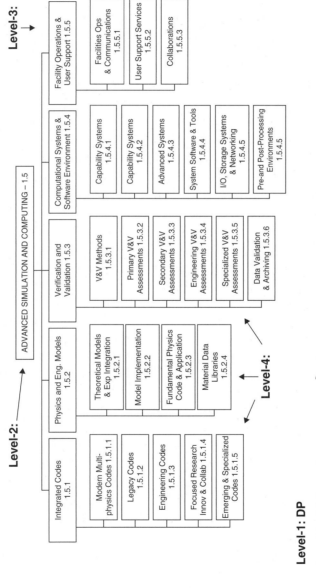

National Work Breakdown Structure

Level-2: → ADVANCED SIMULATION AND COMPUTING – 1.5

Level-3: →

Integrated Codes 1.5.1
- Modern Multi-physics Codes 1.5.1.1
- Legacy Codes 1.5.1.2
- Engineering Codes 1.5.1.3
- Focused Research Innov & Collab 1.5.1.4
- Emerging & Specialized Codes 1.5.1.5

Physics and Eng. Models 1.5.2
- Theoretical Models & Exp Integration 1.5.2.1
- Model Implementation 1.5.2.2
- Fundamental Physics Code & Application 1.5.2.3
- Material Data Libraries 1.5.2.4

Verification and Validation 1.5.3
- V&V Methods 1.5.3.1
- Primary V&V Assessments 1.5.3.2
- Secondary V&V Assessments 1.5.3.3
- Engineering V&V Assessments 1.5.3.4
- Specialized V&V Assessments 1.5.3.5
- Data Validation & Archiving 1.5.3.6

Computational Systems & Software Environment 1.5.4
- Capability Systems 1.5.4.1
- Capability Systems 1.5.4.2
- Advanced Systems 1.5.4.3
- System Software & Tools 1.5.4.4
- I/O, Storage Systems & Networking 1.5.4.5
- Pre-and Post-Processing Environments 1.5.4.5

Facility Operations & User Support 1.5.5
- Facilities Ops & Communications 1.5.5.1
- User Support Services 1.5.5.2
- Collaborations 1.5.5.3

Level-4:

Level-1: DP

Level-2: ASC

Level-3: ASC Subprograms ⎱
Level-4: ASC Products   ⎰ **Shown Above**

Level-5: ASC Projects

FIGURE 6.5 EXAMPLE OF A GRAPHIC WBS AND AN INDENTED (LIST) WBS

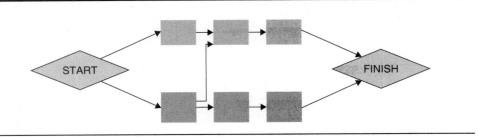

FIGURE 6.6   EXAMPLE OF A PROJECT NETWORK DIAGRAM

A project can best be understood by a thorough understanding of its parts. The work breakdown structure breaks the project down into many small, manageable tasks called work packages. The process of deciding who will perform these tasks and how they will be arranged provides the structure for the actual work of the project.[6] Without a well-defined and thought-through work breakdown structure, a project runs the risk of becoming disorganized, with a likely result that important tasks will be misscheduled, underallocated, or overlooked altogether.

After consulting the project's WBS, the next step in project planning is to identify **task relationships**.

The sequence in which detailed tasks—work packages—are performed is determined by the relationship between the tasks. This is best accomplished by establishing a link between an individual task's predecessor tasks and successor tasks. Scheduled through time, associating the sequence of a project's tasks with predecessor and successor relationships will provide a **project network diagram**.

Network diagrams (as shown in Figure 6.6) are commonly called PERT charts. PERT stands for **program evaluation and review technique**, one of the first formal methods developed for scheduling projects and programs. PERT relies heavily on network diagrams, so for many people the terms PERT chart and network diagram are synonymous.

While a network diagram is essential in calculating the project schedule, it can be difficult to decipher on a large project. There is a good alternative that displays both the schedule information and the task relationships.

Gantt charts, named after Henry Gantt, who developed them in the early 1900s, have become the most common method for displaying a project schedule (see Figure 6.7 for an example). The great advantage of the Gantt chart is its clarity: The horizontal axis shows the schedule and the vertical axis lists the work breakdown structure.

The initial schedule represents the combination of task sequence and task duration. But it's called an initial schedule because it hasn't taken into account people and equipment limitations. The next planning step uses the initial schedule as a starting point and balances it against the resources available to the project.

---

6.   Ibid., pp. 120–152.

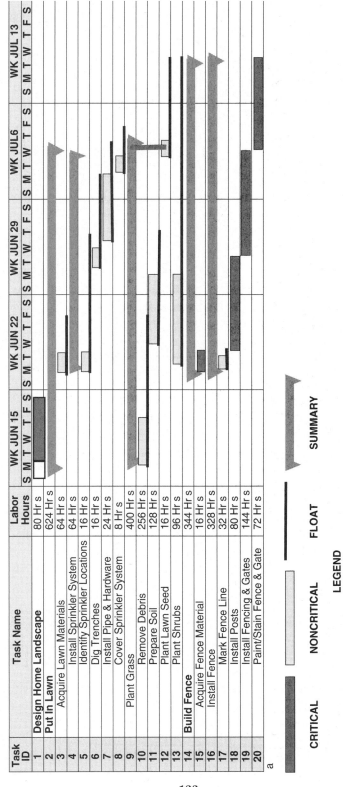

Task ID	Task Name	Labor Hours	WK JUN 15 S M T W T F S	WK JUN 22 S M T W T F S	WK JUN 29 S M T W T F S	WK JUL6 S M T W T F S	WK JUL 13 S M T W T F S
1	**Design Home Landscape**	80 Hrs					
2	**Put In Lawn**	624 Hrs					
3	Acquire Lawn Materials	64 Hrs					
4	Install Sprinkler System	64 Hrs					
5	Identify Sprinkler Locations	16 Hrs					
6	Dig Trenches	16 Hrs					
7	Install Pipe & Hardware	24 Hrs					
8	Cover Sprinkler System	8 Hrs					
9	Plant Grass	400 Hrs					
10	Remove Debris	256 Hrs					
11	Prepare Soil	128 Hrs					
12	Plant Lawn Seed	16 Hrs					
13	Plant Shrubs	96 Hrs					
14	**Build Fence**	344 Hrs					
15	Acquire Fence Material	16 Hrs					
16	Install Fence	328 Hrs					
17	Mark Fence Line	32 Hrs					
18	Install Posts	80 Hrs					
19	Install Fencing & Gates	144 Hrs					
20	Paint/Stain Fence & Gate	72 Hrs					

a

CRITICAL   NONCRITICAL   FLOAT   SUMMARY

LEGEND

FIGURE 6.7   EXAMPLE OF A TYPICAL GANTT CHART

133

(b) THE ASSIGNMENT AND LEVELING OF PROJECT RESOURCES. The goal of resource leveling is to optimize the use of people and equipment assigned to the project. It begins with the assumption that, when possible, it is most productive to have consistent, continuous use of the fewest resources possible. In other words, it seeks to avoid repeatedly adding and removing resources time and again, throughout the project. Resource leveling is the last step in creating a realistic schedule. It confronts the reality of limited people and/or equipment, and adjusts the schedule to compensate.

Every project faces the reality of limited people and equipment (resources). The idea is to avoid both over- and underallocation of project resources. Project overallocation can become serious if project managers believe that they have a large supply of a rare resource, such as the unlimited time of a subject expert. In this example, not only can a project schedule become unrealistic, but the manager may also overload a key resource. "Project managers must do their best to avoid resource peaks and valleys, and try to use a consistent set of people on the project at a consistent rate; this is not only more realistic, it is more efficient. This is because every upswing in resources has a cost."[7]

The process of balancing resource allocations for a project is known as **resource leveling** (see Figure 6.8). Resources are the people, equipment, and raw materials that go into the project. Resource leveling focuses only on the people and equipment; the materials needed for the project are dictated by the specifications, and are planned by material planning and control systems, such as enterprise resource planning (ERP) information systems.

The wise project manager will seek to "level" the project's resources through actions such as a consideration of scheduled overtime, additional funding for temporary labor, subcontracting, and so on.

(c) CALCULATE A BASELINE (INITIAL) PROJECT SCHEDULE. The next step in project planning is to **calculate a baseline (initial) project schedule**. Today, due to the complexity and information requirements of most projects, project management software is employed to not only plan a project schedule, but also to continuously replan the project schedule throughout the life of the project. The initial schedule is calculated by using the network diagram and the duration of each work package to determine the start and finish dates for each task, and so forth for the entire project. Schedule calculation provides a set of detailed schedule data for every work package:

- **Early start.** The earliest date a task can begin, given the tasks preceding it.
- **Early finish.** The earliest date a task can finish, given the tasks preceding it.
- **Late start.** The latest date a task can begin without delaying the finish date of the project.

---

7. Ibid.

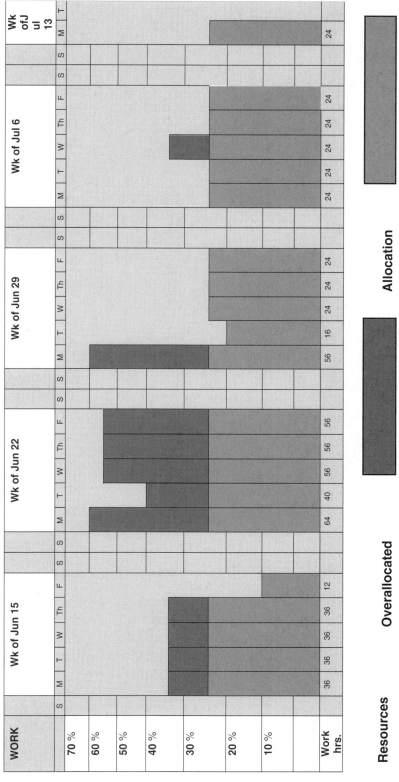

Resources   **Overallocated**   **Allocation**

FIGURE 6.8   RESOURCE LEVELING

- **Late finish.** The latest date a task can finish without delaying the finish date of the project.

A powerful project planning tool of the initial schedule is the determination of the project's **critical path**. When outlined on a network diagram, the critical path is the longest path through the network. A project's critical path information is most often portrayed as either a network diagram, or as a Gantt chart.[8]

It is important to be able to calculate a project's critical path, and to keep a focus on maintaining control over critical path tasks and time allocations. Not every task on a typical complex project is "critical." Noncritical tasks in a project can in reality fall behind schedule without consequence to the overall on-time success of the project. The importance of the critical path is that it highlights those tasks of a project that cannot fall behind schedule, or contribute to unplanned expenditures. In other words—to risk falling behind schedule on any critical path task is to risk falling behind schedule for the entire project.

6.4 STAGE THREE: PROJECT EXECUTION

Project execution is typically the part of the life cycle of a project when the majority of the actual work of the project is performed and the majority of the project budget is expended. The purpose of project execution is to manage every aspect of the project plan *as work is being performed* to make certain the project is successful. Project execution follows a **project execution plan (PEP)**—which is a key document for the management of a project. It is a statement of policies and procedures defined by the project manager, and is usually developed by the project manager for the project sponsor/project director's approval. It sets out in a structured format the project scope, objectives, and relative priorities.

Project execution may be viewed as an outcome of effective project scheduling—and rescheduling. However, the transition is often transparent, as project rescheduling and the actions that flow for rescheduling are prominent in the project execution stage. Thus, a realistic project schedule will emphasize the following ongoing (rescheduling) characteristics throughout the project's life cycle:

- Communicates detailed presentation of the work to be done.
- Applies task sequences in the correct order.
- Accounts for external constraints beyond the control of the team.
- Can be accomplished on time, given the availability of resources.
- Takes into consideration all the objectives of the project (deliverables).

Before formally beginning project execution and control, the project team should review recent project status reports and the project plan. At this point in the

---

8.   Ibid., pp. 140–152.

project, the project plan comprises all deliverables produced during project initiation and project planning:

- Project charter
- Project quality plan (scope, schedule, quality plan, budget)
- Risk management worksheet
- Description of stakeholder involvement
- Communications plan
- Time and cost baseline
- Change control process
- Acceptance management process
- Issue management and escalation process
- Project organizational management plan
- Project team training plan
- Project implementation and transition plan

PROJECT TEAM MANAGEMENT AND TEAM BUILDING

Projects require the engagement of a project team. A team is a group of individuals with a common identity and a psychological attachment, with shared values, norms, and standards of behavior, who work together to achieve a common objective. Each team is unique, because it consists of individuals, each with their own personality, knowledge, and experience. The knowledge and experience of the team members are usually considered during the building of the project team, as to complete any task, especially a project, particular skills are required.[9]

(a) ESTABLISH A TEAM ENVIRONMENT. Project team members must learn to work together to achieve project goals. They must recognize that there is more to teamwork than simply having team members feel good about each other. High-performing project teams are disciplined. Team members participate in all required meetings, are willing to suppress their egos for the good of the group, take their assigned tasks seriously, and continuously strive to improve their skills. High-performing project teams are either empowered to make decisions or are included in decision-making processes. This is the essence of project ownership.

There can be at least three levels of team participation (plus the customer level) and involvement that typically work on a project[10]:

1. **The primary group.** These are the team members who work face-to-face and know everyone else in the group. On a project, they are the immediate project team, or task force, whether full time or seconded part time.
2. **The secondary group.** These are the people who work part time on the project and contribute to the work of the primary team, but are not part of

9. J. Rodney Turner, Kristoffer V. Grude, and Lynn Thurloway. *The Project Manager as Change Agent: Leadership, Influence and Negotiation*. London: McGraw-Hill Publishing Company, 1996, p. 80.
10. Ibid., p. 81.

the task force. On a project, these are the functions that contribute through the network organization. However, they must be treated as part of the larger project team, if the team is to be effective.

3. **The tertiary group.** These are people who influence the work of the primary and secondary teams, or who are affected by their work, but have no direct contribution. The tertiary group has two parts: those influencing the work of the project, and those affected by the facility delivered or the product of the facility. The first may consist of family and friends, peer groups, or professional bodies. The second group are people who live in the neighborhood in which the facility is to be built (NIMBYs—not in my back yard) or who will use or operate the facility after it is commissioned, or they may be people whose lives will be irreversibly changed (even by being made redundant) by the operation of the facility.

4. **Customers (consumers).** The final group are the customer(s); the people who will become the recipients of the output of the project deliverables. (Sometimes they are the users, but often not.) The expectations of all of these groups of people must be managed if the project is to be successful, as they have a powerful ability to disrupt.

A problem often encountered by project managers, especially at project startup, is getting a group of individuals to act collectively, to think as a team, and to commit to the idea of both individual and team responsibilities.

(b) THE PROJECT COMMUNICATIONS PLAN.   During project execution, the project manager, project team, and stakeholders will share information using a variety of communication mechanisms. These were defined during project planning and may include:

- Status meetings
- Status reports
- Memos
- Newsletters
- Executive correspondence
- Meeting notes
- Executive meetings
- Steering committee meetings

This information is collected, stored, and disseminated based upon procedures established and documented in the communications plan. While executing the plan, the project manager must be aware of how the organization will use the information, and whether the plan is effective. He/she must be flexible and ready to modify the plan if portions of it are not working as expected or communications needs change within the performing organization.

Using the progress reports prepared by the project team, the project manager should complete a status report to be presented to the project sponsor. In this report, the project manager measures the "health and progress" of the project against the project plan. It is the primary communication vehicle between the project manager and the project sponsor, and should contain the following information:

- Summary of progress to project schedule—a high-level glance at the major project deliverables, with their intended and actual start and end dates.
- Issues and action items—a running list of open and closed issues, including the name of the person responsible for taking action to resolve them.
- Significant accomplishments—a list of the most important completed tasks, or a description of work done toward their completion.
- Significant planned accomplishments for the following weeks—a description of the most important tasks scheduled for completion during the following weeks.
- Deliverable acceptance log—a running diary of actions taken toward acceptance of deliverables. Change control log—a running diary of actions taken toward acceptance of change control.
- Lost time—a description of any situation that occurred that resulted in the project team being unable to perform work.

Other project documents that should be attached to the status report include any change control requests, deliverable acceptance forms, meeting notes, and the risk management worksheet. The status report becomes the point of discussion for the status meeting, the regularly scheduled forum where the project manager presents the project status and discusses issues with the project sponsor.

(c) MANAGING PROJECT CHANGE PROCESSES.   Managing issues involves documenting, reporting, escalating, tracking, and resolving problems that occur as a project progresses. During project planning, the project manager and project sponsor agreed upon and documented the process for managing issues and included the process in the project plan.

The issue escalation and management process addresses the following:

- How issues will be captured and tracked.
- How issues will be prioritized.
- How and when issues will be escalated for resolution.

Issues are usually questions, suggestions, or problems raised by project team members, including the project manager and customer. They are different from changes in that they do not usually have an immediate impact on the project scope or schedule.

More intractable issues or problems—conflict—must be addressed more expeditiously by the project manager and the project team. The same communications tools are used, but the urgency in addressing conflict and its resolution is necessary; otherwise, there will likely be serious risk to the project's success.

6.5 STAGE FOUR: PROJECT CONTROLLING

The controlling functions include a broad cross-section of management skills and activities. These cover common areas such as quality control, budget management, risk analysis, acceptance of project deliverables, communications planning, and change management. We explore these aspects in the following section.

(a) IMPLEMENT PROJECT QUALITY CONTROL. Quality control involves monitoring the project and its progress to determine if the quality assurance activities defined during project planning are being implemented and whether the results meet the quality standards defined during project initiation. The entire organization has responsibilities relating to quality, but the primary responsibility for ensuring that the project follows its defined quality procedures ultimately belongs to the project manager. Quality control monitoring should be performed throughout the course of the project. Some of the activities and processes that can be used to monitor the quality of deliverables, determine if project results comply with quality standards, and identify ways to improve unsatisfactory performance are described below. The project manager and project sponsor(s) should decide which are best to implement in their specific project environment.

- **Conduct peer reviews.** The goal of a peer review is to identify and remove quality issues from a deliverable as early and as efficiently as possible. A peer review is a thorough review of a specific deliverable, conducted by members of the project team who are the day-to-day peers of the individuals who produced the work.
- **Use quality checklists.** Both the project manager and project team members can create and make use of various checklists to be sure items are not overlooked while a product is being developed. Checklists may be simple hardcopy lists of "things to do," or may be generated using more formal, electronic-based tools.
- **Maintain and analyze the project schedule.** This activity should never be taken lightly, regardless of the size of the project. Updating the project schedule on a regular basis while keeping a close watch on the timeline and budget is the basic means used to measure the quality of the schedule.
- **Conduct project audits.** The goal of a project audit is to ensure that the quality assurance activities defined in project planning are being implemented and to determine whether quality standards are being met. It is a process to note what is being done well, to identify real or potential issues, and to suggest ways for improvement

(b) MANAGE THE PROJECT BUDGET. Part of the project manager's job is to ensure that the project is completed within the allocated and approved budget. Budget management is concerned with all costs associated with the project, including the cost of human resources, equipment, travel, materials, and supplies. Increased costs of materials, supplies, and human resources, therefore, have a direct impact on the budget. The project manager must know the extent of his or her authority to make budget decisions. For example, is the project manager allowed to authorize work that requires additional hours of salaried personnel time, or must employee time extensions go through the same approval process as contract personnel or equipment purchases? Often, the project manager must work closely with fiscal and contract personnel in other divisions to track and control costs. A few budget-related characteristics the project manager should examine each time the schedule is updated include:

- **Original contract value.** The original estimated budget (cost) that was approved by the project sponsor.
- **Total approved changes.** The total cost of approved changes as a result of change control.
- **Total current budget.** The sum of the original contract value and the total approved changes. This is the most current approved project budget.
- **Cost to date.** The actual dollars (cost) expended to date on all tasks and materials in the project. The labor costs can be calculated by the scheduling tool based on the time the project manager tracks against the tasks in the project schedule.
- **Estimate to complete.** The dollars (cost) estimated to be expended to complete remaining project tasks. The project manager must verify and assess the impact of team members' revised effort estimates to complete tasks.
- **Forecast total.** The sum of the cost to date and the estimate to complete.
- **Project variance.** The difference between all estimated and all actual dollars. It is calculated by subtracting the forecast total from the total current budget. A positive variance means that the actual cost of the product is less than the budgeted cost. A negative variance means that the actual cost of the product is greater than the budgeted cost.

(c) PROJECT RISK ANALYSIS.   Risks are potential future events that can adversely affect a project's cost, schedule, scope, or quality (CSSQ). In prior phases, the project manager defined these events as accurately as possible, determined when they would impact the project, and developed a risk management plan. As the impact dates draw closer, it is important to continue reevaluating probability, impact, and timing of risks, as well as to identify additional risk factors and events. The project manager must continually look for new risks, reassess old ones, and reevaluate risk mitigation plans. The project manager should involve the whole project team in this endeavor, as various team members have their particular expertise and can bring a unique perspective to risk identification and mitigation. As the risk management is integrated into the status reporting process, this review and reevaluation should take place automatically, with the preparation of each new status report. The risk management plan needs to be constantly reevaluated.

(d) THE PROJECT CHANGE CONTROL PROCESS.   During project planning, the project manager, project sponsor, and customer agreed on a formal change control process that was documented and included in the project plan. The change control process describes:

- The definition of change and how to identify it.
- How requests for change will be initiated.
- How requests for change will be analyzed to determine if they are beneficial to the project.
- The process to approve or reject change requests.
- How funding will be secured to implement approved changes.

Although changes can be expected to occur throughout every project phase, any negative effect on the project outcome should be avoidable if the change control process is executed and managed effectively. The need for change is usually discovered during project execution, as actual task work is being performed. It is during execution that the project team may discover their original effort estimates were not accurate and will result in more or less effort being required to complete their work.

(e) MANAGE ACCEPTANCE OF DELIVERABLES.   The goal of this task is to manage the acceptance of deliverables according to the acceptance criteria management process developed during project planning. The acceptance management process is part of the project plan, and documents:

- The definition of "acceptance."
- The criteria that must be met for each deliverable to be considered "acceptable."
- The number and identity of customers designated to be reviewers of each deliverable—typically reviewers are experts in the subject matter the deliverable covers.
- The number and identity of customers designated to be approvers—approvers have the authority to sign the approval form, indicating acceptance.
- The number of business days in which deliverables must be either approved or rejected by the reviewers and approvers.
- The number of times a deliverable can be resubmitted.
- The escalation process that will be followed if a timely decision on approval or rejection of a deliverable is not met.

The acceptance management process must be followed throughout the project.

(f) EXECUTE COMMUNICATIONS PLANS. During Project Execution the Communications Plan is carried out so that required information is made available to the appropriate individuals at the appropriate times, and new or unexpected requests receive a prompt response. Communications must continue to be bidirectional during project execution. The project manager must provide required information to the project team and appropriate stakeholders on a timely basis, and the project team and stakeholders must provide required information to the project manager. The project manager should periodically assemble the project team to review the status of the project, discuss their accomplishments, and communicate any issues or concerns in an open, honest, constructive forum.

(g) MANAGING ORGANIZATIONAL CHANGE.   The project manager, with the active participation and support of the customer and project sponsor, must be able to manage the specific activities that will adequately prepare the performing organization for any anticipated changes.

- **People.** Planned workforce changes must be executed in careful coordination with the Human Resource Department.
- **Process.** The redesign of existing business processes affected by the implementation of the product of the project, and the development of corresponding procedures, must be effectively managed.
- **Culture.** Specific plans were developed based on the extent of the "culture shock" the product of the project was expected to introduce into the performing organization and its business strategy, established norms for performance, leadership approach, management style, approach to customers, use of power, approach to decision making, and employee roles.

6.6 STAGE FIVE: PROJECT CLOSEOUT

Often, the most neglected project management activity is closing out the project. The reporting and accounting tasks associated with the closeout are not often viewed as exciting as developing the product of the project.[11] The real evidence that the project is complete will come from the customer of the project.

Formal acceptance of the finished product or acknowledgment of project phase completion signifies that the work is complete. The project manager must plan for customer acceptance from the very beginning of the project—and acceptance criterion should be found in the project charter itself.

The purpose of the *project closeout stage* is to formally acknowledge that all deliverables produced during project execution and control have been completed, tested, accepted, and approved by the project's customers and the project sponsor(s), and that the product or service the project developed was successfully transitioned from the project team to the performing organization. Formal acceptance and approval also signify that the project is essentially over, and is ready for project closeout. Some project closeout activities may be classified as project closeout objectives. These typically include:

- Obtain acceptance by the customer of the project deliverables.

---

11.   Verzuh, p. 243.

- Document lessons learned.
- Facilitate project closure.
- Preserve project records and tools.
- Release resources.

To facilitate project closeout objectives, the project manager should conduct the following activities:

- Notify all project participants of the change in status of the project.
- Communicate product or service improvement ideas that may not have been implemented during the project.
- Detail any open tasks or unresolved issues.

Methods used for the accomplishment of these objectives would include:

- *Conduct final status meeting.* Once the product of the project has been successfully transitioned to the performing organization, the project manager should prepare the final status report and conduct the final status meeting. The project schedule must be up to date for all completed project and project management life-cycle phases. This is the final opportunity for all participants to confirm that the product of the project has been successfully developed and transitioned. Any outstanding issues or action items must be transitioned from the project team to the performing organization.
- *Preserve project materials, tools, and information.* Storage, archival procedures, and retrieval mechanisms for all aspects of the project should be ensured as a part of acceptance and closeout activities. The project manager must ensure that all documents or records that will be provided with the product are produced. Examples of documentation include:
  - o User manuals
  - o Online help
  - o Assembly or usage instructions

6.7 A KEY KNOWLEDGE AREA: PROJECT PROCUREMENT MANAGEMENT[12]

The Project Management Institute has adopted a planning view of the knowledge area related to procurement and its fundamental engagement in the project management process. The steps identified in project procurement management follow the

---

12.   Project Management Institute, pp. 284–310.

PMI publishes the standard PMBOK, *Project Management Body of Knowledge*, and offers two levels of certification:

A *Certified Associate in Project Management (CAPM)* has demonstrated a common base of knowledge and terms in the field of project management. It requires either 1,500 hours of work on a project team or 23 contact hours of formal education in project management.

A *Project Management Professional (PMP®)* has met specific education and experience requirements, has agreed to adhere to a code of professional conduct, and has passed an examination designed to objectively assess and measure project management knowledge. In addition, a PMP must satisfy continuing certification requirements or lose the certification.

project management five-stage process discussed earlier in this chapter. Taken from a contract management overview, the knowledge "steps" are:

1. Plan purchases and acquisitions
2. Plan contracting
3. Request sellers' responses
4. Select sellers
5. Contract administration
6. Contract closure

(a) PLAN PURCHASES AND ACQUISITIONS.   The "plan purchases and acquisitions" process identifies which project needs can be met by purchasing or acquiring products, services, or results outside the project organization and which project needs can be met by the project team during project execution. This phase includes a review of the risks associated in each make-or-buy sourcing decision. This also includes a decision on which contract type is most appropriate for the needs of the project. A critical component of the procurement planning process is the formulation of the **contract statement of work (CSOW)**. The CSOW is written to be clear, concise, and complete. It includes a description of any collateral services required. The CSOW may be modified as required as it moves through the procurement process until it is incorporated in a signed contract.

(b) PLAN CONTRACTING.   The approach taken to perform the plan contracting process is to collect information from the following project processes and their documents: the procurement management plan; the CSOW; project make-or-buy analyses; and the project management plan. The use of standard procurement forms will greatly enhance management of the procurement process during the project's life cycle.

(i) Evaluation Criteria.   Evaluation criteria are developed and used to rate or score proposals. They can be objective (e.g., "The proposed project manager needs to be a certified project management professional [PMP]") or subjective (e.g., "The proposed project manager needs to have documented previous experience with similar projects"). Evaluation criteria are often included as part of the procurement documents.
    The evaluation of bidder response to the contract solicitation can rest on many elements. A few of these are:

- **Understanding of need.** How well does the seller's proposal address the contract statement of work?
- **Overall or life-cycle cost.** Will the selected seller produce the lowest total cost of ownership (purchase cost plus operating cost)?
- **Technical capability.** Does the seller have, or can the seller be reasonably expected to acquire, the technical skills and knowledge needed?

- **Management approach.** Does the seller have, or can the seller be reasonably expected to develop, management processes and procedures to ensure a successful project?
- **Technical approach.** Do the seller's proposed technical methodologies, techniques, solutions, and services meet the procurement documentation requirements or are they likely to provide more than the expected results?
- **Financial capacity.** Does the seller have, or can the seller reasonably be expected to obtain, the necessary financial resources?
- **Production capacity and interest.** Does the seller have the capacity and interest to meet potential future requirements?
- **Business size and type.** Does the seller's enterprise meet a specific type or size of business, such as small business, female-owned, or disadvantaged small business, as defined by the buyer or established by governmental agency and set as a condition of being awarded a contract?
- **References.** Can the seller provide references from prior customers verifying the seller's work experience and compliance with contractual requirements?
- **Intellectual property (IP) rights.** Does the seller possess the IP rights in the work processes or services they will use or in the products they will produce for the project?

(ii) Request Sellers' Responses.   A few of the possible approaches used in the collection of sellers' responses are bidders' conferences, advertising, and the development of a qualified bidders list.

(iii) Select Sellers.   The **select sellers** process team receives bids or proposals and applies evaluation criteria, to select one or more sellers who are both qualified and acceptable. There are many possible selection elements: price, total cost of ownership, technical competencies, single or dual sourcing, sole sourcing, and others. Evaluation tools can employ any of the following techniques: a weighted decision matrix, independent estimates, a formal screening system, contract negotiation, a supplier rating system or matrix, expert judgment, and proposal evaluation scoring. At the end of this process, a contract is awarded to the selected supplier or suppliers. A contract is a mutually binding legal agreement that obligates the seller to provide the specified products or services, and obligates the buyer to pay the seller. A contract is a legal relationship subject to remedy in the courts.

(iv) Contract Administration.   Both the buyer and the seller administer the contract for similar purposes. Each party to the contract ensures that both it and the other party meet their contractual obligations and that their own legal rights are protected. The **contract administration** process ensures that the seller's performance meets contractual requirements and that the buyer performs according to the terms of the contract. Contract administration includes application of the

appropriate project management processes to the contractual relationship, and integration of the outputs from these processes into overall management of the project. Contracts can be amended at any time prior to the close of the contract by mutual consent and negotiation.

(v) Contract Closure. The contract closure process supports the close project process, since it involves verification that all project work and deliverables were acceptable. The contract closure process also involves administrative activities, such as records maintenance to reflect final results. Early termination of a contract is a special case of contract closure, and can result from a mutual agreement of the parties or from the default of one of the parties. The rights and responsibilities of the parties in the event of an early termination are contained in a termination clause of the contract.

6.8 SUMMARY

The Project Management Institute (PMI) has developed the *project management body of knowledge (PMBOK)*. It identifies processes and knowledge areas generally accepted as best practice within the project management discipline.

The PMBOK recognizes five basic process groups and nine knowledge areas typical of almost all projects. The basic concepts are applicable to projects, programs and operations. The five basic process groups are project initiation, project planning, project execution, project controlling, and project closeout.

Procurement in a project management environment has unique challenges in keeping pace with the process. While planning for purchases and contracts is required both in the context of sound business principles and the tightly integrated project, execution to planned timing is paramount. The key is to incorporate best procurement practices into project management activities.

KEY TERMS

Project management body of
    knowledge (PMBOK)
Project Management Institute
Project life cycle
Project charter
Cost/scope/schedule/quality (CSSQ)
Work breakdown structure (WBS)
Task relationships
Project network diagram
Program evaluation and review
    technique (PERT)

Gantt charts
Resource leveling
Calculate a baseline (initial) project
    schedule
Critical path
Project execution plan (PEP)
Contract statement of work (CSOW)
Select sellers
Contract administration

NEGOTIATIONS

LEARNING OBJECTIVES

1. Draw a graph demonstrating the role of supply and demand in establishing the "equilibrium price." Label the axes "price" and "supply available".
2. Describe the role of a cross-functional team in negotiating and selecting the best supplier for your organization.
3. Name some techniques for doing a successful negotiation.
4. List the necessary elements in a negotiation plan.

Your organization naturally seeks to obtain the maximum value for its investment in goods and services. Not surprisingly, so does your supplier; both organizations seek to gain the highest possible benefit from all of their business transactions.

So when there is much value at stake, both parties generally come together to reconcile their differing positions. This process is referred to as **negotiations**.

As you have learned in previous chapters, any business transaction involving commercial buying and selling requires both a valid offer and acceptance. Between these two elements, however, there typically lies a gap of expectations and requirements: Your budget, for example, allows a certain amount of spending for a particular purchase, but the supplier's offer contains a significantly higher amount. Obviously, this creates a gap. How do you reconcile these two seemingly oppositional positions so that each organization can achieve its respective goals? In these circumstances it is critical to engage the supplier in some form of negotiations.

A major portion of the buyer's time will be spent conducting negotiations with suppliers to obtain more favorable terms for their organization. That is not to say that you continually engage in petty haggling with your suppliers. However, when the outcome of a procurement activity is critical to the organization's goals, a successful conclusion can never be in doubt: You will need to meet the goals and expectations of your organization as well as ensuring that the supplier continues to value your business. Negotiation is most likely to occur when the conditions for competitive bidding (see Chapter 3) are not present, such as when there is a sole- or single-source situation. It may also be required even when competitive bidding has taken place. Despite the fact that you have issued a request for proposals (RFP) and selected the most appropriate supplier, there may still be gaps in filling all of your organization's needs. Negotiation, therefore, requires much additional planning, research, and, most importantly, precise execution in order to achieve a successful outcome and meet your organization's objectives. How this is accomplished and the sequence in which it logically progresses is the subject of this chapter.

7.1 ASSESSING THE NEGOTIATING ENVIRONMENT

It is important that you first assess the current situation prior to conducting actual negotiations. Assessing the negotiating climate typically involves gaining an understanding of market conditions for the particular commodity or service being purchased and the position of the supplier in that market. Market conditions generally refer to circumstances such as the availability of supply in relation to actual demand or the number of suppliers in the marketplace available to create a competitive situation. What is the market share for each of the major players, and how aggressive is the battle for market share? How profitable are companies in the industry, and what constitutes a typical profit margin? What is the economic outlook for this particular segment of the economy?

In addition, it is important for you to assess the relationship you have with the supplier. Often, this can determine the atmosphere during the negotiation and have an important impact on how you and your team develop your negotiation strategy. With this information come insights into the supplier's objectives and, as a result, many clues that tell you what supplier strategies to expect during the negotiations.

In this section, you will explore the nature of the competitive environment and how your understanding of it can assist you in your negotiations.

(a) THE COMPETITIVE ENVIRONMENT.   When the competitive environment is limited by the lack of **qualified suppliers** or by intellectual property rights, competitive bidding is unlikely. In this circumstance, negotiations may be the only way to achieve organizational objectives. You can assess the likelihood of conducting competitive bidding by using the chart in Table 7.1. This table describes the specific circumstances in the marketplace and the degree to which their presence fosters competitive bidding. Keep in mind that, as mentioned in the table, there can be no bidding if only one supplier can meet your requirements.

(b) NATURE OF COMPETITION.   **Competition** is available in virtually all markets for goods and services. What you have to assess is the nature of that competition so that you can effectively formulate your procurement strategies. Higher competition generally results in lower prices and a greater willingness by suppliers to provide additional services.

Competition can be evaluated from a number of perspectives:

- **Number of qualified or qualifiable suppliers in the market.** Higher numbers generally foster greater competition.
- **Impact of the buyer.** Greater procurement volume encourages vigorous competition for your business in markets where competition exists.
- **Barriers to entry for the particular product or service.** The lower the cost to establish new businesses in the particular market, the greater is the competitive pressure.
- **Capacity.** Often related to the number of suppliers, higher levels of unused **capacity** within an industry can foster greater competition.
- **Dominant brand.** Effective branding strategies that make one supplier or one product more desirable than others result in less vigorous competition.

COMPETITIVE CONDITION	DEGREE FOSTERING COMPETITIVE BIDDING
Multiple qualified or qualifiable suppliers	High
Contracting is feasible	High
Competitive environment is regulated	Medium
Contract recently negotiated	Medium to low
Product or service is covered by patents	None
Clear specifications or SOW exists	High
Government controlled resource	None
Attractive volume	High
Only one source of supply	None

TABLE 7.1   UNDERSTANDING THE COMPETITIVE ENVIRONMENT

- **Ability to substitute.** Products or services that are easily substituted by those from other industries are more highly competitive.
- **Role of market forces.** When analysts speak of market forces, they generally refer to factors—economic, physical, and political—influencing and affecting buying and selling at a particular time. These factors may exist within a specific industry or a geographical location or over the course of an entire economy. To some extent, the very nature of competition itself is dynamic and in continual flux, so that when you evaluate a given set of conditions—capacity or **barriers to entry**, for example—at any specific time, you do little more than freeze a frame in a never-ending film.

From the point of view of procurement function, supply and demand are two of the most important market force factors, and you need to pay attention to them very closely. Often in flux, supply and demand influences prices in many different ways. While supply and demand will theoretically reach equilibrium over time so that the supply of a given item exactly matches the demand for it, in reality this is rarely the case. More often than not, the ratio of supply and demand continually moves higher and lower, with fluctuating prices reflecting any imbalance. Figure 7.1 shows how prices can increase as a result of reduced supply because buyers tend to bid up prices to meet their requirements. Buyers compete with one another to obtain scarce goods and services. Keep in mind, however, that as prices increase, with all other factors remaining constant, new capacity will usually enter the market to take advantage of the perceived profit, eventually creating additional supply that once again brings prices lower. The ratio of supply to demand always

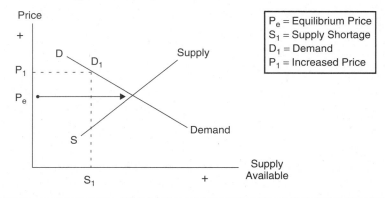

Supply Shortage

Explanation: In this example, the point P_e represents the equilibrium point at which supply and demand are equal—shown by their intersecting lines. When the available supply decreases along the line S to the point S_1, well below the demand line, prices rise to P_1.

P_e = Equilibrium Price
S_1 = Supply Shortage
D_1 = Demand
P_1 = Increased Price

FIGURE 7.1   THE EFFECT OF SUPPLY SHORTAGE ON PRICE

affects prices. When supply is more plentiful than demand, suppliers must lower prices to make buying more attractive; when demand outstrips supply, buyers compete for the few available resources and prices rise.

> Supply shortages can also result from an unexpected increase in demand or some physical situation such as a plant shutdown that severely limits production.

In Figure 7.1, the point P_e represents the equilibrium point at which supply and demand are equal—shown by their intersecting lines. When the available supply decreases along the line S to the point S_1, well below the demand line, prices rise to P_1.

(c) EARLY INVOLVEMENT.   Early involvement by the procurement group is one of the fundamental keys to employing successful negotiation strategies. The later the involvement of the Procurement Department in sourcing decisions, the less leverage will be available for negotiating favorable terms. In other words, the greater the supplier's certainty that it will receive the order, the less likely it will be to engage in serious negotiations.

Early involvement is essential to avoiding being locked into a single source prematurely without sufficient negotiating leverage to influence critical terms of the contract. This is especially true during the new product development cycle and when engaging a new supplier. Figure 7.2 depicts graphically how the influence of the Procurement Department diminishes as the course of the supplier engagement progresses. As you can see, involvement during the initial phases of the engagement allows the Procurement Department to exercise greater influence and incorporate more robust processes than it can when it is engaged later in the development process. Furthermore, the actual impact of that engagement also diminishes with later involvement.

7.2 GATHERING INFORMATION AND ANALYSIS

Information, as they say, is power. Having the right information available when needed is always critical to a successful approach to strategy formulation. It is important to know at least as much (and perhaps more) about the conditions that may influence the negotiation of the supplier. By being informed, your team will be able to develop realistic and workable strategies and avoid the embarrassment of establishing unreachable goals. Having the right facts can also preclude the supplier from springing negotiation surprises as tactics.

Each team member should be responsible for gathering a portion of the information that is needed to adequately prepare for both developing strategies

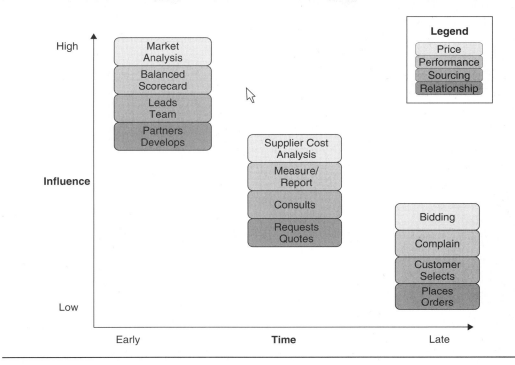

FIGURE 7.2 FACTORS INFLUENCED BY THE PROCUREMENT DEPARTMENT'S EARLY INVOLVEMENT

and actually participating in the tactical negotiations. Price analysis and market conditions, noted previously, are just a few aspects of your analysis, but there are many more outlined next.

(a) ANALYZING THE SUPPLIER'S SITUATION. In gathering information, you might first want to consider looking at the situation from the supplier's point of view: What motivates their position and what are they likely to value the most? Conversely, what concessions might they be willing to make to achieve their goals?

(i) Financial Needs. It is relatively easy to assess a U.S. corporation's financial condition if it is **publicly held** (with stock trading on an open stock exchange) since the Securities and Exchange Commission (SEC) regulations require public disclosure of important financial data. From publicly accessible reports such as those filed with the SEC and from the reports of market analysts tracking its stock performance, it will be possible to gain some relative understanding of the supplier's financial picture and insight into its level of motivation to obtain your business. Obviously, the greater the financial need, the greater is the supplier's incentive to offer concessions.

With a privately held organization, gathering this information may be difficult. You will often need to obtain information available through an industry organization or professional association or through other sources familiar with the supplier's operations. The supplier's competitors will often have comparative data to share with you based on marketing surveys they have conducted, but you will naturally want to take into account the source and the simple fact that suppliers are not in the habit of passing along good news about their competition.

(ii) Existing Relations.   There are many reasons a supplier wants to maintain its favored position with you. Replacing a valuable customer can be costly, and the supplier has already "sunk" the costs of acquiring your business. Prior to negotiations, your team should completely analyze the motivational factors that will likely drive concessions to you. Some of the questions you might want to ask in this regard include:

- How much does a supplier value the status of its existing relationship with your organization? Are you a reference account?
- How does your business impact the supplier's bottom line?
- How does your volume affect its position in the marketplace?
- Does your organization require more or less customer service than others?
- Are your business needs relatively easy to forecast?
- Are your volumes consistent over time?
- Do you pay your invoices in an acceptable time frame?
- Are your organizations engaged in joint product development?

(b) ANALYZING YOUR ORGANIZATION'S POSITION.   You will likely know a great deal more about your organization and its specific needs than you will about your supplier's, so the exercise of gathering and analyzing your own position will encourage your team to more clearly identify areas where concessions may be required. This exercise should flag those concerns for further research into the supplier's situation so that you enter the negotiation with at least some understanding of its likely position. This is really the first step in planning the negotiation process and developing a strategy. You will want to cover some of the same areas we discussed in the preceding section on the supplier's needs and will certainly want to review some of the following requirements:

(i) Urgency.   When does your organization need the product or service you will be negotiating? If it is needed urgently, you may want to prepare to negotiate accelerated delivery by trading concessions in other areas such as price or transportation methods. On the other hand, if the requirement can be met over a period of time, allowing the supplier to fulfill it when time and resources are not being otherwise used, this might prove a useful concession to achieve better prices.

(ii) Priority of Needs.   When you initially evaluated a key supplier, you may have measured its performance on a weighted-average matrix to help in the

Category	Percentage
Cost	40%
Quality	25%
Technology	20%
Service	15%

Table 7.2 Supplier Evaluation Weighting

selection process. If you recall from the previous chapter, we actually developed a hierarchy of importance by assigning values to each of the categories: cost, quality, technology, and service.

In establishing the priority of needs for a particular negotiation, you will want to review your selection matrix to help determine the approximate priority of the organization's needs. Table 7.2 shows an evaluation matrix similar to the one we developed in Chapter 3. If we assigned the following values to our selection process, then we would likely want to assign a similar set of values to our negotiation priorities.

In terms of concessions, then, we would likely trade elements of service (the lowest value on the list) for pricing concessions (the highest value on the list).

(iii) Internal Constraints.   Unknown conditions within your organization may preclude your team from fully leveraging its negotiating position, and they need to be identified prior to establishing a strategy. For example, it may be impossible to precisely define a scope of work for a construction project renovating an existing building. Contractors rarely know what they will find when opening a wall or ceiling. As a result, you will likely be unable to develop a firm fixed price for the project. Other contracts may be similar where quality, delivery, and liability are dependent on a set of conditions that are not known at the time of negotiation.

In addition to unknowns, there may be internal management pressures to achieve certain goals beyond the value that they may be conceivably add. Using a proprietary architectural design to beautify the lobby of the headquarters building may hamper your ability to negotiate with the contractors; nevertheless, it would be unrealistic for a buyer to consider altering an architect's design.

You may also want to consider situations where trade-offs will require an additional investment by your organization. For example, if shortened lead times are critically necessary and the supplier has no flexibility in its manufacturing processes, you may need to develop longer-range forecasts. This may require the addition of a staff planner or a more sophisticated software system. With this knowledge, you will be able to properly evaluate the costs of items that will not be effectively negotiated.

7.3 PREPARING FOR THE NEGOTIATION

Once you have reviewed the general negotiating climate and have a relatively clear understanding of the forces operating behind the scenes, so to speak, you need to prepare for conducting the negotiation itself. This involves a great deal of planning that builds your confidence through a keen understanding of the circumstances you will likely encounter during the actual negotiation. It is also a continual process of fact finding and analysis that leads and guides your strategy.

In preparation, you will likely want to select and orient your cross-functional team to ensure that you are all working together as a team toward the common objectives. With your team in place, the primary focus of your planning will be to carefully review the supplier's proposal from the perspective of your organization's needs. To what extent are your needs being addressed, and where are there critical gaps that fall short of your objectives? The more you know about the contents of the proposal, the less likely you will be caught off guard by any omissions or issues that have not been clearly thought out. Planning for negotiations, in a way, also involves understanding the needs and objectives of your supplier, anticipating its most likely position on any key issue in relation to yours. If you and your supplier can avoid creating surprises with unexpected issues both during and after the contract negotiations, the chances are that the actual performance will run smoothly.

This section will guide you through the processes normally conducted in preparation for negotiations. We will cover some of the ways you might select and assess the team and how you will formulate objectives and develop strategies.

(a) SELECTING AND LEADING THE NEGOTIATING TEAM. In any significant negotiation, you will first want to form a support team composed of technical domain experts, the financial group, and members of the user groups—likely the same people who participated in the preparation of the RFP and the supplier selection. This team should always be led by the senior representative for Procurement who is participating in its activities to ensure that business objectives are met and that the negotiations are conducted in an atmosphere conducive to continued collaboration. The Procurement representative will also be responsible to ensure the negotiations are carried out with integrity and in an ethical manner.

(i) Selection Criteria. It is naturally important that key members of the user group—the stakeholders, as they are sometimes called—actively participate in the negotiation process for a number of reasons. First, there are technical issues that will arise during the course of discussions that only they will be qualified to answer. Second, as the users, they are in the best position to understand the importance of the various elements of the offer and so can determine when specifications can be relaxed, as well as the value of certain trade-offs. Third, as **subject matter experts (SMEs)**, the users are in the best position to evaluate what service levels should be established and the metrics used to evaluate performance. And lastly, the users are the successors of the negotiated bargain—the group that must live with the resulting conditions—and they will inherit not only the wins, but the losses as well.

In addition to members of the user group, you should ensure that you have representation from the various business units such as Finance, Operations, or Facilities. These are the support staff who can provide additional skills—based on their functional roles—to the team when needed. You should select team members according to their behavioral skills as well. Behavioral skills include such qualities as decisiveness, intelligence, business savvy, problem-solving abilities, drive to achieve, patience, and the ability to communicate. It will be up to you to determine what behavioral skills will be needed and who within the broad stakeholder community best demonstrates them.

(ii) Assessing the Team's Strength and Weaknesses.   It is a good idea for the members of the team to jointly assess its collective strengths and weaknesses in advance. By doing so, team members will develop a more realistic understanding of the constraints they are operating under and what technical skills are available to effectively maneuver to a favorable concession as a result. Externally imposed deadlines can often generate situations that create bad decisions, or the lack of authority to make a decision can lead to a stalemate.

(iii) Communicating with Team Members.   One of the most important roles the team leader has is that of the communicator and project manager. The team leader is responsible for seeing that participants know what factual information is needed and who should be gathering it. Information should have a clear distribution channel so that everyone can be updated on relevant information as it becomes available. Exercise caution, however, to ensure that there is not so much information generated that it inundates the team and creates data overload.

The team leader also needs to define the individual roles that may be necessary during the course of the negotiation and to help assess which members are best suited to each specific task. This is likely to include deciding who will become the team's spokesperson and how decisions to accept or reject offers will be made. Signals need to be developed that can indicate to other members when offers are acceptable and when they are not, similar to the way they might be used in a sporting event when the coach wants to send a specific play to team members. The team also needs to know who will make the final decisions and the authority level of each of the negotiators.

TEAM NEGOTIATION ADVICE FROM PETER B. STARK AND JANE S. FLAHERTY

Peter B. Stark and Jane S. Flaherty, authors of *The Only Negotiating Guide You'll Ever Need*, explain that there are times when negotiating as a team is a wise decision:

- Having more than one team member can provide access to more expertise. Of course, this is only an advantage if each team member truly has something essential to add to the negotiation process.
- Generally, when more people are thinking about alternative ways to generate win-win outcomes, success is more likely.
- There is strength in numbers. Presenting a case as a unified group packs considerable power.
- The focus is less likely to be on one individual's personality.
- If you decide to negotiate as a team, the following guidelines will prove helpful:
- Determine what types of expertise are needed to support your side of the negotiations.

  Find people who have the needed expertise; are good, confident communicators; and work well as a team.

  Hold planning meetings prior to the negotiation to agree on team goals, strategies, and tactics.

  Ensure team members will be available to provide their expertise throughout the negotiation.

  Select a lead negotiator or team captain.

  Select a scribe to keep accurate notes during both the planning meeting and the negotiation.

  Assign roles and responsibilities for each team member.

  Practice! Pull together another team of people to represent the counterpart and then rehearse your negotiation. A dry run can be extremely helpful in raising the confidence level of all team members.

Reprinted with permission from *The Only Negotiating Guide You'll Ever Need* by Peter B. Stark and Jane S. Flaherty. For more information, visit: www.everyonenegotiates.com.

(b) FORMULATING OBJECTIVES AND DEVELOPING STRATEGIES.   Once the team has been selected and is operationally in place, your next step is to lead the development of a plan for the actual negotiation. It is always best to put this plan in writing so that you and your team members can use it as a guide in future negotiations.

As a first step in developing the plan, team members should list their objectives and the anticipated objectives of the supplier. Objectives can be based on the identified gap between initial expectations in the sourcing process and those actually achieved. Under each objective, indicate the likely impact of not achieving the objective. Then rank the objectives on this list by priority, focusing on developing a strategy for those that are most critical. The strategy will outline what initial offer you can expect from the supplier and what you are willing to counteroffer. (You might call these "take-aways" and "give-aways.") You will also need to determine a position at which you would be willing to accept the offer and one where you would be willing to walk away altogether for each of the key objectives. Your assessment of the situation, such as current market conditions, will play a critical role in this process, for without it you will likely not be able to understand the supplier's needs and motivation.

TIPS AND TECHNIQUES

Gap analysis can be viewed as the process of assessing (measuring) the difference between the current condition and the desired outcome.

It is sometimes helpful to go one step further and have your team run through a mock negotiation exercise where you set the stage by reviewing general market trends and ask some of the team members to assume the supplier's role. What objectives are they likely to have? What concessions are they likely to make? At what point in each of the elements do you feel the supplier will concede, and at what point are you willing to simply walk away?

As you answer these questions for your own position and then compare them to the answers you come up with for the supplier's anticipated position, you will gain a preview of how the actual negotiations may develop and how you can best respond to specific offers or demands. This is much like scripting a football playbook where time, field position, score, and other key elements in the game are assessed using a **decision tree** to determine what play should be logically called next. Indeed, you should consider having this script put into written form so that each member of your team has the opportunity to review it periodically during the course of the negotiations.

(i) Objectives.   When your supplier selection team established its initial requirements and began the process of determining the most qualified supplier, it also developed a set of expectations. These expectations were based on your organization's needs. Whatever needs are not fully satisfied in the supplier's response, even when that response is the best one received, will need to be further negotiated. You will likely have performed a gap analysis prior to constructing your negotiating plan, so you can compare what you have to what you actually wanted. This can form the basis for determining what you will want to negotiate and your negotiating objectives.

In this section, we'll discuss the few elements you might want to consider including in your checklist such as price, quality, service levels, capacity or volume, the length of the contract, and managing specifications. Shown in Figure 7.3 is an

Negotiation Template Planning Sheet					
Your Major Issues (Ranked in Order of Importance)	Your Goal	Likely Initial Supplier Position	Your Fallback Position #1	Your Fallback Position #2	Your "walk-away" Position
Delivery	June 30th	August 1st	July 1st	July 10th	July 15th
Payment Terms	2% 10 Net 45	Net 30	2% 10 Net 30	1% 10 Net 30	Net 30
Warranty Period (Months)	12	6	10	9	6
Supplier Spare Parts Response Time (Hours)	8	36	12	15	24

FIGURE 7.3   NEGOTIATIONS PLANNING TEMPLATE

example of a planning template that outlines your organization's objectives and compares it with the likely objectives of the supplier's organization.

PRICE

Despite the fact that you understand the nature of value and the concept of total cost of ownership, the focal point of any negotiation is usually price. The seller wishes to reasonably maximize profit, and the buyer wishes to obtain the best possible price. In most cases, the ideal position for both is a fair and reasonable price. For the most part, the best way to determine a fair and reasonable price is through the current pricing in an open market, such as a commodities exchange. On an exchange, commodity prices fluctuate openly in response to supply and demand, so the trading price at any given time reflects the current price a buyer is willing to pay and the current price at which a seller is willing to sell.

In the absence of a public exchange, however, the buyer can turn to the competitive bidding process. When properly executed, the competitive bidding process can approximate an open market exchange. But even when the competitive bidding process is used, there may be some further need to negotiate price. For example, while a specific contract may have an agreed-upon fixed price, the buyer will also want to fix the rates for changes and perhaps prenegotiate the conditions under which the contract may be extended for an additional period of time. This may or may not have been addressed in the initial proposal or competitive bid.

TIPS AND TECHNIQUES

PRICE ANALYSIS

It is important for the lead negotiator to understand when quoted pricing represents an acceptable offer. The reasonableness of a particular price can be established through an analysis of a number of factors such as market conditions, volume of the purchase, overall volume given the supplier, nature of the specifications, and risk. It can also be determined through benchmarking and whatever other comparative analysis is available to the buyer. Always keep in mind, however, that price is not necessarily directly related to the supplier's cost. In fact, the process of price analysis typically evaluates price without regard to its components of cost and, in most commercial environments, without consideration of the supplier's net profit or operating margin.

When evaluating and negotiating price, you also need to consider some of the auxiliary elements that immediately and directly affect price, such as shipping costs and disposal costs, and the terms of payment. Insofar as these can be directly associated with a clearly measurable price factor, they can be evaluated as part of the price package. Conceding a point or two on the price list in exchange for more favorable payment terms (e.g., Net 30 extended to Net 45) can be calculated as a cash value.

QUALITY

As negotiations progress, you will likely find that increased quality specifications result in higher prices and that relaxing some of the noncritical specifications may result in lower prices. To the extent possible, the technical group on your team should review the specifications as part of the planning process. Knowing where specifications and tolerances can be relaxed and where they cannot needs to be determined largely in advance and should be included in the negotiation plan.

SERVICE LEVELS

In many cases, service levels are included in the statement of work in the form of a service-level agreement (SLA). As with quality specifications, service levels, too, can be relaxed and traded off as a concession to receiving some other benefits in exchange. Required lead time that can be extended through some improved planning on your end and early placement of orders may prove beneficial to the supplier and could result in a greater commitment to on-time delivery. Or you may be willing to make some pricing concessions in order to obtain just-in-time (JIT) delivery or the benefit of establishing a supplier-managed inventory (SMI) program.

Service levels can also be evaluated in terms of engineering support provided by the supplier and the impact of this support on your operations. If one of your organization's key objectives calls for being the first to market, engineering support from the supplier can be a crucial factor in getting you there.

CAPACITY/VOLUME

Whenever the potential for limitations in a supplier's production or service levels exist as a result of forecasted changes in market conditions, you will need to address it contractually. During periods of constrained capacity and shortages when supplier's cannot keep up with demand, you will want to ensure that your organization has the protection it needs by locking in specific commitments from the supplier for certain amounts of its capacity or specific volumes based on your anticipated needs. This, of course, is always a trade-off, since in exchange for guaranteed capacity, the supplier usually wants a guaranteed volume of business.

LENGTH OF CONTRACT

Another point of negotiation occurs when there may be considerable risk involved in the fluctuation of prices, and you (or the supplier) wish to lock in pricing for a given period of time. If your team sees prices rising, you will want a longer term for the contract at the current pricing; the supplier, seeing the same trend, will want to shorten the contract period, hoping that increased prices will result in additional revenue. The opposite is true, of course, when prices appear to be falling.

There are many other reasons for negotiations to occur around the length of the contract. The supplier naturally wants to be assured of your organization's business—all other things being equal—for as long as possible. You may want a longer contract period to avoid the additional cost of switching from one supplier to another.

MANAGING SPECIFICATIONS

The technical users on the team are generally responsible for determining the specifications. Often, you will find that the tighter the specifications are (in terms of typical industrial capabilities), the more you will have to pay. Tighter specifications may also mean additional inspection time (and cost) that interferes with the smooth operation of the supplier's production. It is always advisable, in situations where specifications are critical, to maintain a **want position**, a **need position**, and a **can accept position** so that you are flexible enough to earn concessions for more critical factors.

(ii) Establishing Priorities.   As previously described, organizing the priority of your team's objectives can be one of the most important aspects in any negotiation planning process. Based on team discussions and consensus, it is possible to organize each of the stated objectives into a priority list or, at the least, indicate if they are high, medium, or low. During the actual course of negotiations, you will want to be certain to maintain these priorities to avoid wasting time by negotiating for relatively unimportant objectives.

Establishing priorities also relates to determining the amount of time devoted to the actual negotiations. Setting deadlines and the number of sessions reminds everyone that there is an objective to be reached. With this in mind, little time should be devoted to minor issues until the major ones are resolved. However, the order in which you negotiate specific items, critical or minor, can be varied to meet the team's overall strategy.

(iii) Preparing Psychologically.   Psychological preparation generally means preparing well enough to develop a high level of confidence in the validity of your position. As mentioned earlier in this chapter, confidence develops from having a firm grasp of the conditions in the marketplace and understanding the position of both parties relative to their competitors. Gathering facts and analyzing the supplier's position, as well as your own, leads to a clear understanding of what concessions are required and what concessions are going to be impossible to obtain. Attempting to achieve that which is impossible can only lead to disappointment and confrontation. Conversely, lowering expectations below what is truly possible

can lead to demoralization and a sense of loss following the negotiations. The best practices today have buyer and supplier teams working collaboratively so that both achieve the fullest benefit of the bargain.

*(iv) **Planning Your Agenda.*** As part of your psychological preparation, you will want to have your agenda set up in advance. This provides your team with a sense of direction and sets your own pace for the negotiation. The timing of the negotiation is always a critical factor in establishing a strong base for leverage. Timing means not only when the negotiations start and end, but when individual items will be open for discussion. This gives you the opportunity to achieve key objectives first before relinquishing key concessions. Negotiations often move much like card games, where one player can use cards discarded by the other.

*(v) **Conducting Practice Sessions.*** Finally, it can be quite useful to have your team practice for the actual negotiations by holding some realistic practice sessions. During these sessions, team members can take turns in the anticipated role of the supplier and gain some insight into the situations that are likely to occur during actual negotiations. You can make the process even more realistic by bringing in participants from other groups and creating a somewhat competitive environment by offering relatively substantial prizes.

7.4 CONDUCTING THE NEGOTIATION

When it is time to actually conduct the negotiation, you will employ a myriad of techniques and tactics. For example, one of the best practices in preparing for and actually conducting negotiations is to continually ask questions whose answers provide a better understanding of the situation and the needs of both parties. Asking questions also helps control the pace and direction of the negotiations, which can be especially useful when you need to bring the discussion back to its key points.

To a large degree, your tactics will depend on the overall strategy you and your team developed during the planning phase. Implementing your strategy essentially amounts to how you approach the negotiations—cooperatively in a **win-win mode** or win-lose in an adversarial mode. Win-win modes tend to encourage collaboration in the negotiation process. Win-lose strategies tend to rely on power to control the negotiation process.

The following section reviews many of the more traditional tactical aspects of conducting negotiations that you will probably use. Although it is unlikely that they will all fit your personal style of negotiating, keep them in mind and include them as part of your playbook. You never know when you might need a special effect.

(a) CREATING THE CLIMATE. Establishing the climate is one of your first concerns just prior to and during the negotiation process. Climate refers to the physical aspects of where the negotiations are taking place, as well as the general mood of those conducting the negotiations. It encompasses both the physical atmosphere and the nature of the personal interaction.

> Supplier representatives often understand this all too well and have been taught to do as much as possible to keep the lead negotiator or decision maker in a good mood. However, it is generally no longer considered acceptable to conduct serious business negotiations over an expensive lunch or dinner with wine.

(i) Location.   There is a maxim in sporting events that the home team has the field advantage. Most of the spectators are fans of the home team, and the team likely plays the majority of its games on that particular field. It's hard to say how true this is, but there are some related aspects to consider when choosing the actual location where you will conduct negotiations. Typically, negotiations are held at the buyer's office, although there is no hard-and-fast rule about that. If negotiations are conducted at your site, you may be subject to more interruptions by routine business matters than you would be at some other place, but you will have the comfort of familiar ground, as well as the convenience of having support staff and records nearby.

In times past, it was thought that there was a critical psychological advantage to holding negotiations in a familiar environment, and you may have heard that the seating arrangements around the conference table can provide an advantage. There may be some truth to this when high-stakes international political outcomes are involved, but such details rarely influence the kind of business negotiations you will be routinely conducting. This is not to imply that some element of cat-and-mouse intrigue will not be present during your negotiations, since there is often a strong desire on the part of participants to "ink the deal" with favorable terms. It is more important, however, that regardless of where you are, you consider any potential negative impact the environment may have and take whatever steps necessary to counter it.

As part of an awareness of your surroundings, you must also be aware of the **body language** and the physical actions of those in the negotiations. Learning to read these signs can be useful in determining the mood and status of your supplier's team.

> It is universally accepted that the crossed-arm posture (usually sitting with arms folded across the chest, but sometimes seen with the hands held behind the head) represents an unwillingness to listen or to accept what is being said. See what you can do to get your suppliers to open up their posture and demonstrate they are becoming more receptive to your proposals.

(ii) Developing a Collaborative Atmosphere.   A collaborative atmosphere, it is felt by many, is the most conducive to negotiating in environments where long-term relationships are important. While the popularity of win-win negotiations rises and falls with time, there can be little doubt that positional or adversarial contact rarely produces the best results. If your team takes a competitive stance, it is likely the supplier's team will do the same. You should have already developed your priority list of objectives prior to your first session, so you might want to consider that the supplier has done the same. If your discussions are congenial and nonconfrontational and you listen well, you will come away with an understanding very early in the negotiations of what exchanges of value can take place.

That is not to say there is any reason to pretend you and the supplier are best friends. However, you will benefit from good relations if you consider that the supplier's representative is as anxious as you are to do a good job.

You should also keep in mind that sales personnel have generally been given a great deal of training in the tactics of negotiations. Any "tricks" you have learned are likely to be known by one or another member of your supplier's team. Remember the objective of any negotiation is to reach an agreement, so there is little value in playing games. If your position is firm, let that be known. If you are not clear about the implications of a concession, ask questions and hold a caucus with your team.

An important part of developing a collaborative negotiation is to avoid imposing artificial deadlines. If there are absolute time constraints, you should indicate so at the beginning of your negotiation and stick to them. By the same token, you should not let deadlines be imposed upon you either. To maintain your future credibility, it is critical that you honor your commitments. Do not make decisions before you feel completely ready, regardless of the circumstances.

(iii) Allowing for Cultural Differences.   When conducting negotiations with personnel from nations other than your own, the most important rule to remember is that **cultural differences** will invariably have an impact. Even when the parties are speaking the same language, the native speaker may have a different conception of the terminology than the person speaking a second language. Similarly, body language and expressions take on different meanings in different cultures. The only certain way for you to understand this is to do your homework diligently and become familiar with as many of the nuances of the supplier's culture as you can. Sometimes, it helps defuse this potential problem if you take the initial step (sensitively, of course) of informally discussing these differences together.

Some professional tips include:

- Negotiation is always a delicate activity, requiring determination and diplomacy.
- Recognize the cultural principles that negotiators from other countries may be operating under. In the United States, decisions are frequently unilateral,

while in Japan, for example, decisions require consensus. Negotiators in the United States value flexibility, whereas their counterparts in Japan find changing a decision to be a sign of weakness.

- Understand the role of relationships in other cultures—some driven by family ties and long-standing friendships—that render negotiations as much a ritual as a pragmatic approach to making a deal.
- Keep a historical perspective. How have the parties, and the countries, dealt with one another in the past? Previous animosities may require special attention.
- Be informed and up to date on the legal differences between countries. Often, what is acceptable practice in one country can result in criminal charges in another. Understand the legal obligations in the particular country you are engaged with and how they are adjudicated. Contracts are dissolved under different conditions and with different limitations in various countries, and dispute resolution processes vary widely.

NOTE

Travelers' guides, such as those published by Fodor and Lonely Planet, are excellent tools for helping you to understand the business and cultural customs in various countries (www.fodors.com, www.lonelyplanet.com).

(b) ADOPTING A NEGOTIATING STYLE.   While there is an endless array of negotiating styles, and small libraries can be filled with the texts describing them, there are two basic types of negotiators: collaborative negotiators, who seek to develop outcomes that enhance the sense of accomplishment of both parties (win-win), and power (or positional) negotiators, who seek to prevail in achieving their objectives regardless of the impact on the other party. Even after you spend many years in Procurement, it is unlikely you will consistently use one or the other.

(i) Tactics.   The **tactics** you will likely use for negotiations are closely related to the specific style you adopt, and there appear to be endless compendiums of them strung along like so many pejorative proverbs. Here are a few of the more common tactics:

- Generally, more can be gained by listening than by talking. Accordingly, take copious notes and review them frequently.
- Question how your statements will align with your objectives—pronouncements can be pointless or even counterproductive.
- Avoid accepting the first offer.
- Always ask questions, especially when there is useful information to be learned.

- Do not make concessions without receiving equal consideration. This does not necessarily mean that every concession need result in some consideration … but do keep track.
- Attend to deadlines; establish them sparingly and only when necessary.
- Keep your wits about you and avoid reacting emotionally.
- Issues need to be prioritized. When reaching an impasse on one, park it for a while and go on to the next.
- Take breaks whenever you feel the need. Do not attempt to fight fatigue.
- Refrain from bluffing, and use only data you can prove. Imagine the embarrassment and loss of face that could result in being discovered.
- Last and final offers should mean exactly what they say.
- Understand and use body language as a communication tool for your advantage.

(ii) Sole-Source Tactics.   Negotiating with a sole source can provide a measure of challenge. As long as your organization is able to maintain its objectives from a marketing perspective, you will likely find little to negotiate. Typically, sharing the risk in new product development or distributing the burden of inventory will produce some benefit to both parties. However, if profitability becomes significantly impacted through changing market costs or products reaching their end of life, your organization may want to initiate steps to avoid financial loss prior to discontinuation. In this case, you and the supplier will need to work closely together to monitor the profitability for both sides and make recommendations regarding the timing of any changes in terms and conditions.

(c) DOCUMENTING THE NEGOTIATION.   It is important to properly document negotiation activities so that personnel unfamiliar with the specifics of the project will be able to clearly understand what occurred should the need arise. Documentation should be approached from two points: first, documenting the negotiation plan and its objectives and comparing the objectives to actual outcomes as a way of determining the team's effectiveness and, second, providing an executive summary of the actual negotiation so that auditors will be able to assess its impact, and approving authorities will be able to understand what you are requesting.

The negotiation plan should contain information that describes, at a minimum, the team's objectives, its strategy, and the strengths and weaknesses of its position, along with a similar assessment of the supplier's position. Often, it is useful to include an opening position and bottom line (least acceptable) position for each of the key objectives. Your team should also prepare likely scenarios for the supplier's position. When the negotiation has concluded, you should review the original planning document and describe where the objectives were met and where they fell short.

The executive summary should describe the objectives of the contract and the negotiation, what was achieved in relation to initial goals, the cost and benefits to the organization, and any alternative courses of action that may be possible. Any future follow-up action should also be included in this summary.

7.5 SUMMARY

Conducting successful negotiations requires careful planning and organization. As a first step in your planning process, you should prepare an assessment of current market conditions for the industry and organizations with whom you will be engaged. Assessing the negotiating environment includes developing an evaluation of the competitiveness of the particular industry and what impact you and your supplier have in that market. Be sure to consider aspects such as overall industry capacity, pricing trends, availability of substitute products, and other factors that will help establish an understanding of the competitive forces potentially influencing the outcome of your negotiations.

You will also want to look closely at the supplier's situation to assess elements of its current condition that might affect its motivation. What are its financial needs, and how does your organization fit in with them? Similarly, you will want to have a full understanding of the factors influencing your organization. Establish the urgency of the requirements and a prioritized set of needs and understand any significant internal constraints. Early involvement in the contracting process will assist your efforts to effect a favorable outcome.

If the outcome of the negotiation will significantly impact your organization, you will likely want to form a support team composed of key internal users, a finance representative, and someone from the quality assurance group. With the help of the team, you can then formulate your guiding objectives and strategies using many of the same criteria you used during the supplier selection process.

When it comes time for the actual negotiation, your team should have completed a detailed plan prioritizing needs, outlined roles and responsibilities, selected a location, and discussed the various likely scenarios that might occur and how you will deal with them. You should also consider what negotiating style might produce the best results and what tactics you can use to enhance it.

All of the planning and strategy development should be documented so that others will be able to understand what occurred. Using an executive summary to describe objectives and outcomes will help you gain internal approval and describe any follow-up actions that will be required.

KEY TERMS

Negotiations	Dominant brand
Qualified suppliers	Capacity
Unqualified suppliers	Ability to substitute
Barriers to entry	Equilibrium price
Competition	Publicly held (corporations)

Selection criteria

Subject matter experts (SME's)

Decision tree

Negotiations planning template

"Can accept" position

"Want" position

"Need" position

Win-win mode

Body language

Cultural differences

Tactics

Sole-source tactics

LEVERAGING COMPUTER SYSTEMS

LEARNING OBJECTIVES

1. Describe the differences between *a personal computer, a minicomputer, a mainframe and a workstation*.
2. Describe a computer network and name four types of computer networks discussed in the chapter.
3. List four opportunities for the Procurement Department to utilize *e-procurement processes*.
4. Define the "make-or-buy decision" and list the questions a Procurement Manager should ask to make the decision to fulfill software requirements.

The supply management landscape has changed rapidly over the past several years, largely as a result of computerization and Internet utilization. Procurement departments are becoming increasingly inclined to move routine transactional processes, such as placing purchase orders (POs), to computer-based platforms to gain efficiency and better utilization of employee time management. This **reengineering** process has paralleled, for the most part, the widespread acceptance of automated systems across the entire spectrum of our organizations and the increasing use of the Internet for business.

Today, organizations are increasingly turning to computerized tools to integrate all of the elements in the **procure-to-pay** process. By doing so, they are realizing the financial benefits of increased productivity and reduced cycle times generated through the automation of routine processes such as requisition and purchase order generation, quotation, bidding, order tracking, expediting, supplier payment, and procedural compliance. Today, tools are widely available to assist procurement departments to time their buying decisions based on market trends in pricing and availability. Indeed, the current trend to **Web-based sourcing** using tools that automate and speed up many of the more tedious procurement processes such as requests for information (RFIs) and requests for proposals (RFPs) has enabled organizations to improve their supplier selection and reduce prices through standardization methods that would otherwise be cost prohibitive. Using these tools, organizations have even been able to manage their buying power in some of the smaller spending areas, such as maintenance, repair, and operations (MRO), which would have been impossible just several years ago.

Buyers and sellers have shared equally in these benefits through the transparency of supply capacity and product demand, producing greater collaboration and alignment between their organizations. Partners are now able to share supply and demand data in real time, and the result has been savings for both. This has been especially apparent in the recent trend to supplier-managed inventory programs (or **consigned inventory**), where inventory is stored at the buyer's site and paid for only as used. Widespread adoption of methods such as this has freed up enormous resources across the **supply chain**. Just as buyers have benefited from the ability to find more sources more easily, suppliers have benefited from the ability to reach larger markets without additional cost.

In this chapter, we review the most commonly used computer-based technology applications and their function in the organization. We also cover the computerized system tools being used in supply management and how they link to the organization's broader **information technology** structure.

8.1 USING BASIC INFORMATION TECHNOLOGY PROCESSES

Before delving into the specifics of procurement applications, and by way of an introduction to the subject matter, it would be worthwhile to go over some of the fundamentals of computerized systems by looking at the basic terminology, along with the types of **platforms** in use and the nature of the **software applications** developed for them.

(a) COMPUTER BASICS.   As computer systems evolve, the language describing their individual elements naturally changes, too. However, you will need to be familiar with some of the basic terminology to effectively manage your internal systems, regardless of their brand or configuration. Here are some of those terms most commonly used:

(i) Data Processing Terms.   Basic data processing terms describe the fundamental principles used in information technology:

- **Bits/bytes** are the basic building blocks of computer technology. A bit is one binary digit—the smallest unit of computer programming—taking the form of a one or a zero. A byte is a grouping of eight bits that make up a single character.
- **Data** represents the basic information assembled from bits and bytes that is put into a computer.
- A **record** consists of an individual set of data, such as a name or an address.
- A **file** contains a set of related records that are usually stored in one place.
- A **digital system** is a system in which information is conveyed as data in a series of bits and bytes.

(ii) Hardware Terms.   Computer hardware refers to the elements of a computer system that you can actually touch. The major terms used to describe computer hardware include:

- The **central processing unit (CPU)** is really the brains of the computer and is responsible for performing most of the computational work.
- **Storage media** consists of a variety of products such as hard disk drives, memory chips, magnetic tape, CD-ROMs, and DVDs on which data is stored either optically or magnetically.
- **Input devices** are the hardware tools used to enter data into the system. They include keyboards, scanners, readers, memory devices, and disks.
- **Output devices** are the hardware components used to store or display information such as printers, monitors, and the devices listed above as storage media.
- **Communication devices** are used to transmit data between computers and across networks. They include modems, broadband routers, switches, and wireless receivers.

(iii) Computer Types.   There is a traditional set of computer types that we commonly refer to when we describe the kind of devices we commonly use. Today,

however, virtually all appliances and automobiles use embedded computers to one extent or another, so the list that follows is incomplete to the extent that it does not attempt to describe all computational devices.

- The **personal computer (PC)**, desktop or laptop, is the most visible computer in use today and makes up the majority of devices we employ.
- The **minicomputer** is one step above the PC and is designed for limited multiuser applications, such as those that might be found in smaller organizations.
- The **mainframe** is used to run major applications that require a great deal of computational power and storage capacity. They are also used to run large networks that communicate with thousands of terminals, sometimes located around the world.
- **Workstations** are devices that generally consist of dumb terminals used to access data on a mini or mainframe computer in a client/server environment. However, in today's networking systems, quite frequently PCs are used as both stand-alone systems and as workstations.
- The **personal digital assistant (PDA)** is a relatively small, portable device with only limited processing capability that connects to a computer to obtain information from calendars, address books, and lists of project items. PDAs are often combined with cell phones to provide maximum utility.

(iv) Network Terms.   Computer networks consist of a series of computers linked together to exchange information. Some of the more common terms that reference computer networks include:

- **Local area network (LAN)** is a geographically restricted network, most commonly contained in one building.
- **Wide area network (WAN)** is a network that covers a large geographical area.
- The **Internet** is the largest computer network in the world, connecting millions of computers.
- **TCP/IP** is a networking standard. Transmission control protocol refers to that segment of the standard that is used to move data between applications; Internet protocol refers to the standard governing the movement of data between host computers.
- **Virtual private network (VPN)** is a data network that uses telecommunication lines and the Internet to exchange information but is secured by a **tunneling protocol** and secure firewalls.
- **Network operating system (NOS)** is the software used to operate the network.
- **File transfer protocol (FTP)** is a standard used in moving information across a network or the Internet.

- A **firewall** is a specialized software application that prevents unauthorized access to the network at the point where it connects to public systems.

(b) PLATFORMS. The term "platform" refers to the various underlying elements of a computer system: the software being used (such as the **operating system**), the hardware being used to run the software, and the method of storing and distributing data. This section addresses the latter usage and describes the fundamental configurations used in automated procurement systems.

(i) Centralized Systems. A **centralized computer system** is a single computer—often called a **mainframe**—operating from one location but usually serving many users. These are most commonly used in a **client/server** configuration, where a **workstation** (or "dumb" terminal) without any processing capability is linked to a mainframe that does all the computational work. This model, in its simplest form, is shown in Figure 8.1. The major advantage of the centralized computer system is that it can be maintained and operated by fewer personnel since it is located in one place.

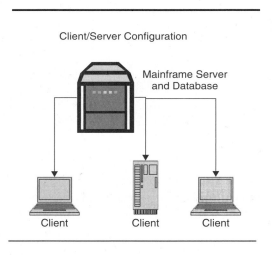

Client/Server Configuration

Mainframe Server
and Database

Client   Client   Client

FIGURE 8.1   CLIENT/SERVER SYSTEM

(ii) Distributed Systems. **Distributed systems** are a collection of computer systems (both hardware and software) dispersed across several sites but operating as one cohesive unit. Their interaction is generally transparent to the users.

Networks are a form of distributed system that consists of a group of computers linked together electronically so that their users can share information. The most common types of networks are the LANs, where computers are geographically close to one another (typically, at the same location) and WANs, where they are further apart and generally linked by some form of telecommunications media. This model is shown in Figure 8.2.

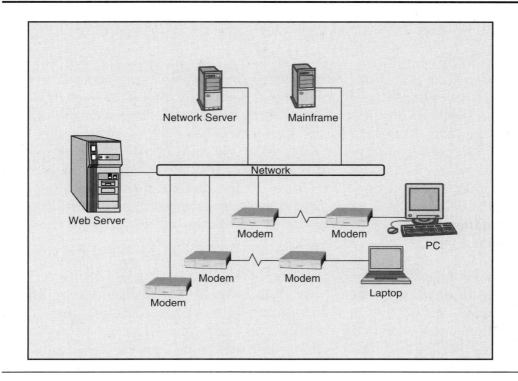

FIGURE 8.2   NETWORK SYSTEM

The major advantage of the distributed system is that it is modular and can be built or reconfigured fairly easily over large distances.

(c) SOFTWARE APPLICATIONS.   Software is a program or set of instructions that make the computer run or perform specific functions. As you know, software can be purchased as **off-the-shelf** items (sometimes referred to as "boxed") or as **customized** applications. Typically, the more common software applications such as word processing or spreadsheet software will be purchased in its packaged form through distributors or directly from the manufacturer. However, buyers always have the option of downloading the software directly from the producer's Web site or buying it already installed on their computers. In some states, boxed software is taxable, while the same software downloaded from a Web site is not, making it an attractive way to save money.

When buying mission-critical applications—such as financial or manufacturing software—organizations often find that the "packaged" version does not meet all of its needs. Consequently, applications are quite typically modified—customized—by the original or third-party programmers so that they can meet these special needs.

It is sometimes helpful to categorize software types so that you can understand where a particular program fits in the computing process. There are two basic types of software:

1. **Systems software. Systems software** provides the instructions that make the computer run. Utilities and operating systems such as Microsoft Windows, MacOS, and Linux are typical examples. Systems software also manages the communications and interface aspects of the network.
2. **Applications software**. **Application software** enables the user to carry out specific tasks such as writing letters using word processing programs or performing financial analysis using spreadsheets programs. The term also applies to the broader, more scalable systems such as **enterprise resource planning (ERP)** applications used to manage an entire organization.

8.2 USING SOFTWARE FOR PROCUREMENT

You will likely find that while much of the software used in procurement applies to processes used by everyone in the organization, some of it is naturally dedicated to the procurement process only. Procurement professionals need to become familiar with virtually all the software used by the organization since the procurement team will be responsible for its purchase. In addition, you should also understand that your role requires particular expertise in applications used primarily for procurement and supply management. When your organization seeks to acquire new or upgraded programs that impact your area, you should expect to be called upon for your knowledge of software tools dedicated to the procurement function.

This section outlines the software applications most commonly used by organizations, grouping them by general applications and applications specific to procurement operations.

General software applications encompass a broad spectrum of software used in today's organization. Here are just a few of them:

(a) DESKTOP APPLICATIONS.   So-called desktop applications include a variety of commonly used software programs, many of which are released and sold in bundled configurations called suites. Microsoft Office is an example of this, containing word processing, spreadsheet, e-mail, database, and presentation software—all typically designed to be used by the general public as well as the experts. In addition to the traditional office suites, there are numerous others available to manage files, scan documents, keep track of appointments and contacts, and manage finances. Some of the more commonly used include:

- **Word processing** programs such as MS Word or WordPerfect enable the creation and editing of text materials for letters, documents, reports, and tables.

- **Spreadsheets** allow the user to organize, analyze, and manage numerical data, create graphs and charts, and generally provide surprisingly powerful number-crunching capability, enabling the sorting and conversion of data through formulas.
- **Contact management** programs enable users to store and keep track of extensive lists of people. Typically, these tools are used in sales to manage customer relationships by maintaining records of contacts, projects under way, and customer preferences.
- **Database management** software allows for the management of relatively large amounts of data through powerful sorting and classification processes, enabling the user to organize and aggregate information logically. Typical **database management systems (DBMS)** in use today are those using relational models that organize data into rows and columns showing the relationship between elements. Two of the most common relational databases in use are Microsoft SQL and Oracle. The relational database has largely facilitated rapid access to large amounts of information, replacing the slower method of hierarchical databases that stored information in tree formats, where data had to be accessed through its corresponding root element.
- **Project management** tools allow users to track complex projects by individual task and timeline. Project management software is often used as a "game plan" to ensure that all participants are aware of their responsibilities and as a means to inform management of the timely progress of the project.

(b) WEB ACCESS AND E-MAIL. **Web browsers** such as Internet Explorer or Netscape provide yet another dimension to software applications, enabling users to effectively access the vast amount of information available through the Internet. As an adjunct to networks, the browser also provides the key user interface to the **World Wide Web**, where information and profiles for just about any organization can be found.

Networks leverage the Internet through the use of a single, common standard: TCP/IP, which stands for transmission control protocol/Internet protocol. It is the basic communication language or protocol that allows computers to exchange information over the Internet.

Combined with browsers, **search engines** such as Yahoo! and Google provide some of the most powerful resources for the buyer. Search engines allow the user to quickly find and consolidate information found on the Internet for just about any specific subject, product, or service. Today, these tools have become so efficient that they can (and frequently do) return thousands of "**hits**" for a search objective in a fraction of a second.

Perhaps more than any other tool, **e-mail** has revolutionized the way we communicate in computer-enabled societies. E-mail allows the immediate transmission of individual messages across the Internet and instantaneously enables individuals or groups to communicate vast amounts of information in real time.

Along with the vast potential that tools such as these have for enhancing and accelerating business processes, occurs a particularly unpleasant downside: **information overload**. Simply stated, this phenomenon occurs when individuals receive more information than they can process or absorb. While no official studies have yet been made public, information overload appears to be largely counterproductive and stress inducing.

(c) GRAPHICS. Graphics tools include programs for creating and viewing illustrations, photography, diagrams, and blueprints. We commonly use Adobe Acrobat, an application offered free by the publisher, to enable users to open and view document files that have been converted to a specific format that does not require you to have the original application in order to view it. Our engineers use AutoCad to design and document manufactured parts, and we typically use programs such as Visio to document process flows in graphical format.

(d) SECURITY. Ensuring that computer systems and files are maintained securely has become a major issue for organizations today. There has been a serious proliferation of malicious software distributed surreptitiously—**viruses**, **worms**, and **spyware**—that can have devastating effects on an organization's operations. So-called **firewalls** have been developed that allow limited access to a particular internal system by blocking material and users coming from systems outside the organization that do not have preauthorization to enter. In addition, software to filter viruses and worms are commonly deployed across networks to also help block these attacks.

Additional security devices commonly used include **encryption** and **digital signatures**:

- **Encryption**. Involves the coding (or scrambling) of messages or data so that only the designated recipient can access them. The most common method in use is the **encryption key**. To decipher an encoded message, both the sender and receiver use the same code. In **public key encryption**, there are two keys: a public key, which is available to anyone, and a corresponding private key, which only the sender can access. Using this method, any party can send a message encrypted with the subscriber's public key, but only the subscriber has the private key needed to decrypt it.
- **Digital signatures**. Consist of encryption technology and a **public key infrastructure (PKI)** used to determine the authenticity of a message and the identity of the sender to ensure that it has not been changed. Often, third parties are used as the certificate authority to manage and certify the authenticity of the signature.

(e) SUPPLY MANAGEMENT APPLICATIONS. In addition to those general applications and processes described above, you will also need to develop a basic

a collection of networked parties known as the World Wide Web, who use the TCP/IP standard to access and transfer data between one another. The Web uses **hypertext markup language (HTML)** as the standard code through which Web site displays are enabled and a **uniform resource locator (URL)** for identifying individual Web sites.

Since the World Wide Web is essentially a public system, parties often wish to connect privately to one another using an exclusive network called an **extranet** or **virtual private network (VPN)**. Basically, these use the same protocols as do the public networks, but general access is restricted through the use of passwords and other forms of coding to exclude unrecognized visitors. Similarly, organizations often establish procurement networks within the confines of their firewall, called **intranets**, to maintain internal security and control of information until it is ready to be transmitted to the supplier.

Some of the more common applications using e-procurement processes are described below:

- **Requisitioning**. Automating the requisitioning process is one of the most logical steps to reducing the transactional processing load in the Procurement Department. Since the user has to complete the requisition anyway, this electronic process begins by converting the organization's paper requisitions to electronic ones. Often, these are created within the bounds of an existing system such as an Oracle or SAP ERP application. However, once the requisition has been submitted, it can be approved electronically by authorizing parties (leaving a clear, auditable trail) prior to submission to the buyer.

  Upon receipt, the buyer can automatically convert the requisition to a purchase order and transmit it electronically to the supplier. Typically, **electronic purchase orders (EPOs)** are transmitted via e-mail or electronically created FAX, although companies using EDI can transmit them through their VAN.

- **Electronic catalogs**. Often, the basis of an electronic requisitioning system is an electronic catalog, typically maintained by the supplier and stored on either its Web site or the client's intranet. An electronic catalog is similar in organization to a paper catalog but is stored and accessed through the computer. Typically, users access the catalog for selection, and once the item they wish to purchase has been identified, it can be submitted directly for approval. Following approval, it is routed directly to the supplier, bypassing procurement altogether since procurement has already approved the catalog's content and negotiated the pricing with the supplier. Except for its automatic transmittal to the supplier, an electronic catalog order is treated in exactly the same manner as any other order.

  By simplifying the ordering process for end users, the Procurement Department can often save significant cost by driving purchases through a single supplier under a contracted discount rather than using a variety of suppliers selling at list.

- **Automated RFP, RFI, and RFQ.** In addition to automating the purchase order process, many organizations have also tied their RFPs, RFIs, and RFQs to automated systems as well. This enables buyers to construct them from preexisting templates and transmit them electronically to a much wider supply base than would ordinarily be possible under traditional methods. The electronic method also allows for automated scoring of the suppliers' responses, removing the tediousness of detailed analysis by the buyer and speeding the process of selection enormously. This also helps avoid maverick purchasing of high-value items by using the excuse that the process just takes too long. It has been shown that an electronic RFP process can reduce the time it takes to go to contract from several months to only a couple of weeks.
- **Competitive bidding events and reverse auctions.** Automated methods for submitting bids have proven quite effective in obtaining cost reductions since the widest possible supply base can be easily accessed using the computer. With increasing popularity, competitive bidding has turned to the **reverse auction (RA)** to drive substantial price reductions.
- The RA is conducted in much the same manner as a traditional auction except for the fact that suppliers are bidding the price **down**. Buyers have the ability to set the highest acceptable bid (or reserve price) prior to the auction, and typically disclaimers give them the right to award to any party regardless of their position in the bidding.

TIPS AND TECHNIQUES

"What about relationships and special service?" is the typical question coming from the user. Well, experience has shown that while auctions provide significant savings, they typically result in the incumbent winning the bid!

Reverse auction companies have also developed ways to automatically transform bids from suppliers weaker in service or quality to the same level as their better counterparts, adding the extra cost to their bids by a predetermined factor. This results, for example, in adding a price factor to a supplier whose lower quality may result in 10 percent fewer usable parts of 10 cents per dollar bid to make it equal to the supplier who has perfect quality.

(iv) Inventory Management/Supplier-Managed Inventory. In addition to the inventory management processes created by MRP that have enabled significant reductions in the volume of inventory, today we are experiencing a trend toward **supplier-managed inventory (SMI)** whereby the supplier owns the material stored at your facility until you actually use it. This process is frequently combined with **evaluated receipts settlement (ERS)** whereby payment is initiated by the

pull order, rather than a supplier's invoice. The advantage to the supplier is automatic payment, typically without delay, and the elimination of the need to initiate an invoice. Combined with **electronic funds transfer (EFT)**, which automatically transmits payment to the supplier's bank account, this system has led to tremendous reductions in transactional processing.

(v) Contract Management. Software that tracks and maintains updates to contracts can be extremely useful to larger organizations, where individual divisions may not be aware of existing contracts at other divisions and thus not able to take advantage of lower pricing. What is equally typical, often one division will go through the tedious process of contracting for something already under contract by another division, resulting in enormous time and energy drains with no payback.

(vi) Cost Management, Spending Analysis, and Supply Base Optimization. One of the keys to cost savings is through consolidating spending volumes going to several suppliers under one contract to obtain the greatest discount. This process is known as supply base optimization. Cost management software helps **rationalize** an organization's spending by analyzing the exact categories and suppliers of actual spending during a particular period. From this data, you should be able to formulate a strategy for combining purchases to leverage volume. Many organizations, unfortunately, have no idea of their spending by category or commodity since an analysis through manual processes would be nearly impossible. That, however, is changing, and one of the most rapidly growing categories of software is in this area.

Before an effective program of supply base optimization can be implemented, an organization needs to develop a sourcing strategy. A sourcing strategy defines how many suppliers the organization deems as appropriate and the circumstances in which it is willing to depend on a single source. Without a clearly articulated sourcing strategy, an organization will not be able to establish its procurement objectives in a prioritized manner. The supply base optimization program can then be charged with identifying spending categories and key suppliers, reviewing and measuring contract compliance, monitoring changes within critical industries through supply intelligence and market research, and tracking cost savings.

Identifying spending data is the tedious task of tracking down the internal and external systems that have spend data in them. Fortunately, specialized software is available today to assist with the process of locating and consolidating information from multiple sources and "translating" that information to a common, reliable database. In system terms, the software standardizes and enriches spending data so that organizations can utilize it to determine commodity spending patterns.

(vii) Supplier Scorecards. Another of the key benefits from automation is the maintenance of **supplier scorecards**. These are typically the basis for the periodic business review and the ongoing evaluation of supplier performance, and normally

require a great deal of clerical time in tracking and recording specific data. Use of automated tools, combined with a centralized processing system such as ERP, enables buyers to pull period reports for on-time delivery, pricing trends, and returns at the touch of a key.

(viii) Asset Tracking.   **Asset tracking** is most often maintained by the Finance Department, so Procurement has only limited ability to determine when assets were approaching the end of their useful life so that replacements could be efficiently planned. In addition, organizations often find themselves purchasing new equipment for one location when surplus exists in another. Currently, greater effort is being given to enabling the involvement of procurement in the management of assets so that these costs can be further reduced.

(ix) Preventative Maintenance.   In environments where equipment is frequently used, the ordering of spare parts has placed heavy burdens on the Procurement Department. There is, however, software becoming increasingly available that ties the scheduled replacement of parts directly to an electronic ordering system, eliminating the need for buyer involvement on a day-to-day basis.

(f) IMPACT OF AUTOMATION ON PROCUREMENT ORGANIZATIONS.   The overall impact of current trends toward automation of the transactional processes has led to a transformation in recent times of the procurement function itself. With the burden of processing purchase orders largely removed from the buying team, organizations are beginning to find more use for their staff in the strategic functions of cost reduction, risk mitigation, and supplier development. This has resulted in a general trend toward upgrading the quality of the procurement staff and placing more of a burden on the Procurement professional to recruit talented staff and to reengineer existing process to enable a more strategic, proactive approach. In today's organization, the enlightened Procurement professional has been given more and more responsibility as an overall business manager charged with ensuring that best practices are implemented throughout the supply community.

8.3 SOURCING SUPPLY MANAGEMENT TOOLS

The Procurement Department plays a dual role in the selection and acquisition of supply management software: providing domain expertise for the development of the statement of work and the typical support role in supplier selection. Generally, the information technology (IT) group will handle the actual specification development since their team will be providing ongoing support and maintenance for any software installed.

The following section reviews some of the basic aspects the Procurement professional should consider when engaged in this process.

(a) SOFTWARE.   As outlined in the sections above, the software requirements for supply management generally include systems related to MRP processes and systems related to e-procurement. From a sourcing standpoint, organizations generally opt for inclusion of new or additional modules in their existing ERP framework. However, many of the applications for e-procurement have been developed only recently—spending analysis, for example—so organizations find that they are faced with a number of issues: Should they create applications themselves or should they acquire third-party systems that may not be compatible with their existing systems? Or should they postpone acquisition for the present time and wait until the provider of their existing software platform gets around to developing the process as an additional module?

(i) Make or Buy. The **make-or-buy decision** for software largely depends on the immediacy of the return on investment and the availability of market-based applications that suitably meet the organization's requirements. In addition, you must also assess the risk factors that may be involved. Use these questions as a brief checklist:

TIPS AND TECHNIQUES

QUESTIONS TO ASK BEFORE THE MAKE-OR-BUY DECISION

Expertise available
- Can you successfully engage commercial resources that will be able to develop applications to meet your organization's needs?
- How well can you define your requirements?

Potential Risks
- What issues are related to the successful implementation of the project?
- What potential risk exists down the road?

Costs
- Are the costs fully understood?
- What potential exists for unknown costs surfacing during the project?
- Will customization add significantly to the overall cost?
- What are the ongoing costs for maintenance?
- How do licensing fees compare?

Fit
- To what extent will customized software better fit the organization's specific needs?
- How easy will it be to migrate to your platform?

(ii) Customized vs. Off-the-Shelf. Similar to the make-or-buy decision is the consideration to customize purchased software to meet the perceived special needs of your organization. The temptation, of course, is to bring in the new system to operate exactly as the old system to increase the comfort level of the users. However, you should consider not only the initial cost to customize but the ongoing cost of maintenance since the publisher's upgrades to existing software may eliminate the customization already installed or require additional support prior to deployment.

You should also keep in mind that there will be ongoing support required and consider the impact of potential turnover of the supplier's staff.

(iii) Training.   During the selection process for software, training issues should not be overlooked. At the very least, you will want to determine the overall cost of training and if it will be held in house or at a remote location requiring travel. You should also determine the impact to existing operations during the training as a result of lost time.

(iv) Outsourcing.   Outsourcing IT applications has become relatively common today, especially favoring suppliers who manage networks, help desks, and Web sites. Most organizations feel that it is no longer part of their core competencies to manage the complex infrastructure required to support fully developed systems. In addition, the coming of age of **application service providers (ASPs)**— software providers who, in effect, rent software that they then maintain on their site—has lent additional credibility to the improved return on investment of leasing as these suppliers move into supporting essential functions for the organization. As the IT function moves offshore to find less expensive labor, the outsourcing formula becomes even more attractive.

While outsourcing continues to remain a risk-focused decision, organizations are increasingly finding that where core competencies are not involved, the benefits of dedicated expertise and reduced cost far outweigh the loss of control.

8.4 SUMMARY

Automation is becoming a way of life for today's Procurement professional as the variety of tools available for transactional processing expands. As a result, the Procurement professional has had to learn new skills to manage technology, including a basic understanding of how computer technology works. The Procurement professional's vocabulary should include standard data processing terminology and a familiarity with the hardware and network requirements common in contemporary organizations. In addition, it is increasingly accepted that the Procurement staff will have adequate facility with the more commonly used business software applications such as word processing and spreadsheet management.

Supply management applications are changing rapidly as well, and virtually every function has seen some form of automation. Organizations are increasingly turning to ERP to ensure process uniformity across operations to supplement their original implementations of financial and human resource programs. MRP and EDI are now becoming simply modules in a broader spectrum of applications. The recent trend to Web-based processes has also affected procurement, and buyers are learning that the automation of traditional methods such as competitive bidding provides significant advantages. However, along with the benefits these processes offer is the downside of potential information overload.

One of the side effects of this process is that the Procurement professional is increasingly becoming the organization's domain expert when it comes to selecting software and systems that automate supplier management. As a result, you will find that you are now applying the same decision-making processes (such as make or buy) to your own department as you previously applied to your customer.

KEY TERMS

Reengineering
Procure-to-pay
Web-based sourcing
Consigned inventory
Supply chain
Information technology
Platforms
Software applications
Bits/bytes
Data
Record
File
Digital system
Central processing unit (CPU)
Storage media
Input devices
Output devices
Communication devices
Personal computer (PC)
Minicomputer
Mainframe
Personal digital assistant (PDA)
Encryption
Digital signatures
Encryption key
Public key encryption
Public key infrastructure (PKI)
Materials requirements planning
    (MRP)
Manufacturing resource planning
    (MRPII)
Computer-aided manufacturing
    (CAM)
Electronic data interchange
    (EDI)

American National Standards Institute
    (ANSI)
ANSI X 12 standard
Field
Value-added network (VAN)
XML (Extensible markup language)
Electronic procurement or
    e-procurement
HTML (Hypertext markup language)
Uniform Resource Locator (URL)
Extranet
Virtual Private Network (VPN)
Electronic purchase orders (EPO's)
Reverse auction (RA)
Supplier-managed inventory (SMI)
Evaluated receipts settlement (ERS)
Electronic funds transfer
Local area network (LAN)
Wide area network (WAN)
Internet
TCP/IP
Virtual private network (VPN)
Network operating system (NOS)
File transfer protocol (FTP)
Operating system
Centralized computer system
Mainframe
Client/server configuration
Workstation
Network
Systems software
Applications software
Enterprise resource planning (ERP)
Database management systems
    (DBMS)

Web browser

World Wide Web

Search engines

"Hits"

E-mail

Information overload

Viruses, worms and spyware

Supplier scorecards

Asset tracking

Preventative maintenance

Make-or-buy decision

Customized

Off-the-shelf

Application service providers (ASPs)

QUALITY

LEARNING OBJECTIVES

1. Define *quality assurance* and describe the Procurement Manager's role in achieving it.
2. Define *standard deviation* and create a hypothetical example showing tolerances at *three standard deviations* above or below the average of the process.
3. List the sequential steps in *root cause analysis*, including the seven steps in taking corrective action.
4. What is Six Sigma? List the six steps which can be remembered with the acronym *DMAIC*.

Virtually all organizations strive to improve the quality of their products and services. In fact, quality is often the most critical aspect of the product or service we buy, so it is not surprising to learn that a great deal of effort is spent identifying the degree to which our purchase conforms to the established quality requirements.

In its supplier management role, one of the key responsibilities of the Procurement Department is to ensure that the organization's quality requirements are being met consistently in order for it to maximize the value from its purchase. But "quality" itself seems to be so broad a subject that we are often at odds as to what exactly we mean when we speak of it.

We turn, therefore, to a review of the basic concepts of quality management in this chapter to ensure you understand what quality means, how it is measured, and how we go about achieving its full value. Here, let's look at how you will generally manage your quality activities, how you will measure your suppliers' performance, and how you will go about ensuring that your organization's overall quality objectives are being achieved.

9.1 MANAGING QUALITY PERFORMANCE

Managing quality performance has a number of aspects: First, we need to define what we mean by quality and how it fits into our overall organizational strategy; second, we need to understand where our organization is currently operating in the range of acceptable performance; and, third, we need to determine how we intend to improve it.

(a) QUALITY ASSURANCE.   Quality assurance plays a significant role in the Procurement Department's daily activities. To a large extent, it drives many of our fundamental processes. Taken in its broadest functional terms, quality assurance is a set of activities through which we define, measure, evaluate, and accept the products and services we purchase, often within the structure of the organization's policies and standard operating procedures. Quality assurance also includes the formal process of identifying and correcting specific problems and deficiencies, and the methodology used to do so.

Larger organizations usually have separate departments called quality control or quality assurance and often have special job titles that accompany the function, such as quality engineer or supplier quality engineer. Supplier quality and manufacturing quality sections are typically distinct within the enterprise, with the supplier quality function generally included within the procurement organization. In addition to maintaining incoming inspection processes, supplier quality engineering groups have the responsibility for identifying, monitoring, and correcting quality problems originating within suppliers' operations.

(b) DEFINING QUALITY.   **In procurement, when we refer to quality, we generally speak of the contractual obligation we've formed with the supplier to provide products or services that conform to a given specification or statement of work. Generally speaking, there are two aspects to this conformance: First, we consider how closely a product or service matches our requirement, referring to our specification as the baseline metric. In this aspect, we measure the precise deviation (or **allowable tolerance) from a given number to determine if it meets specification. Second, we consider the actual frequency with which a product or service meets the specification. Here, we want to know how often individual elements in a given lot of goods fall outside the acceptable limits.

As an example of how we might look at conformance to specifications, please consider this: If the wall of an aluminum tube is specified to be 1/32nd of an inch thick (0.03125) with a tolerance of $+/- 0.0001$ of an inch, a tube measuring between 0.03124 and 0.03126 would be within an acceptable range. One measuring 0.031265, however, would not. So, in this particular case, any submission outside the specified range would not meet our requirements.

However, we recognize the fact that there are inherent variances produced in the manufacturing of aluminum pipe that prevents the absolute conformance to this specification all the time. Therefore, we measure how often within any given shipment we can expect to find individual tubes that do not meet this tolerance. We might specify this by requiring that 99.9997 percent (Six Sigma) of the material sampled falls into the $=/-$ range. If it does, we accept the entire lot; if it does not, we reject the entire lot.

(c) EMPLOYING QUALITY SYSTEMS. Measuring and sampling incoming material, then, is one way to control and manage our suppliers' quality, especially in a product-focused, manufacturing environment. A system most often used for this is **statistical process control (SPC)**, and it will be discussed in some detail later in this chapter. However, for your reference, here are some other commonly used quality system tools:

(i) Certification.   **Supplier certification** is one way of reducing (or eliminating altogether) the need for incoming inspection. In certifying a supplier, the buying organization typically determines that the supplier's internal system for measurement and control of quality is sufficient to ensure it will meet the minimum quality level required without performing further incoming inspections. Often, certification will be provided on a part-by-part basis rather than as an overall blanket endorsement, so suppliers will need to "qualify" or recertify for each new part they produce.

When a supplier has been certified, it means that your organization will rely solely upon the supplier's internal controls to produce acceptable quality. This process usually works fine, but there is one significant caveat: Since certification is based on the supplier's current processes (and equipment), your organization will need to know in advance when a supplier changes any production processes so that you can either recertify the process or reintroduce incoming inspection. The need for a proactive, compliant communication system to monitor these activities is evident, and you should carefully include this as a requirement in your supplier certification agreement.

You should understand, also, that the Uniform Commercial Code (UCC) requirement to inspect incoming materials in a reasonable period of time after receipt will still apply, and your organization will assume responsibility for the goods even if no incoming inspection is actually performed. In your agreement, you should extend liability for nonconforming parts to the supplier until the materials are actually used.

(ii) Acceptance Testing.   Used most frequently when purchasing capital equipment, **acceptance testing** is a method used for determining if a particular piece of equipment is functioning at its expected output level. This usually requires an engineering or manufacturing sign-off and a formal acknowledgment of acceptance (or rejection) communicated to the supplier.

The acceptance testing process is also commonly used for testing the first article submitted for approval prior to the supplier's actual manufacture runs and may represent a first step in the certification process.

(iii) Inspection Process.   When used, the inspection process will usually specify a range of inspection frequency, extending from 100 percent inspection of all products to no inspection at all, or any level in between. In most cases, the buying organization may specify routine lot sampling on a random basis or at specific lots or time intervals, or it may require actual, on-site audits of the process used by the supplier to measure quality metrics.

The location of the inspection is important, too. It is generally agreed that the earlier in the production process the inspection can take place, the less costly will be the corrective action. As a result, requirements may specify that the inspection will take place on the supplier's manufacturing line or at final assembly, or even as a separate process prior to shipment. Inspection may also be called for at your plant at various operational stages, as well: at the receiving dock, upon release to manufacturing, or even at your final assembly stage.

Similarly, in a service environment, the results or output of the service can require inspection at a variety of times and places. While it is not usual to perform acceptance testing as one might for equipment, there may be a requirement within the statement of work (SOW) that calls for some method of services inspection at specified time intervals as part of gathering the metrics for a service-level agreement.

(d) MEASURING QUALITY PERFORMANCE.   It's an old adage that you tend to get what you measure for, since we have a known tendency to work toward specific goals. For this reason, the ongoing measurement of quality performance becomes critical to the success of any serious effort to generate improvements, keeping in mind, of course, that there are numerous methods for measurement in common use today. Choosing the right measurement depends, to a large degree, on what we intend to accomplish.

Most of the time, the measurements we receive relating to quality performance will be based on some specific testing sequence. These measurements will tell us if the material we are receiving conforms to our specifications or if the process being used to produce the products has the capability of doing the job. In the section that follows, we will examine briefly those methods you are most likely to encounter.

(i) Statistical Process Control (SPC).   SPC has been previously defined in Chapter 2 as a system that measures the actual distribution of events from the beginning to the end of a given process. It is a method of monitoring, controlling, and, ideally, improving a process through statistical probability analysis. Its four basic steps include (1) measuring the process, (2) eliminating variances in the process to make it consistent, (3) monitoring the process, and (4) improving the process to its best target value.

When applied to quality measurement, it allows us to determine if the output of our process is within the desired range of control. As you will recall, two key measures are used in SPC: the upper control limit (UCL)—the highest point of measurement at which performance is acceptable—and the lower control limit (LCL)—the lowest point of measurement at which performance is acceptable. Between these two points, events are considered acceptable, and the process is considered to be in control.

We generally use statistical process control (SPC) to measure the tolerances of products produced during rapidly repeating operational cycles, such as the output from automated machinery. In this environment, we determine the range of tolerance mathematically as three **standard deviations** above or below the average of the process.

TIPS AND TECHNIQUES

Standard deviation is a statistical measure of the variability or dispersion within a set of data points. It is calculated from the deviation or mathematical distance between each data value and the sample statistical mean, and is usually represented by the Greek letter "S" for sigma. The more dispersed the data is, the larger the standard deviation. For data that follows a normal distribution, approximately 68 percent of all data will fall within one standard deviation of the sample mean, 95 percent of all values will fall within two standard deviations, and 99.7 percent of all data will fall within three standard deviations.

(ii) Tolerances.   By definition, tolerance refers to the amount of deviation from our specification data points we are willing to accept. Tolerance is usually given in the same unit of measure or dimension as the specification, as we noted in the example given earlier in the chapter in the section on Defining Quality.

The concept of **tolerance stack-up** is used to measure the cumulative variations of each of the items in an assembly that goes into a final product. Tolerance stack-up analysis is used to determine if a form, fit, or function problem exists when manufacturing tolerances combine in a finished part or assembly. Tolerance stack-up analysis is typically performed by either assuming worst-case allowable dimensions or by using statistical analysis of tolerances.

(iii) Pareto Charts.   The **Pareto chart** is a type of quality analysis used to determine if a few categories or units account for the majority of the total occurrences. The chart simply displays events in the order of their frequency.

TIPS AND TECHNIQUES

The commonly used Pareto principle (or 80/20 rule) was originally defined by J. M. Juran in 1950 and named after Vilfredo Pareto, a nineteenth-century Italian economist who studied the distribution of the world's wealth. Pareto concluded that the majority (80 percent) of the world's wealth was in the hands of a minority (20 percent) of its population.

Figure 9.1 represents an example of a Pareto chart showing the percentage by category and the cumulative percentage of defects in a hypothetical failure analysis.

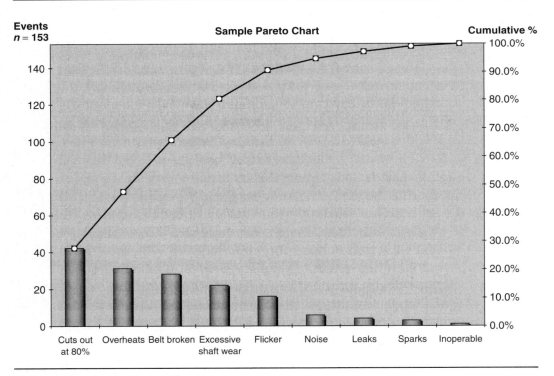

FIGURE 9.1   PARETO ANALYSIS CHART
Source: www.qualityspctools.com/parresults.html.

(iv) C_{pk}. C_{pk} is a process **capability index**. Process capability analysis entails comparing the performance of a process against its specifications. A process is capable if virtually all of the possible variable values fall within the specification limits. This is measured numerically by using a capability index, C_p, with the formula:

C_p = USL − LSL

6s

where USL = upper specification limit and LSL = lower specification limit and
s = standard deviation.

This equation indicates that the measure of process capability is how much of the observed process variation (USL minus LSL) is covered by the process specifications. In this case the process variation is measured by 6 standard deviations (+/−3 on each side of the mean). If C_p is greater than 1.0, then the process specification covers almost all of the process observations.

However, the C_p index does not account for a process that is off-center. This equation can be modified to account for off-center processes to obtain the C_{pk} index as follows:

This equation takes the minimum distance between our specification limits and the process mean and divides it by 3 standard deviations to arrive at the measure of process capability.

(v) *Benchmarking.* As it relates to quality considerations, **benchmarking** is the process of measuring your organization's performance against others within the same business sector or industry to determine what constitutes **best-in-class performance** and how it has been achieved. This comparison can form the basis for a quality improvement program targeting those areas where quality gaps or deviations exist. Benchmarking is also frequently used in conjunction with **strategic value analysis** and planning to help establish goals and allocate resources according to an overall organizational system of priorities.

Philosophically, benchmarking can be considered simply as the search for better methods. It is a way of identifying areas that need reengineering, change, and improvement. It is also a blend of both qualitative and quantitative research that can be tedious and painfully difficult to gather, consuming a great deal of resources. For this reason, many organizations turn to consultants and research organizations that are in the business of gathering this information as a way of accelerating the improvement process.

9.2 ENSURING QUALITY PERFORMANCE

Doubtlessly, one major compliance issue in most organizations involves the notion of getting full value for the price paid. So it is not surprising that ensuring quality performance from suppliers is generally an excellent way to improve the value of purchased goods and services. You should continually ask the question: How do I know that my organization is receiving the full value of its contractual spending? Ensuring quality performance is certainly one proven way.

Let's examine, then, some of the concepts and tools relating to ensuring quality performance from your suppliers.

(a) ENFORCING QUALITY REQUIREMENTS.   The process that **enforces** quality compliance is the key to successfully ensuring that your organization's quality policies and requirements are met by your suppliers. In most organizations with a formal quality program, the central tool for this is the **corrective action process**. Surrounding this process is the accurate documentation of quality standards and their conveyance to the supplier as well as developing an analysis of the root cause of the issue so that ongoing progress toward resolution of the problem can be properly monitored.

(i) Documenting Quality Requirements.   Without proper documentation, quality requirements are rendered virtually meaningless. In most cases, documentation will be related to supplier conformance issues and incoming inspections, but don't overlook the need to maintain accurate records of supplier site visits (when performed) and the history of their qualification or certification process. The qualification process establishes the supplier's level of capability, and it is important that you refer to this (as a baseline) when assessing the supplier's ongoing level of support. In many organizations, quality reporting is required on a periodic basis and is usually incorporated into the formal supplier business review process.

(ii) Conveying Standards.   As part of the documentation process, your organization needs to have a system in place that defines the standards of conformance so that all parties will have a baseline point of reference when reviewing quality performance. Often, these will take the form of a set of written specifications and a system for organizing them, usually some body of standard operating procedures (SOPs), where the measures of conformance we use are typically referred to as key performance indicators (KPIs).

(iii) Corrective Action Process.   Many organizations employ the *corrective action* process whenever standards of quality conformance are not met by suppliers. This tool is traditionally used to document and convey notification of supplier nonconformance and to similarly document the requirements and steps necessary to correct the noncompliant situation. The goal of the process is to eliminate the cause of the problem.

NOTE

Many organizations have robust and well-defined procedures for handling corrective actions. One example of a Supplier Corrective Action Request (SCAR), used by the Harris Corporation, can be found at www.govcoom.harris.com/suppliers/become/H-450-2.pdf.

ISO 9000:2000 defines corrective action as an action to eliminate the cause of a detected nonconformity or other undesirable situation. Accordingly, the component steps for the process include:

1. Recognize the problem and its effect.
2. Determine the root cause.
3. Determine and implement a short-term action plan (often called the "containment" phase).
4. Determine and implement a comprehensive action plan.
5. Determine and implement a preventive action plan.
6. Follow up to ensure compliance.
7. Audit to ensure the plans are effectively eliminating the problem.

(iv) Developing Root Cause Analysis.   Before you can fully resolve any quality discrepancy, you will need to identify and understand its root cause. A *root cause* is the element (or sequence of events) that, if corrected, will prevent a recurrence of the problem in the future. What is the underlying and fundamental element or chain of events that gave rise to the problem in the first place? For tracing the causal relationship of quality issues, we use a process called **root cause analysis**. Root cause analysis thus provides a structured methodology for determining the causal relationships of various elements in the process being used that may be ultimately responsible for the problem.

As with the corrective action process, root cause analysis also follows a sequential methodology that includes:

1. **Data collection.** This procedure should take place as close in time as possible to the initial discovery of the problem to minimize the loss of information.
2. **Assessment.** The assessment phase includes analyzing the data to identify causal factors, summarizing the findings, and organizing them according to logical categories.
3. **Corrective action.** Identify and implement viable solutions. This means finding answers to several questions, including:
   a. How will the corrective action prevent recurrence?
   b. What new risks will this action introduce?
   c. Does the action fit in with overall objectives?
   d. Are resources available to properly implement the correction?
   e. What are the secondary consequences of implementation?
   f. Can the corrective action be implemented within an appropriate time frame?
   g. Will the results be measurable?
4. **Follow-up.** Determine if the corrective action has had the desirable effect in resolving the problem. If the problem recurs, the original instance should be reinvestigated to determine if it was properly analyzed.

(v) Other Corrective Action Options. When suppliers are responsible for nonconforming goods or other quality issues, there are a number of options open to you:

- **Return.** Nonconforming goods can be returned to the supplier for further action. (Keep in mind, your organization may be responsible for any further damage while the goods are in its care.) Under the UCC, both the buyer and the supplier have a number of options regarding correction including repair or replacement. If services are involved, however, the likely remedy will be to redo the work, or some buyers accept some form of discount.
- **Rework.** Under some circumstances, the buyer may be authorized to rework nonconforming goods or services at the supplier's expense. While this requires a negotiated settlement with the supplier, it might prove less expensive than having the products returned or redeploying personnel to correct the deficiency.
- **Renegotiate.** In the case of nonconforming goods or services that are partially usable, the buyer may choose to accept the existing performance and negotiate a reduced rate.
- **Re-source or Retrain.** Ultimately, you will need to decide how the nonconformance, or continuing nonconformance, affects your organization's relationship with the supplier. Should you consider having the supplier retrain its employees as part of the corrective action, or should you simply find another source for your purchase?

(b) TOTAL QUALITY MANAGEMENT (TQM). **Total Quality Management (TQM)** is an enduring process of continuous improvement focused on increasing customer satisfaction. As a philosophy, TQM requires the active participation of all members of the organization in working toward the improvement of processes, methods, and services, as well as the culture in which they are fostered.

TIPS AND TECHNIQUES

THE POWER OF TQM

In 1993, the Boeing Corporation was placed on a limited production status, a form of probation, by the Air Force as a result of admitted quality problems, late deliveries, cost overruns, and an adversarial relationship. Boeing's leadership stepped in and implemented TQM with the stated goals of total customer satisfaction, incorporating quality in everything they did, and involving the entire team in the optimization of processes. The team focused on the systematic and integrated framework of TQM.

So successful was this approach that in 1998, this team was the winner of the National Quality Award, and today they are contenders for the Malcolm Baldrige Award.

(i) Deploying TQM in Procurement. Likely the most commonly used implementation of TQM in procurement is the use of the supplier scorecard combined with the supplier business review. It is through this process that procurement has

the opportunity to address ongoing product quality or quality of service issues in a meaningful way. By measuring and monitoring performance on a regular basis and by utilizing the dynamics of a cross-functional team, continuous improvement processes can become extremely effective tools for developing greater customer satisfaction.

(ii) Kaizen. **Kaizen** is a discipline very closely related to TQM. We generally understand Kaizen to mean "improvement." Originally a Buddhist term, Kaizen comes from the words, "renew the heart and make it good." Closely related to the western concepts of TQM and continuous improvement, adaptation of the Kaizen concept also requires changes in "the heart of the business," corporate culture and structure, since Kaizen enables companies to translate the corporate vision in every aspect of a company's operational practice. Thus, in the workplace Kaizen means continuous improvement involving everyone as a group or team, from the CEO to the delivery van driver. Proponents of this way of thinking believe that continuous development and improvement is critical to the organization's long-term success.

(iii) Quality Functional Deployment (QFD). **Quality Functional Deployment (QFD)** is another adjunct of TQM. As a system, it links the needs of the customer or end user with the design, development, engineering, manufacturing, and service functions. The concept develops from a consideration that in today's industrial society there is a growing separation between producer and consumer. QFD is meant to help organizations discover both spoken and unspoken needs, translate these into actions and designs, and focus various organizational efforts on achieving a common goal of customer satisfaction. QFD thus seeks to create a culture where organizational goals are formulated to exceed normal expectations and provide a level of enthusiasm that generates both tangible and perceived value.

(c) EMPLOYING QUALITY SYSTEMS. Two major quality standard systems are in use today that, in many ways, complement one another and enable organizations to provide greater customer-focused quality assurance. The key elements of these systems, Six Sigma and ISO, are briefly outlined in the section that follows.

(i) Six Sigma. **Six Sigma** is a quality movement and improvement program that has grown from TQM. As a methodology, it focuses on controlling processes to $+/-$ six sigma (standard deviations) from a centerline, which is the equivalent of 3.4 defects per million opportunities (where an opportunity is characterized as chance of not meeting the required specification). Six Sigma fundamental tenets include reducing the variation within a process, improving system capability, and identifying essential factors that the customer views as crucial to quality.

Six Sigma methodologies incorporate six steps corresponding to the acronym *DMAIC*:

Define customer requirement and improvement goals
Measure variables of the process
Analyze data to establish inputs and outputs
Improve system elements to achieve performance goals
Control the key variables to sustain the gains

You can obtain further information about this process by visiting the American Society for Quality's Web site at www.asq.org.

(ii) ISO Standards.   **ISO**, the **International Organization for Standardization**, was established in 1947 as an effort to consolidate widely dispersed methods of approaching quality standards. Its stated goal was to facilitate a means of coordinating, developing, and unifying industrial and technical quality standards. Based in Geneva, Switzerland, ISO is staffed by representatives from standards organizations in each of its member countries, working through committees that establish standards for industry, research, and government.

(iii) ISO 9000.   In 1987, ISO issued a series of quality management and quality assurance standards as the ISO 9000 series that has, today, seen adoption by more than 500,000 organizations in 149 countries. This body of standards now provides a framework for customer-focused quality management throughout the global business community and has been widely acknowledged as providing the paradigm of assurance that customers will consistently find uniform quality in the products and services they purchase. Organizations are today certified as having achieved the standard through examination by an ISO registrar and may then use that certification as an assurance that standardized methods are being employed.

The 1994 editions of ISO 9001, ISO 9002, and ISO 9003 have been consolidated into a single revised document, which is now represented by ISO 9001:2000. ISO suggests that the greatest value is obtained when organizations use the entire family of standards in an integrated manner. It is suggested that, beginning with ISO 9000:2000, organizations adopt ISO 9001:2000 to achieve a first level of performance. The practices described in ISO 9004:2000 may then be implemented to make the quality management system increasingly effective in achieving organizational goals. ISO 9001:2000 and ISO 9004:2000 have been formatted as a consistent pair of standards to facilitate their use. ISO maintains that using the standards in this way will help relate them to other management systems and many sector-specific requirements (such as ISO/TS/16949 in the automotive industry) and will assist in gaining recognition through national award programs.

For the Procurement Department, ISO compliance generally means implementing a series of quality assurance procedures that cover:

- An evaluation process for the selection of qualified vendors.
- A periodic review of supplier performance, along with remedial action for unsatisfactory performance.
- Documentation of quality requirements in the purchase order.
- Quality control procedures for incoming material.
- Establishment of quality systems and monitoring at suppliers' plants.
- Procedures for tracking supplier defects and resolving quality issues with them.
- Implementation of supplier training programs.
- Collaboration in establishing joint quality assurance programs.

(iv) ISO 14000. ISO 14000 is a series of international standards on environmental management. It provides a framework for the development of an environmental management and evaluation system, and the supporting audit program. The standard does not prescribe environmental performance targets, but instead provides organizations with the tools to assess and control the environmental impact of their activities, products, or services. The standards currently address environmental management systems, environmental auditing, environmental labels and declarations, environmental performance evaluation, and life-cycle assessment.

To learn more about this important set of standards, you might want to visit the ISO Web site at www.iso.org.

9.3 SUMMARY

Managing quality at the supplier level is one of the key areas where procurement departments can add value. This generally means working closely with your internal quality assurance team to ensure that your suppliers are fully measuring up to their contractual obligations.

Understanding quality management requires that you first have a clear definition of your organization's quality objectives and improvement programs. You can then use this information to develop and manage supplier certification and qualification programs as well as monitoring the day-to-day quality performance of suppliers through statistical processes and inspections. Some of the common methods you will be expected to work with include SPC, C_{pK}, Pareto charts, and benchmarking the performance of other organizations to determine best-in-class measures.

Ensuring the quality performance of your suppliers will include documenting and conveying your organization's standards and requirements as well as your participation in remediation activities such as corrective action processes, root cause analysis, and exercising a variety of other options available to supply management under the UCC.

You will also be required to understand various TQM processes (along with Kaizen and QFD), how they are structured and how they are deployed in procurement. This will mean developing a working knowledge of the principles and objectives of the predominant quality systems such as Six Sigma and ISO.

KEY TERMS

Quality assurance (QA)
Allowable tolerance
Statistical process control (SPC)
Supplier certification
Acceptance testing
Standard deviation
Tolerance stack-up
Pareto charts
Capability index (C_{pk})
Benchmarking
Best-in-class performance
Strategic value analysis

Enforces
Corrective action process
Root cause analysis
Total quality management (TQM)
Kaizen
Quality Functional Deployment
    (QFD)
Six Sigma
International Organization for
    Standardization (ISO)
ISO Standards

CHAPTER 10

PROCUREMENT'S INTERNAL RELATIONSHIPS

LEARNING OBJECTIVES

1. Name five approaches to achieving good organizational communication.
2. Describe cross-functional teams and list the opportunities for Procurement Managers to bring the team's expertise to bear on organizational issues.
3. List the characteristics of most cross-functional teams which should be considered when evaluating their contribution to an organization.
4. Describe the impact of the Sarbanes-Oxley (SOX) legislation on procurement policy management and the need for training.

The Procurement Department's organizational support role requires extensive coordination and collaboration with other internal departments. While some of these departments—for example, legal and finance—actually provide services to your procurement team, all of them constitute the collective customer base that depends on you to provide critical procurement and supply management functions. You will be working collaboratively with many of these groups on cross-functional teams engaged in the development of a new product or service, for instance. You may also work with them in resolving quality issues in a manufacturing operation, or, even more likely, selecting a new supplier. Consequently, you will likely spend a major portion of your time working with them. For this reason, it is important that you understand other internal departments' corresponding roles in your organization and the common activities they perform in fulfilling their missions.

In this chapter, you will first examine the roles of the major organizational groups you are likely to encounter and how these roles interface with those of your department. We then review the processes used to communicate with other departments and how you can best initiate and reinforce collaborative working relationships with each of them. And, finally, we examine how you can drive operational improvements within the Procurement Department to better serve your internal customers.

10.1 UNDERSTANDING KEY DEPARTMENTAL ROLES

During your career, you will quite possibly never encounter two enterprises with exactly the same organizational structure. However, in the section that follows we will try to describe the roles of the departments you will most commonly encounter so that you can gain a better understanding of how best to develop good working relationships with them. To provide some logical structure, you will find these grouped by their broader functional responsibilities: administrative and support, production or service, sales and marketing, and engineering and design.

Figure 10.1 shows an organizational chart for a typical manufacturing organization. You might find this useful as a reference map as you go through this section.

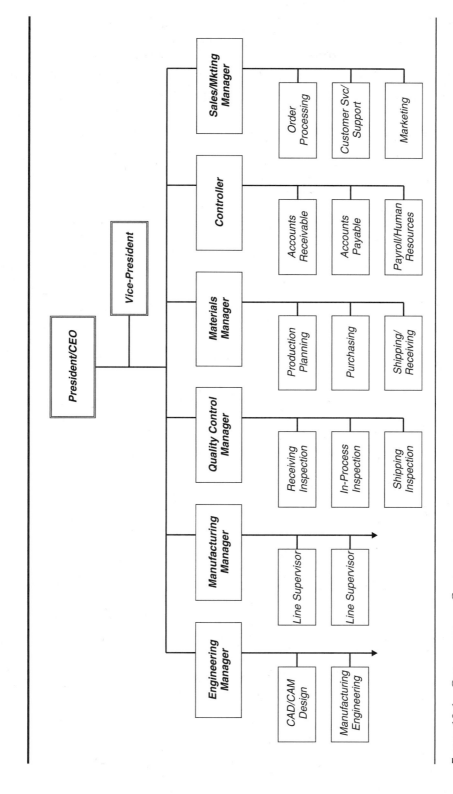

FIGURE **10.1** ORGANIZATIONAL CHART

(a) ADMINISTRATIVE AND SUPPORT FUNCTIONS.   Administrative and support departments generally include those groups that provide the foundation for the smooth, day-to-day tactical operation of the organization as well as those that perform general management activities that serve the entire organization. Typically, within this subsection you will find the following:

(i) Senior Management.   **Senior management** includes the organization's major executive functions such as the chief executive officer (CEO) and president. In public corporations, it also applies to the board of directors, typically lead by a chairperson.

Increasingly, procurement departments have been gaining visibility at the senior management level as a result of the need for improved cost structures and the expanding complexity of managing the supply community for competitive advantage. As a result of this visibility, procurement professionals are finding that they must develop more finely tuned communication skills and the ability to deliver highly effective summary presentations. Generally speaking, you will find that senior management, as a result of the very nature of its role, has less time to spend on individual subjects than other organizational managers. To maintain credibility at this level, you will need to address your presentations to the competitive forces driving overall organizational mission and strategy.

(ii) Finance, Accounting, and Treasury.   These three groups manage virtually all of the organization's monetary funds and provide the foundation for substantiating procurement performance. They are often the audit compliance watchdogs of organizational spending, and they plan the cash flow that ensures your suppliers are paid in a timely manner. Establishing close communications and good working relationships with these groups will enhance your department's fiduciary performance by helping to ensure the effectiveness of decisions that create financial obligations.

(iii) Legal.   Much of the Procurement Department's activities are based on legal principles, and these principles are in continual flux, being modified often by actual decisions of the judiciary branches of state and federal governments. Consequently, you will find your organization's **Legal Department** to be an excellent support function for guidance on how specific legal technicalities can affect your business relationships with suppliers and how courts are currently interpreting statutory law. Through this guidance you will be able to provide more effective support to your internal customers by mitigating risks to the organization and ensuring decisions with potential legal implications are being made correctly.

(iv) Facilities.   **Facilities** departments are responsible for maintaining the physical infrastructure of the workplace and planning for effective space utilization.

To the extent that your needs for inventory storage will vary with changing economic conditions, close coordination with this group can be important. You will also find that this department provides a large amount of your transactional processing workload due to the wide variety of materials and services required to support the organization's physical facilities.

(v) Human Resources. **Human resources (HR)** departments are generally responsible for recruiting new employees, as well as developing and managing personnel policies and employee benefits. Often, HR departments also support training as part of the employee development process, so you may find that your department's training needs can be coordinated and assisted through its resources. As a professional, you will find that HR offers support by providing up-to-date information on employee management affairs and regulations governing the workplace.

(vi) Information Technology. Your **information technology (IT)** group is generally responsible for all the computer and telecommunications requirements in the organization. It supports the organization's internal data and communications networks, enterprise resource planning (ERP) systems, and can provide the integration services necessary to interface with multiple software platforms should you be working toward automating your supply base. In addition, the IT organization is a large user of procurement services, so it is increasingly important that you are tuned in to planning for its future needs.

(vii) Logistics. Frequently an integral part of the supply management function, **logistics** services support the organization by handling finished goods distribution (in a manufacturing environment) and inbound freight. An effective logistics group can add significant value to procurement activities by supporting the just-in-time (JIT) processes that reduce inventory and by providing support for reduced costs associated with inbound shipments. The Procurement Department can assist logistics operations by ensuring close adherence to shipping policy and using preferred carriers.

(b) PRODUCTION FUNCTIONS. **Production** is a term widely used to refer to manufacturing, mining, or services that otherwise generate tangible goods or materials (such as baking and brewing). Production operations generally include the functions of manufacturing operations planning, quality assurance, and the maintenance of related equipment.

(i) Manufacturing Operations. Procurement supports manufacturing operations by ensuring it has delivered the proper supply of quality materials in the required quantity and at the right time. Failure to do so often results in unfortunate conditions where orders are unable to ship on time and the organization loses revenue.

In extreme cases, the inability to ensure supply can lead to plant shutdowns, loss of customers, and layoffs. For this reason, the Procurement Department's responsibility to its manufacturing partners becomes very clear, and its management of the supply community is a mission-critical obligation.

Procurement is also charged with the responsibility to reduce the costs of materials used in the manufacturing operation. This, too, is a mission-critical function since often an organization prices its end product relative to the costs of materials and labor. Improved supplier pricing can lead to a more competitive pricing strategy.

(ii) Planning.   **Planning** is one of the keys to the successful operation of most manufacturing operations. Unless customer demand can be accurately forecasted, there is no guarantee that the available supply of materials will be sufficient to meet production objectives. In most operations, demand planning includes forecasting the mix of the various products customers might order, as well as the quantities that will be needed.

In some operations, the buying function is combined with the planning function in the form of a *buyer-planner* so there are times when the planning function actually falls in the Procurement Department. In these situations, it is not unusual to find the Procurement Department itself reporting to manufacturing management and becoming an integral part of the production environment.

(iii) Quality Assurance.   Quality assurance is a production function tasked to ensure a given standard of quality. In manufacturing environments there are generally two groups engaged in quality assurance: an internal group monitoring manufacturing performance and a supplier-focused group monitoring the quality of incoming materials used in manufacturing. Considering the critical nature of these functions, procurement departments are typically closely allied to quality management teams and often work collaboratively on cross-functional teams. As the role of outsourcing expands and organizations find themselves more closely tied to outside manufacturing sources, this function takes on even greater importance. Today, the management of quality from subcontracting service organizations—whose products are often shipped directly to the customer and never seen at the plant site—is becoming an increasingly important issue, leading to the increased use of supplier quality engineers deployed directly to procurement departments.

(iv) Manufacturing Maintenance.   The Procurement Department also closely supports manufacturing operations by ensuring that spare parts and tools are available so that maintenance activities can take place when needed. In machinery-intensive manufacturing operations, downtime due to the loss of even one piece of equipment can severely limit production capacity. Ensuring the supply of spare parts and maintenance-related supplier services becomes as critical as the material that goes directly into manufacturing of the organization's products.

(c) SALES AND MARKETING.   Sales and marketing activities impact procurement in a variety of ways: increased sales activities and merchandising campaigns generally create added demand that requires planning for additional flows of material, and slower market demand requires greater agility in manufacturing to support the increased customer service required to gain business in a highly competitive environment.

The potential benefits from strong relationships between supplier management groups and the sales and marketing efforts of the organization are frequently overlooked. The supplier community represents a special source of potential sales for your own organization for rather obvious reasons: Purchasing your goods or services increases their sales. What could be simpler? Yet it might be surprising to learn that few organizations have programs to market to their supply bases.

TIPS AND TECHNIQUES

> There is nothing illegal or unethical about selling to your suppliers as long as the sales are not directly related to your specific purchases. A so-called tying contract, where a purchase of goods or services from the supplier is contingent upon a corresponding purchase from your organization, is usually illegal. However, there is nothing wrong with saying, "My organization prefers to purchase goods and services from its own customers."

(i) Product/Business Development.   Product managers and business development managers are generally charged with overseeing specific product lines within the enterprise and have broad responsibilities for developing new business opportunities. Consequently, the groups they manage often have important roles in the development of new products and end-of-life discontinuation of existing ones. As a source of information regarding the potential needs of the organization, these groups can provide the Procurement Department with invaluable information that can be useful in formulating supply strategies and determining future directions for supplier partnerships.

(ii) Public Relations.   The public image of your organization can significantly affect your relationships with suppliers. A strong, positive public image suggests that businesses associated with your organization will benefit beyond the direct profit they earn from their dealings with you, and they are more likely to offer concessions to gain your business. You can leverage this even further by ensuring that key executives of your suppliers are on the mailing list for press releases and other public relations materials … but be sure to send them only as long as the news continues to be favorable.

(iii) Advertising/Sales Collateral.   Most of the advertising done by your organization will be placed with professional advertising agencies by staff members with marketing backgrounds and expertise, since vendor selection for this service can be highly subjective. Nevertheless, there can be significant opportunity for cost savings through the purchase of printed materials and promotional merchandise that should not be overlooked. Sourcing and supplier management can work very well when you stick to providing collaborative input on the business aspects of procurement and consider that aesthetic considerations may be the key driver in a successful marketing campaign.

(iv) Distribution.   Distribution is one of the key physical aspects to sales management whose importance should be evident. Physical distribution processes—conveying goods or services to the customer—typically involve a host of disciplines such as warehousing, packaging, inventory management, security, transportation and **traffic**, information technology, and customer service, just to mention a few. Distribution is a critical strategic function in any organization that generates a strong demand for purchased services and will often require the Procurement Department's assistance. You should work closely with this group to ensure that you have a clear understanding of its needs.

Similarly, distribution groups are in an excellent position to forecast incoming demand and sales trends, and so represent a primary source of planning information that can assist you in developing relevant supply strategies.

(d) ENGINEERING AND DESIGN FUNCTIONS.   Engineering and design functions are typically separated into those groups working on new products and technical research and development, and groups working with manufacturing operations and factory systems. Early involvement by the Procurement Department in the **new product introduction** process can assist in aligning future strategies with sourcing needs and provide a smooth transition to new materials or suppliers. The Procurement Department can often help accelerate the process by introducing potential suppliers to the organization's business requirements and taking the initial steps toward qualification.

(i) Research and Development (R&D).   The research process focuses on the discovery of new technology and methods, while the development process seeks ways to exploit them through practical application. The Procurement Department's ability to identify and develop new sources of supply can become a strategic resource to the organization when it is employed early in the design specification process.

(ii) New Product/Service Introduction (NPI).   New product or service introduction is the complete business process of developing new products for the market. It typically covers the complete product life cycle from initial discovery of opportunity, product/service conception, design and development through to production, market launch, support, enhancement, and even retirement.

Other titles are often used to describe the NPI process, such as new product development (NPD). The exact meaning of the terms vary with different organizations; however, today the NPI process is characterized by a distinct functional division, notably between marketing, engineering (or R&D), and production, and NPI is likely to be seen as a cross-functional business process, involving both internal groups and external suppliers or partners.

In conjunction with the R&D functions, the introduction of new products or services requires a great deal of planning by the Procurement Department to ensure that new suppliers have been properly qualified and have the required capability to deliver. Early involvement by Procurement is no longer just desirable; it has become a necessity to the organization to ensure a smooth product introduction ramp-up from the development phase to actual marketing and distribution.

10.2 DEVELOPING GOOD WORKING RELATIONSHIPS

Throughout the procurement process, your effectiveness and your department's effectiveness will depend largely on the strength of your relationships with suppliers and your internal customers. For this reason, it is critical that you understand how to engage others proactively and how to establish the foundation for effective collaboration.

In this section, we review the ways good communication skills can assist your efforts and how you might better assist your organization as a participant in a collaborative working environment.

(a) COMMUNICATING WITHIN THE ORGANIZATION.   Good communication skills are the essential cornerstone to building meaningful relationships with other internal departments. Unless your customers clearly understand your goals and objectives and how you work to achieve them, you run the risk of being held at arm's length and excluded from critical internal communication activities. Similarly, those in your department need to have a clear understanding of the activities of other groups you will provide services for in order to more effectively meet their needs. If the communication is not clear and timely, both groups run the risk of misunderstandings that can result in ineffective team performance. Keep in mind that improving total operational performance is your primary objective in developing effective communications. To do so, you will require the active participation of those with whom you interface.

(i) Establishing Credibility and Trust.   Your ability to execute to plan can be the key to establishing credibility and trust with other groups. Thus the need to accurately communicate your performance objectives and progress toward them frequently and appropriately becomes apparent. To the extent that you can do this prior to engaging in activities that affect other departments and solicit their input regarding your approach and how best to meet their needs, you will find that you

are effectively establishing credibility and trust. You can do this best by aligning your activities to support the departmental goals of your internal customers.

Gaining visibility also assists your efforts in developing credibility and trust. The more your customers know about your value-adding activities, the more likely they are to engage you in future sourcing efforts. Far too often, the Procurement Department is viewed as being stuck in administering meaningless details and transactional processes that seldom amount to any significant benefit to other departments. You can change this perception by creating frequent opportunities to "market" your strategic services and communicating success stories.

In this age of communication, there are virtually unlimited tools available to exchange information. In fact, there are so many avenues for information delivery, buyers often complain of information overload. To avoid inflicting numbing overcommunication on your customers, you will want to select the most effective channels for gathering and disseminating information and use only those most appropriate to individual situations. Here are some of the more common methods.

(ii) Customer Surveys.   The customer survey is one method commonly used for gathering information. Properly employed, the survey can focus input on specific issues and root out problems before they interfere with operations. The survey can also gather opinions and assess the perceptions customers have regarding departmental performance and effectiveness.

TIPS AND TECHNIQUES

LEVERAGING AN EFFECTIVE SURVEY

A national biotech company used several dozen travel agents in the 20 states where it had either a sales office or manufacturing operation. Because the company utilized so many travel agents, the level of service it experienced was relatively low, while the cost of service was high. Some of the travel agencies even proposed a consolidation, offering lower prices. To ensure that the company used the best travel services and agents, its Procurement Department polled all end users of travel services via a survey that the Procurement Department developed and distributed. The results of the survey showed which of the many travel agency service providers met the expectations of the internal end users and which service providers did not. The survey input enabled the Procurement Department to eliminate the nonperforming suppliers much more objectively because the decision was based on the input of the end-user customer. At the same time, additional business was moved to the service providers that met the expectations of the end user. The result: greater user satisfaction, improved supplier performance, and less procurement management (and fewer travel agents).

(iii) One-on-One Meetings.   Individual meetings with your key customers can provide an opportunity to exchange information and ideas in a private setting. Personal conversations are often very productive simply because, by the nature of their privacy, they encourage collaboration and an open exchange of opinion.

Although these meetings tend to be somewhat informal, it is always a good idea to prepare an agenda in advance so you and your customer can stay organized and both of you can come away with a sense of having accomplished a meaningful dialogue.

(iv) Team Meetings.   Held periodically, team meetings can be an excellent venue for communication. One of the greatest advantages is that you are able to pass along exactly the same information to all members of the team. You will also benefit from the interchange of ideas that typically occurs in a team environment, and you will find it an opportunity for gaining consensus in reaching decisions.

(v) Newsletters and Web Sites.   Newsletters and information posted on a Procurement Department Web site, while certainly less personal than face-to-face meetings, can offer the advantage of reaching large numbers of readers with relatively minimal effort. When used regularly to convey relatively important information rather than minutiae, these tools can provide a focal point for dispensing up-to-date information. Keep in mind, however, that typically these tools provide only one-way communication and are not often effective substitutes for the interaction that goes along with face-to-face interaction.

(b) GAINING EARLY INVOLVEMENT.   Early involvement by the Procurement Department in sourcing and new product introduction activities benefits the organization in several ways. Involving the Procurement Department in the initial stages of supplier contact enables the organization to leverage cost reduction and supplier management efforts at a time when they can be best influenced. Then, as the buying organization gains a clearer understanding of the product needs and cost restraints, sourcing strategies and negotiating tactical plans can be more highly focused on achieving the customers' goals rather than simply reacting to compliance issues. With the procurement team focusing on the business requirements, the technical team's time and energy is available to pursue optimal solutions.

From the supplier's perspective, early involvement by the Procurement Department enables a smoother transition from the development phase to the operational working environment. When the Procurement professional explores terms and conditions early in the process, he can resolve potential contracting obstacles prior to their becoming "deal-breaking" roadblocks. By establishing solid relationships early, the Procurement professional also clears the way for more collaborative negotiations with suppliers since both parties will have a better understanding of one another's needs and a greater opportunity to produce mutually beneficial results.

Strategic leverage increases with early involvement in the procurement process. As suppliers gain certainty that their company will receive the order, the incentive for creative solutions tends to diminish. You might want to use the following table as a guide because it outlines the specific development stage (in the left column) and the areas readily influenced through the Procurement Department's active role in the process at that stage (in the right column). See Table 10.1.

STAGE	AREAS OF INFLUENCE
PRODUCT CONCEPTION	
	Commodity strategy
	Alternative materials
	Supplier investment
	Comarketing development
PRODUCT DESIGN	
	Sourcing strategy
	Total cost of ownership
	Quality requirements
	Partnerships and alliances
PRODUCT ENGINEERING	
	Supplier qualification
	Make-or-buy decisions
	Value analysis
	Negotiation of cost-based pricing
PRODUCTION PLANNING	
	Negotiation of availability
	Schedule creation
INTRODUCTION	
	Negotiation of volume-based pricing
	Negotiation of schedule allocations
	Schedule influence

TABLE 10.1 INFLUENCE AT STAGES OF INVOLVEMENT

10.3 PARTICIPATING IN CROSS-FUNCTIONAL OPERATIONS

A cross-functional team is composed of representatives from various segments of the organization with complementary skill sets and perspectives. In most organizations, the cross-functional team shares a common goal, and its members are equally accountable for the team's results. Typically, projects related to strategic sourcing activities and the ongoing management of critical suppliers is where you will most likely participate and where your input can be most valuable. In many cases, you will even find yourself leading these teams, so it is important you understand the role you bring to the team and where you can be expected to add value.

In the section that follows, we will review the various roles and responsibilities of the Procurement Department in cross-functional team participation and how you can be most effective in helping to build successful teams.

(a) SUPPLY MANAGEMENT ROLES AND RESPONSIBILITIES.   The Procurement Department works with a number of typical operational and development teams where specific supply management expertise is useful. The most common of these teams include:

(i) New Product Development.   As we discussed earlier in the chapter (in the Engineering and Design Functions section), procurement departments have an important role in new product development teams to provide sourcing and supplier management assistance.

(ii) Sourcing and New Supplier Development.   Closely related to developing and introducing new products is the development of new suppliers. Typically, procurement departments will take a leading role in this business process, sourcing and helping to qualify potential new suppliers.

(iii) Cost Reduction.   Specific products or service lines may require reduced cost to effectively compete with others in the marketplace. Cross-functional teams review all aspects of internal and supplier-related costs with an objective of reducing the purchase price. Often, teams will adopt the value analysis methodology by looking at all the parts that are used in a particular product with the objective of reducing cost without impairing functionality.

(iv) Cycle Time Reduction.   The cycle time for ordering and receiving purchased parts and service can often become the gating factor in delivering to the end customer. Organizations have come to realize that there are trade-offs of value to simply achieving the lowest possible price, and you will frequently find yourself discussing the need for cycle time reduction with your suppliers.

(v) Budget.   Input from the Procurement Department on budget teams focuses on pricing trends and expected pricing in the future. Often, the Procurement Department will be asked to forecast prices for areas of major commodity or category spending.

(vi) Capital Equipment.   The procurement group is often asked to participate in the selection of capital asset equipment as the business lead in negotiating price and delivery terms.

(vii) Information Technology.   Procurement departments take part in IT sourcing activities, both as a using group and as the buyer. As organizational computer and telecommunications systems become more fully integrated and more resources are dedicated to them, Procurement spends increasingly more time working with this group.

(viii) Quality Assurance.   Since the quality of your own product or service is often largely dependent upon the quality of purchased goods and services, the Procurement Department will be asked to assume an important role in ensuring the specified quality requirements are met by suppliers.

(ix) Evaluating Teams.   Under what conditions will a cross-functional team likely produce value? This, of course, is a topic for organizational design debate. However, there are circumstances that are generally recognized as favoring the use of a team and others that tend to reduce its benefits. From a procurement perspective, you should be able to distinguish those desired outcomes that will benefit from team involvement and those that will be hindered. Here are just a few aspects you should consider:

- **Speed.** Overall, cross-functional teams tend to reduce the time it takes to reach objectives, especially in the product development process, where ongoing coordination between functional elements can be critical. Speed is a critical factor in product and system development, and cross-functional teams allow many parts of the development process to take place concurrently.
- **Degree of change.** Massive degrees of change generally require a great deal of communication, and teams can become excellent tools for introducing and communicating change throughout the organization. By jointly developing a plan for communication and through joint crafting of the messages, teams can help ensure that the rest of the organization is in sync with the overall objectives of the change.
- **Organizational culture.** To a large degree, organizational culture determines the effectiveness of team outcomes. In cultures where teams actually manage processes and have the decision-making authority, team outputs are extremely effective. In cultures where tradition prevails, the teams may need to develop additional management buy-in for its recommendations, thus slowing the process considerably.
- **Decision making.** It has been shown that collectively teams make better decisions and produce more effective outcomes than any of their individual members, substantiating the adage that "two heads are better than one." However, teams can often take a lot more time debating issues prior to reaching a decision than an individual would take to reach a decision alone.
- **Leveraged expertise.** In a team environment, individual members gain the benefit of having subject matter experts to rely upon for technical information. This often reduces the time it takes to understand a specific problem. However, there is a downside: Frequently, individuals feel that the circumstances in their organizations are unique and substantially different from others in the industry. This thinking tends to restrict the options available to the team and often generates friction. Procurement professionals often refer

to this as the NIH syndrome—not invented here—to describe the reluctance of some to use new ideas.

- **Consensus building.** Consensus generally means that everyone on the team agrees to support an action or decision, even if some of them are not in full agreement. Consensus contrasts with voting where the majority rules. To the extent that teams are responsible for making strategic and operational decisions, consensus building has an important function because individual members of the team are required to provide public support for its decision. If the disagreement is strong, members will not be inclined to provide the needed effort and consensus will not be achieved.

- **Complacency.** Teams, especially those of long standing, have a tendency toward entropy and can become complacent. Generally, one finds that goals are not updated and perhaps are no longer as valid as they were in the past. Under these circumstances, it is difficult for meaningful action to take place, and the individual members of the team become demotivated. This is one of the major pitfalls of the team process and seems to suggest that teams should be project oriented with a clearly established time for disbanding.

(x) Developing Effective Teams. There is a tendency for teams to develop within a specific growth pattern, similar to that often referred to in organizational development literature as the four phases: forming, storming, norming, and performing. Table 10.2 provides examples of these phases and what you might expect to encounter in each of them.

STAGE	DEVELOPMENT STEPS
Initial team organization	The team is chartered and formed. Team members learn about the project and one another.
Defining needs and goals	The team establishes goals and objectives consistent with its assignment. The team develops a preliminary time line for completion.
Developing solutions and action plans	The team develops and refines potential solutions and builds consensus for one of the alternatives.
Achieving objectives	The team implements its plan, measures progress, adjusts actions to meet situation, and celebrates success.

TABLE 10.2 TYPICAL STAGES OF TEAM DEVELOPMENT

Team effectiveness depends upon the establishing measurable goals early and developing a timeline with milestones for their achievement. These measurements work best if they parallel the team's expected deliverables. For example, if the team was established to develop cost savings, you would want to identify and measure:

- Anticipated cost savings.
- Method of measuring cost savings.
- Timeline for producing cost savings.
- Milestones.
- Duration of the project or completion criteria.

10.4 REENGINEERING SUPPLY MANAGEMENT

As part of your duties, you will likely be called upon occasionally to lead or participate in formulating new procedures or revising existing ones. As organizational policy changes to meet changing economic or regulatory conditions, elements within the organization, such as supply management, also require realignment. Change also sometimes develops from newly available technology that offers greater efficiency or from new processes rolled out organizationally.

Dealing with change is a necessary skill that must be learned and continually employed as part of our professional lives. In procurement departments, change has an even more profound effect on others, and you must also learn to continually consider how to assist internal customers as well as suppliers through these changes. This section reviews the scope of operations in most procurement departments so that you can more clearly understand the functions that you will be responsible for improving. This section also discusses how change is best managed throughout the organization and supply base.

(a) UNDERSTANDING THE SCOPE OF OPERATIONS.   When you consider the overall scope of procurement and procurement operations, you can easily understand how it touches virtually every function within the organization. For the purpose of providing some reference points and as an aid to understanding how typical procurement activities usually relate to one another, we've provided the following listing, which contains most of the common roles and responsibilities carried out in procurement departments. Notice that they are grouped into three main categories: procurement, materials management, and other supporting roles.

(i) Procurement.   The procurement function manages the acquisition of goods and services, conducting a broad range of functional services that are used by all departments in the organization, as shown in Table 10.3.

(ii) Materials Management.   The materials management function is responsible for the planning of supply requirements and the internal handling of purchased materials, as shown in Table 10.4.

(iii) Other Supporting Roles.   The Procurement Department indirectly supports a variety of activities within the organization. They are shown in Table 10.5.

COMMODITY EXPERTISE

> Industry analysis
> Market analysis
> Commodity analysis
> Benchmarking
> Forecasting

SOURCING

> Locating potential suppliers
> Supplier prequalification
> RFx preparation and response analysis
> Evaluation of supplier capabilities
> Competitive bidding
> Supplier selection leadership

CONTRACTING

> Contract formation
> Negotiation of terms and conditions
> Management and administration of contract
>   compliance
> Termination

SUPPLIER DEVELOPMENT AND MANAGEMENT

> Conducting performance reviews
> Implementing continuous improvement
>   programs
> Developing cost reductions
> Auditing

RISK MANAGEMENT

> Risk assessment and evaluation
> Risk mitigation
> Ensuring supply
> Supplier ratings and approved supplier list
> Regulatory compliance

LICENSING

> Protection of intellectual property rights
> Licensing compliance

QUALITY MANAGEMENT

> Supplier qualification
> Quality assessments
> Quality improvement programs

TRANSACTIONAL PROCESSING

> Issuing purchase orders
> Expediting supplier shipments
> Returned goods documentation
> ERP and systems implementation
> Procurement card management
> E-procurement solutions

TABLE 10.3   PROCUREMENT FUNCTIONAL SERVICES

LOGISTICS/SUPPLY CHAIN MANAGEMENT

> Transportation and customs management
> Receiving
> Packaging
> Physical distribution of finished goods
> Internal movement of materials

PLANNING

> Production planning and master scheduling
> MRP management
> Capacity planning
> Forecasting
> Just-in-time manufacturing

INVENTORY MANAGEMENT

> Warehousing and stores operations
> Part master maintenance
> ABC inventory control
> Economic ordering quantity analysis

SURPLUS DISPOSAL

> Hazardous materials handling
> Scrap sales
> End-of-life product sales
> Surplus equipment sales

TABLE 10.4 MATERIALS MANAGEMENT FUNCTION

PROJECT MANAGEMENT

> New product introduction projects
> Information technology and systems projects
> Manufacturing/services improvement programs
> Plant engineering and relocation projects
> Policy and procedure revisions
> Audit preparation
> Value analysis

FINANCE AND BUDGET

> Cost center maintenance
> Pricing forecasts for budgets
> Spending analysis
> Cost analysis
> Accounts payable support
> Return on Investment analysis

TABLE 10.5 OTHER SUPPORTING ROLES

(b) MANAGING THE CHANGE PROCESS. Charles Darwin, the nineteenth-century British evolutionist, is perhaps the preeminent student of change and one of the first to explore the way in which change affects our lives. "It is not the strongest species that survive," he wrote, "nor the most intelligent, but the ones who are most responsive to change."

In order to improve organizational effectiveness, especially when responding to dynamic changes in the business environment, you must learn to master change. Despite its seeming randomness, change must be managed so that you can implement new methods. To a large extent, this means developing clear plans for structuring changes and communicating them to those within the organization who will be affected. People are generally resistant to change unless they fully understand it, and even then only accept it with some trepidation. Unless you can manage change in measured increments, you run the risk of overwhelming them.

There are several factors that influence the effectiveness of change that you should take into consideration:

- The impetus for significant change needs to come from senior management or it gains little support.
- Your agenda for change must be shared by everyone, and you need to have a mutual vision of how the change will provide benefits to the entire organization.
- You need to have access to the resources—time, money, staff, and expertise—to implement the changes smoothly.
- Plan ahead, define each step, check before acting, and communicate so that there are no surprises; absorb feedback and make allowances to correct mistakes as required.
- Whenever possible, introduce change at the prototype level first, testing to see if it will work as expected and making any needed changes before going forward. Choose opportunities for learning rather than just attempting to prove the concept through a successful first test. Mistakes are opportunities for learning.
- It is important to deal with emerging issues as soon as possible so that dissatisfaction and frustration do not take root.
- Provide continual feedback to your team on progress—both success and failures.
- To the extent possible, avoid micromanagement. Overstructuring finite details can be disenfranchising to team members and will only serve to slow the process by reducing initiative.
- Remember that if change moves too quickly, you may end up leaving a good many employees confused and in the dark as to what is expected of them. It is probably best to include in your plan a segment of time for feedback and questions as a way of ensuring you are moving ahead smoothly.

In your procurement role, you will most likely encounter the need for change that results from new or redefined Procurement Department roles and from changes in organization policy required by legislation such as that recently encountered through the Sarbanes-Oxley Act.

(i) Redefining the Role of Procurement.   As transactional processing methods improve efficiency, fewer procurement employees are being assigned to routine buyer duties. More and more, organizations are coming to rely on their procurement departments to drive profitability improvement programs that translate to increased shareholder value and introducing innovation.

(ii) Forming and Communicating Organizational Policy.   Organizational policy needs to receive periodic reviews to ensure that it reflects up-to-date thinking. This is especially true for procurement activities, which must adapt to continually changing legislation and regulatory requirements, as well as industry standards such as ISO. Ethical conduct has recently come under serious scrutiny in the business sector, and many organizations—especially those publicly held—are struggling to revise policy to conform to new criteria. Recently, the Institute for Supply Management published a set of guidelines called "Principles of Social Responsibility" to provide guidance on what constitutes socially responsible conduct. (You can find an outline of the program at the Institute of Supply Management's Web site: www.ism.ws.) Since its intention is to include this criteria in supplier selection and qualification audits, this will likely result in a flurry of new internal policies to ensure compliance.

(c) PROCUREMENT POLICY AND PROCEDURES TRAINING.   Internal organizational procurement policy and procedures are often complex and not readily accessible, so they need to be supplemented with training and extended communication activities. Fostering a better understanding of the requirements and benefits of compliance with these policies will greatly assist you in carrying out the organization's procurement strategy and objectives. Directing this task falls naturally in the hands of the Procurement professional.

Meeting external regulations for public corporations has become a real issue with the passage of the Sarbanes-Oxley Act (SOX). Policies and procedures must be documented. SOX requires that key financial and accounting processes must be clearly stated and presented. In addition, all financial software applications must be documented.

(i) Formulating Training Needs.   Internal procurement training requirements address two main areas, each with a somewhat distinct focus:

1. **Procurement Department standard operating procedures (SOPs).** SOPs address the "how to" of procurement, defining the specific tasks

required to perform any given operation. Examples of typical procurement procedures include how to qualify a supplier for inclusion on the approved supplier list or how to add a new supplier to the database. Training is typically required when new procedures are implemented and when existing procedures are revised. It is also important to have a structured training program to initiate new employees into the Procurement Department to reduce the risk of costly mistakes.

Additionally, SOX requires organizations to standardize and update their procedures to ensure SOX documentation compliance. As a result, many organizations are discovering that their procedures are either incomplete, outdated, or do not adequately conform to regulatory requirements. It is clear that much training will be needed to ensure compliance with regulatory requirements as broad based as this.

2. **Organizational policy regarding procurement**. Most organizations have policies regarding who can purchase materials and services and who can approve purchases and their limit of authority. Policies also typically specify who can obligate the organization to contractual relationships in the course of business activities. In addition, many organizations specify codes of ethical conduct for dealing with suppliers and for maintaining internal confidentiality.

While much of this policy may be strictly common sense, it is, nevertheless, prudent to ensure compliance through some method of organized training.

(ii) Developing Training Materials. The format for training materials is generally determined by how the materials are intended to be used. Procedural and policy materials are often developed for classroom training or on-the-job training since this type of material often requires detailed explanation and coaching. Technical materials are often developed in manuals and used primarily for reference as needed. You will find that there are occasions when both systems will be useful.

(iii) Delivering the Training. How the training is delivered is often as important as the content of the training itself. Some training is best handled in a classroom environment, while other training can be delivered through **computer-based training (CBT)** or other methods of self-directed study. Sometimes it is more effective to develop combinations of training types such as instructor-led, Web-based training (known as **blended learning**) or classroom training followed by on-the-job coaching.

It is widely accepted, however, that formal training should be provided only "as needed" to reinforce a specific skill requirement at the time of implementation. Skills are most effectively learned when they are introduced where there is some previous context on which to base their value. Thus the focus of training should be developmental rather than purely remedial and should be presented in that context.

10.5 SUMMARY

Successful interaction with other departments within the organization should be a key element in the Procurement Department's strategy. To accomplish this, you will need to develop a thorough understanding of the roles and duties of your internal customers and process partners. While no two organizations have exactly the same structure, most can be organized according to broad operational categories: administration, production (or service), sales and marketing, and engineering and design.

Your effectiveness within the organization will depend, to a large extent, on how well you can develop strong working relationships. Developing relationships with other departments (and employees) requires that you employ sound communication and trust-building techniques. Using appropriate channels and tools effectively is also an important element in this process. By building trust you will be able to gain early involvement in the sourcing and contracting processes, which will further enable you to contribute effectively in your organizational role.

Procurement departments typically participate in or lead cross-functional teams in most areas of the organizations, so you will be required to understand your role and responsibilities as a member of these teams. You will also need to know how these teams are formed, how the team process is carried out, and what the requirements are for effective team management. In order to improve operations and better meet organizational expectations, you should completely understand the scope of operations in the Procurement Department and the major functions that go along with it. This will assist you in managing the change process, helping to formulate policy and procedures, and providing communication and training to your staff and other departments within the organization.

KEY TERMS

Senior management
Finance, Accounting and Treasury
Legal Department
Facilities
Human Resources (HR)
Information Technology (IT)
Logistics
Production

Planning
Manufacturing Maintenance
Product/business development
Research and Development (R&D)
New product introduction (NPI)
Standard operating procedures (SOPs)
Computer-based training (CBT)
Blended learning

CHAPTER 11

SUPPLIER RELATIONSHIP MANAGEMENT

LEARNING OBJECTIVES

1. List steps to take to manage productive supplier relationships.

2. Explain what is meant by "certifying suppliers" and describe the difference between certification and qualification.

3. Define the "standard markup model" and create an example using a hypothetical supplier's bid.
4. Name five rules for conducting successful meetings.

No progressive organization can operate in a vacuum. The Procurement professional is uniquely positioned for adding strategic value to the organization by finding business opportunities to build strong relationships with other organizations in the supply chain, leveraging their innovation to seed fresh ideas and business processes. These supply relationships foster new learning that helps develop improved methods and generate new business opportunities.

In the multifaceted business climate of today, information gained from supply chain partners is often the key to competitive success. Consequently, managing supplier relationships is one of the most important functions performed by the Procurement Department. It requires strategy, skill, and patience; it is a complex process that demands comprehensive attention in order to prove successful. And, most importantly, it has to be learned and practiced.

This chapter reviews several key aspects to managing supplier relationships. To begin with, we examine the steps you can take to develop the groundwork for more productive strategic supply relationships. Then, we review the more common day-to-day tactical activities of a Procurement Department in its interface with the supplier community and how you can make these activities more meaningful. Finally, we look at how you can effectively represent your organization through interaction with external supply groups.

11.1 MANAGING PRODUCTIVE SUPPLIER RELATIONSHIPS

Productive supplier relationships do not just happen: As with any relationship of value, they demand effort and perseverance. In your role as Procurement professional, there are a number of disciplines you will have to master in order to better encourage strong supply relations. In this section, we review the more commonly used processes that enable and improve relations with your suppliers.

(a) CREATING GOOD WORKING RELATIONS. You create good working relations with your suppliers through fair and consistent treatment, enhanced by the judicious use of communication tools and by holding regular meetings. The benefits of building solid relationships can be enormous. When your working relationship is strong, suppliers are more likely to cooperate with you by moving up lead times when a product or service is needed immediately or by taking a return of product for your convenience. A close, collaborative relationship also makes it easier to negotiate terms and prices with your suppliers and helps avoid disputes since your organization's business will be highly regarded.

The following sections outline some of the more common ways to enhance working relationships:

(i) Meeting with Suppliers Regularly. You will want to arrange meetings with your key suppliers on a regular basis. Often, these meetings will take the form of a formal supplier review or an executive conference. Such meetings provide the opportunity for the management of both organizations to get together to exchange technology or business development road maps so that strategic relationships can be better aligned and leveraged. At other times, you may want to meet less formally to review your immediate plans and ways that the supplier can provide support. Sometimes, you may be able to help the supplier resolve an internal problem that your organization has already solved.

While it is impossible to meet regularly with all of your suppliers, there are a number of other ways you can maintain regular contact:

1. **Supplier surveys.** Periodic surveys of suppliers can provide information on how effective your organization has been in developing them as a resource. They can also help identify problem areas that are generating additional cost to your organization. Sometimes, it is just good business practice to be open and listen to how suppliers view you as a customer.

2. **Improvement teams.** Regardless of the criticality of their role in supplying your organization, with good working supplier relationships you provide an extra incentive for suppliers to participate in cost reduction projects and to work on multifunctional teams to help improve overall operations, keeping in mind that your best suppliers do not have a monopoly on good ideas. Inviting a talented supplier representative to participate in an improvement project, even if it does not directly relate to the product or service supplied, makes good business sense since it is another way to leverage the talent within your supply base.

3. **Reciprocal visits.** You should visit the supplier's facility as often as possible. By putting a face to a name, you will be inviting the supplier's personnel to connect with your organization and create a common bond. Visits will also enable you to become more familiar with how the supplier's operation works so that you can better leverage its capabilities and strengths, as well as understanding its limitations.

Holding a supplier open house—Supplier Day, as it is sometimes called—will introduce the supplier's team to your organization and enable them to see first hand how their products or services are employed. This can be an extremely powerful tool for personalizing your organization's needs, thus strengthening the bonds between you.

(ii) Improving Communication. Interorganizational communications are most effective when they are bidirectional and when they involve all levels of personnel. Effective communication can produce remarkable results. For example, forecasts of trends affecting your organization, even generalized ones, can reduce cycle time by

preparing your suppliers to respond more rapidly to anticipated needs. To the extent that information such as this can be collaboratively shared, you will find that fill rates improve and that service levels rise. Information that provides a window into your operations can also be reassuring to supplier sales teams. Knowing which of your product lines are moving quickly, what products you intend to discontinue, and what new products you intend to introduce can be valuable intelligence to the supplier's sales organization, especially when it correlates with information from other sources.

You will also want to tap your suppliers as resources for trend information that will assist your internal customers by helping to determine the best time to place their orders. Often, sales departments have better access to market information that can be valuable assets when properly used.

There are a number of other ways your department can work with suppliers to better leverage information and improve communication. Here are just a few of the more commonly used methods:

- **Web site.** Information about your company and your procurement team can be posted on a public Web site. Some organizations actually establish a supplier section where information of special interest to suppliers— Invitations to Bid, for example—can be distributed. Visit the HP Web site at http://h30173.www3.hp.com if you would like to see a good model of one.
- **Focus groups.** The **focus group** is a useful method for gaining supplier feedback. Typically set in a somewhat structured environment led by a professional facilitator and consisting of between 9 and 12 individuals, the group is brought together to examine a specific subject and share opinions. It can be a particularly effectively way to test new ideas and gain feedback prior to implementation.
- **Newsletter.** A newsletter can be used to address the supply community specifically with information that will help them better understand what is happening inside your organization. Using word processing software makes it relatively easy to publish a newsletter at your desk, and it can be quite effectively distributed at no cost through e-mail.

(iii) Reverse Marketing.   Michiel R. Leenders and David L. Blenkhorn[1] identified the concept of **reverse marketing** by pointing out that the traditional relationship where the seller takes the lead by seeking out the buyer is being replaced in many instances by one where the buyer actively searches for suppliers to fill a specific need. This practice occurs when there are few or no suppliers available, and you will have to employ some aggressive recruiting and persuasion in order to develop a source to meet your organization's needs. Reverse marketing generally sees the buyer making the offer, even to the point of suggesting the selling price.

---

1.   Leenders, Michiel R., and David L. Blenkhorn. *Reverse Marketing: The New Buyer-Supplier Relationship*. New York: Free Press, 1987.

(b) RESOLVING RELATIONS ISSUES. Reinforcing good business relationships with your supplier takes some measure of attention to detail and effort as there are numerous daily activities that, when not well performed, can lead to disputes and concerns. Normally, these issues are relatively minor and part of the normal course of business; however, when failure to perform routine supplier support activities becomes the rule rather than the exception, you will run the risk of having them result in diminished performance levels.

While it is difficult to generalize the kinds of problems you may encounter, here are some of those that have been frequently mentioned in procurement literature:

(i) Paying Invoices on Time. Cash flow is important to every business enterprise, and the finance team at your supplier will continually monitor and rate your account on how timely the payments are made by your organization. Accounts that are continually past due present a problem. If you consider that money has a time value, the longer it takes to collect the payment, the lower will be the actual profit. As a result, late payments actually cut into the supplier's operating margin. While an occasional late payment can be overlooked, a pattern of late payments may require the supplier to raise its prices in compensation.

An associated issue related to late payments is the handling of invoices. It's extremely frustrating for the supplier's Accounts Receivable staff to find an overdue payment and discover that the buying organization has no record of ever receiving it. No matter how you look at it, this will require significant duplication of effort to correct. To reduce lost invoices, be sure suppliers have the correct address for submitting them to your organization and, if needed, have the suppliers include an individual's name or a mail stop in the address.

TIPS AND TECHNIQUES

Organizations can maintain effective alignment with their suppliers by exchanging *aging* reports. The supplier's aging report shows when the invoice was submitted and how many days old it is, while the buyer's shows how long the invoice has been received and when payment will be made based on the existing terms. In this way, each party can proactively identify problem payments before they get out of hand.

(ii) Maintaining Confidentiality. Any information given to you by the supplier should always be considered confidential and never disclosed to third parties outside your organization. Most of the time, buyers and sellers exchange confidentiality agreements or nondisclosure agreements early in their relationship that requires both to maintain certain levels of confidentiality. Regardless of the existence of such legal documents, it is of the utmost ethical importance that information given to you in confidence never be shared with your suppliers' competitors.

(iii) Dealing Fairly and Equally with Suppliers. To maintain credibility requires that you treat all suppliers fairly and consistently, avoiding the perception that you

favor one over the others. If your organization maintains a system of priorities based on the level of supplier qualification or certification, you will be obliged to follow it. However, you should continually encourage suppliers to work toward the preferred status, offering help and guidance as needed.

Many organizations develop close partnerships with some of their suppliers, including joint ventures and similar programs. Be sure to disclose this information to suppliers who are new to doing business with you so that they do not waste effort in focusing on areas that will likely yield no results.

TIPS AND TECHNIQUES

> Trust is a key element in relations with your suppliers. One way to establish and continue to maintain trust is by always keeping your word.

(iv) Avoiding Illegal Situations.   On the opposite end of the spectrum, there are many actions that may superficially appear to be solidifying relationships, but that may bring up issues with restraint of trade. Providing preferred treatment to suppliers who also buy your products can be one of them. While it is legal, and often preferable, to buy from one's suppliers, trading purchase for purchase can be seen as a tying contract, which is illegal. So long as price, quality, delivery, and the other fundamentals of supplier selection override decisions of personal preference, you will likely be viewed as exercising sound ethical judgment.

(c) CERTIFYING NEW SUPPLIERS.   Every organization has its own method for certifying suppliers. Some are general and based on conformance with specific qualifications, such as being ISO certified. Some require certification by a third-party examiner. Others are more specific to the needs of your particular organization such as ISO/TS 16949, which is an international quality management system standard for manufacturers of automotive parts. Perhaps you require a specific environmental policy or conformance to specific rules of social responsibility in order for your suppliers to reach certified status. You may find that some of these requirements are readily achievable while others may be established only by your own organization. In this case, you may need to develop a program for communicating your requirements and assisting the supplier in achieving them.

TIPS AND TECHNIQUES

> Certification should not be confused with qualification. Supplier qualification is a process used to determine if a particular supplier is capable of handling a specific job. Certification means that the supplier has met certain criteria and levels of performance—often determined through field audits—that enable it to be considered by your organization as an ongoing applicant for business.

(i) Mentoring.   **Mentoring** is a form of teaching and guidance that assists individuals and organizations to reach a certain level of performance. Often, mentoring is an educational process where the mentor serves as a role model or teacher, providing opportunities for growth to less experienced organizations. It is based on encouragement, constructive comments, openness, mutual trust, respect, and a willingness to learn and share.

Often, an established organization will assist a newly developing one through this kind of mentorship, but for the process to work well, there has to be some mutual benefit. In some cases, the benefits can be an additional source of supply that makes an otherwise closely held industry more competitive. At other times, it can be the means to support small, minority businesses to ensure that they get a fair share of your business.

11.2 DEVELOPING CONTINUOUS IMPROVEMENT

Continuous improvement as a quality concept was discussed in Chapter 8 in relation to the buyer's responsibility in managing suppliers. In this section, we look at it a bit further from the aspect of obtaining alignment with supplier activities.

(a) GAINING EARLY SUPPLIER INVOLVEMENT.   Early supplier involvement in new product design can beneficially influence both cost and cycle time by leveraging the supplier's process strengths and relying on the expertise of its staff to enable optimal solutions. Often, it makes sense to involve multiple tiers of supplier so that you can assure alignment of processes within the immediate supply chain. This is best accomplished through cross-functional, multiorganizational teams that search out the methods and processes that best leverage all of their strengths.

(i) Working Collaboratively.   Supplier involvement in your organization's operations will generally focus on areas of mutual goals. Activities can range from the typical unilateral problem solving to participation in activities that reach far into your organization. The benefit of this close collaboration is that both organizations are able to leverage their individual strengths toward the development of a single process that divides the workload and responsibilities accordingly. Real gains, however, occur when technology and expertise pass freely among partners so that knowledge is shared as it is jointly developed, providing a competitive advantage to the entire supply chain. From this effort, products that are brought to the marketplace are likely to add more value and, because they are not easily copied, offer greater sustainability.

(ii) Forming Partnerships and Alliances.   Partnerships and business alliances are generally formed to fill specific needs, such as the joint development of a new product or service that would fall outside the capabilities of each of the participants if they were to attempt to go forward alone. This need is generally defined through

some specific market research or opportunity analysis, following a formal path of internal examinations and recommendations by management. Typically, a business case is prepared prior to approval, outlining the strategic benefits and potential threats.

For the supplier's contribution, the alliance generally requires an additional investment in equipment or staff. The buyer's contribution usually comes in the form of an exclusive contract to buy certain volumes of specific items. When the alliance involves joint development, cross-organizational, cross-functional teams are generally formed, bringing the two organizations' strategic objectives into alignment.

It is typical for organizations engaged in partnerships or alliances to form contracts governing roles and responsibilities, as well as the accrual of benefits. Successful partnerships are based on the full involvement of each of the partners, so it is important to develop clear measurements for how effectively each partner is meeting its commitments.

(iii) Maintaining Partnerships and Alliances.   To maintain the relationships, there must be continuing benefit to both parties. Successful long-term partnerships generally have high management visibility and support, so resources continue to be made available as long as there is a clear willingness by the working teams to continue to engage.

(iv) Strengthening Supplier Relations.   There is no general rule for strengthening supplier relationships: Many of the processes outlined earlier that are used to form the initial relationship can continue to be used to strengthen it. However, please keep in mind that it is the Procurement Department's responsibility—your responsibility—to develop and maintain valuable working relationships with suppliers.

Experience shows that one of the most important ingredients in strong relationships is trust. Trust is a characteristic and quality that typically develops when there is open and honest communication between parties, and when both respect the behaviors of one another. Fundamental to this is keeping one's word and honoring all of your commitments.

(b) IMPLEMENTING SMALL/DISADVANTAGED BUSINESS PROGRAMS.   In order to have an effective corporate supplier diversity development program, both commitment and involvement from senior management is usually required. The major goal of developing a supplier diversity program is to provide all potential suppliers equal access to procurement opportunities generated by your organization.

A written supplier diversity development policy is used to formalize the goals and objectives of the program. By formalizing the program with senior management support, you can generally ensure the dedication and support of the

Procurement staff. In order to meet the formalization of the process, a comprehensive buyer training and accountability road map must be developed. This accountability road map must include tracking and reporting systems that show the results of awarding procurement business to small and disadvantaged suppliers. To ensure success, effective communication of the program objectives needs to be developed to internal customers, existing suppliers, and potential suppliers.

TIPS AND TECHNIQUES

MINORITY BUSINESS DEFINED

The National Minority Supplier Development Council defines a minority-owned business as a for-profit enterprise, regardless of size, physically located in the United States or its trust territories, which is owned, operated, and controlled by minority group members. "Minority group members" are United States citizens who are Asian, Black, Hispanic, and Native American. Ownership by minority individuals means the business is at least 51 percent owned by such individuals or, in the case of a publicly owned business, at least 51 percent of the stock is owned by one or more such individuals. Further, the management and daily operations are controlled by those minority group members. See www.nmsdcus.org.

(i) Locating Qualified Minority Suppliers.   Effective identification and sourcing from minority suppliers is paramount to long-term success. There are many minority supplier directories that can assist in this effort. Attendance at small business and minority and female-owned trade shows is also effective in identifying such suppliers. Various industry contacts can also serve as informational networking in locating qualified minority suppliers within various commodities.

The following URLs can assist in sourcing of minority suppliers:

- Diversity Information Resources, Inc.: www.DiversityInfoResources.com
- DiversityBusiness.com: www.div2000.com
- DiversityInc.com: www.diversityinc.com
- Dynamic Small Business Search: http://dsbs.sba.gov/dsbs/dsp_dsbs.cfm
- Industry Council for Small Business Development: www.icsbd.org
- Minority Business Development Agency: www.mbda.gov
- Minority Business Entrepreneur Magazine: www.mbemag.com
- Minority Business News: www.minoritybusinessnews.com
- National Minority Business Council Inc.: www.nmbc.org
- National Minority Supplier Development Council Inc.: www.nmsdcus.org
- Women's Business Enterprise National Council: www.wbenc.org

(ii) Developing and Managing Programs.   Making small business and minority suppliers known within your organization is core to the development of any comprehensive procurement diversity program. The identification of the potential suppliers' capabilities is the domain of any procurement policy and supplier

development strategy. To be truly effective, such information must be effectively communicated to the entire organization.

In order to determine if your supplier diversity development strategy is effective, a measurement and reporting system must be established to monitor results in a timely fashion. Many corporations use such reporting systems to establish various types of rewards and recognition programs for outstanding results for diversity suppliers and procurement commodity groups alike.

11.3 PRICING FACTORS AND SUPPLY

The basics of supplier selection based on pricing were initially discussed in Chapters 2, 3, and 7. In this section, however, we will round out those discussions by reviewing some of the factors that govern the actual pricing you will encounter.

(a) UNDERSTANDING MARKET CONDITIONS.   While strong relationships, as well as negotiation skill, have an important role in determining the prices your organization will be asked to pay for any particular product or service, **market conditions** at the time will also play a major role. Market conditions consist of a number of factors such as supply and demand, the overall economic climate, production capacity, competition, and numerous other elements that affect even the psychology of buyers and sellers. Since pricing is often a measure of your ability to manage the supply base, let's look more closely at some of the elements that affect your ability to control pricing from your suppliers.

(i) Supply and Demand.   You will recall in Chapter 6 we examined the role of market forces through supply and demand and stated that the imbalance of one in relation to the other directly affects pricing. "The ratio of supply to demand always affects prices. When supply is more plentiful than demand, suppliers must lower prices to make buying more attractive; when demand outstrips supply, buyers compete for the few available resources and prices rise." This is a fairly timeless concept.

However, there are times when an increase in pricing does not result in a corresponding decrease in demand. Automotive fuel is a paradigm example, with consumers purchasing the same amount regardless of the fluctuation in pricing. When this occurs we say that the price is "inelastic," that is, it does not move in direct relationship to supply and demand.

(ii) Economic Factors.   Overall economic conditions are generally what drive supply and demand. When the economy is strong, consumers tend to have ample cash to spend. This generally strains production capacity, creating shortages and raising prices. Conversely, when consumers have little cash to spend, capacity is plentiful and prices tend to spiral downward.

What causes these cycles? Good question! The best answer is that at any given time, no one really knows. Economic cycles have been noted since the beginning of recorded time but, while theories abound, no agreement is readily available. In hindsight, however, we can always point to situational factors such as "the market was oversold" as causes for creating a downturn. Overall, though, we consider upturns and downturns to be naturally occurring phenomena that will always be with us.

INDUSTRY CAPACITY

Within any given industry, capacity can be measured by the percentage of utilization of resources. As we approach 90 percent of utilization, overtime tends to rise, and orders that were once profitable require increases in prices to sustain them. If you can adequately forecast these trends, you will likely be able to take very productive steps to take advantage of them.

SUPPLIER CAPACITY

Individual supplier capacity can be constrained from time to time as well, based on an influx of large orders or the unexpected loss of production capacity due to disaster. This may require you to move orders to a secondary source without the benefit of favorable pricing. Effective procurement professionals are always alert to the conditions affecting their most important suppliers and generally tend to avoid sole-sourcing situations for this very reason.

AVAILABLE LABOR

In unionized environments, conditions can change whenever a contract is under negotiations. Negotiation failure frequently results in strikes and work stoppages, followed by resultant shortages. Stockpiling in advance of a potential labor dispute can drive prices up even before the negotiation has concluded.

(b) COST-BASED PRICING MODELS.   In addition to general market conditions, prices can be governed by supplier costs and *markup* strategies. Despite the fact that we may never have full access to the supplier's costs, there are a number of profit models we can examine to get the full picture.

(i) Standard Markup Model.   Using a typical markup model, the supplier calculates the unit cost and then adds a percentage to cover overhead and profit. The overhead is generally comprised of all the operating expenses for the organization and converted to a percentage of direct costs. For example, if an organization allocates 20 percent of its costs to direct materials and labor, and 40 percent of its costs to overhead, the cost ratio of overhead costs to direct costs is 2:1 (40/20 = 2). This means that the supplier determines the price by adding an overhead and profit factor to its estimated product or service cost. Let's look at an example where the

supplier's desired profit is 10 percent and the direct cost of the product is deter-mined to be $1.80.

$$\text{Selling Price} = \text{Total Cost} + \text{Profit}$$

$$\text{Total Cost} = (\text{Direct Cost} + (\text{Dirrect Cost} \times \text{Overhead}))$$

$$= (1.80 + (1.80 \times 2))$$

$$= 5.40$$

$$\text{Selling Price} = 5.40 + .54$$

$$= 5.94$$

(ii) Specific Rate of Return Model. When the supplier expects to receive a specific rate of return for an investment, the calculation is based on the total cost of the investment plus the cost to produce the product or service. This figure is then multiplied by the rate of return desired in order to arrive at the selling price. As a simplified calculation it might look like this, given a 15 percent rate of return:

$$\text{Selling Price} = \text{Average Cost} + \text{Desired Rate of Return}(15\%)$$

$$\text{Average Cost} = \frac{(\text{Total Investment} + \text{Total Cost to Produce})}{\text{Anticipated Sales Volume}}$$

$$= \frac{\$150,000 + \$100,000}{100,000 \text{ Units}}$$

$$= \$2.50 \text{ per unit}$$

$$\text{Selling Price} = 2.50 + .375$$

$$= 2.875$$

(c) PRICE ANALYSIS METHODS. While there are many elaborate ways to analyze prices, in your day-to-day activities you will likely have only little time to do overly academic studies. From a practical point of view, the easiest and most produc-tive method of analysis is to compare the prices being offered with some form of benchmark. Here are some of the more commonly used tools to consider:

- **Trend analysis** employs statistic methodology to determine where prices are heading or how one price compares to another. Some of the more commonly used statistical methods used in procurement include:

  o **Linear regression analysis** calculates a mathematical formula for the best-fitting straight line through a series of data points. By extending the calculation of this line to an event in the future, we can develop a forecast. The upper chart in Figure 11.1 shows the actual prices paid for purchases over a 26-week period. This data can then be used to calculate a trend line, which is shown as the dotted line in the lower chart. We can then use this trend line to forecast anticipated volumes, shown as the extension of the trend line in the lower chart.

○ **Exponential smoothing** is an adjustment technique that takes the previous period's forecast and adjusts it up or down based on what actually occurred in that period. It accomplishes this by calculating a weighted average of the two values. As an historical projection, it allows the user to give more weight to the most recent data.

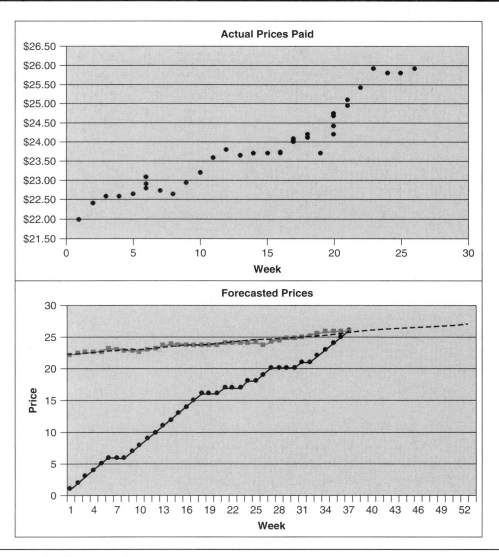

Figure 11.1   Example of Linear Regression Analysis

- **Comparative analysis** can take a number of forms, ranging from benchmarking industry standards to a side-by-side comparison of quoted prices. Table 11.1 shows an example of a price list analysis that compares the prices from three suppliers at different volume levels. As you can see, no single supplier has the best price throughout the volume range. How you make your selection will depend upon the volume you purchase and how well you can negotiate aggregated volumes over a period of time to obtain the highest discount.
- **Product analysis** or **functionality analysis**, as it is sometimes called, examines products or services in terms of the functionality they provide, evaluating each element as a separate cost factor so that a comparative analysis of features can be made. This comparison helps determine the value and desirability of added functionality and can also help compare products considered to be as disparate as apples and oranges.

Quantity	Supplier A	Supplier B	Supplier C
1,000	1.10	1.12	1.09
2,500	0.84	0.88	0.84
5,000	0.78	0.80	0.80
10,000	0.64	0.66	0.68
25,000	0.52	0.51	0.54
50,000	0.48	0.46	0.49

TABLE 11.1   SIDE-BY-SIDE COMPARISON OF PRICES

11.4 REPRESENTING THE ORGANIZATION

One of the key functions of the Procurement staff is managing the interface with suppliers and others outside the organization. This function requires an extremely tactful approach since in many ways your contacts are the "public," and you must be certain the messages you give are in alignment with organizational policy. Close contact with your organization's public relations or communications teams will help ensure you are up to date on your organization's current positioning and that you are providing the correct message.

(a) MEETING SALES PERSONNEL.   When effectively organized, meetings with sales personnel should always prove productive. While you have only the perspective of your own organization from which to gauge industry developments, your sales counterpart typically meets with several organizations during the normal course of business. Without compromising confidentiality, the sales representative can provide you with a host of ideas on how to improve operations.

As a result, it is important that you follow some specific protocol in dealing with sales personnel. To do so requires that you clearly understand the role of the sales professional.

(i) The Role of the Sales Professional. Sales methods, of course, vary from organization to organization, industry to industry, and country to country. There are, however, a certain set of roles that are universal to virtually all those in sales. These roles generally include:

- Researching and prospecting for potential customers.
- Establishing rapport with a potential customer.
- Identifying the customer's needs.
- Matching the customer's needs with product offerings.
- Presenting the offer, asking for the sale, overcoming objections.
- Making the sale and closing.
- Providing ongoing customer support.

TIPS AND TECHNIQUES

Sales training can be an extensive and detailed process, often quite mysterious to the buyer. For an excellent resource for learning more about selling techniques and the selling profession, go to www.businessballs.com/salestraining.htm.

Keep in mind, however, that unlike the procurement agent or buyer, the salesperson is rarely an agent of the organization and is therefore not empowered to commit the organization to contractual obligations. To do so generally requires an individual at the management level.

(ii) The Role of Procurement. The Procurement Department provides the initial interface with sales personnel and is responsible within the organization for responding to initial sales inquiries. In this role, the Procurement Department must decide if there is any potential in the offering and if the salesperson has the ability to add value to the process. In addition, it is the Procurement Department's function to work with the sales representative to further identify organizational needs that might fit and to introduce the sales rep to others in the organization who may have an interest in the products or services being offered.

The procurement team also has the opportunity through its interface with sales personnel to learn how others in the same marketplace may be conducting operations (without asking for confidential information) and can pass along this information to others in the form of intelligence.

It is also worth noting that Procurement should be informed of any supplier visits paid directly to the user so that it can monitor information being disclosed. This helps ensure that other suppliers, should there be a competitive situation, gain access to the same information.

(iii) Extending Organizational Hospitality. Sales staff should be treated at all times with courtesy and respect, as valued representatives of their organizations.

Here are some guidelines you might want to refer to when meeting with sales personnel:

- Meet promptly and courteously with sales representatives making scheduled calls.
- Offer as much hospitality as possible during your meeting.
- Provide equal opportunity for all representatives to present their products when you have a specific need.
- Maintain confidentiality at all times.
- Show concern for the representative's time and expense.
- When unable to provide the business being sought, explain the reasons as clearly as possible.

(iv) Handling Inquiries, Protests, and Complaints.   The Procurement Department handles numerous inquiries in the normal course of conducting business. Obviously, it is important that these be reviewed promptly and handled expeditiously as well as courteously. While many of these inquiries are simply prospecting efforts by sales personnel, many of them involve pending business and often require coordination with other departments in the organization.

When an inquiry refers to a current bid process or an open request for proposals (RFP), the buyer must be certain to respond accordingly to all participants as a measure of fairness and good business conduct. If the question materially affects the bidding, it may be necessary for the buyer to publish a formal addendum to the bid solicitation or the RFP addressing the issue.

From time to time, suppliers will want to protest an award decision or file a complaint regarding unfair treatment. Most organizations have well-defined processes to handle this, including requirements for filing the objection in writing along with appropriate documentation. As part of an appeals process, some organizations provide for an escalation path to management or a standing committee for further review and action. In many cases, a contract or policy calls for a formal dispute resolution process involving a neutral third party.

Regardless of the process used by your organization, it is important both that the suppliers understand the review process and that it be conducted expeditiously so as not to disrupt normal operations for either party.

(v) Professional Conduct.   Professional conduct is paramount to maintaining credibility with suppliers. Many organizations have a specific code of conduct, but if yours does not, consider using the one established by the Institute for Supply Management.

TIPS AND TECHNIQUES

PRINCIPLES AND STANDARDS OF ETHICAL SUPPLY MANAGEMENT CONDUCT

LOYALTY TO YOUR ORGANIZATION

JUSTICE TO THOSE WITH WHOM YOU DEAL

FAITH IN YOUR PROFESSION

From these principles are derived the ISM standards of supply management conduct. (Global)

- Avoid the intent and appearance of unethical or compromising practice in relationships, actions, and communications.
- Demonstrate loyalty to the employer by diligently following the lawful instructions of the employer, using reasonable care and granted authority.
- Avoid any personal business or professional activity that would create a conflict between personal interests and the interests of the employer.
- Avoid soliciting or accepting money, loans, credits, or preferential discounts, and the acceptance of gifts, entertainment, favors, or services from present or potential suppliers that might influence, or appear to influence, supply management decisions.
- Handle confidential or proprietary information with due care and proper consideration of ethical and legal ramifications and governmental regulations.
- Promote positive supplier relationships through courtesy and impartiality.
- Avoid improper reciprocal agreements.
- Know and obey the letter and spirit of laws applicable to supply management.
- Encourage support for small, disadvantaged, and minority-owned businesses.
- Acquire and maintain professional competence.
- Conduct supply management activities in accordance with national and international laws, customs, and practices, your organization's policies, and these ethical principles and standards of conduct.
- Enhance the stature of the supply management profession.

Approved January 2002

(vi) Participating in Meetings and External Events.   From time to time, Procurement Department staff will be required to represent the department or the organization in meetings and at outside events. For this reason, it is important that you understand how to conduct an effective meeting and how to prepare successful presentations.

MEETINGS
There are a few simple rules for conducting meetings that will help you make them more effective:

- Select the right participants based on the topic and input from others who might be interested in attending.

- Extend invitations in sufficient time to ensure everyone who wishes to attend will have ample time to make arrangements.
- Prepare an agenda and distribute it in advance of the meeting.
- Ensure that the meeting facilities are sufficient to hold the number invited and have the necessary supplies.
- During the meeting, ensure that those who wish to participate in the discussion are provided with ample opportunity.
- Follow the agenda, including starting and ending on time.
- Maintain focus during the meeting.
- Periodically evaluate progress during the course of the meeting.
- Take and post notes as appropriate.
- Reach consensus or decision if and as planned.
- Following the meeting, publish notes and provide an opportunity for further input.

Presentations

Preparing and delivering an effective presentation is one of the most important skills you can develop and should not be difficult to achieve if you follow a few basic rules consistently. Many guides to effective presentations list the following as important considerations:

- Define the desired outcome of your presentation.
- Stay focused on your topic.
- Prepare your presentation with your specific audience in mind.
- Be in touch with your surroundings.
- Prepare carefully; use a script if needed.
- Organize material and present it in a logical sequence.
- Deal with one concept at a time.
- Leverage appropriate visual aids; be simple.
- Test regularly for clarity to be sure you are communicating with your audience.
- Deliver your material clearly.
- Define acronyms and unfamiliar terms.
- Maintain your audience's attention through eye contact.
- Encourage participation.
- Stay on schedule.

Ultimately, the most important consideration in meetings and presentations to bear in mind is to maintain your sincerity at all times. Most audiences feel uncomfortable around affectation.

11.5 SUMMARY

In this chapter, we reviewed the requirements for managing productive supplier relations and how creating good working relationships required a measure of effort. Meeting regularly with your suppliers, conducting surveys to garner input, and initiating reciprocal site visits are just a few of the ways to enhance relations. We also reviewed many of the tools available for improving communications with suppliers and how best to resolve ongoing relationship issues.

We then turned our attention to ways in which new suppliers could be certified and how to develop continuous improvement programs for existing suppliers. We looked at how early supplier involvement assisted better performance in procurement and the advantages of working collaboratively through supplier partnerships and alliances.

This chapter also covered the fundamentals of establishing and managing a supplier diversity program, including sourcing minority suppliers, as well as developing and managing programs.

As a key part of supplier relationship management, we examined how supplier pricing operates in response to market conditions and profit strategies. This included a look at pricing methods and analysis of pricing trend data.

We concluded the chapter with an examination of how the Procurement Department represents the organization with suppliers, handling supplier inquiries and protests, reviewing a standardized code of ethical conduct. And, finally, we reviewed how to conduct effective meetings and prepare presentations.

KEY TERMS

Focus group

Reverse marketing

Mentoring

Continuous improvement

Market conditions

Linear regression analysis

Exponential smoothing

Functionality analysis

CHAPTER **12**

FINANCIAL DECISIONS FOR SOURCING

LEARNING OBJECTIVES

1. List three steps in performing the make-or-buy analysis.
2. Name the "intangible factors" which should be considered before making an outsourcing decision.
3. Describe the benefits of buying vs. the benefits of leasing.
4. Describe the organizational considerations which influence financial strategies.

During the normal course of business, you will be required to assist in making many financial decisions related to the acquisition of goods and services for the organization. Many of these decisions will involve determining whether to acquire the goods and services from suppliers through direct purchase or if the organization can more efficiently provide them itself by using internal resources. In addition, determining whether to buy or lease is another typical business decision that must be made on an ongoing basis. These decisions are generally referred to as **make or buy** and **lease or buy** because they require a comparative analysis of those alternatives.

In addition, there are numerous other financial leveraging strategies that you will need to understand, such as how commodity markets operate and how the cost of money through interest rates is determined—factors that are most often driven by conditions in the marketplace. In this chapter, we will explore the processes for preparing for some of these key financial decisions and their importance to the modern organization.

12.1 PERFORMING MAKE-OR-BUY ANALYSIS

Make-or-buy analysis, as its name implies, is the process that determines if the organization should produce a particular product or service in-house or if it should turn to a third-party supplier and simply purchase it from them. Many companies in the semiconductor industry, for example, have increasingly turned to "fabless" operations, choosing to outsource the production of silicon die products, which requires large investments in sophisticated tools and equipment, to third parties who have already invested huge amounts of money in developing their state-of-the-art facilities. Today, approximately two-thirds of all semiconductor companies delegate manufacturing operations to outside foundries, focusing instead on what they consider to be their own core competencies and design and marketing strategies.

In the following section, we will examine the dynamics of make-or-buy analysis, looking at the process dynamics as well as the strategies behind them.

(a) MAKE-OR-BUY DYNAMICS.   There are numerous opportunities for *outsourcing* the products your organization manufactures or the functions your organization performs internally by contracting them to third parties. Commonly targeted services include business functions such as information technology, facilities management, payroll management, logistics, and with more increasing frequency, procurement itself. It is also becoming increasingly more common for manufacturing operations to outsource entire product-line assembly functions to firms specializing in material procurement, assembly, and testing. The benefits of outsourcing generally include reduced labor costs resulting from the transfer of operations to lower-paid workers, along with lower material prices due to the larger economies of scale with consolidated volumes purchased by third manufacturers. The offsetting disadvantages include loss of control and, sometimes, loss of scheduling flexibility.

Generally, make-or-buy decisions are conducted by a cross-functional team so that the benefit of all perspectives can be obtained and evaluated. Before deciding the viability of buying products or services currently handled internally, the team will need to look carefully at a number of factors and gather information from a number of sources.

(i) Viability Study.   The first step in a make-or-buy decision is determining if buying the product or outsourcing the service is viable. This depends largely on the existing supply base. You will likely find that this is actually a sourcing process involving finding suppliers capable of handling your organization's business. You will need to locate suppliers that have personnel with the proper skill set, as well as available equipment and facilities, to handle your needs. If you and your team are unable to locate viable suppliers, you are faced with either developing existing suppliers to handle your needs or continuing to do it in-house.

If the marketplace for your requirement has a limited number of suppliers, you will also want to analyze the risk involved. Are there viable backup alternatives should the supplier you choose encounter difficulties? Do the physical logistics involved add significantly more costs and process complexity to your operations? How financially solvent are the potential providers—are they capable of making the financial investments required by developing technology?

You will also want to look into the resources required for managing the supplier. Will the supplier become a critical factor in producing your end product, requiring close audit tracking and frequent business reviews? Will the outsourcing engagement require engineering or quality staff to work closely with the supplier on a continuing basis? Will these support resources be available?

(ii) Requirements.   The next step in the process is determining your organization's exact needs. This part of the process is very similar to the one we outlined in the section on developing requirements in Chapter 2. You will need to develop a clear specification or statement of work (SOW), as well as an estimate of future requirements volume or frequency of service. This is necessary for two reasons: first, to establish a baseline for the current costs to your organization, and second, to enable a relatively accurate quote from potential suppliers. Without either of these, you may not be able to determine accurately if there are financial advantages to buying.

(iii) Conducting Analysis.   Having located viable sources and defined the exact requirements, the final step is actually conducting the analysis. To do this, you will first need to prepare a request for proposal (RFP) or request for quotation (RFQ) to go out to the potential suppliers. Once the RFP and RFQ are returned and analyzed, you will have enough data to do a comparative analysis between your current operating values—primarily cost—and those of the proposed outsourcing. As with any RFP or RFQ comparison, you will want to analyze and compare the elements of quality, cost, technology, and service. Most importantly, you must be certain you are receiving equal or greater value from the supplier before making a final outsourcing decision.

The team's initial analysis will likely focus on those elements you consider tangible, such as cost, lead times, and scheduling flexibility. If, following this analysis, the team continues to find potential value in an outsourcing engagement, it should continue with the analysis and turn to a number of subjective criteria before making the actual decision.

In performing a basic analysis—with a new product, for example—cost and capacity may be the critical factors. In the analysis of cost, you will want to be sure to consider direct costs such as material, labor, and freight and indirect costs such as receiving, inspecting, and stocking, as well as scrap and the cost of resolving quality issues.

(b) SUBJECTIVE MAKE-OR-BUY ANALYSIS FACTORS. There are several intangible factors that should be considered by the team before coming to a final conclusion as to whether or not to actually go forward with the outsourcing engagement.

(i) Strategy. In the long term, your team will want to determine how well the proposed outsourcing fits with the overall organizational strategy. Prior to making a recommendation, you will want to explore a number of questions such as these:

- Is the process or product a critical part of the organization's core competency? If so, your team must weigh the pros and cons of placing this in the hands of a third-party supplier.
- Does learning from the development of this product or service drive learning in other business function areas? You will want to determine if this will weaken any existing technology development.
- Will your outsourced business provide adequate incentive to suppliers to continue participating? If there is not sufficient revenue from the outsourcing to continue to engage suppliers, you should consider the effect that future capacity constraints might place on the supplier.
- Can you actually reduce internal costs sufficiently enough to offset the acquisition costs? You need to analyze the true cost reduction to the organization as a result of outsourcing. Unless buying can produce reduced staffing by eliminating existing head count, the calculated savings may be "soft." You will also want to be certain that reduction in staffing in one area does not result in the need for increased staffing in another. For example, will outsourcing a manufacturing operation require additional quality and procurement personnel due to quality or delivery issues?
- To what extent will the organization be able to reverse its sourcing decision in the future, bringing back in-house the product or service if the supplier should fail? This is often a key strategic decision because the equipment and expertise needed to produce the outsourced item may require heavy investment to replace at some future date.

(ii) Risk.   Although risk assessment is difficult or impossible to quantify, its evaluation is a critical part of any outsourcing determination. In the words of the famous Murphy: "Anything that can go wrong will go wrong." Therefore, when conducting any risk analysis, one should not hesitate to evaluate every one of the factors and assumptions made in the initial sourcing comparative analysis.

In performing risk analysis, you need to carefully balance the specific, expected benefits of the engagement with factors that you may not be able to control. For example, you will need to determine the effect of capacity constraints in the supply community hampering future production operations. Conversely, you will want to gauge the impact that a business downturn will have on your selected supplier. Will your supply needs continue to be met?

You will also want to analyze, where possible, the potential impact that changing technology may have on future requirements. With relatively low volumes, you may be unable to convince a supplier to invest in future research and technological development. This condition might favor keeping the product or service in - house. Similarly, with a new product or service about to be introduced to the market, your organization will want to determine if the resources that must be acquired to produce the product or service will result in an internal return on that investment. In these circumstances, turning to a supplier with existing capability may prove more effective.

TIPS AND TECHNIQUES

Some elements of risk cannot be tolerated at any level. Lack of statistical process control (SPC) tools, for example, should immediately disqualify a potential supplier for technology-driven parts.

(iii) Quality Considerations.   There is virtually no factual data to support the assumption that buying a product or service rather than making it will result in diminished quality. According to a recent survey, in fact, the majority of companies outsourcing found that work skill quality actually improved following the engagement, and 70 percent reported an increase in the quality of outsourced business processes.

As always, successful buying programs require a clear definition of quality and the definitive documentation of the business processes required for its support. Many organizations choose to outsource simply because they have little or no documented control of subordinate processes in the first place. Suppliers often have better process documentation in place and greater control of quality simply because the product or service is a core competency for them.

(iv) Support Capability.   Support capability refers to the ability to develop advanced product technology. Supporting new product development in some areas is often a financial burden for the buying organization but a core competency for the supplier engaged in providing the service to a wide spectrum of customers.

Suppliers are usually in a better position to absorb the costs of development simply because they can distribute it over a wider customer base.

Similarly, supporting business processes has become, for some organizations, a core competency due to their large customer base. Many have dedicated engineering staffs to work with customers during the product development cycle to ensure alignment between the design and the manufacturing process. Many are global and have multinational support. Most have sophisticated customer service systems capable of tracking customer orders and repair status on a 24/7 basis.

(c) OUTSOURCING BUSINESS PROCESSES. Today, outsourcing entire business processes, such as manufacturing assembly, information technology, or logistics, is a common occurrence. While the process sometimes appears more complex and the resulting risk may be higher because of the broadened scope, it invariably follows a process similar to the make-or-buy analysis.

Outsourcing is defined as the transfer of a previously performed function from the organizational staff to a third-party supplier. As we noted earlier in this chapter, there are a host of such functions within the organization that have become subject to potential outsourcing. The prime drive appears to be lowered cost from the engagement, likely as a result of efficiencies the supplier is able to achieve by spreading the overhead across a larger group of users. However, many organizations are experiencing improved service as a result of the greater human resources available to the supplier in times of customer need.

The following sections discuss the make-or-buy process and some important elements you should consider when sourcing these services.

(i) Needs Analysis. Needs analysis should be performed by a cross-functional team composed of subject matter experts and those familiar with the processes being used internally at the current time. Be sure to include stakeholders as well, so that all user groups are represented.

Your team must define the requirements in terms of a statement of work (SOW), just as it would with any other service. At a minimum you will want to have:

- A detailed description of the work to be performed.
- Costs of the present operation, by function.
- Required service levels—how you intend to measure performance.
- Critical risks in the engagement.

(ii) Decision-Making Process. From these elements, your team should be able to incorporate its needs into an RFP and submit it to qualified or qualifiable suppliers. Be certain to include your typical contract terms for this type of engagement so you can determine quickly if suppliers are not willing to accept your existing business and legal terms. You should also be able to construct an assessment criteria matrix to objectively rate the suppliers' responses to your RFP once received.

Based on the initial responses (or noticeable lack of response), your team will need to decide if the potential exists to actually conduct the proposed outsourcing. You'll base this decision on the nature of the responses and the costs being proposed. If it appears to be feasible, proceed to the supplier selection process; if not, consider revising the SOW or dropping the outsourcing project.

(iii) Supplier Selection. Many organizations use a preestablished selection criteria based on comparative rating methodologies that rates suppliers on the basis of proposed cost, service levels, technology capability, quality, and the level of ongoing investment in the process you are outsourcing. We reviewed this in Chapter 3, and you may want to refer back to it for further details.

12.2 PERFORMING LEASE-OR-BUY ANALYSIS

Leasing is an alternative to buying that's used primarily when acquiring **capital equipment**. In many respects, leasing can be considered similar to renting.

Lease-or-buy analysis is the process of comparing the overall costs associated with leasing compared to owning a particular asset. Depending on the cost of capital for a given organization, the lease may provide significant advantages. Lease payments are typically expensed rather than capitalized, so they can be directly related to the accounting period in which they occur. While it is common for an equipment lease to require a long-term contract, there is usually little or no down payment needed.

Consider Table 12.1 and the comparison between the two options.

(a) LEASING FEATURES. A lease agreement grants the **lessee** possession of equipment or property for a stated period of time and at an agreed-upon rate of payment. The lessee is not the owner of the asset but commonly bears all responsibility for maintaining it in good working order. At the end of the lease, the lessee may have the option of purchasing the equipment at a *fair market value* or at a previously agreed-upon amount if such a clause is included in the contract.

BENEFITS OF BUYING	BENEFITS OF LEASING
No fees for early termination	Little or no cash to obtain the equipment
Can be sold at any time	Payments are considered expenses and may provide tax advantages
Total costs are usually lower over time	Several disposal options at end of lease
Use of the equipment can extend far after it is paid for	Does not affect bank line of credit
	Little fear of obsolescence

TABLE 12.1 BENEFITS OF BUYING VS. LEASING

(i) Lease Types.   There are several common types of leases that you should become familiar with:

Finance lease. A financing device whereby a lessee can acquire an asset for most of its useful life. Generally, a finance lease is noncancelable during the term of the lease. Leases of this type are generally net to the lessor, so the lessee is responsible for maintenance, taxes, and insurance.

Full-payout lease. A lease in which the actual cash payments will return the lessor the full equipment cost plus a satisfactory return over the lease term.

Leveraged lease. A lease in which the lessor borrows a portion of the purchase price of the leased equipment from institutional investors. In a typical transaction, 20 to 40 percent of the purchase price is provided by one or more investors, who become owners and lessors of the equipment. The balance of the purchase price is borrowed from banks or other sources of capital.

Net lease. A lease in which the fees are payable net to the lessor; that is, the lessee pays all out-of-pocket expenses such as taxes, insurance, and maintenance. The lease, therefore, only addresses the equipment itself. All costs in connection with the use of the equipment (usually hard to predict) are to be paid by the lessee over and above the agreed rental payments. Most finance leases are net leases.

Operating lease. A short-term lease whereby a user can acquire an asset for a fraction of the useful life of the asset. The lessor may provide services in connection with the lease such as maintenance, insurance, and payment of personal property taxes. From a strict accounting standpoint, the specific requirements of Financial Accounting Standards Board (FASB) Standard 13 (discussed later in the chapter) must be met for a lease to be qualified as an operating lease.

(ii) Lessors.   **Lessors** are persons or entities who own the property being leased (e.g., real estate or equipment), which a lessee receives use and possession of in exchange for a payment of fees. Lessors typically include banks, manufacturers of equipment, third-party owners, and capital funding organizations.

(b) DECISION-MAKING FACTORS.   As with any decision, leasing provides a number of considerations, both favorable and unfavorable. The next sections discuss some of those you should usually consider.

(i) Advantages of Leasing.   Some of the advantages to leasing include:

- **Better cash flow.** Leasing gives you access to the asset with minimal up-front payments and spreads the cost over time. You can pay for the asset with the income it generates while minimizing the drain on your working capital.

- **No debt.** An operating lease preserves your credit options and does not influence your credit limit because it is generally classified as expense, not debt.
- **Maximize financial leverage.** Your lease can often finance everything related to the purchase and installation of the asset and may free up cash flow to pay for items such as training.
- **Cash flow management.** Lease payments are usually constant, making cash management more predictable.
- **Tax advantage.** Operating lease payments are generally tax deductible just like depreciation charges but are made with pretax money. Cash purchases, in contrast, are made with after-tax money.
- **Flexible time frames.** Leasing contracts can be structured to fit your requirements. You can use an asset as long as you need it without owning it forever.
- **Protection against obsolescence.** Depending on your end-of-lease option, you can return the asset to the lessor.

(ii) Disadvantages of Leasing.   Some of the disadvantages to leasing are:

- **More expensive.** A finance lease is usually more expensive than an outright cash purchase because the payments include finance charges. However, leasing may cost less than other forms of financing.
- **Additional guarantees required.** Depending on the credit rating of your company, the lessor might require additional guarantees. These may be provided by officers of your organization or your bank and could affect your organization's credit rating or financial standing with bankers reviewing debt-to-asset ratios.
- **Fixed term.** It may be impossible, or very costly, to terminate a leasing contract early.
- **Locked interest rates.** Interest rates are usually fixed throughout the lease, which may prove a disadvantage in times of falling interest rates.

(iii) Cost Factors.   Any lease analysis must consider typical total cost of ownership factors such as acquisition cost, operating costs, and maintenance and disposal. Acquisition costs typically include the down payment (if required), taxes, shipping costs, installation, and financing or loan fees. Operating costs typically include any enhancements to the original equipment, consumables, and energy/fuel consumption. Maintenance factors include preventative maintenance, spare parts, and down time. Disposal costs include reconditioning costs, facility removal costs, shipping, early lease termination fees, and "fair market value" salvage value.

Here are some of the more subtle cost factors that you will need to take into account in any complete analysis:

- **Return of asset reconditioning.** If you choose to return the asset at the end of your lease, the condition to which it must be reconditioned and the place where it must be returned are important cost factors to consider.

- **Notice period.** If your lease includes an automatic option to renew, take note of any time periods in which you must give notice in case you do not want to renew the contract. Some leasing companies will automatically renew the contract if you fail to give notice.
- **Purchase rights.** When returning the asset at the end of your lease, a predetermined fixed price offers more option than the fair market value, which theoretically is always available to you.
- **Maintenance responsibility.** Clarify which service and maintenance programs are included in the lease. If you are responsible for service and maintenance, make sure it is in line with the manufacturer's recommendations.

(iv) Budget Considerations.   Organizations needing to balance the need for new technology with budget constraints find that leasing helps stretch budget dollars with monthly payments that are often lower than purchase installments. With a lease, organizational cash remains untouched and available for other profitable uses. In addition, leasing often expands financial resources without affecting established credit lines.

Many companies realize significant tax benefits from leasing their technology. Monthly lease payments are generally tax deductible and can be treated as a business expense. Conventional bank financing typically requires a minimum balance. With leasing, there is no minimum balance or down payment required.

(v) FASB 13.   The FASB established standards of financial accounting and reporting for leases by lessees and lessors for transactions and revisions entered into on or after January 1, 1977. For lessees, a lease is a financing transaction called a capital lease if it meets any one of four specified criteria; if not, it is an operating lease. Capital leases are treated as the acquisition of assets and the incurrence of obligations by the lessee. Operating leases are treated as current operating expenses.

For lessors, a financing transaction lease is classified as a sales type, direct financing, or leveraged lease. To be a sales type, direct financing, or leveraged lease, the lease must meet one of the same criteria used for lessees to classify a lease as a capital lease, in addition to two criteria dealing with future uncertainties.

Leveraged leases also have to meet further criteria. These types of leases are recorded as investments under different specifications for each type of lease. Leases not meeting the criteria are considered operating leases and are accounted for like rental property.

12.3 FORMULATING FINANCIAL STRATEGIES

The Procurement Department is in one of the best positions in the organization to influence and improve the bottom line by leveraging relationships and information from the supply community. But to do so, the professional must understand existing processes and strategies within the organization so that, for example, creating a cost saving in one operating area does not resurface as financial burden in another.

In this section, let's examine some of the finance-based avenues and tools available to you to better perform your job.

(a) ORGANIZATIONAL CONSIDERATIONS.   The type of organization you are employed by will have a large influence on the nature of its financial strategies and will require different approaches from the Procurement Department. Consider some of the various ways organizations might respond to similar situations depending upon their sectors and organizational structures.

(i) Commercial.   Commercial enterprises can be divided into two sectors:

1. **Public corporations.** Public corporations, businesses whose stock is publicly owned and traded on one of the many stock exchanges, owe a measure of fiduciary due diligence to their many stockholders. In addition to its efforts to reduce cost, the Procurement Department must follow standard operating procedures so that the public can rely on the management's ability to produce profit. The department is always under audit scrutiny and must ensure that procedures are followed at all times.
2. **Privately owned enterprises.** Businesses that are privately held are free to develop financial strategies within the constraints of their mission and the direction provided by the owners. The Procurement Department's responsibility, however, remains the same: to provide value for the organization.

(ii) Nonprofit.   Nonprofit organizations include schools, churches, charities, and other organizations working for the benefit of the community. Obviously, with nonprofit organizations, the "profit" motive is largely absent. Nevertheless, these organizations want to stretch their operating budgets as far as possible in order to better fulfill their mission, and the Procurement Department can serve the mission by enabling a fixed budget to be leveraged that much further.

(iii) Government.   Government procurement requirements are possibly the most stringent and certainly the most complex in regard to process and procedure compliance. Procurement departments in these environments must conform to a host of complex and sometimes obscure regulations originally designed to ensure that the public is protected while receiving the most value for its tax dollar and that suppliers are treated fairly and equally. This has unfortunately made the procurement process more cumbersome than most would like it to be, and it's certainly more difficult for the purchaser to achieve outstanding results. To many, conformance to the prescribed process and completion of proper documentation have become more important considerations than desirable results. While improvements

in the system to make them more strategically responsive to financial objectives are taking place all of the time, it is by nature a slow process, and we (the authors) have unbridled admiration for those who manage to consistently produce outstanding results despite the often formidable obstacles and roadblocks.

(iv) Procurement Structure. How the procurement organization is structured and where it resides in the organization can definitely affect its performance and fit with the organization's overall financial and operational strategies. An astute Procurement professional will make every possible effort to ensure that those in the organization developing the strategic goals understand how the current structure of the procurement group both supports and hinders those goals.

While there are likely infinite variations of Procurement Department structure, the next sections list some of the standard types you are likely to encounter.

Centralized

A centralized Procurement Department exists when it is the sole authorized agency to purchase goods and services for the organization. This group supports the entire organization, regardless of location or the nature of operations. The advantage of this structure is that it supports compliance to organizational policy, and it can better leverage the supplier community through combined volumes. The downside is that it is extremely difficult to find expertise capable of servicing a product or diverse organization.

Lead/Divisional

In a lead/divisional Procurement Department, the procurement groups are distributed across the organization to support local user groups, and each procurement group places its own purchase orders. However, the group with the greatest expertise in a specific area is responsible for negotiating prices and contracts for the entire organization.

Cooperative

Centralized buying services, known unofficially as **cooperatives** or **buying consortiums**, have become relatively popular recently. They are able to save money by combining the volumes of several customers and making one purchase. Several of these have become successful and quite well known.

Tips and Techniques

Consortiums need to have a common basis for organization in order to comply with antitrust regulations when receiving preferential pricing. One significant requirement is that the organizations participating in the buying have a significant similarity, such as being part of the same industry or being engaged in a similar nonprofit mission. Be sure to check with your legal counsel before proceeding with forming a consortium.

(b) MONETARY CONSIDERATIONS.   Related to the development of financial strategies are a number of elements that will affect how and when purchases are made. Here, we'll look at some of the more common areas where procurement and financial influences overlap.

(i) Depreciation.   It is generally recognized that equipment and certain other assets purchased by an organization have a finite useful life, at the end of which they will theoretically no longer be of any salvage value. **Depreciation** is the process of allowing for and recording this decline in value over a specified period of time. If, for example, a copier machine cost $100,000 and has a recognized useful life of five years, then each year it would depreciate by another $20,000.

This has two important considerations: First, since depreciation is an expense for tax reporting purposes, it represents a **liability** on the organization's books. Second, the "book" value or asset value also declines at this rate, reducing the organization's book value on the **balance sheet** and, potentially, the possible resale or salvage value.

This needs to be taken into consideration when preparing **return on investment (ROI)** analysis and when calculating costs for a make-or-buy/lease-or-buy decision.

(ii) Bond and Currency Markets.   Purchasers involved in foreign trade understand that currencies fluctuate frequently, rising or declining in value against the U.S. dollar or other base currency. If you are purchasing in foreign currencies, you need to know how this can affect the future price of your purchase at the time of contracting. If your base currency—let's use U.S. dollars for this example—declines relative to the purchase currency, you will need more dollars to pay the invoice. If the opposite is the case, the supplier may receive less than expected in terms of global market value.

To maintain the stability of your transaction (and to some extent, the profitability of your purchase), you can often use a process called **hedging**. Hedging is a strategy designed to reduce the risk of fluctuations in forward-looking contracts requiring payment in a foreign currency. Your organization's actions will depend on how it forecasts currency changes: If it expects the foreign currency to decline in value relative to the dollar, it will place aside the dollars needed for payment, purchasing the foreign currency when it appears to be at its lowest point. However, if the currency is expected to increase in relation to the U.S. dollar, it might prove wise to purchase the foreign currency as soon as the contract is signed.

Tips and Techniques

Currency hedging is best left to experts because of its inherent financial risk. To date, no one has figured out how to predict the future value of any currency very far in the future. Most organizations rely on their treasury group to handle this or use an outside broker who is an expert in the currency under consideration.

(iii) Commodity Markets.   To constitute a **commodity**, products must be relatively standardized, undifferentiated, and capable of trading in a formalized market environment, such as an exchange. In the past, typical commodities have been related to metals, lumber, agricultural products, chemicals, and fuels. They are typically traded on open exchanges where the price fluctuates according to supply and demand. In these open exchanges, it is possible to purchase a number of so-called instruments that can reduce risk of future fluctuations, including the purchase of contracts for future delivery at a designated date and at the price specified in the contract, regardless of the actual market price at the time of purchase. Contracts can be created and sold even for product not yet physically owned by the seller. Once created, these contracts can then be bought and sold as desired.

These financial instruments all have one aspect in common: risk. As you know, it is impossible to forecast where prices are heading from one period to the next. Expert advice, sound forecasts of demand, and lots of diligent scrutiny are the minimum requirements for success in mastering commodity markets.

(iv) Interest Rates.   **Interest rates** can have a significant impact on purchasing decisions, especially those related to timing. As interest rates rise, companies pay more to the lenders for additional capital, thus raising their costs and their selling prices. For the same reason, buyers are under increased pressure to reduce inventory and the price of equipment purchased.

(v) Payment Terms.   **Payment terms** refer to the agreement between buyer and seller regarding the timing and method of payment for goods and services supplied. Payment terms are closely related to interest rates because in many senses they represent a loan to the buyer by the seller for the period between receiving the product or service and the time that it takes for the payment to actually reach the sellers' coffers.

Payment terms for purchases generally follow a standard format, indicating the number of days in which the payment is due and any discounts that can be taken for payment at some specific, earlier date. For example:

- Net 45 means that payment in full is due in 45 days.
- Net 10th prox means that payment in full is due on the tenth day of the following month.
- 2 percent 10/Net 30 means that payments received within 10 days of the invoice date will receive a 2 percent discount and the balance is payable in full in 30 days.

Some organizations maintain the policy that payment is due from receipt of the invoice rather than its date since this is easier to verify. Most sellers invoice upon shipment, so this does not seem unfair, especially in a situation where the product being shipped takes weeks to arrive.

(vi) Buyer Financing. There are always situations where suppliers require advance payment, either to ensure that the contract can be started or to provide financing for equipment and materials in quantities not affordable at the supplier's current level of operation. Sometimes organizations advance loans to suppliers or provide equipment already owned in order to help them along. This practice has its pros and cons. Nonetheless, organizations must ensure fairness to other suppliers and conformance to applicable laws and regulations.

(vii) Cash Flow. The term "cash flow" is often used rather vaguely. Operating cash flow is the cash generated by the business after changes in working capital; net cash flow is the amount of money left after expenses at any particular time period. It may not be a good time to make large purchases when cash flow is at a low point because funds may need to be borrowed to cover the bill. Timing purchases to coincide with cash inputs can prove an effective tool in adding to the bottom line.

(c) LEGAL ASPECTS. While most of the legal aspects affecting procurement have been outlined in Chapter 4, as a professional you should be reminded of the importance of tracking legal developments so that you are in full compliance with the law, Sarbanes-Oxley (SOX), for example, which requires reporting commencing in November 2005.

(i) Tax Laws. While you will not have direct responsibility for taxes, you will need to know some basic principles under which tax laws operate so that you can take them into account when making certain procurement decisions. For example, in many states, purchases for products being resold (or that go into products being resold) do not require the payment of sales tax. In many areas, taxes on inventory are assessed just as they would be for real property. Software downloaded via the Internet is usually exempt from sales tax (considered a service rather than a product), while the same software purchased in a box will be subject to tax.

Tips and Techniques

Use tax is a tax levied on goods that are bought outside the taxing authority's jurisdiction and then brought into the jurisdiction. This tax is designed to discourage the purchase of products that are not subject to a sales tax.

(ii) Regulations. As noted, most of the regulations governing procurement operations relate to commonly used processes. These include regulations governing antitrust, intellectual property, environmental health and safety (including hazardous materials), international trade, and the Uniform Commercial Code. You will likely be required to track changes to these regulations as the compliance source for your organization.

12.4 SUMMARY

One of the Procurement Department's most frequently used analytical tools is the make-or-buy analysis. This comparative analysis enables you to determine whether or not outsourcing a product or service or manufacturing or performing it in-house is the most advantageous path for your organization. There a number of dynamics that must be considered, including specific analysis of needs and requirements, technical viability, risk, quality, and service capability. There is also the ever-important aspect of price to consider.

Similar to considerations you must take to determine whether to outsource a product or service or not is the process of determining whether to lease or buy. Leasing has a number of additional considerations that should be taken into account, including the impact on cash flow, tax liability, cost factors, budget considerations, and regulatory requirements. There are various lease types to consider, and they differ from one another significantly, each providing its own advantages and disadvantages.

There are also a number of financial tools you will be required to understand and use as part of developing strategies. Divided into two aspects—organizational and monetary considerations—these covered organizational and procurement structures and common financial factors such as depreciation, payment terms, interest rates, bond and commodity markets, financing, and cash flow.

KEY TERMS

Make or buy
Lease or buy
Leasing
Capital equipment
Lessee
Full-payout lease
Leveraged lease
Net lease
Operating lease
Lessors

Cash-flow management
Cooperatives or buying consortiums
Depreciation
Liability
Balance sheet
Return on investment (ROI)
Hedging
Commodity
Interest rates
Payment terms

MATERIAL MANAGEMENT AND SUPPLY OPERATIONS

LEARNING OBJECTIVES

1. Name the three classifications for inventory discussed in the chapter.
2. Calculate the turnover for $200 million of annual inventory used, with current inventory valued at $20 million. Explain the importance of the turnover calculation.
3. Explain the meaning of "MRPI II" and describe its importance in good management of inventory.
4. Name and define two concerns a Procurement Manager will have when dealing with disposal of materials.

Controlling the flow, storage, and stocking levels of materials is another of the key functions of supply management. Organizations, particularly those engaged in manufacturing operations, consider material management a core competency because production processes and materials go hand in hand. The effective flow of materials can, and often does, significantly affect the overall productivity—and thus the costs—of the manufacturer.

Because, in many instances, there is a great deal of capital invested in stored inventory, how the inventory is controlled and managed can also affect the organization's profitability. When profit is viewed as a return on the investment, it becomes clear that maximizing that return will depend largely on how rapidly existing inventory can be consumed and converted back into cash. Obviously, if all other conditions are equal, the organization with the smallest ratio of inventory to sales will likely be the most profitable.

In this chapter, we will examine the various methods of controlling inventory so that it can be used as a valuable resource to support operations rather than as a black hole for cash. These controls include strategies and methods for ordering and stocking materials, as well as effective processes for disposing of inventory that is no longer needed.

13.1 INVENTORY CONTROL AND MANAGEMENT SYSTEMS

Organizations that own and manage inventory are constantly seeking ways to reduce the size of that inventory in order to reduce the amount of nonproductive funds that are thus tied up. As most of you know, inventory generally doesn't do anything except consume valuable space and require a lot of cycle counting. For organizations that require inventory for perhaps justifiable reasons, such as using it as a buffer for unreliable supply or large swings in demand, the challenge comes with managing it so that as little as possible is needed. From this effort, a number of systems have been developed for determining when to order inventory and automating the management process. We'll describe some of these systems in this section.

(a) TYPES OF INVENTORY. Inventory is generally classified according to its functional type and, if used in manufacturing, its current state of production. Thus it is typical for material to be classified as **raw material (RM)**, **work-in-process (WIP)**, or **finished goods (FG)**. Raw material, in turn, can be classified as **direct material** (i.e., material that goes directly into the product being manufactured) or **indirect material** (material that supports manufacturing operations but does not ship out with the final product). In addition, there are inventories of materials you maintain that are not directly related to any production functions, such as MRO (maintenance, repair, and operations), as well as supplies and marketing support materials.

Before we look at how these inventories are managed, it might be useful to define their various natures. Let's start with raw materials.

(i) Raw Material Classifications. Raw materials, as the title implies, are materials in their basic state as they have been received and to which no manufacturing operations have been performed. They are in the first stage of the transformation process to the final manufactured product.

There are two major categories of raw materials:

1. **Direct material.** Direct material is the primary classification for raw materials in manufacturing operations. It is only the material that, after manufacturing processes are applied, ships out to a distributor or the final customer. If, for example, you manufacture hammers, then steel would be your primary direct material.

   The level of inventory for direct material is considered one of the manufacturing organization's key financial indicators. To demonstrate effective management of inventory, organizations use the term *turns*, referring to the number of times the inventory of direct materials will turn over during a period (usually a year). In simplest form, inventory turnover is calculated as the number of times the inventory is sold during the period or as the ratio of inventory to sales. Inventory turnover is also calculated as the cost of goods sold divided by the average level of inventory on hand.

2. **Indirect material.** Indirect material is the class of materials in the manufacturing process that does not actually ship to the customer as part of the final product. For example, the gas used to heat the furnaces that melt the steel in the manufacture of hammers is an indirect material. Similarly, the water that cools the metal is also an indirect material.

(ii) Work-in-Process (WIP).   Work-in-process describes manufactured goods that have not yet been completed. However, in order to be considered WIP, some labor other than handling and storage must have been directly applied. Components and assemblies are the typical types of WIP in most manufacturing operations.

(iii) Finished Goods.   Finished goods are those products that have completed the manufacturing production process and for which all necessary labor operations have been completed. Depending on the industry, finished goods are usually packaged and ready for shipment.

(iv) Non-Production-Related Materials.   Non-production-related materials are those not used in manufacturing at all, but rather that support the administrative operations of the organizations. MRO items such as light bulbs, copy paper, maintenance, construction, and janitorial supplies are a few examples. Nonproduction materials may also include inventories of promotional materials such as advertising flyers and catalogs. Many of them are managed by the same inventory management methods used in manufacturing so that their levels can remain as low as possible.

Capital goods are also a form of large expenditure assets tracked by the organization as though it were inventory. Capital goods are assets purchased for long-term use, such as machinery and other equipment that **depreciate** or lose value over a predetermined period of time.

(b) THE ROLE OF INVENTORY. Inventory has a specific role in manufacturing entities, and inventories are maintained by these organizations for a number of specific reasons:

- Inventory protects the organization from the uncertainties of supply and ensures that material is readily available when it is needed. Inventory buffers are most common in operations where demand and lead times vary considerably and are hard to predict.
- Inventory is often held in anticipation of a seasonal demand or other specific increase in demand or for a particular customer order. It can also be the result of canceled sales orders.
- Some situations result in inventory being created by the minimum quantity of orders required by a supplier or as a result of ordering larger amounts to receive special price breaks.
- Extra-large WIP inventories are often created through long production cycle times.

Regardless of the specific reason for maintaining the inventory in the first place, inventory must be closely controlled and monitored since it absorbs a great deal of the organization's available working capital. For a review of inventory management, let's look at the systems typically used to keep inventory to a minimum.

(c) SYSTEMS FOR MANAGING INVENTORY. Inventory management systems are tools used to control inventory so that materials are on hand when needed while minimizing the financial liability to the organization. Fundamental to these tools are the various ordering strategies you ultimately employ and the automated systems that support these tools.

(i) Ordering Strategies. An inventory ordering strategy is basically a method for determining the quantity of materials to be ordered and the timing for delivery of that order. There are several common methodologies in use that you should be familiar with that we will discuss in this section.

ORDER POINT REORDERING

The **order point** method of inventory replenishment establishes a predetermined minimum level of inventory that, when reached, will trigger a reorder. The calculation subtracts incoming orders from the stock on hand to determine when the reorder point has been reached. This method may require the calculation of a **safety stock**, typically based on the anticipated amount that will be used during the lead time it takes to replenish the stock. The actual formula is:

On-Hand Inventory − Incoming Orders − Safety Stock (if used)

= Reorder Point

FIXED ORDER QUANTITY

The fixed order quantity rule (sometimes called FOQ) states that the quantity ordered is the same fixed amount each time an order is required to cover a potential shortage, regardless of how much is actually needed to cover that shortage. Table 13.1 shows the incoming demand for a number of given weeks and the effect of this demand on the available balance of inventory at the end of each week. From the information in the bottom row, you can see that, based on a lead time of two weeks and a fixed order quantity of 200 parts (a number determined, perhaps, by the minimum order the supplier requires)—you will need to place an order in Week 3 to cover a planned deficit of 135 parts in Week 7 and in Week 5 to cover a planned deficit of 35 parts. Notice that while the shortages are different quantities, the amount ordered is always the same. Week 8 shows a question mark in the quantity to order because you do not have demand figures to cover the two-week lead time.

WEEK #	1	2	3	4	5	6	7	8
Demand	150	0	70	0	175	0	90	60
Net Balance	110	110	40	40	(135)	65	(35)	(135)
Planned Receipts	0	0	0	0	200	0	200	0
On Hand End of Week	110	110	40	40	65	65	165	30
Quantity to Order	0	0	200	0	200		0	?

TABLE 13.1   FIXED QUANTITY ORDER METHOD

PERIODIC ORDER QUANTITY

The **periodic order quantity** rule (sometimes called POQ) requires that the quantity ordered be enough to cover requirements for a fixed number of periods. Table 13.2 shows the same demand as Table 13.1, and you can see that orders are placed in the same intervals (every two weeks), but the orders are placed in the amount needed to cover the shortage during the two-week period following receipt. Notice that, in Week 5, 150 parts need to be ordered to cover the cumulative demand for Weeks 7 and 8 (90 + 60). Since you are ordering every two weeks exactly, your next scheduled order in Week 7 shows a question mark because you don't know what the demand will be in Week 9, at the end of the two-week lead time.

LOT FOR LOT

As the title implies, with a **lot-for-lot** (**L4L** or **LFL**) system, you order exactly what is needed for a given period. With respect to the quantity, you always order exactly enough to avoid a stock outage while ordering as little as possible. With respect to timing, you always order in time to ensure that no outages occur. Using the same figures used for Table 13.2, you can see in Table 13.3 that the only change is that the order originally placed in Week 5 for 150 parts is split into two orders one week apart, for 90 and 60 parts, respectively.

WEEK #	1	2	3	4	5	6	7	8
Demand	150	0	70	0	175	0	90	60
Net Balance	110	110	40	40	(135)	0	(90)	60
Planned Receipts	0	0	0	0	135	0	150	0
On Hand End of Week	110	110	40	40	0	0	60	0
Quantity to Order	0	0	135	0	150	0	?	0

TABLE 13.2 PERIODIC ORDER QUANTITY METHOD

WEEK #	1	2	3	4	5	6	7	8
Demand	150	0	70	0	175	0	90	60
Net Balance	110	110	40	40	(135)	0	(90)	60
Planned Receipts	0	0	0	0	135	0	150	0
On Hand End of Week	110	110	40	40	0	0	60	0
Quantity to Order	0	0	135	0	90	60	?	0

TABLE 13.3 LOT-FOR-LOT ORDERING METHOD

ECONOMIC ORDER QUANTITY

Economic order quantity (EOQ) is another inventory ordering model that attempts to minimize total inventory cost by answering the following two questions.

- How much should I order?
- How often should I place each order?

This model assumes that the demand faced by the firm is linear, that is, the rate of demand is constant or at least nearly constant. It also assumes that the purchase price of the product is not dependent on the quantity ordered at any given time but determined between purchaser and supplier in advance based upon the anticipated number of units to meet the demand over the coming period, typically annually.

The goal of the EOQ formula is to minimize total inventory cost. Inventory costs are assumed to be made up of total holding costs and ordering costs. Holding costs include the cost of financing the inventory along with the cost of physically storing and managing the inventory. These costs are usually expressed as a percentage of the value of the inventory. Ordering costs include the costs associated with actually placing the order. These include a labor cost as well as a material and overhead cost.

The basic economic order quantity formula is calculated as the square root of twice the annual usage times the ordering cost, divided by the carrying cost per unit. It's shown in the following formula:

$$E00 = \sqrt{\frac{2(\text{Annual usage in units})(\text{Order cost})}{(\text{Carrying cost per unit})}}$$

As an example, say that the usage for a particular part is 15,000 per year. Let's also assume that the organization orders the parts three times per year and that the average cost of placing an order is $129. Thus, the numerator in this calculation would appear as:

$$2 \times (15{,}000 \times 129) = 3{,}870{,}000$$

Carrying cost, the denominator in the formula, consists of the cost of storage and handling plus the theoretical cost of interest for the value of the inventory should it be financed. Calculating the carrying cost is a bit more difficult. Let's take some shortcuts in establishing the interest cost by assuming the average daily inventory volume is 7,500 parts, and each part costs $1.10. This means that there is an average daily value of $8,250 on hand (7,500 × 1.10 = 8,250). If interest rates were 5 percent per year, the interest for one day would be approximately $1.13 per day ((.05/365) × 8,250 = 1.13). Calculating the annual interest cost per unit is as follows:

$$\text{Average Interest Cost/Unit} = (1.13 \times 365)/7{,}500 = \$0.055$$

Continuing the calculation requires a determination of the storage and handling costs. Let's assume that 7,500 parts (the average daily inventory) uses 50 square feet of storage at a monthly cost of $0.45 per square foot or $22.50 per month. If you multiply this by 12 months and then divide by the average number of parts stored, you can calculate the average storage costs per unit:

$$\text{Average Storage Cost/Unit} = (22.50 \times 12)/7{,}500 = \$0.036$$

The remaining calculation requires an estimate of the handling costs per unit. Let's assume that the handling costs are simply the cost of cycle counting. If you cycle count four times each year (once per quarter) and it takes 10 minutes (0.1667 hour) at an average labor cost of $18 per hour, the cost would be calculated as follows:

$$\text{Handling Cost/Unit} = ((18 \times 0.1667) \times 4)/7{,}500 = \$0.002$$

You now have the denominator for the formula:

$$\text{Carrying Cost} = \text{Interest Cost} + \text{Storage Cost} + \text{Handling Cost}$$

$$= (0.055 + 0.036 + 0.002) = \$0.093/\text{Unit}$$

Using these numbers to complete the formula:

$$\text{Square Root of } (3{,}870{,}000/0.093) = 6{,}451 \text{ parts per order}$$

Using this formula, you would then order parts approximately twice per year at an interval of 157 days. To calculate this, you divide the parts per order by the annual requirements and then multiply 365 by that fraction:

$$\text{Days to Reorder} = 365 \times (6{,}451/15{,}000) = 156.95$$

Using EOQ effectively requires strict adherence to a number of requirements:

- Demand is known with certainty.
- Demand is relatively constant over time.
- No shortages are allowed.
- Lead time for the receipt of orders remains constant.
- The order quantity is received all at once.

If you are lacking any one of these criteria, use caution because your calculation will probably have a wide margin of error.

(ii) Automated Processes. Managing inventory through automated processes has become fairly common as a result of the widespread use of ERP systems. Most organizations maintain computerized **perpetual inventories** that automatically add incoming receipts to the quantity on hand and then subtract issues from that amount to provide an up-to-the-minute tally of the inventory on hand. In addition to using automated systems, many organizations today also rely on their suppliers to manage and keep track of inventories that are held on consignment. Ultimately, this may prove to be the most effective way of managing inventory because, among other factors, it enables the supplier to integrate usage in its customer's facility with its own planning strategy. (Supplier-managed inventory is discussed later in this section.)

MRP AND MRPII

As discussed in Chapter 8, material requirements planning (MRP) and manufacturing resource planning (MRPII) are computerized, time-based priority planning techniques that calculate material requirements and schedule supply to meet changing demand across all product lines. MRP, the initially developed system, was created in the United States and Canada during the 1960s. MRP takes into consideration customer orders and planning forecasts to determine inventory requirements. MRPII is essentially MRP but with some additional features. Typically, an MRPII package includes elements such as cost information, management reports, and the ability to model situations through "what-if" analysis. It may also include *capacity requirements planning*, a tool that determines the loading at a workstation or throughout the entire factory so that capacity constraints can be reflected in the planning process.

TIPS AND TECHNIQUES

MRPII stands for manufacturing resources planning, signifying a concentration on the planning of all manufacturing resources, rather than limiting planning to just the material requirements. The "II" designation is used to distinguish this form from its MRP predecessor.

When relevant data has been gathered regarding the status of parts, assemblies, and resources, the lead time of every component can be determined based upon a variety of manufacturing conditions. As soon as an incoming customer order is received, the backlog for the manufacturing organization and the delivery time for product can be calculated. An MRP system can call attention to constraints such as overloaded production centers, the effect of incoming orders, changes in capacity, shortages, delays in manufacturing, and delays by suppliers so that effective action can be taken to reduce them in a timely fashion.

From a systemic perspective, MRP relies on two basic types of information to calculate requirements:

1. **Structural information.** Structural information is information about the organization's items (parts or components) and how each of the different items is related to one another. It includes important ordering information for each item such as lead time, lot (or batch) size, and where the item is obtained from (for example, whether it's purchased or manufactured in-house). The key point about structural information is that it changes relatively infrequently.

2. **Tactical information.** Tactical information is information about the current state of manufacturing; for example, sales orders (real and forecast) pending, the master production schedule, on-hand inventory levels, and unfilled purchase orders. Obviously, the key point about this information is that it changes frequently.

DEMAND CONCEPTS

In procurement, **demand** generally means the actual or projected usage of the items you are monitoring. The concept of demand is very closely related to the MRP process and is an integral aspect of inventory management. For this reason, demand is typically classified in terms of the conditions that generate it. Thus, there are two basic types of demand:

1. **Independent demand** is any demand for a product or service that is generated externally, usually by customer orders. It is usually difficult to predict and quantify.

2. **Dependent demand** is dependent in quantity, quality, and timing on its related independent demand, usually in the form of an incoming customer order or aggregation of orders. The materials needed to fulfill such incoming orders are by nature dependent upon that order in the first place. An independent order for a computer from an assembly facility, for example, creates a dependent demand for a motherboard and a certain set of other specific subassembly components. MRP and MRPII systems are primarily dedicated to tracking these dependencies and calculating dependent demand patterns as a primary function in inventory control.

In most MRP systems, the dependent demand generated by "exploding" the bills of material (BOMs) for incoming orders does not assume an infinite capacity for capacity-constrained resources (such as machines and people). Therefore, specific methods are required to schedule capacity-constrained resources. This scheduling process usually generates a manufacturing plan, and it is the responsibility of the Procurement Department or materials control group to ensure that the materials are available as required by the plan.

DEMAND PLANNING

Demand planning is a process of collaboration among all of the participants—sales, operations, finance, as well as affected groups in the supply community—in the demand forecasting process. Each needs to receive and provide data.

Demand planning is also a critical element in enabling a more comprehensive process like a collaborative planning, forecasting, and replenishment process (CPFR). It employs the demand forecast as the foundation for its planning and offers guidance on how the forecasted elements will be actually used. Demand planning allows the organization to make accurate customer demand predictions to better manage inventory replenishment with forecasting.

CPFR is a set of standardized business processes shared between trading partners. As in demand planning, collaborating partners develop forecasts and operational plans based on mutual objectives and measures.

(iii) Just-in-Time Inventory Management. Meeting the requirements of a manufacturing plan and at the same time allowing for maximum flexibility and last-minute changes due to customer order changes requires a truly flexible demand management system. **Just-in-time (JIT) inventory management** processes (also known as lean or stockless manufacturing) were developed for just this reason.

JIT and MRP are two distinctly different systems for controlling production. While MRP is based on meeting predicted demand during a period of time, JIT is based on actual usage. JIT is a means of market pull inventory management conducted in an environment of continuing improvement. Use of JIT methods results in considerably reduced inventory and enhanced customer response time. However, to be successful it requires a systemic and highly cooperative approach to inventory receipt, throughput, and delivery.

Although JIT was developed for production environments, the process can be extended to all business environments. The basic concept is to receive what is needed just in time for it to be used. This, in effect, places the responsibility on the supplier to get what is needed to where it is needed, just before it is needed.

JIT is also a management philosophy that works to eliminate sources of manufacturing waste by producing the proverbial "right part in the right place at the right time." In theory, waste results from any activity that adds cost without adding value, such as moving and storing. JIT is thus designed to improve profits and return on investment (ROI) by reducing inventory levels (increasing the inventory turnover rate), improving product quality, reducing production and delivery lead times, and reducing other costs (such as those associated with machine setup and equipment breakdown).

(iv) Supplier-Managed Inventory (SMI). The concept of SMI or **vendor-managed inventory (VMI)**, whichever you prefer to call it, is a logical progression from ideas that generated JIT inventory management in the first place. The goal of both is to build enough flexibility into the manufacturing system (or the supply chain itself) so that customer demand can be met in as short a time frame as possible. In today's business environment, the consumer wants immediate gratification and will likely turn to another product if the one chosen is not available relatively instantly.

SMI places the responsibility on the supplier to meet incoming customer demand (or rapidly changing forecasts). Often working from the manufacturer's MRP outputs, the supplier assesses incoming demand and plans operations accordingly to ensure that material is available for production exactly when it is needed. Although in most SMI applications the supplier is responsible for managing the inventory, the buying organization pays for it when received as it would if it had ordered the material directly. Consequently, there must exist a very close partnership built upon mutual trust in order for the management of materials to be confidently turned back to the supplier. In these situations, however, the materials management group (or Procurement Department) must closely monitor activities, working with the supplier on a continuous improvement process.

The ultimate extension of SMI is consignment inventory. Managed in essentially the same way as SMI, the major difference is that the supplier owns the inventory until it is actually withdrawn from stock for production. To be considered true consignment, the stock must be located at the buyer's facility and owned by the supplier with no contingencies for automatic purchase of obsolescent stock.

(d) INVENTORY ECONOMICS. Since manufacturing organizations often have a great deal of capital resources tied up in inventory, minimizing inventory can result in better overall financial performance. However, there should always be a balance maintained between inefficient use of inventory and the needs of meeting market demand. In general, you will want to consider how to maximize the return on the organization's investment in inventory. In this evaluation, you may want to consider that ROI is a ratio that measures how much over how long. So you can conceivably improve the performance of inventory investment both by reducing the overall size of the inventory, and therefore its value, and by shortening the length of time your organization owns it, and thereby its rate of return.

(i) Inventory Turnover. One typical measure of the efficient use of inventory is its **turnover ratio**. Inventory turnover measures the speed that inventory is used relative to sales. It's typically calculated by dividing annual sales by average inventory, using the average inventory over an accounting period rather than just an ending-inventory value. Inventory turnover can also be calculated by dividing the

total annual value of all inventory used (or issued) by the amount of inventory currently on hand:

$$\text{Annual Inventory Used}/\text{On-Hand Inventory} = \text{Turnover}$$

For example, if the annual inventory used was \$100 million and the current inventory is valued at \$10 million, the turnover rate would be 10 times annually. Low turnover is an indication that inventory is too high for the accompanying level of sales.

(e) LEAD-TIME CONSIDERATIONS.   As noted earlier in this chapter, inventory can be used to buffer stock outages caused by suppliers and to support variable customer demand. Strategically, the consideration of when to carry inventory and how much should be held can be rationalized according to the service levels the organization is attempting to achieve. Service levels can be measured in terms of the frequency of stock outages and the seriousness of the effects of the outages, such as production stoppages or order cancellations. For the most part, these effects can be financially evaluated and related to the cost of carrying various levels of inventory, with strategic decisions made according to the degree of support desired.

13.2 PHYSICAL MANAGEMENT AND INVENTORY ACCOUNTING

In order to effectively manage inventory, it must be properly maintained, reported, and carried on the business records. Automated systems rely on a virtual accuracy of 100 percent in order to properly maintain minimal amounts of inventory. In a JIT environment, even the smallest discrepancy can result in a planning or financial disaster. In this section, we review some of the methods and tools available to maintain accurate records and account for discrepancies.

(a) CONTROLLING INVENTORY.   Inventory control refers to the activities and methods used by organizations to receive, track, maintain, and issue materials. It also includes the management of inventory from a financial standpoint to ensure that it is accurately accounted for and valued. This process involves the actual physical storage, handling, and issuance of materials, as well as the record keeping that goes along with it.

(i) Stores.   Organizations that maintain substantial amounts of inventory usually manage it by keeping it in specific locations. These stocking locations are usually referred to as **stores**. The general function of the stores operation is to physically manage and issue parts and supplies to internal groups as they are needed. There are two broad systems for managing stores:

1. **Open stores.** When the value of inventory or the need for security is relatively low, or when access to it is required quite frequently, materials

may be stored in open locations that are accessible directly by production staff, known as **open stores**. Record keeping is typically loose, relying primarily on physical cycle counting to reconcile on-hand inventory levels.

2. **Closed stores.** Conversely, when inventory must be tightly controlled because of its value, scarcity, or potential safety issues, it is generally maintained in a limited-access stockroom, called **closed stores**. Here, receipts and issues are closely recorded and often require authorized signatures or approvals before inventory release.

(ii) Storage and Retrieval Systems.   Within the storage facility, and regardless of its type, material is physically stored using various systems for stocking and retrieval:

- **Specified locations.** In some storage schemes, designated bins or storage shelves are allocated for the same specific items of inventory. This enables rapid retrieval when goods are uncontrolled because the staff becomes familiar with where materials are actually located and can find them quite easily.
- **Random-access locations.** In automated storage and retrieval systems, inventory locations are stored on a computer system. When inventory is received, it is automatically allocated the first open space designated on the computer system and physically placed in that location. When it is needed, the material is found by using the computer system to report its exact location.
- **Automated storage and retrieval systems.** Automated storage and retrieval systems rely on computerized mechanical systems—often robotic—to store and retrieve material with little human intervention. Parts are delivered to specified locations either on demand or in accordance with a manufacturing schedule.

(iii) Record Systems.   Today, most inventory record-keeping systems are automated. However, depending on the system used for controlling inventory—open or closed stores, for example—inventory records are updated on a **periodic** or **perpetual** basis.

Periodic updating requires that physical counts are taken at designated intervals and used to update the records of quantities on hand. This system is most commonly used for small parts such as nails or screws or liquids that are difficult to account for precisely.

Perpetual inventory is used when precise and up-to-date accounting is required. This system records exact receipts and issues as they occur so that the on-hand inventory is precise.

(iv) Cycle Counting.   **Cycle counting**, physically counting inventory to ensure its accuracy, is used to update inventory records when usage varies imprecisely or is nonstandard (as may be the case with commodities, liquids, and fasteners) and when inventory accuracy is critical. It is also commonly employed when auditing or verifying the actual value of the inventory at a specific time.

The timing for cycle counting often follows a specific schedule based on the value of the inventory as segmented according to the typical Pareto principle of **ABC analysis**, where the most valuable materials are counted most frequently: A items may be counted monthly, B items quarterly, and C items annually. Cycle counts are also taken more frequently for parts that are used more frequently since there may be a higher risk of inaccuracy.

(b) RECONCILING DISCREPANCIES.   The difference between the recorded inventory and the actual inventory found on hand when it is physically counted requires some form of reconciliation. Most commonly, the recorded inventory is adjusted to reflect the actual inventory counted during the cycle count. However, you should always keep in mind that such variation has financial implications, and how it is accounted for financially depends upon the organization's policy. Low-value errors associated with high volumes of transactions are common and typically tolerated. Generally, such losses are absorbed by an overhead variance account. However, loss of valuable inventory through damage or theft can become a serious financial issue if it becomes commonplace, so you will want to ensure that proper safeguards are in place so that it does not become a serious issue. Judicious use of closed stores for inventory security may circumvent such problems.

13.3 DISPOSITION SURPLUS ASSETS

Most organizations, at one time or another, generate surplus materials, scrap, or obsolete equipment that may have value to others outside the organization. Surplus materials and equipment can be generated in a number of ways:

- Scrap or waste generated by manufacturing operations.
- Excess purchases.
- Obsolete material and supplies.
- Discontinued finished products.
- Decommissioned equipment.

Converting these nonproductive assets to cash or, at the very least, minimizing the cost of their disposal, can certainly add financial value to the organization. Nevertheless, it is surprising to learn that many organizations have no process or system at all for effectively handling these assets.

ONE OF OUR AUTHOR'S (FRED SOLLISH'S) FIRST VISIT TO CORPORATE STORAGE

As a newly appointed procurement manager, Fred was assigned the task of supervising the revamping of his organization's 5,000-square-foot storage facility. He was told it was used mostly for retired records. Although it sounded simple, he was immediately challenged: on his first visit, Fred was unable to open the door because it was apparently blocked by something inside. With some help, he was able to raise the rollup receiving door and was presented with a startling scene: equipment and surplus materials were randomly piled everywhere, from floor to ceiling, covering every available square foot of the facility. It was impossible to enter without climbing upon or over something.

Fred hired a disposal firm, which inventoried the usable equipment and placed it in an already scheduled auction for a similar firm. The company recovered close to $90,000. What's more, with all the equipment and surplus removed, they found that the records occupied a very small portion of the warehouse. The company sent them to a records storage facility and turned in the lease on the warehouse, saving another $2,200 per month.

(a) DISPOSAL STRATEGIES.   The Procurement Department is a natural resource for surplus disposal since it has continuing contact with both internal users and suppliers. With knowledge of the needs of internal users, Procurement has an opportunity to find secondary uses for surplus within the organization. Procurement may also have specialized knowledge about where the material or equipment was purchased from initially and may have access to reselling channels through them. There are two main concerns you'll have as a Procurement professional when it comes to disposal of materials: The first are your legal obligations, and the second is the disposal of hazardous materials. Let's discuss these in more detail.

(i) Legal Aspects.   Before beginning any disposal operations, you should first acquaint yourself with any key legal aspects that might be associated with the specific items you are proposing to dispose of, such as transfer of legal title, liabilities, and implied warranties. You will also want to be certain that you prepare the appropriate sales "as is" documents. Since legal requirements can be as varied as the materials and equipment you are giving up for disposal, it is imperative to get the proper legal counsel prior to going forward.

(ii) Hazardous Materials Disposal.   Hazardous materials must be disposed of in accordance with applicable laws and regulations. In the United States, the U.S. Environmental Protection Agency (EPA) defines the nature of specific hazardous materials and prescribes the methods for their disposal. The U.S. Department of Transportation (DOT) prescribes the method for transporting hazardous materials and their required documentation. There are also numerous state and

local regulations governing the disposal of hazardous waste. New York State, for example, has enacted a series of regulations that is intended to supplement those of the federal government. (For more information, visit *www.dec.state.ny.us/website/dshm/regs/370parts.htm*.)

(iii) Other Environmental Considerations.

ISO 14000 is a group of environmental management standards developed by the International Organization for Standardization in 1996. It is designed to provide an internationally accepted framework for environmental management, measurement, evaluation, and auditing, to provide organizations with the tools needed to assess and control the environmental impact of their activities. In addition to environmental management systems, the standards address environmental auditing, environmental labels and declarations, environmental performance evaluation, and life-cycle assessments.

In Europe, the *WEEE (waste electrical and electronic equipment)* regulation, which was designed to tackle the issue of surplus TV and computer equipment recycling, requires the original equipment manufacturer to take back all surpluses for disposal. With an effective date of August 2005, this regulation will require manufacturers and importers to recycle a large variety of equipment from customers ranging from mobile phones to tea kettles. Further, businesses are expected to provide for the recycling of existing electrical and electronic equipment that will become waste in the future.

The *Basel Convention*, an international agreement on the control of cross-boundary movements of hazardous wastes and their disposal was adopted in 1989 by a United Nations–sponsored conference of 116 nations held in Basel, Switzerland. It restricts trade in hazardous waste, some nonhazardous wastes, solid wastes, and incinerator ash.

The *Kyoto Protocol (http://unfccc.int/resource/docs/convkp/kpeng.html)*, also known as the *Kyoto Agreement*, is a United Nations–sponsored agreement to prevent global warming signed by 38 developed countries. At a summit held in 1997, those signing the treaty agreed to reduce their emission of *greenhouse gases* by the year 2012. Greenhouse gases are gases such as carbon dioxide (CO_2), water vapor, methane (CH_4), nitrous oxide (NO_2), and other trace gases that trap heat in the atmospheres and produce a greenhouse effect that causes an increase in global temperatures. However, by 2002, several countries, including the U.S. and Japan, had all but reneged on their promises. The use of public areas for landfill has also come under tighter regulation all around the globe by local governments, and many countries have enacted regulations supplementing those issued by their respective governments. By focusing on landfills, environmental movements have addressed two major issues: First, there is an urgent need to develop more sustainable resources through recycling, and one way to drive recycling is through limitations on the amount of solid waste allowed in landfills. Second, the gases emitted by landfills are considered a source of global warming.

(b) DISPOSAL METHODS.   Depending on their nature and the legal and environmental considerations governing them, surplus materials and equipment can be disposed of in a variety of ways. To be truly effective, however, the process requires proper planning, organization, and assessment. Not surprisingly, the market demand for surplus materials and equipment follows a similar pattern as its newly manufactured counterparts. It would be wise for you to understand the nature of the marketplace so that you can make informed decisions on the value and salability of your organization's surplus.

The methods for asset disposal are fairly common and are listed below. The challenge lies in matching the material with its optimum method of disposal, which will, of course, depend on the nature of the materials and the needs of your organization. Following are some of the disposal methods you may utilize as a Procurement professional:

- **Return.** One of the easiest alternatives is to return excess material or equipment to its original manufacturer. Often this also provides the best value since the supplier can offer a credit on future sales that can be timed to the actual revenue generated by your organization. Keep in mind, however, that if you are a small buyer of these items, you will not likely have a great deal of leverage to compel the supplier to accept the return.
- **Reuse.** Another excellent method of disposal is to transfer the materials or equipment internally to another department that can use it. This not only avoids the expense of disposal, but it may also save money by avoiding the direct purchase of similar materials.
- **Sale.** Sale of excess assets provides an excellent way to generate cash. However, keep in mind that your sale of this material will likely compete with the sale of new products and may be discouraged by your supplier. Also keep in mind that it might be costly to find potential buyers and to make the sale.

   One alternative is to consign the material to a third-party reseller who already has channels for moving this. You will likely have to pay a large percentage of the revenue, but using a third party might provide the path of least resistance for you.

   You may also want to explore surplus auctions. These are conducted both live and online. Be cautious, however, of the effort involved not only in selling but in collecting the funds.
- **Trade-in.** Trading in old equipment for credit toward the purchase of similar new equipment may also prove effective, if the need to purchase new equipment actually exists. Even when the value of the surplus is low, this may be an easy way for the supplier to offer you a discount and may save you the trouble of actually having to go through the physical disposal process yourself.

- **Donation.** Depending on the material or equipment, donating it to a charitable operation may provide excellent community relations and may also offer a tax deduction (if your organization is otherwise profitable). Donating surplus materials and usable equipment fulfills a social responsibility, as well.

TIPS AND TECHNIQUES

> Don't count on your ability to give the surplus away to charity. Many charities are inundated with such donations and have little ability to use or accept them.

- **Cannibalization.** If you have no use for the entire surplus product (or equipment), you might want to consider tearing it down for usable spare parts. While this is not a preferred use for excess assets, it may prove more profitable than having to put it in a landfill or sell it for scrap.
- **Scrap.** Again, depending upon the exact nature of the surplus, scrap dealers may have a use for it and may be willing to purchase it and pick it up if the price is right. You can expect, at best, to realize a few pennies on the initial dollar your organization spent for its purchase. However, as previously noted, regulations such as WEEE may soon spawn new recycling industries that of necessity find increasing value in scrap materials.

13.4 SUMMARY

Managing and controlling inventory, often one of the major assets of the organization, is another key area where the Procurement Department can add value. To accomplish this effectively requires an understanding of the various reasons for keeping inventory, such as safety stock and economic ordering methods, as well as being familiar with the specific classifications of inventory such as direct and indirect materials, work-in-process, and finished goods. The Procurement professional must also be able to implement and utilize various common systems for managing inventory levels and reordering stock. These systems are often automated and include MRP and MRPII, along with various demand-based strategies such as JIT and SMI.

In this chapter, you also looked at various methods for managing and controlling inventory, including stores, storage and retrieval systems, and records systems. In this role, the Procurement professional will also need to know how to maintain accurate inventory counts and reconcile discrepancies that may occur.

As a central focus for managing the disposal of surplus and obsolete assets, the procurement team is frequently responsible for determining the most valuable method of disposal for the organization.

KEY TERMS

Raw material (RM)
Work-in-process (WIP)
Finished goods (FG)
Direct material
Indirect material
Capital goods
Depreciate
Order point
Safety stock
Periodic order quantity (POQ)
Lot for Lot (LFL)
Economic order quantity (EOQ)

Perpetual inventories
Demand
Just-in-time inventory management (JIT)
Supplier-managed inventory (SMI)
Vendor-managed inventory (VMI)
Turnover ratio
Stores
Open stores
Periodic or perpetual
Cycle counting
ABC analysis

LOGISTICS

LEARNING OBJECTIVES

1. List ten activities which typically are part of Logistics Management, as described in the chapter.
2. Explain the need for a high level of "integration" required in a Supply Network.
3. Name eight regional trading alliances and governing bodies described in this chapter. Describe recent events involving the *"European Union"*.
4. The U.S. Department of Homeland Security is one of the most recent government agencies to have an impact on logistics management. Name five functions that come within the scope of the agency.

The term "**logistics**" derives from an ancient French military term for soldiers' barracks or quarters, **loger**. Interestingly, the early supply arm of the military was known as Quartermasters, a group markedly inefficient during Napoleon Bonaparte's historical march to Moscow, where the lack of an effective supply management process resulted in the loss of an entire army. Barely 5,000 of the original force of over 500,000 returned home; starvation and cold resulting from the inability to properly supply the army accounted for the majority of the loss.

In the business world, logistics can be equally important and can have the same fatal effects if managed poorly, although the victim is typically the corporate entity rather than its individuals. Today's concept of supply chain management recognizes this importance and seeks to develop effective, efficient processes that focus on controlling the flow of materials from origin to end user. This process is critical to the effectiveness of globalization.

14.1 THE LOGISTICS PROCESS

In this section, we turn our attention to the multiple aspects of logistics to examine how the discipline affects the commercial organization.

(a) DEFINITIONS OF LOGISTICS.   In today's complex commercial environment, with its ever-expanding global reach and a focus on process integration between business enterprises, it is hardly surprising that definitions associated with the term "logistics" have likewise evolved. The views of what constitutes the boundaries of the study and practice of logistics are varied. One definition describes logistics as:

> The process of strategically managing the procurement, movement and storage of materials, parts and finished inventory (and the related information flows) through the organization and its marketing channels in such a way that current and future profitability are maximized through the cost-effective fulfillment or orders.[1]

The **Council of Supply Chain Management Professionals** (**CSCMP**, previously known as the Council of Logistics Management [CLM]), offers a more expanded view that logistics is intimately intertwined with supply chain management processes:

> Logistics Management is that part of Supply Chain Management that plans, implements, and controls the efficient, effective forward and reverse flow and storage of goods, services and related information between the point of origin and the point of consumption in order to meet customers' requirements.[2]

From a supply management perspective, it is most important to consider the *management* of logistics as a body of knowledge and practice that:

> Logistics Management activities typically include inbound and outbound transportation management, fleet management, warehousing, materials handling, order fulfillment, logistics network design, inventory management, supply/demand planning, and management of third party logistics services providers. To varying degrees, the logistics function also includes sourcing and procurement, production planning and scheduling, packaging and assembly, and customer service. It is involved in all levels of planning and execution—strategic, operational and tactical. Logistics Management is an integrating function, which coordinates and optimizes all logistics activities, as well as integrates logistics activities with other functions including marketing, sales manufacturing, finance and information technology.[3]

Based upon this definition, we may view the scope of logistics management as shown in Figure 14.1.

The scope of logistics management requires that we should view logistics as an integrative, process-oriented set of activities. This requires the orchestration of materials, human resources, and information not only within a business enterprise, but also between the numerous enterprises that constitute a supply chain/supply network.

---

1. Martin Christopher. *Logistics and Supply Chain Management: Creating Value-Adding Networks*, 4th ed. FT Press. UK: Pearson Education, Ltd., 2011, p. 4.
2. Council of Supply Chain Management Professionals (CSCMP). "Supply Chain Management/Logistics Management Definitions." Oak Brook, IL, 2011. *www.cscmp.org/AboutCSCMP/Definitions.asp*.
3. Ibid.

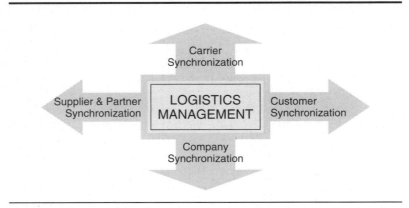

FIGURE 14.1   THE SCOPE OF LOGISTICS MANAGEMENT

(b) THE MILITARY DIMENSION OF LOGISTICS.   In military logistics, experts manage how and when to move resources to the places they are needed. In military science, maintaining one's supply lines while disrupting those of the enemy is a crucial element of military strategy, since an armed force without food, fuel, and ammunition is defenseless.

Logistics has been around for as long as there have been armies and navies with which cities, territories, and nation-states have attempted to exert their will via military force on others. The earliest known standing army was that of the Assyrians at around 700 B.C. The need to feed and equip a substantial force along with the means of transportation (i.e., horses, camels, mules, and oxen) would mean that it could not linger in one place for very long.

The U.S. Department of Defense places a strategic emphasis on the study and application of logistics. The U.S. Air Force Institute of Technology identifies the acquisition of materials and the management of information associated with the deployment and sustainability of its weapons systems as **Acquisition Logistics**. This view encompasses everything involved in acquiring logistics support equipment and personnel for a new weapons system. The formal definition is "the process of systematically identifying, defining, designing, developing, producing, acquiring, delivering, installing, and upgrading *logistics* support capability requirements through the acquisition process for Air Force systems, subsystems, and equipment."[4]

The U.S. Department of Defense also places an emphasis on the ongoing support of its weapons systems in the field, long after manufacture and delivery. Critically, this view of military logistics stresses the critical nature of spare parts provisioning. **Integrated Logistics Support (ILS)** encompasses the unified management of the technical logistics elements that plan and develop the support

4.   Air Force Institute of Technology, Graduate School of Acquisition and Logistics. Wright-Patterson AFB. Dayton, OH: In *Logistics World*, Logistics Dictionary. Matthew D. Cox, 1997. *www.logisticsworld.com/logistics/glossary.asp*.

requirements for a weapons system. This can include hardware, software, and the provisioning of training and maintenance resources.[5]

(c) THE COMMERCIAL DIMENSION OF LOGISTICS. From organizations such as Toyota came the then-revolutionary philosophies of just-in-time (JIT) and Total Quality Management (TQM). From these philosophies have arisen and developed the competitive strategies that world-class organizations now practice. Aspects of these that are now considered normal approaches to management include Kaizen (or continuous improvement), improved customer-supplier relationships, supplier management, vendor-managed inventory, customer focus on both the specifier and user, and, above all, recognition that there is a supply chain along which all efforts can be optimized to enable effective delivery of the required goods and services. This means a move away from emphasizing functional performance and a consideration of the whole chain of supply as a total process. It means a move away from the "silo" mentality to thinking and managing "outside the (functional) box." In both commercial and academic senses, the recognition of supply chain management as an enabler of competitive advantage is increasingly coming to the fore. This has resulted in key elements being seen as best practice in their own right, and includes value for money, partnering, strategic procurement policies, integrated supply chain/network management, total cost of ownership, business process reengineering, and outsourcing.

However, the history of logistics in the U.S. commercial sector is best characterized as a view of logistics as a loose collection of functional specialties, with little integrative ability. While this may be said of many business enterprise functions, the problem of "**functional silos**" has been particularly acute in the field of logistics. In many ways, the evolution of modern logistics has paralleled the development of emergence of process integration both within business enterprises, and more recently, throughout the supply chain. This trend is demonstrated in Figure 14.2.[6]

In traditional organizations, work within a firm was performed by specialists who often worked in isolation from one another and, most frequently, competed with one another for scarce resources and funds. Additionally, functional isolation

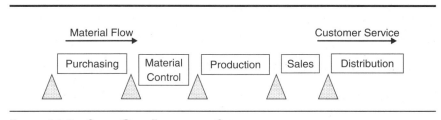

FIGURE 14.2 STAGE ONE: FUNCTIONAL SILOS

5. University of Scranton/Defense Logistics Agency, from "Integrated Logistics," *HUM—The Government Computer Magazine*, December 1993, Walter Cooke. In *Logistics World*. Logistics Dictionary. Matthew D. Cox, 1997. *www.logisticsworld.com/logistics/glossary.asp*.

6. Adapted from: Martin Christopher. *Logistics and Supply Chain Management: Creating Value-Adding Networks*, p. 19.

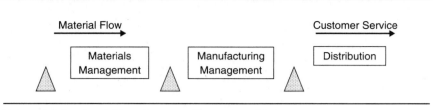

FIGURE 14.3   STAGE TWO: INTERNAL FUNCTIONAL INTEGRATION

was complicated by fragmented information flows and transactions. Consequently, little attention was paid to the needs of the customer. Under the umbrella of logistics, organizational silos were further fragmented as evidenced by further organizational specialization, such as warehousing, material handling, transportation (often organized as inbound freight and receiving, and outbound freight and shipping), fleet operations, where applicable, and distribution operations.

After World War II, the concept of materials management introduced some degree of functional integration internal to the firm (Figure 14.3).

In this stage of development, many firms reduced the organizational conflict in consolidating many of the functions associated with the manufacturing process and the acquisition and planning of material requirements. Further, links with distribution requirements driven by customer demand were organizationally linked within the firm. This internal integration was mostly driven by acquired information capabilities with the development of material requirements planning (MRP) and distribution requirements planning (DRP information systems in the late 1950s through early 1980s). The next stage in the integration of business logistics may be characterized by effectively linking internal functional information systems, as shown in Figure 14.4.

Once again, the potential of the integration of previously isolated functional silos and their activities was made possible by the introduction of more powerful information systems, such as manufacturing resource planning (MRP II) and distribution resource planning (DRPII). The introduction and development of these powerful planning systems continued throughout the 1980s and early 1990s.

The next evolutionary stage in the integration of logistics processes may be illustrated as shown in Figure 14.5.

During the period of the mid-1990s and today, powerful **enterprise resource planning (ERP)** information systems have enabled the integration between suppliers,

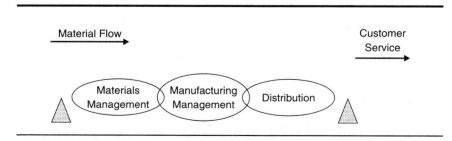

FIGURE 14.4   STAGE THREE: INTERNAL PROCESS INTEGRATION

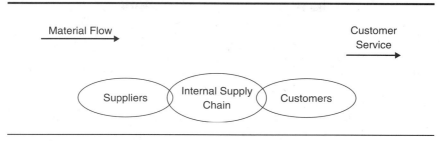

FIGURE 14.5   STAGE FOUR: PROCESS INTEGRATION BETWEEN A FIRM, ITS SUPPLIERS, AND CUSTOMERS

the business enterprise, and its customers. The potential for vastly improved planning and scheduling of materials and finished goods to better serve the enterprise's customers is still emerging. This potential has demonstrated the effectiveness of a process view of not only a particular business, but has given rise to a realization that customer satisfaction may be best served through the application of the concept of supply chain management (SCM).

(d) LOGISTICS MANAGEMENT AND SUPPLY CHAIN MANAGEMENT.   Modern logistics management has evolved into a potent strategic competitive weapon in global business. The contemporary view of SCM lends itself to a continued evolution of logistics as a core competency for any business enterprise. To understand this point, one must examine supply chain management as a concept that demands the utmost in the seamless integration of information regarding manufacturing and production capabilities, supplier performance, inventory, and customer service and demand management. Instead of viewing logistics management and its processes as a series of functional relationships, it is more appropriate to view the set of complex and seamless relationships between a firm's suppliers, the internal competencies of the firm, and the needs of its customers as a "network" that spans all functions of all constituents of a "chain"[7] (Figure 14.6).

The supply network model in fact suggests integration well beyond a supply chain management model. The collaborative efforts of multiple channel members assemble to meet the real needs of the end customer, so that the requirement for seamless value-added processes is very real. When we seek to further integrate the entirety of the processes in such an environment, we are combining the objectives of both customer requirements management (CRM) and **supplier relationship management (SRM)**. The result is a concept known as **value chain management**. Thus, VCM may be defined as:

> The integration and optimization of all resources, starting with the vendor's vendor. It integrates information, materials, labor, facilities, logistics, etc. into a

---

7.   James D. Reeds. Adapted from David N. Burt, Sheila Petcavage, and Richard Pinkerton. Supply Management, 8th ed. New York: McGraw-Hill/Irwin, 2009, p. 625.

time responsive, capacity managed solution that maximizes financial resources and minimizes waste, i.e. optimizes value for both the Supply Chain Network and the customer's customer.[8]

Further, the characteristics of global value chains requires the coordination between all network processes. Such networks are typically fast, virtual, highly flexible, oriented toward future customer demand, and are uniquely positioned and configured along product lines. The implication is that such network relationships must address highly complex and changing customer demand and supply patterns. The idea of a "one-size-fits-all" supply chain management business strategy is not realistic.

Modern logistics management will most likely evolve toward a greater use of highly focused and flexible cross-functional and cross-enterprise teams to accomplish its objectives. As a result of this trend, logistics management will receive top management attention, and occupy a strategic focus in the business enterprise. This is an important challenge for logistics management, as not all business enterprises have developed an integrated view toward the study and application of logistics.

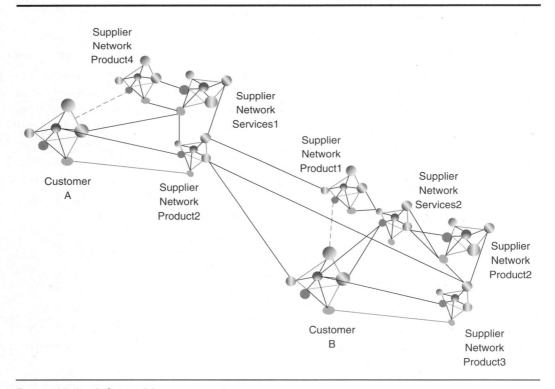

FIGURE 14.6   A SUPPLY NETWORK

8.   Gergard Plenert. *The eManager: Value Chain Management in an eCommerce World*. Dublin: Blackhall Publishing, 2001, p. 30.

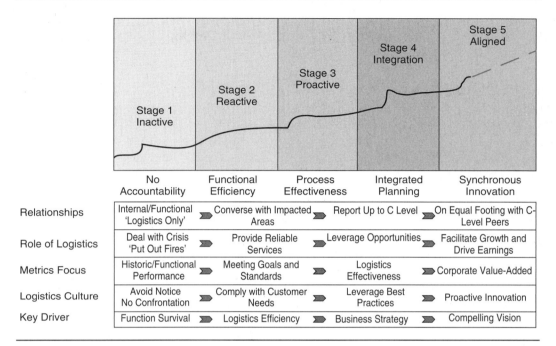

	No Accountability	Functional Efficiency	Process Effectiveness	Integrated Planning	Synchronous Innovation
Relationships	Internal/Functional 'Logistics Only'	Converse with Impacted Areas	Report Up to C Level		On Equal Footing with C-Level Peers
Role of Logistics	Deal with Crisis 'Put Out Fires'	Provide Reliable Services	Leverage Opportunities		Facilitate Growth and Drive Earnings
Metrics Focus	Historic/Functional Performance	Meeting Goals and Standards	Logistics Effectiveness		Corporate Value-Added
Logistics Culture	Avoid Notice No Confrontation	Comply with Customer Needs	Leverage Best Practices		Proactive Innovation
Key Driver	Function Survival	Logistics Efficiency	Business Strategy		Compelling Vision

FIGURE 14.7   FIVE-STAGE MODEL OF SUPPLY CHAIN AWARENESS

This is illustrated in a recent study aimed at increasing the awareness of top business executives of the strategic potential of logistics management (Figure 14.7).[9]

While there has been considerable development in the integration of logistics processes *within* many firms, the CSCMP study indicates that the biggest challenge that lies ahead for the majority of business enterprises is the attainment of effective process alignment *between* firms.

14.2 MODES OF TRANSPORTATION

When we think of methods to manage the flow of goods, we immediately think of transportation and how we can best move the equipment and materials we need for operations into our facilities, and how we can move the products we make to the consumer. In most cases, the decisions we make are likely based on trade-offs between cost and time; air freight, for example, is faster than ocean vessels but proportionally more expensive.

The role of transportation under logistics management has changed significantly over the past three decades. The deregulation of the U.S. transportation industry in 1980 proved an important departure from a previous time wherein

---

9.   Karl B. Manrodt, Brian Gibson, and Stephen Rutner. "Communicating the Value of Supply Chain Management to Your CEO". Oak Brook, IL: The Council of Supply Chain Management Professionals, 2005, p. 12.

transportation was viewed as mostly a commodity to be purchased from the lowest bidder. In the scenarios of supply and value chain management discussed earlier, it is imperative that the selection of the very best transportation service providers has an important impact on successful business strategy.

(a) A LOGISTICS PERSPECTIVE ON TRANSPORTATION.   A consideration of transportation capabilities will focus on the movement of products, the storage of products, the costs of transportation, and the various players in a typical transportation cycle.

(i) Product Movement.   Goods may be moved by a number of means and methods, commonly referred to as transportation *modes*:

- **Air.** Aviation or air transport refers to the activities surrounding mechanical flight and the aircraft industry. Aircraft include fixed-wing (airplane) and rotary-wing (helicopter) types. Air transport capability is limited by load size, weight lift capacity of an aircraft, and aircraft availability. Dedicated airfreight services, such as Federal Express, UPS, and DHL have managed to become profitable, despite the inherent limitations of airfreight capabilities. No particular commodity dominates the traffic of goods carried by airfreight.
- **Water transport.** Goods carried by ship fall into three distinct waterborne categories of transport: internal river, coastal and intercoastal freight, and international freight. Additionally, categories such as barge and powered versus nonpowered shipping vessels should be considered.
- **Pipeline, oil and gas.** Pipeline transportation is a significant element of the U.S. transportation system. In addition to petroleum products, the other major product that is transported by pipeline is natural gas. Similar to petroleum, natural gas pipelines are owned and operated by private business enterprises. In comparison with other modes of transportation, pipelines are unique in that they operate on a 24/7 basis. Unlike other modes, there is no empty container that must be returned. Pipelines have the highest fixed cost and lowest variable cost among transportation modes. High fixed costs result from the right of way for pipelines, construction, and other requirements for safety and control.
- **Rail.** Rail transport refers to the land transport of passengers and goods along railways or railroads. Rail transport makes highly efficient use of space: a double-track rail line can carry more passengers or freight in a given amount of time than a four-lane road. As a result, rail transport is the major form of public transport in many countries. In Asia, for example, many millions use trains as regular transport in India, South Korea, Japan, China, and in European countries. However, outside of New York City, rail transport as a form of public transit in the United States is rare. Very few major U.S. cities other

than New York, Chicago, Boston, and Philadelphia can lay claim to any significant use of local rail-based passenger transport; meanwhile, Amtrak is the only nationwide passenger rail system in the country. Commercially, world rail transport has had a mixed record. Most rail systems, including urban rapid transit (metro/subway) systems, are highly subsidized and have never or rarely been profitable; however, their indirect benefits are often great. With the advent of containerized freight in the 1960s, rail and ship transportation have become an integrated network that moves bulk goods very efficiently with a very low labor cost. An example is that goods from east Asia that are bound for Europe will often be shipped across the Pacific and transferred to trains to cross North America and be transferred back to a ship for the Atlantic crossing.

- **Road.** (motor or "highway"). Highway transportation in the United States has greatly expanded since the end of World War II. A road is an identifiable route or path between two or more places. Roads are typically smoothed, paved, or otherwise prepared to allow easy travel; though they need not be, and historically many roads were simply recognizable routes without any formal construction or maintenance. In urban areas, roads may pass along and be named as streets, serving a dual function as urban space and route.

- **Intermodal transportation.** Intermodal transportation combines two or more transportation modes to take advantages of economies of scale, with an objective of providing service at the lowest total cost. For example, **piggyback service** combines the flexibility of motor freight for short distances with the low line-haul cost associated with rail transport for longer distances. The most common example of **piggyback** transport is the trailer-on-a-flatcar (TOFC) or container-on-a-flatcar (COFC). Another example of intermodal transportation is that of the **containership**. The *fishyback,* **trainship**, or *containership* concept loads a truck trailer, railcar, or container onto a barge or ship for the line-haul move.

(ii) Transportation Participants.   One way in which to better understand the scope of logistics is to examine the participants in a typical transportation transaction (Figure 14.8).

Most transportation decisions involve at least six parties: a shipper, a destination party (usually called a consignee), carriers and agents, governments, the Internet, and the public.

- **Shipper and consignee.** The shipper and consignee have a common interest in moving goods from origin to destination within a period of time at the least possible cost. Related services would include scheduled pickup and delivery times, estimated or actual delivery transit time, and a guarantee of accuracy in information between the parties.

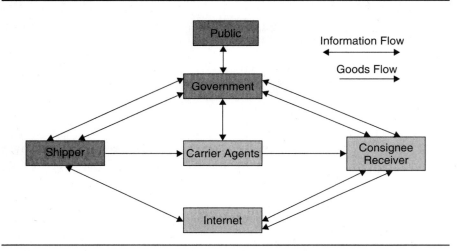

FIGURE 14.8   RELATIONSHIPS BETWEEN TYPICAL TRANSPORTATION PARTICIPANTS
Source: Bowersox, et al. p. 331.

- **Carrier agents.** The carrier represents a business that performs a transportation service. It needs to maximize its revenue while moving goods, while at the same time, reducing costs associated with labor, fuel, and vehicle costs. To further reduce costs, most shippers seek to consolidate shipments and coordinate pickup and delivery times in order to achieve economies of scale.
- **Governments.** Governments have a vested interest in transportation because of its effects on the economy and general social well-being of its citizens. Because of the direct impact of transportation on the economy, governments have been traditionally involved in the practices of carriers. In the United States, a more recent emphasis on carrier safety and security, in addition to traditional financial review, is evident in the formation of the Department of Homeland Security in 2001.
- **Internet.** A wide assortment of Internet-based transportation information services have developed in the last decade. These transportation information capabilities are most typically referred to as aspects of *e-commerce*. Two distinct e-commerce marketplaces have emerged that greatly simplify transportation information flow. One area of transportation e-commerce involves matching carrier carrying capacity to available shipments. Yet another form of transportation e-commerce provides information on the purchase of fuels, equipment, spare parts, and related operating supplies. Also, real-time traceability of goods is now possible as a result of the adoption of bar code and radio frequency identification technologies.
- **The public.** The public is concerned with transportation accessibility, expense, and effectiveness as well as environmental and safety standards.

14.3 TRAFFIC MANAGEMENT

In its simplest form, traffic management governs the scheduling of shipments and receipts, managing the overall transport of goods and material. Many changes have taken place in this area since 9/11, and the impact of increased worldwide security has been profound.

(a) THE TREND TOWARD THE OUTSOURCING OF LOGISTICS SERVICES. The question of outsourcing all or a part of the logistics management function for any firm should be the result of an extensive, strategically driven decision by a business enterprise's top management. In all likelihood, such an important decision should also take into consideration valued inputs from a firm's key customers and suppliers as well. A typical decision matrix is illustrated in Figure 14.9.[10]

(b) DEGREES OF LOGISTICS OUTSOURCING: 3PL AND 4PL.

(i) 3PL. A **third-party logistics provider** (abbreviated 3PL) is a firm that provides outsourced or "third-party" logistics services to companies for part or sometimes all of their supply chain management function. Third-party logistics providers typically specialize in integrated warehousing and transportation services that can be scaled and customized to customers' needs based on market conditions and the demands and delivery service requirements for their products and materials. A 3PL provides integrated logistics services (i.e., the complete set of logistics activities from the buyer to the seller).

(ii) 4PL. *"A 4PL is an integrator that assembles the resources, capabilities, and technology of its own organization and other organizations to design, build and*

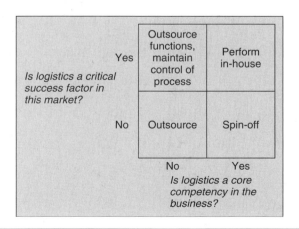

FIGURE 14.9 LOGISTICS OUTSOURCING DECISION MATRIX

---

10. After Martin Christopher, pp. 281–284.

run comprehensive supply chain solutions." The term 4PL is something that every organization has its own interpretation of and ideas on what exactly a 4PL should offer. To add more complexity to the interpretation, the following groups of service providers actually provide "4PL type" services:

- Consultants
- IT service providers
- "E" marketplaces
- Financial institutions
- Private organizations
- Logistics service providers (3PL activities)

A true 4PL organization would then build a set of activities focused around a specific set of supply chain initiatives and goals, generally with the attributes shown in Figure 14.10.[11]

The 4PL architecture is still in the conceptual stage. As conceived, however, the 4PL, a logistics planning and control organization, manages all of the details related to the daily conduct of business. This group provides customer visibility, control, performance metrics management, reporting, daily problem solving, and so on. Additionally, this planning and control group would manage specific logistics issues related to knowledge transfer, business development, and functional support.

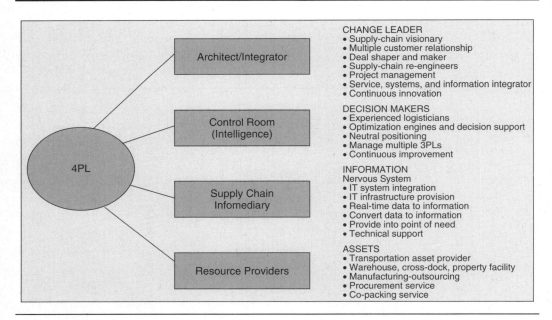

FIGURE 14.10   4PL ARCHITECTURE

---

11.   Ibid., p. 296.

14.4 CUSTOMS

For various reasons—generally revenue generation and market regulation—nations have established tariffs for products and materials entering (and departing) their countries. These tariffs are typically regulated by the respective national customs agency. There is no universal system that applies to all countries and all situations, despite the fact that many countries today adhere to some community of regulation, such as the European Common Market (EC) or **the North American Free Trade Agreement (NAFTA)**, explained in their respective sections.

(a) SCOPE OF U.S. CUSTOMS REORGANIZATION.[12]   Established in 1927, the U.S. Customs Service and its organizations were formed to regulate immigration into the United States, as well as regulate the traffic of goods both into and out of the country. In the United States since the terrorist attacks of September 11, 2001, there has been a considerable reorganization and integration of customs functions at the federal governmental level. The various functions are now under the organizational control of the **U.S. Department of Homeland Security**.

The U.S. Customs Service (now part of **U.S. Customs and Border Protection or CBP**) was the portion of the U.S. federal government dedicated to keeping illegal products outside of U.S. borders. It also regulated what could leave the United States and was partially responsible for who could enter the United States.

Operations were divided into two separate sections—the first of which was the **Office of Field Operations (OFO)**, which handled duties and tax penalties along with helping to prevent contraband from entering the United States. It was primarily made up of inspectors that served as the "front line" of customs by monitoring and policing all international ports of entry into the United States, (land, sea or air); by screening incoming and outgoing international shipments of cargo; and by inspecting informal entries of dutiable goods by individuals through personal transport or shipment through international postal carriers (government and private). Inspectors also handled operations regarding smuggling of contraband into the United States and controlled the exportation of controlled or strategic resources from the United States. Other OFO personnel included import specialists, intelligence officers, and other contracted personnel responsible for record keeping and handling protest and tax penalty arbitration, along with other record support functions.

Import specialists provided the backbone of OFO by providing expertise concerning proper classification of goods for the purpose of charging duties. The primary resource for determining duty classifications is the two-volume Harmonized Tariff Schedule for the United States or HTSUS, which is updated annually. Import specialists were divided into commodity teams (CTs), which are assigned specific types of goods to specialize in. For example, one team may be assigned vehicles, vehicle components, and ball bearings, and another may be

---

12. Wikipedia—the Online Encyclopedia. "United States Customs Service." Accessed February 3, 2012. http://en.wikipedia.org/wiki/United_States_Customs_Service.

assigned clothing, textiles, and toys. Each CT is assigned a more senior import specialist, whose job it is to train import specialists who are new to a particular commodity team. These individuals are usually *de facto* experts in the analysis of goods that they are assigned and are often called upon to physically inspect goods entering (or petitioning to enter) the United States. They are primarily engaged in activities concerning formal entries, which are handled by customs brokerage houses, but they also provide assistance in informal entries.

The other half of the U.S. Customs and Border Protection Service was the **Office of Investigation (OI)**. The OI consisted of specialized sections of special agents who are divided by common crimes regarding international affairs. Primary sections included financial crimes, narcotics, strategic, and computer forensics. The OI also included an internal affairs section that monitored and investigated allegations of misconduct and criminal activity within both the OI and the OFO. As part of the reorganization associated with the creation of the Department of Homeland Security, the OI was transferred to U.S. Immigration and Customs Enforcement on March 1, 2003.

(b) GLOBAL CUSTOMS ISSUES AND LOGISTICS. It is sufficient to repeat that each nation engaged in today's global commerce maintains its own set of customs laws, regulations, and organizational infrastructures. This fact makes it a challenge to effectively engage in the seamless, efficient, and effective transfer of goods among the world's many trading nations. For example, moving goods across a border often requires the payment of excise tax, often collected by customs officials. Animals (and occasionally humans) moving across borders may need to go into quarantine to prevent the spread of exotic or infectious diseases. Most countries prohibit carrying illegal drugs or endangered animals across their borders. Moving goods, animals, or people illegally across a border, without declaring them, counts as smuggling. The rationalization of trading agreements between international and regional trading partners, as well as an unprecedented trend toward the disaggregation and outsourcing of the various aspects of the means of production and distribution, has resulted in an overall simplification or "harmonization" of customs regulations and procedures.

Within the environment of global trade, however, it should be noted that each nation is unique in how it executes its own customs requirements—and it is recommended that for any international trade and customs transaction, the specific customs authorities in each nation must be consulted. Frequently, such specialized and comprehensive knowledge is provided by third-party service providers (customs agents, freight forwarders, or brokerage firms). The trend toward harmonization—alignment—of international customs procedures and regulations is generally encouraged by:

- The similarity of consumer demand of like goods throughout the world (*examples:* cell phones, television sets, and consumer electronics in general).
- The increasing scarcity of raw materials and the continuing search for new sources of supply.

- The need to serve growing consumer demand in new markets with great sales potential to a rising middle class (*examples:* the People's Republic of China and India).
- The availability and access to standardized high-speed data transmission and associated technologies (*examples*: bar-coding and radio frequency identity tags).
- Cost advantages in both labor and materials offered by global strategic sourcing.

(c) THE WORLD CUSTOMS ORGANIZATION. For more than 50 years, the **World Customs Organization (WCO)** has provided leadership in expanding the avenues of international trade. The WCO's accomplishments are both numerous and varied. The organization's success has been driven by a clear-minded adherence to a simple principle: The more simple and harmonized the world's customs procedures, the more prosperity for international trade and the world at large. By following this principle, the WCO has scored many triumphs across the entire spectrum of customs-based issues. For example, the WCO created and administers several international agreements that facilitate world trade. The major international conventions created or administered by the WCO include:

- The *Harmonized System Convention* (the basis for the U.S. import and export schedules).
- The General Agreement on Tariffs and Trade (*GATT) Customs Valuation Agreement*.
- The *Nairobi* and *Johannesburg Conventions*, both dealing with the sharing of information.
- The *1973 Kyoto Convention* on customs procedures.
- The *1999 revised Kyoto Convention*, formally known as the *International Convention on the Harmonization and Simplification of Customs Procedures*.

In June 2002, the WCO Council unanimously adopted a resolution on the security and facilitation of the international trade supply chain proposed by the United States that has resulted in the development of numerous guidelines, benchmarks, and best practices. Together with the WCO, U.S. Customs and Border Protection (CBP) has been actively drafting and writing best practices, guidelines, and standards relating to the security of international supply chains. While much has been accomplished, the work continues both at CBP and the WCO.

As in a domestic logistics environment, important decision elements will be encountered in an international setting. Some of these are:

- Port selection.
- Desirability of free trade zones.

- Customs regulations and procedures unique to individual nation states and trading blocs.
- Total cost decisions.
- Financial and currency exchange considerations.

14.5 LOGISTICS IN THE CONTEXT OF INTERNATIONAL TRADE

An emerging view of logistics and supply chain management as an appropriate strategic business perspective in the development and maintenance of global commerce and trade is noteworthy. SCM, with a high dependence upon the flawless execution of logistics strategies, is a vehicle that promises to lift the traditional views of logistics from a set of descriptive analyses focused on activities *within* a firm, to one which underscores the importance of high levels of organizational integration and interdependence. Further,

> Global sourcing may be important to a firm's competitive position as a means to access raw materials, improve quality, lower cost, or access technology. … Pursuing a global procurement strategy successfully requires that a firm possess a supply chain orientation and the skills to deal with the complexities and uncertainties of the global environment.[13]

(a) THE INFLUENCE OF GLOBALIZATION ON LOGISTICS. An ideal "globalized" business environment could be described as one in which neither distance nor national borders impede economic transactions. This would be a world where the costs of transportation and communications approached zero, and the barriers created by differing national jurisdictions (nation-states or regional economic organizations) had vanished.

According to Sir Anthony Giddens of the London School of Economics and Political Science, the debate over both the meaning and consequences of globalization may be viewed from two perspectives[14]:

- **The radical perspective:**

  > … not only is globalization very real, but that its consequences can be felt everywhere. The global marketplace, they say, is much more developed than even two or three decades ago, and is indifferent to national borders. Nations have lost most of the sovereignty they once had, and politicians have lost most of their capability to influence events. It isn't surprising that no one respects political leaders any more, or has much interest in what they have to say. The era of the nation state is over.

13. Nancy W. Nix, "Supply Chain Management in the Global Environment". In John T. Mentzer (ed). *Supply Chain Management*. Thousand Oaks, CA: Sage Publications, 2001, p. 44.
14. Sir Anthony Giddens, *Runaway World: How Globalization is Reshaping Our Lives,* Revised edition. London: Routledge, 2002, p. 29–30.

- **The skeptical perspective.**

> The notion of globalization, according to the skeptics, is an ideology put about by free-marketeers who wish to dismantle welfare systems and cut back on state expenditures. What has happened is at most a reversion to how the world was a century ago. In the late 19th Century there was already an open global economy, with a great deal of trade, including trade in currencies.

(b) DEGREES OF GLOBAL AND REGIONAL ECONOMIC INTEGRATION. In surveying the global business environment, there are considerations beyond the context of the values and beliefs of the individual, and the characteristics of the single business enterprise. Such considerations should focus on the array of economic interactions, and ultimately, the forms of economic interaction that take place at the regional and interregional level. Such an analysis must take into account the effects of globalization and the trend toward global economic integration. There are several degrees of economic integration, which range from loose trading affiliations to virtual full economic and political union. It is within this landscape that modern logistics management must operate. The following narrative is intended to provide a general familiarity with global trading issues the logistics professional will most likely encounter.

Table 14.1 presents the numerous forms of international trade organizations.

(c) REGIONAL TRADING ALLIANCES AND GOVERNING BODIES. There are numerous international trade agreements between global trading partners and numerous contracts between business enterprises. However, it is important to note the existence of the world's major trading blocs.

(i) The European Union (EU).   The **EU** is an intergovernmental and supranational union of 25 democratic member states from the European continent. The EU was established under that name in 1992 by the Treaty on European Union (the Maastricht Treaty). However, many aspects of the EU existed before that date through a series of predecessor relationships, dating back to 1951. The EU nowadays has a common single market consisting of a customs union, a single currency managed by the European Central Bank (so far adopted by 12 of the 25 member states), a common agricultural policy, a common trade policy, and a common fisheries policy. A common foreign and security policy was also established as the second of the three pillars of the European Union. The Schengen Agreement abolished passport control, and customs checks were also abolished at many of the EU's internal borders, creating a single space of mobility for EU citizens to live, travel, work, and invest. [The most important EU institutions include the Council of the European Union, the European Commission, the European Court of Justice, the European Central Bank, and the European Parliament. The European Parliament's origins go back to the 1950s and the founding treaties, and since 1979 its

INTEGRATION FOCUS	CHARACTERISTICS	EXAMPLE
The Free Trade Area	All barriers to the trade of goods and services among member countries are removed. Ideally, no discriminatory tariffs, quotas, subsidies are allowed to distort trade between member countries. All members are free to determine their own trade policies with regard to nonmembers.	North American Free Trade Association (NAFTA)
The Customs Union	Eliminates trade barriers between member states and adopts a common external trade policy toward nonmembers.	The Andean Pact
Common Market	In addition to the free flow of finished goods, factors of production (labor and capital) are allowed to move freely among members. Thus, a common market is characterized by the free flow of immigration, emigration, and capital.	The European Union (EU)
Economic Union	Possesses the same characteristics of a common market, but additionally exhibits a common currency, the harmonization of member tax rates, and common monetary policy and tax rates.	Evolving: The European Union as of January 2002 instituted a common currency (the Euro) for the majority of its member states.
Political Union	Beyond economic union, a political union seeks an overarching and coordinative political bureaucracy to ensure accountability to the citizens of its member states.	The United States, Canada. Evolving: The EU is gradually moving toward this objective—epitomized in the development of the European Parliament and the Council of Ministers.

TABLE 14.1   LEVELS OF ECONOMIC INTEGRATION
Source: Charles W. Hill. *International Business: Competing in the Global Marketplace*, 9th ed. New York. McGraw-Hill/Irwin, 2012, pp. 223–247.

members have been directly elected by the people they represent. Elections are held every five years, and every EU citizen who is registered as a voter is entitled to vote. The EU's activities cover all areas of public policy, from health and economic policy to foreign affairs and defense. However, the extent of its powers differs greatly between areas. Depending on the area in question, the EU may therefore resemble a federation (e.g., on monetary affairs, agricultural, trade and environmental policy, economic and social policy), a confederation (e.g., on home affairs), or an international organization (e.g., in foreign affairs). Many of the policies of the EU relate in one way or another to the development and maintenance of an effective single market. Significant efforts have been made to create harmonized standards, which are designed to bring economic benefits through creating larger, more efficient markets. The power of the single market reaches beyond the EU borders, because to sell within the EU, it is beneficial to conform to its standards. Once a nonmember country's factories, farmers, and merchants conform to EU standards, much of the cost of joining the Union has already been sunk. At that point, harmonizing domestic laws in order to become a full member is relatively painless, and may create more wealth through eliminating the customs costs.

(ii) The North American Free Trade Agreement (NAFTA). **The North American Free Trade Agreement,** known usually as **NAFTA,** is a free trade agreement among Canada, the United States, and Mexico. NAFTA went into effect on January 1, 1994. NAFTA is also used to refer to the tripartite trading bloc of North American countries. NAFTA called for immediately eliminating duties on half of all U.S. goods shipped to Mexico and gradually phasing out other tariffs over a period of about 14 years. Restrictions were to be removed from many categories, including motor vehicles and automotive parts, computers, textiles, and agriculture. The treaty also protected intellectual property rights (patents, copyrights, and trademarks) and outlined the removal of restrictions on investment among the three countries. Provisions regarding worker and environmental protection were added later as a result of supplemental agreements signed in 1993. This agreement was an expansion of the earlier Canada-U.S. Free Trade Agreement of 1989. Unlike the European Union, NAFTA does not create a set of supranational governmental bodies, nor does it create a body of law that is superior to national law. NAFTA is a treaty under international law. (Under U.S. law it is classed as a congressional-executive agreement rather than a treaty, reflecting a peculiar sense of the term "treaty" in U.S. constitutional law that is not followed by international law or the laws of other states.)

(iii) Association of Southeast Asian Nations (ASEAN). The **Association of Southeast Asian Nations (ASEAN)** is a political, economic, and cultural organization of countries located in Southeast Asia. ASEAN was formed on August 8, 1967, by Thailand, Indonesia, Malaysia, Singapore, and the Philippines, as a nonprovocative display of solidarity against communist expansion in Vietnam and insurgency within their own borders. Following the Bali Summit of 1976, the

organization embarked on a program of economic cooperation, which floundered in the mid-1980s, only to be revived around a 1991 Thai proposal for a regional "free trade area." The countries meet annually. The ASEAN was founded by five states, mostly from maritime Southeast Asia: Indonesia, Malaysia, the Philippines, Singapore, and Thailand. The British protectorate of Brunei joined the ASEAN six days after the country became independent from the United Kingdom on January 7, 1984. The mainland states of Vietnam, Laos, and Myanmar were later admitted. Vietnam joined the ASEAN on July 28, 1995. Laos and Myanmar were admitted into the ASEAN on July 23, 1997. Cambodia became the newest member when it was admitted on April 30, 1999. The Melanesian state of Papua New Guinea has observer status in the ASEAN. Meanwhile, the former Indonesian province of Timor-Leste has applied for observer status in ASEAN. Timor-Leste is widely seen as a member state candidate. The association includes about 8 percent of the world's population, and in 2003 it had a combined gross domestic product (GDP) of about US$700 billion, growing at an average rate of around 4 percent per annum. The economies of member countries of ASEAN are diverse, although its major products include electronics, oil, and wood. The ASEAN countries are culturally rich. They include more Muslims than any other geopolitical entity. About 240 million Muslims live mostly in Indonesia, Malaysia, and Brunei. Buddhism constitutes the main religion of mainland Southeast Asia, and there are about 170 million Buddhists in Thailand, Myanmar, Laos, Cambodia, Vietnam, and Singapore. Catholicism is predominant in the Philippines. ASEAN has governments with widely differing views on governance and political process, including practices in areas such as suffrage and representation. It encompasses styles of government ranging from democracy to autocracy.

(iv) MERCOSUR. MERCOSUR was founded in 1988 as a free-trade pact between Brazil and Argentina. The modest tariff reductions in its first years led to an 80 percent increase in trade between the two partners. In 1990, Paraguay and Bolivia joined MERCOSUR, and the members have committed to the formation of SAFTA (South American Free Trade Area). The ambitious goal is to invite other Latin American nations into the pact, and by 2005, to encourage internal free trade for not less than 80 percent of the goods produced in the region. Some South Americans see MERCOSUR as giving the capability to combine resources to balance the activities of other global economic powers, perhaps especially the United States and the European Union. The organization could also potentially preempt the Free Trade Area of the Americas (FTAA); however, over half of the current MERCOSUR member countries rejected the FTAA proposal at the IV *Cumbre de las Americas* (IV Summit of the Americas) in Argentina in 2005. The development of MERCOSUR was arguably weakened by the collapse of the Argentine economy in 2002, and it has still seen internal conflicts over trade policy, between Brazil and Argentina, for example. In December 2004 it signed a cooperation agreement with the Andean Community trade bloc (CAN), and they

published a joint letter of intention for a future negotiation toward integrating all of South America. The prospect of increased political integration within the organization, as per the European Union and advocated by some, is still uncertain. There are more than 220 million people in this region, and the combined GDP of the member nations is more than $1 trillion a year. Recently, with the new cooperation agreement with MERCOSUR, the Andean Community gained four new associate members: Argentina, Brazil, Paraguay, and Uruguay. These four MERCOSUR members were granted associate membership by the Andean Council of Foreign Ministers meeting in an enlarged session with the Commission (of the Andean Community) on July 7, 2005. This move reciprocates the actions of MERCOSUR, which granted associate membership to all of the Andean Community nations by virtue of the Economic Complementarity Agreements (Free Trade agreements) signed between the CAN and individual MERCOSUR members.

(v) The Andean Community.   **The Andean Community of Nations** (in Spanish: *Comunidad Andina de Naciones*, abbreviated **CAN**) is a trade bloc comprising the South American countries of Bolivia, Colombia, Ecuador, Peru, and Venezuela (which is in the process of leaving the bloc). The trade bloc was called the Andean Pact until 1996 and came into existence with the signing of the Cartagena Agreement in 1969. Its headquarters are located in Lima, Peru. The Andean Community has 120 million inhabitants living in an area of 4,700,000 square kilometers, whose GDP amounted to US$260 billion in 2002.

(vi) Asia-Pacific Economic Cooperation (APEC).   **The Asia-Pacific Economic Cooperation (APEC)** is a group of Pacific Rim countries that meet with the purpose of improving economic and political ties. It has standing committees on a wide range of issues, from communications to fisheries. The heads of government of all APEC members meet annually in a summit called "APEC Economic Leaders' Meeting" rotating in location among APEC's member economies.

(vii) The World Trade Organization (WTO).   **The World Trade Organization (WTO)** is an international, multilateral organization, which sets the rules for the global trading system and resolves disputes between its member states, all of whom are signatories to its approximately 30 agreements. WTO headquarters are located in Geneva, Switzerland. As of December 15, 2005, there are 149 members in the organization, with the latest to join being Saudi Arabia. All WTO members are required to grant one another most-favored-nation status, such that (with some exceptions) trade concessions granted by a WTO member to another country must be granted to all WTO members. Since its inception in 1995, the WTO has been a major target for protests by the antiglobalization movement.

(viii) GATT and the Goods Council.   (www.wto.org/english/tratop_e/gatt_e/gatt_e.htm) GATT covers international trade in goods. The workings of the GATT

agreement are the responsibility of the Council for Trade in Goods (Goods Council), which is made up of representatives from all WTO member countries. The current chairperson is H.E. Mr. Vesa Tapani HIMANEN (Finland).

The Goods Council has 10 committees dealing with specific subjects (such as agriculture, market access, subsidies, antidumping measures, etc.). Again, these committees consist of all member countries.

Also reporting to the Goods Council are a working party on state trading enterprises and the Information Technology Agreement (ITA) Committee.

(d) FOREIGN CURRENCY AND EXCHANGE.　The management of currency during the exchange of products and materials between countries is no insignificant task in global trade and is often best left to the Finance function. However, it is frequently the role of the procurement and logistics sections to negotiate the details of how and when rates are calculated.

(i) The Foreign Exchange Market (FOREX).　**The foreign exchange** (currency or forex) **market** exists wherever one currency is traded for another (see Table 14.2). It is by far the largest market in the world, in terms of cash value traded, and includes trading between large banks, central banks, currency speculators, multinational corporations, governments, and other financial markets and institutions. Shown in Table 14.2 are those currencies that are most widely traded. Retail traders (small speculators) are a small part of this market. There is no single unified foreign exchange market. Due to the over-the-counter (OTC) nature of currency markets, there are rather a number of interconnected marketplaces, where different currency instruments are traded. This implies that there is no such thing as a single dollar rate, but rather a number of different rates (prices), depending on what bank or market maker is trading. In practice, the rates are often very close; otherwise, they could be exploited by arbitrageurs. The main trading centers are in London, New York, and Tokyo, but banks throughout the world participate. As the Asian trading session ends, the European session begins, then the U.S. session, and then

RANK	CURRENCY	ISO 4217 CODE	SYMBOL
1	United States Dollar	USD	$
2	Eurozone Euro	EUR	€
3	Japanese Yen	JPY	¥
4	British Pound Sterling	GBP	$
5–6	Swiss Franc	CHF	–
5–6	Canadian Dollar	CAD	$

TABLE 14.2　TOP SIX MOST TRADED CURRENCIES
Source: Investopedia, Posted August, 2009.

the Asian begin in their turns. Traders can react to news when it breaks, rather than waiting for the market to open.

(ii) Banks.   The interbank market caters for both the majority of commercial turnover and large amounts of speculative trading every day. A large bank may trade billions of dollars daily. Some of this trading is undertaken on behalf of customers, but much is conducted by proprietary desks, trading for the bank's own account. Until recently, foreign exchange brokers did large amounts of business, facilitating interbank trading and matching anonymous counterparts for small fees. Today, however, much of this business is moving on to more efficient electronic systems, such as Bloomberg EBS and TradeBook, Reuters 3000 Matching, and EBS. The broker squawk box lets traders listen in on ongoing interbank trading in most trading rooms, but turnover is noticeably smaller than just a few years ago.

(iii) Central Banks.   National central banks play an important role in the foreign exchange markets. They try to control the money supply, inflation, and/or interest rates and often have official or unofficial target rates for their currencies. They can use their often substantial foreign exchange reserves to stabilize the market. Milton Friedman argued that the best stabilization strategy would be for central banks to buy when the exchange rate is too low, and to sell when the rate is too high—that is, to trade for a profit. Nevertheless, central banks do not go bankrupt if they make large losses, like other traders would, and there is no convincing evidence that they do make a profit trading. The mere expectation or rumor of central bank intervention might be enough to stabilize a currency, but aggressive intervention might be used several times each year in countries with a dirty float currency regime. Central banks do not always achieve their objectives, however. The combined resources of the market can easily overwhelm any central bank. Several scenarios of this nature were seen in the 1992–1993 ERM collapse, and in more recent times in Southeast Asia.

(iv) Commercial Companies.   An important part of this market comes from the financial activities of companies seeking foreign exchange to pay for goods or services. Commercial companies often trade fairly small amounts compared to those of banks or speculators, and their trades often have little short-term impact on market rates. Nevertheless, trade flows are an important factor in the long-term direction of a currency's exchange rate. Some multinational companies can have an unpredictable impact when very large positions are covered due to exposures that are not widely known by other market participants.

(v) Investment Management Firms.   Investment management firms (which typically manage large accounts on behalf of customers such as pension funds, endowments, etc.) utilize the foreign exchange market to facilitate transactions in foreign securities. For example, an investment manager with an international

equity portfolio will need to buy and sell foreign currencies in the "spot" market in order to pay for, and redeem, purchases and sales of foreign equities. Since these transactions are secondary to the actual investment decision, they are not seen as speculative or aimed at profit maximization. Some investment management firms also possess specialist currency overlay units, which have the specific objective of managing clients' currency exposures with the aim of generating profits while limiting risk. While the number of dedicated currency managers is quite small, the size of their assets under management (AUM) can be quite significant, which can lead to large trades.

(vi) Retail Forex Brokers.   Retail forex brokers handle a minute fraction of the total volume of the foreign exchange market. Standard retail services include 24-hour online currency trading, and 100-to-1 leverage. Most retail brokers do not provide direct access to the interbank market, acting as dealers (buying or selling against the customer's order for their own account) rather than as true brokers (arranging a trade for the customer with a third party). The brokers earn money by offering a bid/offer spread that is wider than the interbank spread. Retail traders should be aware of the possibility of retail forex brokers manipulating quoted spot rates, improperly triggering their clients' stop-loss orders, or charging hidden fees.

In the United States, "it is unlawful to offer foreign currency futures and option contracts to retail customers unless the offeror is a regulated financial entity," according to the Commodity Futures Trading Commission. Legitimate retail brokers serving traders in the United States are most often registered with the CFTC as "futures commission merchants" (FCMs) and are members of the National Futures Association (NFA). Potential clients can check the broker's FCM status at the NFA. Retail forex brokers are much less regulated than stockbrokers, and there is no protection similar to that from the Securities Investor Protection Corporation.

14.6 GOVERNMENT ORGANIZATIONS AND ROLES, REGULATIONS, AND CONTROLS

Government has a vested interest in logistics, and in particular, its transportation component, as its critical importance related to reliable service and economic well-being of its citizens. Government desires a stable, secure, and efficient transportation environment to support economic growth.

Since the terrorist attacks on the United States on September 11, 2001, there has been an unprecedented reorganization and realignment of the U.S. government agencies and their various roles and duties as they apply to the movement of goods and services, both domestically and internationally. Some of the major federal agencies that deal with transportation and logistics issues are:

(a) THE U.S. DEPARTMENT OF TRANSPORTATION.[15]   **The U.S. Department of Transportation (DOT)** is a cabinet department of the U.S. government concerned with transport. It was established by an act of Congress on October 15, 1966, and began operation on April 1, 1967. It is administered by the U.S. Secretary of Transportation. Its mission is to "Serve the United States by ensuring a fast, safe, efficient, accessible and convenient transportation system that meets our vital national interests and enhances the quality of life of the American people, today and into the future." The DOT consists of the Office of the Secretary and 11 individual operating administrations:

- Federal Aviation Administration (FAA)
- Federal Highway Administration (FHWA)
- Federal Railroad Administration (FRA)
- Federal Transit Administration (FTA)
- Maritime Administration (MARAD)
- Federal Motor Carrier Safety Administration (FMCSA)
- National Highway Traffic Safety Administration (NHTSA)
- Research and Innovative Technology Administration (RITA)
- Pipeline and Hazardous Materials Safety Administration (PHMSA)
- Saint Lawrence Seaway Development Corporation (SLSDC)
- Surface Transportation Board (STB)

The Homeland Security Act of 2002 authorized the establishment of the Department of Homeland Security, which, on March 1, 2003, assumed management of the U.S. Coast Guard and the Transportation Security Administration, formerly DOT Operating Administrations.

The duties of the chief U.S. DOT agencies are outlined below:

(b) THE FEDERAL AVIATION ADMINISTRATION (FAA).   **The Federal Aviation Administration (FAA)** has the authority to regulate and oversee all aspects of civil aviation in the United States. Along with the European Joint Aviation Authorities, the FAA is one of the two main agencies worldwide responsible for the certification of new aircraft. The FAA issues a number of awards to holders of its licenses. Among these are demonstrated proficiencies as a mechanic, an instructor, a 50-year aviator, or as a safe pilot. The Air Commerce Act of May 20, 1926, is the cornerstone of the federal government's regulation of civil aviation. This landmark legislation was passed at the urging of the aviation industry, whose leaders believed the airplane could not reach its full commercial potential without federal action to improve and maintain safety standards. The FAA became more

---

15. From Wikipedia. http://en.wikipedia.org/wiki/U.S._Department_of_Transportation. Accessed February 3, 2012. See also U.S. Department of Transportation Web site: www.dot.gov/.

involved with the environmental aspects of aviation in 1968, when it received the power to set aircraft noise standards. Legislation in 1970 gave the agency management of a new airport aid program and certain added responsibilities for airport safety. During the 1960s and 1970s, the FAA also started to regulate high-altitude (over 500 feet) kite and balloon flying. In 1979, the Congress authorized the FAA to work with major commercial airports to define noise pollution contours and investigate the feasibility of noise mitigation by residential retrofit programs. Throughout the 1980s, these charters were implemented. In the 1990s, satellite technology received increased emphasis in the FAA's development programs as a means to improvements in communications, navigation, and airspace management. In 1995, the agency assumed responsibility for safety oversight of commercial space transportation, a function begun 11 years before by an office within DOT headquarters.

For more information, visit *www.faa.gov/*.

(c) THE FEDERAL HIGHWAY ADMINISTRATION (FHWA).   The FHWA specializes in highway transportation. The agency's major activities are grouped into two programs: the Federal-Aid Highway Program and the Federal Lands Highway Program. The FHWA's role in the Federal-Aid Highway Program is to oversee federal funds used for constructing and maintaining the National Highway System (primarily interstate highways, U.S. routes, and most State Routes). This funding mostly comes from the federal gasoline tax and mostly goes to state departments of transportation. The FHWA oversees projects using these funds to ensure that federal requirements for project eligibility, contract administration, and construction standards are adhered to. Under the Federal Lands Highway Program (sometimes called "direct fed"), the FHWA provides highway design and construction services for various federal land-management agencies, such as the Forest Service and the National Park Service. In addition to these programs, the FHWA performs research in the areas of automobile safety, congestion, highway materials, and construction methods. The FHWA also publishes the Manual on Uniform Traffic Control Devices (MUTCD), which is used by most highway agencies in the United States. The MUTCD specifies such things as the size, color, and height of stop signs.

For more information, visit *www.fhwa.dot.gov/*.

(d) THE FEDERAL RAILROAD ADMINISTRATION (FRA).   The FRA was created in 1966 to promote safe, environmentally sound, successful rail transportation. The Office of Railroad Development (RDV) is responsible for federal investment and assistance to the rail industry as well as the development and implementation of administration policy concerning intercity rail passenger service and high-speed rail. It sponsors research and development activities to advance science and engineering to improve the technology for railroad safety and work. It provides investment opportunities for small freight railroad projects, primarily through the RRIF program. The Office of Safety promotes and regulates safety throughout the nation's railroad industry. It employs more than 415 federal safety inspectors, who operate out of eight regional offices nationally. FRA inspectors specialize in five safety disciplines and numerous grade crossing and trespass-prevention initiatives: Track, Signal and Train Control, Motive Power and Equipment, Operating Practices, Hazardous Materials, and Highway-Rail Grade Crossing Safety. The Office trains and certifies state safety inspectors to enforce federal rail safety regulations. Central to the success of the rail safety effort is the ability to understand the nature of rail-related accidents and to analyze trends in railroad safety. To do this, the Office of Safety collects rail accident/incident data from the railroads and converts this information into meaningful statistical tables, charts, and reports.

For more information, visit *www.fra.dot.gov/us/content/2.*

(e) THE FEDERAL TRANSIT ADMINISTRATION (FTA). **The FTA** provides financial and technical assistance to the local public transit systems. The FTA is one of 11 modal administrations within the DOT. The FTA functions through a Washington, D.C., headquarters office and 10 regional offices, which assist transit agencies in all 50 states, the District of Columbia, Puerto Rico, the U.S. Virgin Islands, Guam, Northern Mariana Islands, and American Samoa. Public transportation includes buses, subways, light rail, commuter rail, monorail, passenger ferry boats, trolleys, inclined railways, and people movers. The federal government, through the FTA, provides financial assistance to develop new transit systems and improve, maintain, and operate existing systems. The FTA oversees grants to state and local transit providers, primarily through its 10 regional offices. These grantees are responsible for managing their programs in accordance with federal requirements, and the FTA is responsible for ensuring that grantees follow federal mandates along with statutory and administrative requirements.

For more information, visit *http://www.fta.dot.gov/.*

(f) THE MARITIME ADMINISTRATION (MARAD). MARAD administers financial programs to develop, promote, and operate the U.S. Merchant Marine; determines services and routes necessary to develop and maintain American foreign commerce and requirements of ships necessary to provide adequate service on such routes; conducts research and development activities in the maritime field; regulates the transfer of U.S. documented vessels to foreign registries; maintains equipment, shipyard facilities, and reserve fleets of government-owned ships essential for national defense; operates the U.S. Merchant Marine Academy at Kings Point, New York; and administers a grant-in-aid program for state-operated maritime academies in California (California Maritime Academy), Maine (Maine Maritime Academy), Massachusetts (Massachusetts Maritime Academy), Michigan (Great Lakes Maritime Academy), New York (SUNY Maritime College), and Texas (Texas Maritime Academy). The Maritime Subsidy Board negotiates contracts for ship construction and grants operating-differential subsidies to shipping companies. The Maritime Administrator is vested with the residual powers of the Director of the National Shipping Authority, which was established in 1951 to organize and direct emergency merchant marine operations.

For more information, visit *www.marad.dot.gov/index.html* and *www.nvr.navy.mil/marad.htm.*

(g) THE FEDERAL MOTOR CARRIER SAFETY ADMINISTRATION (FMCSA).   The FMCSA's primary mission is to reduce crashes, injuries, and fatalities involving large trucks and buses. In carrying out its safety mandate, the FMCSA:

- Develops and enforces data-driven regulations that balance motor carrier (truck and bus companies) safety with industry efficiency.
- Harnesses safety information systems to focus on higher risk carriers in enforcing the safety regulations.
- Targets educational messages to carriers, commercial drivers, and the public.
- Partners with stakeholders including federal, state, and local enforcement agencies; the motor carrier industry; safety groups; and organized labor on efforts to reduce bus and truck-related crashes.

For more information, visit *www.fmcsa.dot.gov/*

(h) THE NATIONAL HIGHWAY TRAFFIC SAFETY ADMINISTRATION (NHTSA). The NHTSA is responsible for setting safety standards and verifying compliance by automobile manufacturers. It also issues recall notices that ensure full awareness of mechanical problems with cars sold in the United States, and publishes the results of safety tests of various automobiles, to allow buyers to evaluate the anticipated behavior of an automobile in a crash.

For more information, visit *www.nhtsa.dot.gov/.*

(i) THE RESEARCH AND INNOVATIVE TECHNOLOGY ADMINISTRATION (RITA). The RITA is comprised of the Bureau of Transportation Statistics (Washington, D.C.), Volpe National Transportation Systems Center (Cambridge, Massachusetts), Transportation Safety Institute (Oklahoma City, Oklahoma), and the Office of Intermodalism (Washington, D.C.). The main vision of the RITA is to identify and facilitate solutions to the challenges and opportunities facing America's transportation system. The RITA will be part university research lab and part Silicon Valley entrepreneurial company. The agency will foster the exchange of ideas and information in a high-priority incubator committed to research, and get these innovative ideas from the laboratory into the field. The RITA will allow the DOT the opportunity to realize greater collaboration, information sharing, coordination, support, and advocacy for its widespread research efforts.

For more information, visit *www.rita.dot.gov/.*

(j) THE PIPELINE AND HAZARDOUS MATERIALS SAFETY ADMINISTRATION (PHMSA).   The PHMSA has public responsibilities for safe and secure movement of hazardous materials to industry and consumers by all transportation modes, including the nation's pipelines. The agency also overseas the nation's pipeline infrastructure, which accounts for 64 percent of the energy commodities consumed in the United States.

For more information, visit *www.phmsa.dot.gov/*.

(k) THE SAINT LAWRENCE SEAWAY DEVELOPMENT CORPORATION (SLSDC).
The SLSDC is a wholly owned government corporation created by statute on May 13, 1954, to construct, operate, and maintain that part of the St. Lawrence Seaway between the Port of Montreal and Lake Erie, within the territorial limits of the United States. Trade development functions aim to enhance Great Lakes/St. Lawrence Seaway System utilization without respect to territorial or geographic limits.

For more information, visit *www.seaway.dot.gov/*.

(l) THE SURFACE TRANSPORTATION BOARD (STB).   The STB was created by the Interstate Commerce Commission Termination Act of 1995 at the same time the Interstate Commerce Commission was abolished. The STB was created to replace the ICC, which had been charged with playing to the interests of the trucking industry and being generally useless due to deregulation. The STB is an economic regulatory agency that Congress created to resolve railroad rate and service disputes and reviewing proposed railroad mergers. The STB is decisionally independent, although it is administratively affiliated with the U.S. DOT. The STB serves as both an adjudicatory and a regulatory body. The agency has jurisdiction over:

- Railroad rate and service issues.
- Rail restructuring transactions (mergers, line sales, new line construction, and old line abandonment).
- Certain trucking company, moving van, and noncontiguous ocean shipping company rate matters.
- Certain intercity passenger bus company structure, financial, and operational matters.
- Rates and services of certain pipelines not regulated by the Federal Energy Regulatory Commission.

For more information, visit *www.stb.dot.gov/*.

(m) THE U.S. DEPARTMENT OF HOMELAND SECURITY.   Homeland security refers to domestic governmental actions designed to prevent, detect, respond to, and recover from acts of terrorism, and also respond to natural disasters. The term became prominent in the United States following the September 11, 2001, attacks; it had been used only in limited policy circles prior to 9/11. Before this time, such action had been classified as civil defense. Homeland security is officially defined as "a concerted national effort to prevent terrorist attacks within the United States, reduce America's vulnerability to terrorism, and minimize the damage and recover from attacks that do occur," according to the National Strategy for Homeland Security. Because the U.S. Department of Homeland Security (DHS) includes the Federal Emergency Management Agency (FEMA), it has responsibility for preparedness, response, and recovery to natural disasters as well. Homeland security is generally used to refer to the broad national effort by all levels of government—federal, state, local, and tribal—to protect the territory of the United States from hazards, both internal and external, as well as the Department of Homeland Security itself. Homeland security is also usually used to connote the civilian aspect of this effort; "homeland defense" refers to its military component, led chiefly by the U.S. Northern Command headquartered in Colorado Springs, Colorado. The scope of homeland security includes:

- Emergency preparedness and response (for both terrorism and natural disasters), including volunteer medical, police, emergency management, and fire personnel.
- Domestic intelligence activities, largely today within the FBI.
- Critical infrastructure protection.
- Border security, including both land and maritime borders.
- Transportation security, including aviation and maritime transportation.
- Biodefense.
- Detection of nuclear and radiological materials.
- Research on next-generation security technologies.

In the United States, the concept of "homeland security" extends and recombines responsibilities of much of the executive branch, including the Federal Bureau of Investigation (FBI), the National Guard, the Federal Emergency Management Agency (FEMA), the U.S. Coast Guard, the former Immigration and Naturalization Service (INS), the former U.S. Customs Service, the Secret Service, the Transportation Security Administration (TSA), and the Central Intelligence Agency (CIA).

For more information, visit *www.dhs.gov/dhspublic/.*

14.7 SUPPLEMENTAL INFORMATION

Because logistics is such a broad-ranging and key function in procurement and supply management, it is impossible to cover all of the related topics *in their appropriate contexts* in a single chapter. In the following section, we provide some additional information out of context for the sake of brevity, which we hope will be useful.

(a) THE REACH OF INTELLIGENT FREIGHT TECHNOLOGIES.   Intelligent freight technologies monitor and manage physical assets and information flows. Five clusters of technologies can be applied individually or in tailored combinations:

- **Asset tracking** uses mobile communications, radio frequency identification (RFID), and other tools to monitor the location and status of tractors, trailers, chassis, containers, and, in some cases, cargo.
- **On-board status monitoring** uses sensors to monitor vehicle operating parameters, cargo condition, and attempts to tamper with the load.
- **Gateway facilitation** uses RFID, smart cards, weigh-in-motion, and nonintrusive inspection technologies to simplify and speed operations at terminal gates, highway inspection stations, and border crossings.
- **Freight status information** uses Web-based technologies and standards to facilitate the exchange of information related to freight flows.
- **Network status information** uses services to integrate data from cameras and road sensors and uses display technologies to monitor congestion, weather conditions, and incidents.

See *www.ops.fhwa.dot.gov/freight/intermodal/freight_tech_story/exec_summ_intro.htm.*

(b) LOGISTICS AUTOMATION. Logistics automation is the application of computer software and/or automated machinery to improve the efficiency of logistics operations. Typically, this refers to operations within a warehouse or distribution center, with broader tasks undertaken by supply chain management systems and enterprise resource planning systems.

Logistics automation systems can powerfully complement the facilities provided by these higher level computer systems. The focus on an individual node within a wider logistics network allows systems to be highly tailored to the requirements of that node.

(i) Components. Logistics automation systems comprise a variety of hardware and software components:

FIXED MACHINERY

- Automated cranes (also called automated storage and retrieval systems) provide the ability to input and store a container of goods for later retrieval. Typically, cranes serve a rack of locations, allowing many levels of stock to be stacked vertically, and allowing far high storage densities and better space utilization than alternatives.
- Automated conveyors allow the input of containers in one area of the warehouse, and either through hard-coded rules or data input allows destination selection. The container will later appear at the selected destination.
- Sortation systems are similar to conveyors but typically have higher capacity and can divert containers more quickly. They are typically used to distribute high volumes of small cartons to a large set of locations.

Typically, all of these will automatically identify and track containers based on bar codes, or increasingly, RFID tags.

MOBILE TECHNOLOGY

Radio data terminals are handheld or truck-mounted terminals that connect wirelessly to logistics automation software and provide instructions to operators moving throughout the warehouse. Many also have built-in bar code scanners to allow identification of containers.

SOFTWARE

- Integration software provides overall control of the automation machinery and, for instance, allows cranes to be connected up to conveyors for seamless stock movements.
- Operational control software provides low-level decision making, such as where to store incoming containers, and where to retrieve them when requested.
- Business control software provides higher level functionality, such as identification of incoming deliveries/stock and scheduling order fulfillment, assignment of stock to outgoing trailers.

(c) TARIFFS. Customs duties on merchandise imports are called tariffs. Tariffs give a price advantage to locally produced goods over similar goods that are imported, and they raise revenues for governments. For more information, visit *www.wto.org/english/tratop_e/tariffs_e/tariffs_e.htm.*

(i) Rules of Origin. Determining where a product comes from is no longer easy when raw materials and parts criss-cross the globe to be used as inputs in scattered manufacturing plants. **Rules of origin** are important in implementing such trade policy instruments as antidumping and countervailing duties, origin marking, and safeguard measures. For more information, visit *www.wto.org/english/tratop_e/roi_e/roi_e.htm.*

(ii) Antidumping Duty. Duty applied to imports of a particular good from a specified country in order to eliminate the harm being caused by the dumping to the domestic industry of the importing country. Article VI of the GATT 1994 permits the imposition of antidumping duties against dumped goods, equal to the difference between their export price and their normal value, if dumping causes injury to producers of competing products in the importing country.

If a company exports a product at a price lower than the price it normally charges on its own home market, it is said to be "dumping" the product. Is this unfair competition? The WTO agreement does not pass judgment. Its focus is on how governments can or cannot react to dumping. It disciplines antidumping actions, and is often called the "Antidumping Agreement."

For more information, visit *www.wto.org/english/tratop_e/adp_e/adp_e.htm.*

(iii) Ad Valorem Tariff.   An ad valorem tariff is a tariff that is imposed in percentage terms over the value of the good, for example, a 5 percent tariff, which means that the import tariff is 5 percent of the appraised value of the good in question.

(iv) Rates of Duty.   All goods imported into the United States are subject to duty or duty-free entry in accordance with their classification in the HTSUS.

There are three types of rates of duty that may be assessed on goods imported into the United States: ad valorem, specific, or compound (or mixed).

- An ad valorem rate of duty is a percentage of the dutiable or customs value of the merchandise. (This is the rate of duty most often applied in the HTSUS.)
- A specific rate of duty is a specified amount per unit of weight or other measure of quantity (e.g., 10 cents per pound or 5 cents per dozen).
- Finally, a compound (or mixed) rate of duty is a combination of both an ad valorem rate of duty and a specific rate of duty (e.g., 5 percent ad valorem plus 10 cents per pound).

(d) FREIGHT STANDARDS.
- Economic Impact of Inadequate Infrastructure for Supply Chain Integration: *www.nist.gov/director/prog-ofc/report04-2.pdf.*
- Standards Setting Needs for Freight Management: *www.ops.fhwa.dot.gov/freight/intermodal/standards_iso.htm.*
- Concept of Operations for an ESCM Standard: *www.ops.fhwa.dot.gov/freight/publications/concept_ops.htm.*

14.8 SUMMARY

In this chapter, we defined logistics in its broader sense as the segment of supply chain management concerned with the movement of goods and materials, and provided a brief background on its historical importance. We also outlined the key role of logistics as a process in the business environment and how it is likely evolving toward the concept of value chain management.

The overview of transportation modes described the various methods of moving materials through stages from raw material to the consumer, pointing out the optimum use for each of them. In conjunction with transportation, traffic management is the administrative segment of logistics. In reviewing traffic management, we examined the role of the 3PL and 4PL providers.

Since all governments regulate the movement of materials into and out of their countries, knowledge of customs requirements is critical in the management of logistics. While duties are currently established by individual nations, there is an increasing movement toward a harmonized system of tariffs. The Supplemental Information section included a summary of the various types of tariffs in effect today.

Global trade has become increasingly characterized by regional trade agreements such as NAFTA and the EU, with many treaties and pacts focused on improving trade relations and reducing restrictions within the immediate geographical area in response to competitive pressures from other regions. As global trade rapidly accelerates, global organizations such as the WTO have stepped up efforts to unify widely regulated and disparate practices worldwide. In the United States, for example, literally dozens of federal and state agencies are involved in the regulation of trade to one extent or another, from the use of roads and waterways to regulating the traffic in endangered species.

Since money is the common denominator in trade activities, currency transactions also play a major role in logistic activities. Multiple markets exist for the exchange of currency, and we reviewed several of the more important of them.

In concluding this chapter, we examined several elements of logistics out of context, including technology and automation efforts, along with some common concepts in tariff administration.

14.9 LINKS

California Center for Innovative Transportation (CCIT): *www.calccit.org*

National Transportation Research Center: *www.ntrc.gov*

Transportation Research Board (TRB): *www.trb.org*

Defense Logistics Agency: *www.dla.mil*

Foreign relations of the United States: *www.state.gov/r/pa/ho/frus*

Foreign trade statistics: *www.census.gov/foreign-trade/www*

Free Trade Area of the Americas (FTAA): *www.ftaa-alca.org/alca_e.asp*

Hemispheric Trade and Tariff Database: *www.ftaa-alca.org/NGROUPS/ NGMADB_e.asp*

North American Free Trade Agreement (NAFTA): *www.nafta-sec-alena. org/DefaultSite/index_e.aspx*

United Nations Commission on International Trade Law (UNCITRAL): *www.uncitral.org*

United Nations Conference on Trade and Development (UNCTAD): *www.unctad.org*

World Customs Organization (WCO): *www.wcoomd.org*

World Intellectual Property Organization (WIPO): *www.wipo.org*

World Trade Organization (WTO): *www.wto.org*

Customs Service: *www.cbp.gov*

NAFTA Trilateral Web sites: *www.cbp.gov/nafta/nafta_new.htm*

NAFTA Resources: *www.cbp.gov/nafta/resource.htm*

WTO trade topics: *www.wto.org/english/tratop_e/tratop_e.htm*

WTO Glossary: *www.wto.org/english/thewto_e/glossary_e/glossary_e.htm*
Exporting Basics: *www.export.gov/exportbasics/index.asp*
Trade Agreements: *www.ustr.gov/Trade_Agreements/Section_Index.html*
Intermodal Association of North America: *www.intermodal.org*
Council of Supply Chain Management Professionals: *www.cscmp.org*
Customs Service: *www.cbp.gov*

KEY TERMS

Loger
Logistics
Council of Supply Chain Management Professional (CSCMP)
Acquisition Logistics
Integrated Logistics Support (ILS)
Functional silos
Internal process integration
Enterprise resource planning (ERP)
Customer relationship management (CRM)
Supplier relationship management (SRM)
Value chain management (VCM)
Piggyback service
Containership
Piggyback
Trainship
Third-party logistics provider (3PL)
U.S. Customs and Border Protection or CPB
U.S. Department of Homeland Security
Office of Field Operations (OFO)
Office of Investigation (OI)
World Customs Organization (WCO)
The European Union (EU)
The North American Free Trade Agreement (NAFTA)

Association of Southeast Asian Nations (ASEAN)
MERCOSUR
The Andean Community of Nations (CAN)
Asia-Pacific Economic Corporation (APEC)
The World Trade Organization (WTO)
GATT and the Goods Council
The Foreign Exchange Markets (FOREX)
The U.S. Department of Transportation (DOT)
The Federal Aviation Administration (FAA)
The Federal Highway Administration (FHWA)
The Federal Railroad Administration (FRA)
The Federal Transit Administration (FTA)
Intelligent Freight Technologies
Asset tracking
On-board status monitoring
Gateway facilitation
Freight status information
Network status information
Logistics automation
Rules of origin
Antidumping duty
Ad valorem duty

PROVIDING VALUE TO THE ORGANIZATION

LEARNING OBJECTIVES

1. List the seven steps necessary to develop and implement standardization of purchased materials.
2. Define the concept of *"continuous improvement,"* which the authors recommend, and list the steps involved in the continuous improvement process.
3. Describe the role of the *"commodity counsel"* in improving direct materials costs.
4. Name two ways in which the Procurement Manager may support effective new product development.

As you have already learned, the Procurement Department is in a unique position to add value to the organization as the key interface between internal consumers of goods and services and the corresponding supplier community. In this role, the buyer has the opportunity to exert considerable influence on reducing costs and significantly adding to the organization's profit and loss statement's bottom line. This can be particularly effective when applying methods that aid in the **standardization** of materials and provide a proactive supply sourcing approach to the **new product introduction (NPI)** process. You will likely find that the major drivers in these efforts will be initiatives to improve the efficiency of supply management processes and to effectively control the costs of purchased goods and services.

In this chapter, we examine ways that you can effectively improve procurement operations and save money for the organization by standardizing materials and developing other **cost-reduction** activities. We will also examine how these elements can be combined in the new product introduction process.

15.1 STANDARDIZING PURCHASED MATERIALS

Material standardization refers to the process of finding ways to use as few purchased items as possible to perform as many functions as possible. Let's explore the many avenues available to the Procurement Department to formulate material standardization programs.

(a) STANDARDIZATION CONSIDERATIONS. There are a number of factors to consider when looking at material standardization. First of all, materials **standards** can refer to common specifications for designed and engineered materials used within a single organization, an industry, or even an international body of nations. Secondly, standards can apply to materials to enable them to share the same functional specifications. Having the same specifications allows materials to be interchangeable from one environment to another as substitutes. And, finally, standardization can apply to methods for producing and distributing materials. Standardized methods ensure uniform operations, processes, procedures, and therefore, results, throughout the supply base. As an example, imagine the cost and potential unreliability of air travel if every airport in the world performed take-off and landing operations using a different air traffic control system.

(i) Benefits of Standardization. There are many obvious benefits to standardization. It reduces or eliminates one-time processes that produce variability and add cost, and it allows organizations to understand the true cost associated with producing a particular product or providing a service.

Standardized parts reduce the level of inventory since fewer items must be stocked. When parts are standardized across an industry, they tend to become readily available "off-the-shelf" commodity items and therefore require lower levels of stock to support. Standardization also reduces the cost of parts by enabling organizations to purchase a consolidated assortment of parts in greater quantities. This, in turn, can reduce administrative and handling costs since fewer items need to be ordered, received, inspected, stocked, and distributed.

Standardized parts also enable interchangeability and interoperation from one environment to another, regardless of where it is produced, thus reducing engineering and design costs across the supply chain. This also tends to reduce prices as a result of greater competition in the marketplace.

Standardization tends to improve quality through uniform processes and specifications that can be easily understood and measured with most quality systems.

(ii) Standardization Development Processes. The Procurement Department can take the lead in developing a standardization program in the organization simply because it places the purchase orders and therefore has greater access to the organization's overall buying history. While there are many ways to develop a standardization program, most programs share a degree of similarity in their operational process steps.

Here are some common steps you should consider when developing and implementing a standardization program:

Establish team involvement. Cross-function participation helps ensure that all appropriate parties are represented during the development phase, saving the time that would be needed to later obtain their buy-in. Typically, a standardization team will consist of members from procurement, manufacturing, engineering, quality, and finance. Depending on the project, it may also require a member from sales. Organizations often have a semi-permanent standing team for this particular purpose.

Establish team objectives. Determine what outcomes the team would like to have in place at the conclusion of the standardization process. These will likely include goals related to part reduction, inventory reduction, improved pricing through part consolidation, or reduced errors in shipped products.

Gather information. Determine what conditions actually exist currently—how many parts are being used to do similar tasks, for example.

Outline a plan. Develop a proposal and timeline for accomplishing the objectives that the sponsoring team can use to gain team member and management support.

Develop standards. Define and document the industry or commodity standards that will be followed going forward.

Implement the plan. Roll out the plan to the using groups accompanied by specific instructions for meeting plan objectives. Part of this process includes developing an awareness of the program to gain as much support as possible.

Measure results and provide continuous feedback. Periodic surveys can be used to provide information on the efficacy of the program.

(iii) Common Areas for Standardization. There are likely endless areas for standardization in the typical organization. However, you should first consider parts that

are used in relatively high volumes since the opportunity for cost savings will be greatest there. These are often parts that are incidental to the design and function, such as common fasteners, and there will be little resistance to their standardization. Parts that are relatively low in individual value but are frequently ordered, and thus have higher administrative costs to manage, are also prime candidates for consolidation.

You should also consider the standardization process when specifying new equipment. Standardized equipment helps drive standardization throughout the manufacturing process, from maintaining spare parts inventory to training new employees in the equipment's operation.

(iv) Potential Issues. Standards require continuous review and updating, especially when they apply to the organization's direct operations. If they are proprietary standards, applicable only to your organization, someone will need to ensure that changes are conveyed to your suppliers in a timely manner. Whenever new standards are established, there should be a procedure for maintenance that clearly outlines roles and responsibilities for keeping them aligned with present needs and changes in technology.

In the case of externally developed standards, a specific monitoring procedure and system should be in place to ensure that changes made by the originating entity are conveyed to users within your organization. Without this contact, your organization risks the possibility of not remaining aligned with its customers and suppliers.

(b) STANDARDS ORGANIZATIONS. Standards are developed by a wide variety of organizations, both locally and internationally, within or across industries and geographical boundaries. As you will see in this section, standards are also developed by both independent and government-sponsored organizations. What generally unifies various interests to develop standards is their common need for **interoperability**. In computer science, for example, interoperability refers to the ability to exchange and use information across platforms and networks. Without interoperability, computer systems would be unable to communicate with one another and would thus have little value.

(i) Individual Organizations. Each individual organization has its unique disciplines where standards might apply, but there are a number of common areas where standards most often apply.

- **Materials.** For an individual organization, specifications define the standard dimensions, utility, and useful life of purchased parts and supplies to ensure that they consistently meet its needs.
- **Equipment.** Performance, functions, and productivity requirements define the standards in an organization for purchased equipment, along with useful life and, occasionally, physical characteristics and dimensions.

- **Processes and procedures.** Standards for processes and procedures ensure uniform operating environments and repeatable results for various operations that are similar throughout the organization.

(ii) Independent Standards Associations and Functions.   There are numerous organizations—mostly nonprofit and serving a specific community—that identify the need for standards and develop them for common use. Some of the most commonly recognized include ANSI, SAE, and ASTM.

ANSI

The **American National Standards Institute (ANSI)** is the administering and coordinating body for voluntary standards in the United States, although it remains a nonprofit, private organization by charter. It is responsible for approving standards in a number of areas, including those that apply to computers. Originally founded in 1918 as the American Engineering Standards Committee (AESC), its first approved standard was for pipe threads. In 1928, it was reorganized and renamed the American Standards Association (ASA), and it adopted its current name in 1969. ANSI currently provides a forum for over 270 ANSI-accredited standards developers representing over 200 distinct organizations in the private and public sectors. The organizations work together to develop the American National Standards (ANS). For more information, visit www.ansi.org.

SAE

The **Society of Automotive Engineers (SAE)** is an organization that establishes voluntary standards for mobility products, automotive and aerospace components, vehicles, and systems. Founded in the early 1900s, today it represents nearly 85,000 members in 97 countries. Visit www.sae.org for more information.

ASTM

ASTM International, formerly the **American Society for Testing and Materials (ASTM)**, was also formed in the early 1900s, initially to address issues in the railroad industry. Today, its stated purpose is to work toward consensus for "stakeholders involved in issues ranging from safety in recreational aviation to fiber optic cable installations in underground utilities to homeland security." The organization currently represents over 30,000 members. For more information, visit www.astm.org.

(iii) U.S. Government Standards Organizations.   While there are numerous U.S. standards organizations, the **National Institute of Standards and Technology (NIST)**, formerly the **National Bureau of Standards (NBS)**, is the central government-supported agency for standards. Founded in 1901, NIST is a nonregulatory federal agency within the U.S. Commerce Department's Technology Administration. NIST's mission is "to develop and promote measurement, standards, and technology to enhance productivity, facilitate trade, and improve the quality of

life." NIST maintains and promotes **open measurement standards** to facilitate commerce, including the maintenance of the official U.S. time. For more information, visit http://nist.time.gov.

NIST also manages the Baldrige National Quality Program under The Malcolm Baldrige National Quality Improvement Act of 1987.

(iv) International Standards Organizations.   There are also many international standards organizations. Some are independent, while others are sponsored by the United Nations. The most commonly known are the International Organization for Standardization, Underwriters Laboratories Inc., and the Institute of Electrical and Electronics Engineers.

INTERNATIONAL ORGANIZATION FOR STANDARDIZATION (ISO)
This organization was formed to consolidate widely dispersed methods of approaching quality standards. As we discussed in Chapter 8, its stated goal is to facilitate a means of coordinating, developing, and unifying industrial and technical quality standards (www.iso.org).

UNDERWRITERS LABORATORIES. (UL)
This organization is a private not-for-profit institution that was established by the insurance industry to test and rate devices, materials, and systems, especially electrical and electronic products, for safety. Items that pass specific tests can include a UL certificate on the product (www.ul.com).

INSTITUTE OF ELECTRICAL AND ELECTRONICS ENGINEERS, INC. (IEEE)
This nonprofit, technical professional association has more than 360,000 members in over 175 countries. IEEE is the leading authority in technical areas including computer engineering, biomedical technology, and telecommunications. IEEE has 900 active standards with hundreds under constant development (www.ieee.org).

15.2 IMPROVING PROCUREMENT-RELATED PROCESSES

Because an organization's procurement process itself is so highly dynamic and changes often as new technologies are put in place or markets evolve, it is an area rich with potential for cost-reducing improvements. While standardization is one way to improve procurement performance, there are many others. As a procurement professional, you will responsible for developing a mindset in your group that seeks out and embraces **continuous improvement**, responding proactively to changing needs and conditions. Continuous improvement is the ongoing improvement of processes, methods, and products that takes place over a period of time through incremental, progressive steps.

To effectively implement a continuous improvement program in your group, you first need to identify where opportunities for improvement exist and then establish goals. You'll likely find that one of the most productive areas for improvement lies in streamlining your procurement processes themselves. Systematic analysis of the processes used should produce clear documentation of each of the steps in the process being reviewed so that you have a clear picture of existing conditions. You will then want to know how their effectiveness compares to other organizations. This will likely require a bit of benchmarking (as we described in Chapter 9.)

The mechanics of implementing a continuous improvement process requires following these basic steps:

Form an improvement team. As noted in the previous section, Standardization Development Process, cross-functional participation helps ensure that all appropriate parties are represented during the development phase, saving the time needed to obtain their buy-in later.

Initiate a *gap analysis* study. Gap analysis identifies the difference between the existing process and a best practice. For example, if there is a lag in your receiving process of two working days before an incoming receipt is logged into the system (and thus available for use in production), and you find that best practices indicate it should take no longer than two hours, you have measured a gap of approximately 14 hours (assuming an eight-hour workday). It is usually helpful to document each of the steps in the process, along with their associated times, by using a **flowchart**—a step-by-step diagram—so that you can be relatively certain that all process activities are accounted for.

Develop a plan. A continuous improvement plan will be directed toward achieving the team's objective by reducing or eliminating the identified gap over a period of time or with repeated effort. The plan might include such elements as changes to the work flow, elimination of unnecessary steps, or reduction in waiting time. The redesigned process can be documented with a written narrative outlining the new process, along with a new process flowchart. The implementation may also require a project timeline to use for tracking progress. Part of the plan development process will also likely include getting buy-in for the program from management and affected users, so this should be documented as well.

Implement the plan. Assign roles and responsibilities to team members and begin executing the redesigned process. Track progress against the established timeline.

Measure results. Using the same methods employed during the gap analysis, measure the resulting improvement following implementation. If the results are not as anticipated, it may be necessary to audit the implementation process to determine if it was carried out according to plan. You may also have to review the initial analysis and plan to determine if some element was missed.

Repeat the process. Remember, continuous improvement requires incremental steps so the process analysis will be ongoing.

(a) BUSINESS PROCESS IMPROVEMENT (BPI).   As we have learned from nature, in order to survive, entities must change; "evolve or perish" is the way it's often expressed. For an organization, this means continual change in its business processes to meet new challenges in the market and to overcome emerging constraints. In many ways, BPI is synonymous with continuous improvement.

In its simplest form, a business process consists of the planned sequence of operations required to ensure a particular outcome or objective. Business process is most clearly evident in an organization's standard operating procedures.

By its very nature, a business process creates change, transforming an existing condition or constraint into one that produces desired results. Process improvements typically address better performance such as increased profit, larger market share, improved product or service quality, and greater customer loyalty.

(b) MEASURING PERFORMANCE IMPROVEMENT.   As the adage goes, what gets measured gets done. Accordingly, one of the key elements in continuous improvement is the measuring process. Meaningful metrics—those clearly linked to the improvement objectives—can tell you how effectively the improvement is going. Keep in mind, you are concerned with measuring business results and process improvements that directly impact your organization's bottom line. Simply measuring the degree of compliance to a given set of procedures adds little value. It is even possible to follow procedures precisely without producing added value. It is important to also determine the rate of progress being made so that you can estimate the resources required to complete the project. When the rate of improvement diminishes, it may signal the proper time for reengineering the process and repeating the continuous improvement steps.

15.3 CONTROLLING AND REDUCING COST

No organization can survive for long without employing a method for cost control. While much of the impetus for containing costs generates from the user groups or finance group within the organization, the Procurement Department, because of its unique role as the custodian of supplier relationships, generally takes the lead in such projects.

While there are numerous methodologies for containing or reducing cost, those that appear to be the most effective share a systematic approach that tries to look at all aspects of the cost of acquiring the product or service. Far too often, procurement professionals reduce the purchase order price they pay for a product or service just to find that in doing so they have increased some other area of expenses. Only by examining the full cost structure of an acquisition can procurement professionals implement a truly effective cost containment or reduction program.

In this section, we'll explore some of the considerations you will need to evaluate when implementing cost reduction programs, as well as some of the methods typically used in procurement operations to manage these programs.

(a) COST REDUCTION CONSIDERATIONS.   **Cost reduction** must be carefully distinguished from a related process, **cost avoidance**. Cost reduction activities can be regarded as the proactive steps taken to actually lower the costs of the products and services you are currently purchasing from their present levels, while cost avoidance refers to analytical measures used to prevent their increase in the future. As an adjunct to cost avoidance, procurement professionals frequently include the process of **cost containment** (mentioned in the preceding section), which applies most often to a more systematic, project-oriented approach to both cost reduction and cost avoidance at the same time.

Keep in mind, however, that "cost" means more than just the price you pay for the product or service. It also means all of the combined expenses associated with the acquisition, such as the total cost of ownership to the organization over the entire period of time that it's in use, as well as the administrative cost associated with its acquisition and disposal. (We covered this consideration in the section Total Cost of Ownership in Chapter 1.)

(i) Organization of Effort.   Cost reduction efforts can be linked as a supplement to a number of other ongoing programs, such as parts or methods standardization projects or a supplier consolidation project. The benefit of this approach is that you can immediately leverage the synergy of combining efforts within an existing framework and being able to provide additional value through a closely related project. For example, combining a part standardization program with a supplier consolidation effort can result in more benefits than either one alone, but would not require many additional resources since the teams could be composed of the same members.

From another perspective, you may also want to consider working with ongoing engineering efforts or work simplification projects within user departments as a way of developing additional synergy that doesn't require a great deal of dedicated resources. These teams are likely already in place, and it will just be a matter of linking up with them.

One important point you might also want to keep in mind is that cost reduction efforts can be accelerated with strong senior management sponsorship and team member participation. When the need to reduce cost in a particular area is driven from senior management, it seems to receive more attention and thus, a higher priority for team accomplishment. Resources are often more readily available. Similarly, forming a cross-functional team, just as you did in your negotiation efforts, can provide technical resources that can ensure that you are not trading off lower prices for additional internal costs down the road.

(ii) Quality Concerns.   In the effort to reduce cost, it is important to be certain that lower prices are not simply a trade-off for reduced or compromised quality for a product or service. Your goal as a buyer is to continually obtain increased value for the buying organization. You will find that your internal users are very sensitive to the potential for reduced quality and service, so you may have a difficult time convincing

them of the value in your proposed program unless they can see clear evidence that the cost reduction will not adversely affect their own functional operations.

To ensure that there is a proper balance between cost reduction and quality requirements, you will need to be able to understand the quality issues in your organization and effectively communicate them to your suppliers. This often requires a close working relationship with the quality control group. In fact, many organizations, recognizing this need, have embedded quality control into the procurement group in the form of a **Supplier Quality Engineering (SQE)** group. To a large extent, it is this group's responsibility to work with suppliers to achieve the optimal balance of cost and quality and to continually monitor supplier production output performance as a method of ensuring that this cost and quality balance is not compromised. In this role, they often represent the Procurement Department objectives to both internal users and suppliers.

(b) COST CONTROL AND REDUCTION OPPORTUNITIES.   Finding opportunities for cost reduction is not always as straightforward as it may sound. If your organization is like most, the low-hanging branches have already been cleared of their fruit. You are going to have to stretch a bit to find rewarding opportunities. Let's turn our attention now to some of the areas you might want to investigate.

(i) Areas for Cost Review.   Using the concept of ABC analysis (as discussed in Chapter 13), you are likely to find that a major portion of your organization's spending (the 80 percent or A category) falls within the scope of perhaps 20 percent of the products and services you buy. This is a good starting point, because if you can control costs of the major portion of the organization's purchases, you will certainly be successful. Consider too, that even a minor cost reduction in a costly product or service is likely to produce greater results than a significant reduction in a seldom-used one.

NOTE

As you probably know, the Pareto Principle (or 80/20 rule) gets bandied about quite a bit. Do not take it literally; it is used today in its less scientific context simply as an expression of the disproportion of certain types of categorization.

It may also be appropriate to look into the detail of unit costs (cost per unit produced) or total costs (including overhead) within the organization in descending order of their variance from budget objectives. Costs that are higher than your budgeted costs may indicate opportunities to reduce costs in the short term. In general, the larger the cost overrun, the more scope there should be for savings. Costs that are higher than your **standard cost**—the engineering estimate on which your selling price may be predicated—usually indicate opportunities to reduce costs in the longer term. It is also considerably more important to review costs during the initial phases of the product life cycle for much the same reason: the longer the product is in use, the greater will be the accumulated savings.

In a manufacturing organization, the emphasis is generally on savings for direct materials since direct material costs have a greater accounting impact on the ultimate selling price of the product. However, savings can often be generated in much the same way for areas of overhead, such as maintenance, repair, and operations (MRO) or facilities services.

(ii) Internal Approaches to Cost Reduction.   As discussed in Chapter 12, the structure of the buying organization can have considerable impact on the cost of purchased products and services. Centralized buying, lead divisional buying, and cooperative purchasing all have benefits and counter-balancing drawbacks. However, in any given situation, changing the method of procurement from centralized consolidation to locally purchased can have an impact on the cost of a specific product or service and should be routinely analyzed.

A **commodity council**, or commodity team, is perhaps one of the best avenues for determining cost reduction strategies. Commodity councils are generally composed of members from various user departments across the organization and are empowered to develop procurement sourcing policy related to the specific commodity. This ensures a uniform approach to cost reduction with centralized decision making throughout the organization. As the name implies, commodity councils focus primarily on materials rather than services, so there may be a somewhat limited application of this process in any given organization. However, as of this writing, similar concepts are being adopted as spending increases in the service areas.

(iii) External Approaches to Cost Reduction.   Aside from typical negotiations, there are several ways to work with suppliers to help reduce costs, which we discuss in this section.

LONG-TERM CONTRACTS
Generally, extending the length of an agreement to purchase specific quantities can result in price reductions and other concessions from the supplier who's anxious to book forward-looking business.

CONSOLIDATING PURCHASES
Providing the supplier with greater volumes by consolidating purchases across the organization or reducing the number of suppliers for a wider range of products or services can result in lower prices.

CONSORTIA AND POOL BUYING
Consolidating purchases between organizations can also result in lower prices and additional concessions. Interorganizational procurement consortia, however, must meet specific legal requirements regarding competition and trade restraint. As a

result, buying consortia have not been as successful in the private sector as they have been in the nonprofit and governmental sector.

TARGET COST AND TARGET PRICE

These are concepts that rely on the cumulative effects of new technology and on production **learning curves** to help plan future pricing reductions as a result of the supplier's internal cost reductions. They may also be based on the projected dynamics of market conditions such as supply and demand, which are a bit riskier to try to predict.

COLLABORATION AND JOINT VENTURES

Teaming up with suppliers to jointly develop new products or processes can be a way of sharing the cost (and the resulting benefits) to reduce overall costs in the supply chain.

(iv) Value Analysis. Value analysis is a systematic process used in the design or redesign of products and services that is based on providing all the necessary functions at the most economic cost within the required level of quality and performance. The process employs techniques that identify all of the required functions and characteristics of an item and establishes values for each of them, arriving at the lowest overall cost within the scope of its required performance. Value analysis, therefore, links cost and function.

Developed at the General Electric Company during World War II, two employees, Lawrence Miles and Harry Erlicher, are credited with creating value analysis, which almost immediately became a critical part of manufacturing. Because of the war, there were always shortages of materials and component parts. By utilizing value analysis, Miles and Erlicher continually looked for acceptable substitutes for items that were in scarce supply. They found that these substitutions frequently reduced costs or improved the product, or both. What originated from critical necessity turned into a systematic process that they named value analysis.

Looking at it another way, value analysis is a tool for analyzing the value of any specific element's function in relation to its cost, eliminating those elements that add cost without adding corresponding value. For example, it may be possible to eliminate certain expensive housing materials for a machine by improving the shipping container at a lower cost.

15.4 SUPPORTING NEW PRODUCT INTRODUCTION

Today's business model relies on the fact that with shorter and shorter product life cycles, the organization that is first to market a new concept generally maintains the lead in both revenue and profit throughout the product's sales life. As a result, decisions that rely on processes such as make-or-buy analysis or value analysis must be accelerated and started early in the design process.

The Procurement Department supports the organization's design and new product introduction (NPI) process primarily through its sourcing activities. The task here is to find suppliers that can support the requirements generated by new products or services or, if none are available, to work with existing suppliers to develop new capabilities. In this role, the procurement professional acts as a consultant to the design and engineering teams by leveraging the appropriate sources of knowledge and information within the supplier community, often recommending one solution over another as a result of experience with the supply base.

Early Supplier Involvement (ESI) is a process in which manufacturers collaborate with suppliers at the beginning stages of the product development process, often as early as the concept phase. This process works to leverage the specialized domain expertise of the supplier and help accelerate the development of specifications so that the product can reach the market more quickly. As was noted in Chapter 10, the introduction of new products or services requires a great deal of planning by the Procurement Department to ensure that new suppliers have been properly qualified and have the required capability to deliver. Early involvement by Procurement has become a necessity to the organization to ensure a smooth product introduction ramp-up from the development phase to actual marketing and distribution.

During the NPI phase, the procurement professional often works in the role of liaison between the internal design team and the supplier's engineering group to develop a collaborative approach to new product development. Because of the high cost of developing new products or new technologies and the speed at which they are required to reach the market, collaboration within the entire supply chain is of paramount importance. This is where the potential for adding strategic value is at its greatest. Sourcing potential partners for joint ventures or collaborative development is just coming into its own as the concept of outsourcing gains currency. In fact, outsourcing engineering and design functions has become increasingly more attractive because suppliers have the domain expertise as their core competency.

TIPS AND TECHNIQUES

TOO MANY ENGINEERS?

One now-defunct multibillion-dollar company in the high-tech manufacturing sector required more than 3,000 engineers to keep up with its new product development. The development cycle for a new product in this field, including its design and engineering, was about 10 months. The corresponding product's life cycle, however, was only three months. Technology was moving so quickly and the competition was so keen that platforms were going obsolete almost as they were introduced.

As a result of the high-tech boom and the employment opportunities it generated, the average longevity of an engineer in this company was about two years. But it took close to a year to fully train an engineer in the company's processes. Wasn't this a formula that could have predicted the company's ensuing demise?

15.5 SUMMARY

Material standardization is the process of reducing the number of parts being used by the organization to make the products it markets. There are many benefits to standardization, including cost reduction through consolidated procurement volumes and lower inventories. Standardization also enhances quality by concentrating focus since there are fewer items to control. Implementing a standardization program relies on a cross-function team and generally follows a project team methodology.

In addition to relying on internal standardization efforts, there are numerous official and quasi-official organizations that develop and publish standards that can be used in many organizations and often across industries and geographical boundaries. These range from independent standards organizations such as ANSI, SAE, and ASTM International to government standards organizations such as NIST and ISO.

Continuous improvement methods also apply to improving procurement-related processes. There are specific steps involved in this process that include the use of gap analysis and flowcharting, as well as the use of appropriate measurements to assess progress.

Controlling and reducing costs is another key function of the Procurement Department. Procurement professionals need to know the difference between cost reduction and cost avoidance and understand the major areas where cost reduction efforts might be most appropriate. There are internal and external approaches to cost reduction to be considered, as well. Internal cost approaches deal primarily with the strategy for organizing procurement decisions, while external approaches focus on ways to tactically address the marketplace to leverage buying power. Value analysis is another important method of developing cost reductions by examining each individual part in a product to determine if it can be eliminated or if a less costly part or material can be substituted.

Finally, the Procurement Department's support for new product introduction, including early supplier involvement and the increasing collaborative use of suppliers, is vital to the development process.

KEY TERMS

Standardization

New product introduction (NPI)

Material standardization

Interoperability

American National Standards Institute (ANSI)

Society of Automotive Engineers (SAE)

American Society for Testing and Materials (ASTM)

National Institute of Standards and Technology (NIST)

National Bureau of Standards (NBS)

Open measurement standards

Gap analysis

Cost reduction

Cost avoidance

Cost containment

Supplier Quality Engineering (SQE)

Commodity council

Learning curves

Early Supplier Involvement (ESI)

CHAPTER 16

STRATEGIC PLANNING FOR PROCUREMENT

LEARNING OBJECTIVES

1. Name eight procurement strategies described in this chapter.
2. Define "hedging" and give a hypothetical example.
3. List the steps in putting effective forecasting processes into place.
4. Define the term "elasticity" and describe how it impacts business requirements.

Sound procurement planning is the cornerstone of effective supply management. By its nature, planning is focused on the future, so developing effective plans enables the purchaser to proactively address and eliminate potential supply constraints that may arise in future activities. Also in this regard, good planning requires a thorough understanding of the particular market for the goods and services being purchased and where that marketplace is heading. With this knowledge, the purchaser can develop procurement strategies to meet evolving business conditions as they are needed. These important concepts are the focus of this chapter.

16.1 DEVELOPING DEMAND- AND FORECAST-BASED PROCUREMENT STRATEGIES

The situation for the organization can be this critical: forecast accurately to meet changing market conditions or perish. The dilemma is that as the pace of business accelerates, the reaction time available to adjust to changing market conditions diminishes dramatically. Your organization needs to get the product or service to its customers in the right time frame and at a viable market price. Keeping pace with changing marketplace conditions is the only way that organizations can continue to maintain their competitive positions. If your organization is unable to fulfill your customers' needs, you can be assured that another organization will.

Accordingly, procurement strategy, also dynamically linked to changes in the market, requires continual reassessment. Effective practice relies heavily on the ability to employ forecasts of future demand and link them to strategic planning. Minor shifts in buying patterns or new technology, for example, can send significant ripples—sometimes even major waves—through the entire supply chain. As demand parameters change, the procurement professional needs to be certain that these changes are identified and that the organization's supply base is prepared to respond quickly.

NOTE

Demand-based strategies develop from actual customer orders, whereas **forecast-based strategies** are estimates (or, in some cases, best guesses) of customer demand during a future period.

To understand these concepts, let's begin with an analysis of various procurement strategies and how they are commonly implemented. We can then turn our attention to recognizing how these strategies can be supported through market analysis and forecasting.

(a) DEFINING PROCUREMENT STRATEGIES.   In one sense, a procurement strategy can be looked at as the method you and your team choose to employ to buy specific goods or services. Since many goods and services share the same or similar characteristics, it is probably not surprising that these strategies tend to coagulate into several common approaches, which we will discuss in this section.

(i) Procurement for Current Requirements. **Requirements** in a procurement context refer to the amount of any particular material or service you may expect to buy within a given time frame. Current requirements can be loosely characterized as those needed within a three-week to three-month time frame. While they can, of course, be demand-based or forecast-based, depending on the nature of your organization's marketplace sector, you will generally find that the more distant the timeline horizon, the greater the likelihood that you will rely on forecasts.

Organizations that rely on forecast-based planning generally require some form of assurance that the purchase will actually occur before committing their inventory and a specific amount of their production capacity. For example, if you are collaboratively scheduling the next 13 weeks' requirements with your supplier, you may have to commit to a guaranteed purchase for the amount you are predicting you will need in the next five weeks, 75 percent of what you are predicting in the following five weeks, and perhaps 50 percent of what you indicate in the remaining three weeks. Thus, your forecast might look something like that shown in Table 16.1.

(ii) Spot Buying. **Spot buying** (or short-term buying on a hand-to-mouth basis) is a strategy in which minimum amounts are purchased as needed, sometimes even on a daily basis. This approach is often taken when demand is generated at the last minute, when the product is perishable, or when prices are declining and the buyer hopes to benefit in the immediate short term as prices continue to fall. This approach can also be taken to protect cash flow when the organization is cash restricted.

(iii) Volume Purchasing Agreement (VPA). The **Volume Purchasing Agreement (VPA)** is used for larger purchases that will take place on an ongoing basis. The VPA generally sets forth the pricing for specific goods or services over a designated period of time and is based on some agreed volume during a specific time

WEEK	1	2	3	4	5	6	7	8	9	10	11	12	13
GUARANTEE	100%					75%					50%		
PART # AND QUANTITY													
69782, BOARD	65	65	65	60	60	60	50	50	50	50	60	60	60
17962, ASSEMBLY	20	20	20	18	18	18	15	15	15	15	18	18	18

TABLE 16.1   ILLUSTRATION OF FORECASTED REQUIREMENTS GUARANTEE

period horizon. However, it is not usually an actual purchase order or commitment to purchase; it simply fixes prices for a given period of time.

(iv) Forward Purchasing.   Occasionally, the concern for projected market shortages or price increases gives rise to the practice of buying in advance of actual demand or forecasted needs. This process, often referred to as **forward buying**, is generally used to ensure supply at a fixed price when prices are trending upward or market conditions indicate there may be potential shortages in supply.

(v) Speculative Purchasing.   There are occasionally opportunities to profit from buying in larger quantities than your organization requires and reselling the amount in excess of your needs at a profit. This practice generally occurs when the quantity purchased substantially reduces the price paid *and* there is a readily available market for the excess.

(vi) Product Life-Cycle Purchasing.   When a collaborative relationship with the supplier exists, or when both buyer and supplier are jointly developing a product, it may prove advantageous to develop a contract for the life of the product. This reduces the financial risk of product development to the supplier and provides an incentive to go forward with expenses that may be needed for product development. The practice also ensures there will be an ongoing source of supply at stable pricing for the buyer.

(vii) Just-In-Time (JIT) Purchasing.   **Just-in-time (JIT)** is a management philosophy that strives to eliminate waste sources—resulting from any activity that adds cost without adding value, such as moving and storing inventory—by producing and delivering the right part in the right place at the right time. JIT (also known as lean production or stockless production) works to improve profits and return on investment by reducing inventory levels (increasing the inventory turnover rate), improving product quality, reducing production and delivery lead times, and reducing other costs (such as those associated with machine setup and equipment breakdown).

JIT is a means of enabling market demand to drive inventory management and is typically imbedded within an environment of Six Sigma continuous improvement. However, to be successful it requires a systematic and highly cooperative approach to inventory planning, receipt, throughput, and delivery that focuses on smaller lot sizes delivered more frequently.

Although JIT was developed for production environments, there seems to be no reason the concept cannot be extended to all business environments. The basic concept is to receive what is needed just in time for it to be used. This places the responsibility on the supplier to get what is needed to where it is needed, just before the time it is needed.

(viii) Commodity Purchasing. **Commodities** are generally products that have uniform natures and are traded in an open marketplace, usually an exchange. They include many raw materials and natural resources such as aluminum and copper, as well as common agricultural products like grains and live-stock.

On a **commodity exchange**, prices move in relation to projected supply and demand, often in a highly speculative manner. They are traded using financial instruments such as **futures options** (a contract for a specified product and amount to be delivered at some future date), so rarely does any physical exchange take place until the actual time of delivery called for in the contract. In commodities trading on an exchange, a **spot price** is the price of a product available for immediate delivery.

Some examples of popular commodity exchanges include:

- Chicago Board of Trade
- New York Mercantile Exchange
- London International Financial Futures
- International Petroleum Exchange
- Fukuoka Futures Exchange (Japan)

NOTE

A comprehensive listing of worldwide commodity exchanges can be found at the Rutgers University Library: *www.libraries.rutgers.edu/rul/rr_gateway/research_guides/busi/stocks.shtml#A.*

(ix) Supplier-Managed Systems. In **supplier-managed inventory (SMI)**, the supplier is responsible for maintaining the proper level of inventory (often at the buyer's site) based upon an agreed-upon formula of minimum and maximum levels. In an SMI system, the buying organization typically sends a periodic report of current inventory levels and incoming demand (or forecasts), and the supplier then ships the correct amount to maintain the agreed-upon level of stock.

(x) Consignment. Suppliers are sometimes required to maintain inventory that they continue to own and manage at the buyer's site. In a true **consignment** environment, the buyer does not pay for this material until it is actually sold or used in its application. Consignment inventory, despite the fact that it is not billed to the buying organization until it is used, is nevertheless inventory and does not eliminate the wasteful nature of maintaining unsold stock.

(b) IMPLEMENTING PROCUREMENT STRATEGIES. Once a procurement strategy is established, the purchaser should develop an appropriately related technique for its implementation. While there are endless numbers of procurement situations that may arise, some of those most common techniques for dealing with them are outlined in the following sections.

(i) Contracting.   Contracting is one of the most widely used methods for implementing any particular buying strategy, particularly when the procurement volume tied to a strategy is of significant value to the organization and when the objective of the strategy is to reduce risk. In this section, we cover some common contracting techniques.

LONG-TERM (AND MULTIYEAR) CONTRACTING

Extended contracting periods—beyond the typical yearly renewal contract—are used when there is a need to develop partnerships as an inducement for suppliers to invest in initial startup production costs or when internal processes such as implementing a JIT program require close collaboration between the two organizations. These contracts often cover a range of requirements (such as servicing training and spare parts, in the case of capital equipment) as a means of reducing the supply base and providing more value to the supplier.

Contracts of this nature are usually established following a time-consuming, detailed sourcing and selection process, so the buying organization also has a stake in maintaining a long-term relationship to avoid having to repeat the sourcing process. Consequently, these contracts typically include provisions for comprehensive performance criteria, accompanied by a continuous improvement and review program. They may also contain provisions for price escalation (or deescalation) based on predetermined levels of fluctuation in materials or labor—for changes over 5 percent, for example—as a way of sharing the risk of uncertain pricing structures in a dynamic market. These adjustments are often based on changes in a specific published price index or the rate of exchange between the monetary currencies used by the two parties.

LIFE-OF-PRODUCT CONTRACTING

As we pointed out earlier, it is often advantageous for the contracting parties to develop agreements that cover the entire life cycle of the product being sold to offset the risk of the supplier's initial investment and startup costs and to provide a longer basis to amortize its costs. When the cost of new technology, for example, is relatively high, it can provide restraints to effective marketing if the development cost must be recovered in a shorter time frame such as one year.

FUTURE CONTRACTS (AND OPTIONS)

A contract for future delivery—similar to the commodities futures contracts traded on public exchanges—can gain a supplier's commitment for production capacity when demand is random but nevertheless critical. Similarly, it can also fix prices during periods of uncertain supply and demand.

Options—the rights to buy something at a set price for a specified period of time—are also used when constraints to finalizing a purchase exist. This can occur, for example, when a sale is likely but the customer has not fully committed to a particular configuration. Usually, an option such as this is purchased for a fee that is either applied to the purchase should it be completed or given back should the project be cancelled.

CONTRACTING FOR CAPACITY

When overall volume can be estimated but the **product mix** required from a specific supplier cannot be determined, the best solution to ensure supply might be to contract for a portion of the supplier's production capacity in exchange for a firm commitment for volume. The volume may not actually be needed, but by reserving this production capacity in advance, you can reduce the risk of losing potential future sales due to lack of production capacity, or you can increase the chances of gaining last-minute business from unanticipated demand.

(ii) Spot Buying.   Spot buying, as described in the Defining Procurement Strategies section, refers to the practice of purchasing a product on the open market for immediate delivery at the current cash price. Traditionally, spot markets exist primarily for those commodities traded on the futures markets, but in today's practice the term might refer to any purchase made without a contract or blanket order, as might be the case with on-time purchases, or it can refer to purchases made to meet unplanned demand.

Because of the immediacy of its requirement, spot buying rarely allows the buyer time for competitive bidding. For products or services not normally available for purchase through an exchange, the purchase goes to a supplier that is already doing business with the organization and has capacity to meet the volume. If there are no such suppliers available, the next preferable option would be some form of competitive bid, usually taken in the form of quotations. Again, depending on the immediacy of the need, this will likely be possible only in the case of off-the-shelf items.

(iii) Dollar Averaging.   When short-term pricing fluctuates to the extent that it is difficult to determine your organization's basis for selling prices, it is common practice to use the averaged price of the commodity purchased for the recent period. Table 16.2 shows how this can help stabilize the calculations used for cost purposes. Note that the highlighted average price differs from the individual prices paid at each purchase.

(iv) Hedging.   Hedging, in its purest form, is the practice of offsetting the current contracted price by taking the opposite position in the futures market. This enables the organization to protect against any adverse price changes. Let's say, for

DATE	QUANTITY	PRICE/UNIT	TOTAL PRICE	AVERAGE PRICE
MAR 7	210	$ 8.22	$1,726.20	
APR 22	160	$11.70	$1,872.00	
JUN 3	450	$ 7.94	$3,573.00	
TOTAL	820		$7,171.20	$8.75

TABLE 16.2   EXAMPLE OF DOLLAR AVERAGING

example, a U.S. organization signs a contract to purchase some capital equipment for €12 million with delivery and payment due in 90 days. Because of potential fluctuations in the euro, the currency in which the payment is to be made, the organization immediately enters into a financial contract to buy the €12 million at the current exchange rate of $1.28 per euro in 90 days when the payment is due. It also purchases an option to sell the same amount of currency at the same time and at the same rate. In this way, whatever direction, up or down, the currency exchange rate takes, your organization will pay no more than the current market value.

(v) Decision Tree Techniques.   Decision tree analysis is a support tool to help review alternative strategies in a standard format and represents the decision-making process in a graphical format. Decisions that can be made sequentially are shown as branches of a tree, beginning with the initial point of decision and extending to the probable final outcome. Each branch represents a separate set of decisions and probable outcomes.

In procurement, the decision tree is useful in the planning process as a means of evaluating the risk and benefit relationships between possible courses of sourcing action. By assigning a value to both the successful outcome of a particular course of action and its failure and linking it with the probability of an outcome, an expected value can be calculated.

In the example shown in Figure 16.1, a decision tree is employed to determine allocations among four suppliers. For each supplier, a probability factor of a purchase being required at a specific level of demand is estimated. The quoted price is then multiplied by this factor to calculate a probable price outcome. Capacity is calculated at that level of demand for the period during which the requirement exists. Choices based on projected price and capacity can then be made. In this example, demand for 1,000,000 units could only go to Supplier 1, the only supplier with that level of capacity; demand for 750,000 and 500,000 units could go to Supplier 4, which has the best probable delivery price with available capacity.

(vi) Supply Chain Management.   The supply chain is generally referred to as consisting of all organizations involved in the creation of a specific product or service, its distribution to the final consumer, and its retirement and disposal. In

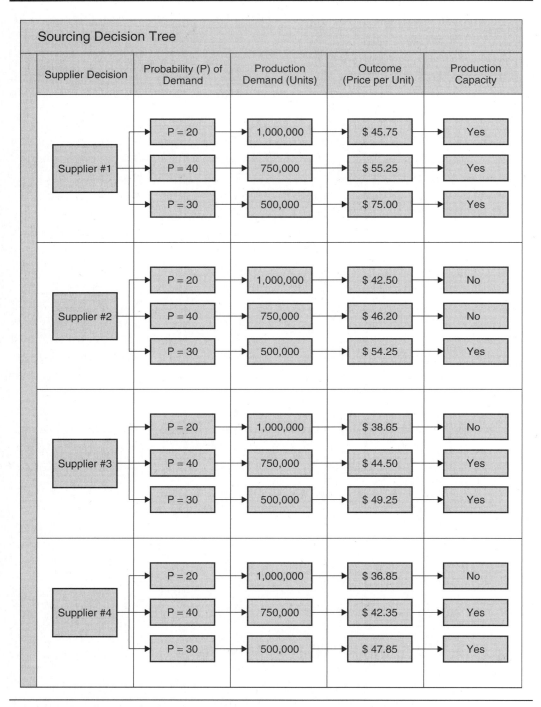

FIGURE 16.1   EXAMPLE OF A DECISION TREE ANALYSIS

broad terms, you can divide the supply chain into two segments: supply management and distribution management. Supply management is concerned primarily with creating the product or service, whereas distribution management focuses on sales, delivery, and customer service.

Supply chain management strategies will vary widely, depending on the industry or market segment to which it is applied, and it would be impossible to formulate a one-size-fits-all supply solution. However, it is safe to say that virtually all strategies will involve the collaboration and integration of multiple organizations as a means to strengthen the group's position in relation to competing supply chains. In some cases this might involve consortium buying (where not legally prohibited) or perhaps even sharing manufacturing production facilities or distribution channels. The key ingredient appears to be leveraging the synergy between trading partners.

16.2 PLANNING PROCUREMENT REQUIREMENTS

Regardless of the strategies or methods developed to secure materials and services, most future focused procurement activities will rely heavily on sound and effective forecasting and planning. Operationally, the forecast enables the buyer to determine the timing required for the actual purchase and provides the supplier with the tools needed to better support the buying organization. Based on internally generated information relating to demand and externally generated information relating to supply, the buyer is able to effectively manage and ensure supply.

In this section we will examine the nature of forecasting and demand planning, as well as the methods available to coordinate planning with your suppliers.

(a) FORECASTING AND DEMAND PLANNING.   As noted earlier in this chapter, demand planning is based on incoming customer orders, while forecasting is based on estimates of future requirements. The distinction between them is primarily their planning horizon. The key to either of these processes, however, is to accurately define and predict future requirements so that the availability of supply can be ensured.

(i) Short-Term Planning.   The challenge of short-term planning is to provide sufficient detail and granularity so that orders for materials can be placed with the suppliers to meet the demand of actual customer requirements. The goal of the short-term plan is to optimize inventory while meeting 100 percent of customer demand in a timely manner. This is usually accomplished by prioritizing incoming customer orders and grouping them according to production capacity. Generally, short-term planning and coordination with the supplier is handled by the organization's operational units—the production control or

manufacturing planning sections, for example—since contracts with suppliers have most likely already been put in place by the Procurement Department for commonly used materials.

(ii) Forecasting. Planning for the longer term requires that procurement professionals develop processes to accurately predict future requirements so that potential supply contingencies or constraints can be proactively met. While opinion-based forecasts are helpful and occasionally used to establish reliable future trends (when expert information is available), the forecasts most common in procurement are fact-based and derived from historical usage data. These are used because they can be mathematically extrapolated to establish future needs. Procurement also uses standard industrial predictors that rely on **change indexes** such as the **Consumer Price Index (CPI)** or **ISM's Report on Business** to help define business trends.

FORECASTING SPECIFIC ELEMENTS
Forecasting supports strategy by providing reasonably accurate predictions for information that can assist the organization's planners to meet future demand in a manner that both ensures supply and develops a competitive advantage. While the precise nature of the information will vary from situation to situation, there are a number of key elements that are typically of special interest to the forecasting processes, and we will discuss them here.

- **Pricing trends.** Supply and demand are the primary drivers of pricing, so it is important to gain an understanding of their future interaction in your marketplace. You also need to have information available regarding the length and severity of pricing movements so that you can better time purchases and contracts for most favorable pricing. Keep in mind, however, that there are numerous other factors that may drive pricing that are difficult to predict, such as natural disasters or wars.
- **Capacity and material availability.** Capacity constraints and the availability of materials can be closely related to economic trends. Examining long-term supply and demand in its relation to future investment in capital and new technology can provide invaluable insights into planning supply operations. In times of severe capacity restrictions, production output allocations from suppliers can be critical to continued operations, so it is important to identify areas where potential constraints may require strong supply partnerships and solid contractual relations.
- **Changing technology.** The introduction of new technology and its timing has serious implications for procurement. For example, in the semiconductor industry, the shift from 200-mm wafers to 300-mm wafers impacts all aspects of procurement, from capital equipment to raw materials to

auxiliary professional services. Detailed insight into the timing of such technology changes is important for planning inventory reductions to minimize financial loss as a result of the changeover and to limit contractual obligations. It is also important simply from a workload balancing perspective, because there will be an obvious spike in procurement activity as a result of most technology conversions.

FORCASTING PROCESSES

In order to effectively develop appropriate forecasting processes, the procurement professional will have to put in place a number of elements:

- Establish forecast metrics. Define those measures that will drive desired planning results, such as planning horizons, scheduling interval buckets, and levels of detail that will be required by others in the supply chain to support your operations.
- Develop and implement collaborative processes with customers so that a continuous stream of **actionable** market information is available as the basis of the forecasts and forecast revisions.
- Create a feedback mechanism so that customers can be made aware of potential supply constraints and pricing changes.
- Acquire systems tools that will prioritize incoming demand and optimize supply operations.
- Determine internal accountability and periodic timing requirements for forecast generation.

(b) COORDINATING FORECASTED REQUIREMENTS WITH SUPPLIERS. Coordinating the information obtained through forecasting activities with your suppliers is equally as important as generating the forecasts themselves. Working collaboratively with your suppliers often means involving them early in the development and distribution of actionable information. Early supplier involvement (ESI) is a process that enables suppliers to participate in the early stages of product development and production planning so that they can better support your organization through their domain expertise. ESI also has the added potential of reducing turnaround time for new product introduction by leveraging the added expertise of the supplier's technical resources.

(i) Supplier Involvement. ESI is an effective collaborative process that adds value in many ways. In supply planning, it enables the supplier to ensure ongoing materials and services consistent with actual customer requirements. It also enables the supplier to better plan the utilization of its resources—especially important if you are a key customer—to help control and reduce manufacturing costs.

Implementing collaborative planning and replenishment processes enables the supply chain to more effectively respond to rapid changes in demand and to improve allocation activities by anticipating the conditions that create peaks and valleys in requirements. Early supplier involvement also provides time to identify potential constraints and select possible alternatives. By encouraging the development of these collaborative processes, you will help ensure the continued balance of supply and demand.

Some of the specific areas you will likely want to focus your efforts at developing collaboration to improve procurement processes are discussed next.

MANUFACTURING PROCESSES AND PLANNING

By working closely with your supplier's team, you have the opportunity to increase its responsiveness to changes in demand by helping to shorten the production planning cycle. Shorter planning cycles generally result in leaner operations through less buildup of inventory and reduced inventory obsolescence. This, in turn, leads to reduced costs to the buyer.

Effective manufacturing and fulfillment planning always involves the optimization of plant and asset utilization and is especially effective when the buying organization's staff understands the supplier's potential constraints. **Constraint-based planning** between collaborative partners is certain to better serve the consumer by ensuring the orderly allocation of resources and providing a mechanism to avoid supply shortages.

CAPITAL REQUIREMENTS

Forecasts of needed equipment—replacements or new acquisitions—can be useful to suppliers in the same way as material requirements. By engaging suppliers early, special requirements can often be included in new equipment being designed without the need for additional engineering cost. Similarly, early involvement helps ensure that production capacity and engineering staff are available to work on your projects when they are needed.

COST REQUIREMENTS

Early involvement of key suppliers can be critical to controlling and reducing costs. As the design process evolves in your organization, the supplier can provide assessments regarding the cost of various alternatives. Often this intervention will prevent decisions that lead to costly mistakes and avoidable lapses in judgment. In a competitive environment, this input can often provide a critical advantage to new product introduction.

TECHNOLOGY REQUIREMENTS

Collaboration and early supplier involvement often results in the added capability of leveraging the expertise of the supplier to identify trends that might materially affect the products or services your organization is marketing. Obviously, you would not encourage investment in tooling or equipment that might become obsolete prior to its return on investment (ROI). However, you would want to encourage your organization to prepare for changes in materials and processes being driven by technology that your supplier may have special access to and can pass along to your organization.

PRODUCT DESIGN

Suppliers often have design expertise in areas that can supplement what is available in your own organization. Knowing what works and what doesn't work in a specific feature can add great value in designing new products, especially in areas where the supplier's expertise is superior to that of your own. Leveraging this expertise often develops from close collaboration and interaction between the two organization's design and engineering teams. To the extent that it is possible for you to encourage and facilitate this level of collaboration, you can help provide further competitive advantage for your organization.

QUALITY REQUIREMENTS

Improved quality at a reduced cost often comes with the early involvement of suppliers in the development of specifications. Here you must assume that the supplier has unique knowledge of the processes and methods being used to fulfill your requirements. By bringing suppliers into the specification development process early, you can frequently assist them in preparing to meet special quality requirements and industry quality standards.

LEAD-TIME REQUIREMENTS

It is important to sufficiently plan for supplier capacity and lead-time requirements. In doing so, you should involve your internal customers in the process to ensure early supplier response. This can often make a significant difference in supplier performance because it allows sufficient time for the supplier to increase capacity to meet your needs in a timely and orderly fashion. Insufficient supplier capacity can often lead to an unreliable source of supply and loss of consumer confidence.

(ii) Disclosure.   Prior to engaging a supplier in any activity that allows access to your organization's confidential information, you must be certain that its staff has the capability of protecting it from unwanted access. Similarly, in order to earn the trust and confidence of your suppliers, you will want to ensure the protection of its information as well. You will not want to shake that confidence by disclosing proprietary information about one supplier to another.

CONFIDENTIALITY

Confidential information can take a surprisingly broad scope, so you must be vigilant with the information you disclose. It will certainly include the obvious such as pricing and intellectual property; it may also include other information that appears to be less sensitive but nevertheless should not be disclosed, such as final positions in bidding events, software systems in use, organizational structure, staffing, and anything related to future business planning.

LEGAL ASPECTS

Typically, organizations use instruments such as a nondisclosure agreement (NDA) to ensure the maintenance of confidential information between it and its customers and suppliers. In developing these documents, it is important to fully define what they cover and how the information being disclosed may be used. Since this can be associated with extensive legal and liability issues, it is not a good idea to simply execute a standard form for every situation. Many companies with extensive intellectual property will require specific legal review by experts prior to executing such documents.

16.3 CONDUCTING MARKET ANALYSIS

Market analysis is a discipline that examines all of the key economic and technological aspects within an industry or industry segment and systematically gathers data that can help predict future trends in that market. It is an important element in procurement planning because it produces information on the composition and growth of the marketplace—suppliers as well as buyers—that can form the foundation of an organization's competitive business strategy. This information can help you determine future pricing trends and what capacity will be available to fill your needs. It can also provide insight into potential new sources of supply.

While market analysis can be as much of an art as a science, requiring advanced skill and learning, there are some basic principles you can employ to answer the fundamental questions posed in procurement planning. We will explore these in the following section.

(a) DEVELOPING MARKET AWARENESS AND EARLY INVOLVEMENT.   The Procurement Department is in a unique position to gather information from the marketplace through its role as the key interface in the supplier relationship. Data available from suppliers often provides the most current perspectives on market trends and technological advances, giving the Procurement Department an opportunity to funnel this information to other groups within the organization that can use it to further their competitive business advantage. In some organizations, the Procurement Department may be called upon to facilitate supplier involvement in major activities, providing expert input on product viability and sourcing strategies.

(i) New Product Introduction (NPI).   Getting early participation in new product development activities from your suppliers can significantly reduce the cycle time

required to bring a new product to market and help avoid major difficulties with design and production failures down the road. The Procurement Department can also leverage the resources of the supply community by proactively seeking input from suppliers regarding possible issues with new products, such as those related to product applications, manufacturing strategies, quality, and pricing. It is important that activities involving suppliers take place as early in the research and development stage as possible to fully leverage their expertise before making any significant commitments to design.

The Procurement Department can add value to the new product development process in a number of other ways as well, including providing advice on the cost impact of various substitution alternatives being considered, negotiating prices with suppliers to meet initial targeted budget requirements, laying the groundwork for future sourcing activities, and coordinating the development of material specifications. By using market-driven data, the Procurement Department can help provide the foundation for design decisions with material choices, determining if adequate supplies will be available in the future and what, if any, capital investments may be required to produce the product. By analyzing the nature of competition within the industry, the purchaser can also advise the organization where opportunities for joint design and development partnerships might be found.

(ii) Source Development.   Market analysis can assist you with the identification of key marketplace suppliers for the products or services you may need in the future. Taking a proactive approach by investigating possible sources in advance of actual requirements will enable you to provide wider competition, which will drive more favorable terms when the time comes for an actual purchase. Identifying secondary (or backup) sources also reduces the risk inherent in selecting a new supplier; without early involvement, you will likely not have adequate time to do so when you must make the actual purchase.

(iii) Technology Impact.   Getting information on the latest developments in technology for the products you buy can become quite challenging, given the time constraints of today. Here, early involvement often includes attending trade shows and working with suppliers who are on the leading edge of technological developments in the industry. You can also subscribe to leading trade journals, many of which are available online, that can deliver periodic summaries of recent developments in technology. Professional associations and industry trade organizations often offer similar information and can provide up-to-date studies and surveys to help you understand the direction and challenges of the industry you are analyzing.

(iv) Market Capacity.   The ability of the market to absorb the volume of your organization's future purchases should not be taken for granted. You should always

be alert to market conditions when you are anticipating significant procurement volumes or when prices could rise significantly as a result of production capacity constraints. An early understanding of the major factors that drive market price will help you to develop offsetting strategies and negotiate in advance the most favorable terms possible.

(b) COLLECTING AND DISTRIBUTING DATA. Sources for information are abundant. Depending upon your objectives, you should therefore restrict your data collection to stay aligned with your objectives. Are you looking for economic information such as pricing trends and capacity, or are you interested in gaining a better understanding of the individual suppliers in the industry? If you are looking for industry or economic data, you may want to consult secondary sources such as government-published data; if you are interested in company-based information, you may want to go to the primary sources such as the companies themselves. A company's Web site is an excellent place to gather public information about potential suppliers and the marketplace they operate in.

GOVERNMENT DATA

There are a number of excellent government sources for industry-specific data available in the United States. Here are a few of those widely used:

- U.S. Department of Labor, Bureau of Labor Statistics, provides data on employment and employment trends: *http://stats.bls.gov/*.
- U.S. Census Bureau, Economic Census, profiles the U.S. economy every five years: *www.census.gov/*.
- U.S. Securities and Exchange Commission (SEC), EDGAR Database, provides information for public companies based on real-time filings and other company information: *www.sec.gov/edgar/searchedgar/webusers.htm*.
- U.S. Department of Commerce, STAT-USA, provides U.S. import and export statistics including the National Trade Data Bank (NTDB), as well as access to Country Commercial Guides and Market Research reports: *www.stat-usa.gov/*.
- U.S. International Trade Administration, Trade Stats, provides trade data and statistics: *www.ita.doc.gov/*.

COMMERCIAL DATABASES

There are also a number of excellent commercial databases available that can provide market information:

- Dun and Bradstreet provide financial information, business ratings, and company profiles on public and privately held companies: *www.dnb.com/us/*.
- Hoover's Online provides business information on publicly held companies: *www.hoovers.com/free/*.

- *Wall Street Journal,* Tech Library, offers a compendium of white papers and free market analysis: *techlibrary.wallstreetandtech.com/data/rlist?t= busofit_10_30_10.*
- ThomasNet is a comprehensive resource for industrial information: *www. thomasnet.com.*

PUBLICATIONS AND GOVERNMENT REPORTS

Several well-known publications and government reports are also available to provide detailed information on business and economic trends. Those more commonly used include:

- ISM *Report on Business* (manufacturing and nonmanufacturing) measures the change in activity levels through polling selected companies and industries and is the basis for the *Purchasing Manager's Index (PMI)*, a highly regarded leading economic indicator: *www.ism.ws.*
- *Survey of Current Business*, published by the U.S. Department of Commerce, Bureau of Economic Analysis, provides up-to-date analysis of economic conditions: *www.bea.doc.gov/bea/pubs.htm.*
- *Federal Reserve Bulletin* contains articles and reports that analyze economic developments: *www.federalreserve.gov/pubs/bulletin/default.htm.*
- The U.S. Government Printing Office (GPO) hosts a Web site with links to useful economic publications from all three government branches, including the *Economic Report of the President* and the *Statistical Abstract of the U.S.: www.gpoaccess.gov/index.html.*
- Industry publications are widely distributed to buyers in their particular areas of interest and are usually free. CMP Media, for example, publishes several online and paper journals (*www.cmp.com*), as does Reed Business Services (*www.pubservice.com/CH.htm*).

(i) Internal Communication. Once you have gathered relevant information, the challenge will be distributing it to others in your organization. While the way you handle this will vary depending on the nature of your organization, it is wise to consider that information should be sent only to those interested in receiving it to avoid adding to the information overload problem.

TIPS AND TECHNIQUES

Try posting market and up-to-date supplier information on a dedicated Web site (or portal) on your organization's intranet server. If properly sorted, this will enable users to access only the data they need. It will also provide the added benefit of giving you statistics on the number of times specific information is accessed so that you can better determine what the users deem valuable.

(c) FORECASTING MARKET TRENDS.   Forecasts of future market conditions provide the procurement professional with information on pricing and potential risk factors. This information is needed to develop effective strategic plans, so it is important that the data be gathered and analyzed in a timely and methodical fashion to avoid errors and incorrect conclusions.

(i) Forecasting Processes and Methods.   Depending on your specific requirements, short-term forecasts (one year or less) can be used for tactical planning, while long-term forecasts can be used to develop strategic plans. There are numerous methods available for use in forecasting, and we discuss some of the more common methods here:

- **Correlation analysis** measures the degree to which changes in one variable are associated with changes in another. Its measure, the correlation coefficient, describes the degree of association (or co-variance) with -1, indicating a perfect negative correlation; through 0, meaning no correlation; to +1, a perfect positive correlation.
- **Regression analysis** is a statistical technique that determines, for predictive purposes, the degree of correlation of one variable (the dependent variable) with one or more independent variables. This determines if a strong or weak cause-and-effect relationship exists between two elements.
- Similar to regression analysis, **trend analysis** seeks to determine variations in the rate of change so that predictions regarding future conditions (such as product demand) can be extrapolated.
- **Time series analysis** is the analysis of a sequence of measurements made at specified time intervals, usually taken from the organization's historical records. Time is usually the dominating dimension of the data, and the measure is usually used to predict trends that may contain cyclical variations.
- **Measures of central tendency** are likely the most common statistics available. They describe the grouping of values in a data set around some common value—the median, arithmetic mean, or geometric mean.
- **Measures of dispersion** (or measures of variability) describe how two sets of numbers differ from one another. They include measures such as range (the difference between the largest number and the smallest), variance (the square of the sum of individual variations from the mean, divided by the number of values in the group), and the standard deviation (the square root of the variance).
- When no verifiable statistical data exists, forecasters often turn to the **Delphi method**, a procedure for developing opinion-based forecasts. The process consists of a series of repeated interrogations of selected individuals. After a set of responses is analyzed, and its recommendations incorporated into a revised interrogation, it is resubmitted to the group for reconsideration, with

encouragement to change the revised version if appropriate until a final composite can be obtained, when no further changes are made.

(ii) Economic Considerations.   Rarely do economic events take place in isolation. There are often complex marketplace interactions between related segments and a general economic environment operating as a support backdrop. These blend to create a specific context in which factors and events can be analyzed. Applying the proper context to the information being analyzed places it in the correct perspective so that accurate conclusions can be drawn and appropriate courses of action established. In order to establish the appropriate context for data review, you should consider the overall business picture of the industry and how it relates to general market and **macroeconomic trends**. In doing so, you can better select the thrust of your analytical efforts, leading to your business and supply plan.

In any free-market economy (such as the United States), price and production levels are established by open-market factors such as supply and demand. On the other hand, in a centrally controlled economy (such as China's), prices can be determined by policies and regulatory administrators; that is, they can be "legislated" without regard to fundamental economic factors. While there are crossovers—for example, government-regulated commodities in the United States such as pharmaceuticals that exhibit both open-market and centralized influences—purchasers generally agree that market factors are the driving forces behind most pricing structures. For this reason, you must pay especially close attention to what you expect conditions to be like in the future.

INDUSTRY AND MARKET ECONOMICS
Products and markets that respond to supply and demand exhibit a degree of price elasticity. **Elasticity** refers to the relative change in demand for a product or service as a response to a change in price or, conversely, the relative change in price in response to a change in demand. When there is little or no response, price or demand is considered inelastic. Similarly, if price elasticity is low, a large movement in price will only produce a small change in demand. Markedly elastic prices are often referred to as "volatile" and require the most attention since they present the greatest risk.

Keep in mind that there is also a principle of equilibrium at work in the supply and demand equation. In the longer term, supply and demand move to match one another and develop a balance so that prices remain fairly stable, but there are other factors to consider, too. Obviously, as the amount of money available to a purchaser changes, the demand curve also changes. The **law of diminishing marginal utility** indicates that additional satisfaction (or utility) decreases as additional units of a product are consumed. This is perhaps the point at which a product line might begin moving into the end-of-life phase, and this helps redirect available purchase funds to more recently introduced products that may have greater utility to the buying organization.

There is also another key economic factor to consider: business organizations seek to maximize profit. When prices drop below actual cost, there is little incentive to continue to produce; however, when profit becomes excessive, competition for the lucrative market increases. For this reason, economists agree that in the long run the supply curve of any particular commodity will tend to reflect the actual cost to produce the good or service. Ideally, the market stabilizes at the point where the marginal cost (the additional cost of the last unit produced) equals marginal revenue (the additional revenue produced by the last unit sold). Competitive markets are thus most likely to exist where the price buyers are willing to pay at a level to at least balance the costs to the supplier.

Perfect competition may never exist, and most suppliers usually operate in an environment of limited or **imperfect competition**. This environment is characterized by the existence of some competitors whose products can provide relative distinction from one another and suppliers having some degree of control over marketplace pricing.

GLOBAL TRENDS

The global economy is characterized by continual change, with some countries or geographical regions holding advantages only in specific commodities. For example, natural resources such as petroleum or timber are common in one area, while low-priced labor is common in another. Countries that have higher efficiency or greater resources in a particular area will always hold a competitive advantage over others, unless somehow restricted by laws or other governmental actions. In some areas, government subsidies or tariffs help local producers of a particular product to compete with outsiders where they would not likely have an advantage. When production exceeds local demand in such situations, products are often *dumped* in other countries; that is, exported at prices well below cost.

BUSINESS CYCLES

Economic conditions tend to move in cyclical fashion, creating what are known as business cycles. While these cycles are by no means regularly timed, as in the case of **seasonal cycles**, they do have certain common characteristics of **expansion** (an increase in **gross domestic product [GDP]**) followed by **contraction** (a decrease in GDP), with specific economic turning points and troughs in between.

(iii) Economic Terms and Indicators.   Forecasting business cycles is not an exact science, but there are certain economic indicators—such as housing starts, stock prices, or ISM's Report on Business—that can be used for short-term prediction of a changing economic phase. The procurement professional can use these indicators to determine the direction of market conditions and develop appropriate procurement strategies.

Econiomic Indicators

Economic indicators are usually statistical signals of changes in an economy's trend. In the United States, the Bureau of Economic Analysis of the Department of Commerce groups these indicators by their timing relationship to the general economy. There are three primary indicators:

- **Leading indicators** are those that forecast changes in the economy before they occur. They include elements such as the money supply, stock prices, commodity prices (raw materials and agricultural products), new unemployment claims, new building permits, new orders for consumer goods, new orders for investments goods, and unfilled orders.
- **Coincident indicators** are economic elements that measure changes in the economy as they occur, providing information related to the present condition of the economy. Personal income and the unemployment rate are examples.
- **Lagging (trailing) indicators** are market indicators that follow general trends in the economy, often continuing either an upward trend after the peak of the economy is signaled by other economic indicators, or a downward trend after a rise is signaled. Examples include business expenditures for new plants and equipment, consumers' installment credit, short-term business loans, and the overall value of manufacturing and trade inventories.

Economic Price Indices

A **price index** is a statistical tool that compares prices from one period (usually a base period) to the next in specific areas of the economy. Numerous indices of this kind exist, but the more commonly used ones in the United States include:

- The **Consumer Price Index (CPI)**, published by the U.S. Bureau of Labor Statistics, is one of the most widely cited examples of a price index. It measures the cost of a representative "market basket" of typically purchased consumer goods that changes in composition very slowly. As a measure of the change in the cost of living, it has become commonly used as an indicator of the degree of *inflation* in the economy. There are two official CPIs, the CPI-U and the CPI-W. The CPI-U is an index of consumer prices based on the typical market basket of goods and services consumed by all urban consumers during a base period. The CPI-W is an index of consumer prices based on the typical market basket of goods and services consumed by urban wage earners and clerical workers during a base period.
- The **Producer Price Index (PPI)** is a group of indexes (also published by the Bureau of Labor Statistics) that measures the average change over time in wholesale selling prices received by domestic producers of goods and services. The index is reported by commodity, industry sector, and stage of processing and is separated into finished goods (those that will

not experience any further change), intermediate goods (those that have had some processing but are not finished), and raw materials (those in their original, unprocessed state).

- The **Implicit Price Deflator** (or GDP deflator) is an index-based ratio that measures inflation by converting output in current prices into a constant-dollar GDP, showing how much of the change relative to the base year's GDP (1992) can be attributed to changes in price levels.

The rate of change in an index can be used to assess changes in direction of the overall economy. An index is calculated from a base period (or year) that is assigned a value of 100. Subsequent calculations are made as a percentage of change from that base period. For example, if the price of market basket of goods during the base period is valued at $1,195.00 (which equals 100) and in the second year it is valued at $1,254, it has increased by 5 percent. This puts the index for year 2 at 105.

INTEREST RATES

Interest rates are the charges assessed by a lender for borrowing money. They are usually expressed as a percentage of the loan over a period of time. Fixed rates are calculated on the basis of a specific periodic rate that remains unchanged and are the same amount for each period, while variable rates change according to changes in a specified index and can vary from period to period. The rates themselves, however, are based on factors such as the borrower's credit risk rating and the relative level of supply and demand for money.

EMPLOYMENT LEVELS

Employment levels are most commonly measured in terms of the rate of unemployment. You should also consider the size of the labor force overall and the number of new jobs created in any given period. These measures help shape public policy. In times of recession with accompanying high unemployment, government-subsidized programs may be used to stimulate employment, which in turn results in an increase in overall economic spending.

GROSS DOMESTIC PRODUCT (GDP)

GDP is the total market value of all the goods and services produced domestically during a given period. GDP equals total consumer spending on final products, business investment, and government spending and investment, plus the value of exports, minus the value of imports. In the United States, it is calculated by the Department of Commerce each quarter and is considered the key measure of economic output. You measure expansion and contraction in terms of GDP.

MONEY SUPPLY

Money supply refers to the amount of money in circulation. There are two main measures: $M1$ measures the funds readily available for spending, that is, currency and liquid bank and investment accounts. *M2* is M1 plus relatively accessible savings, such as small time deposits held for the most part by households. When the money supply figure is up, it is an inflationary factor and, therefore, generates concern that the Federal Reserve will tighten money growth by allowing short-term interest rates to rise. A rise in interest rates often leads to less spending, and a cooling off of the economy usually takes place.

EXCHANGE RATES

Rate of exchange refers to the value of one country's currency in relation to another. Fluctuations in these rates are of considerable concern to buyers engaged in international procurement because of the potential for price erosion as the value of one currency declines in relation to the other. Currency rates are typically established by the central banks in response to market conditions. Countries generally seek a level of exchange that is low enough to encourage other countries to purchase their products (because their currency has greater purchasing power) while not so low that it produces a low rate of return and discourages foreign investment.

BALANCE OF TRADE/BALANCE OF PAYMENTS

Simply defined, the **balance of trade** is the difference between a country's imports and its exports from the rest of the world for any given period. It is an element of the larger **balance of payments**, which reflects additional nontangible flows such as capital investment, dividends, debt payments, and interest payments. A deficit in payments means the country is paying out more than it receives. This has been the case in the United States for more than the past 50 years.

INFLATION/DEFLATION

In its simplest terms, inflation is the measurement of the rate of increase in the general level of prices in an economy, producing a decline in purchasing power of the currency. Inflation most commonly occurs when overall economic demand exceeds the supply of goods and services, driving prices upward. This can be the result of a rise in the money supply increasing at a rate that exceeds the rise in output. It can also result from a steep decline in supply or an increase in demand when industrial capacity is full. Inflation has been relatively stable in the U.S. economy at about 2.5 percent during the past decade.

Deflation is the opposite of inflation and is typically characterized by an actual decline in the general level of prices in the economy and a resulting increase in purchasing power. In the United States, the last major period of deflation occurred during the Depression of the 1930s.

CAPACITY UTILIZATION

The Federal Reserve Board calculates and reports the output of factories, industries, and the entire economy in terms of their **capacity utilization**. When factories are operating above 85 percent of capacity, industrial output is considered to be at full capacity. As the rate approaches 90 percent, it is assumed to be inflationary, while at a figure close to 70 percent, it is considered recessionary.

(iv) Government Policies. Most governments attempt to influence the overall conditions in their economies to help ensure the welfare of their citizens and to influence public objectives. Depending, of course, on the specific circumstances, common objectives might include reducing unemployment, increasing the rate of economic development, managing inflation or deflation, providing higher rates of return for foreign investment, and maintaining price stability. We'll discuss the most widely used government policies in this section.

MONETARY POLICY

Monetary policy controls economic activity by regulating the amount of money available to the public. In the United States, monetary policy is governed by the **Federal Reserve System** through its Board of Governors. An "easy" monetary policy leads to faster money growth and initially lower short-term interest rates in an attempt to increase overall demand, but it may also lead to a higher rate of inflation. A "tight" monetary policy restricts money growth and higher interest rates in the near term in an attempt to reduce inflationary pressure by reducing overall demand. During periods of recession, lower interest rates and higher money growth can help stimulate the economy. During periods of declining unemployment and increasing inflation, the Federal Reserve usually emphasizes monetary restraint by raising interest rates and slowing the growth of money.

FISCAL POLICY: TAXES

Because of its relative size, most governments can influence economic activity through its fiscal policy, both by supporting public spending as a stimulant or by raising taxes to cool off the economy. Conversely, corporate and consumer tax cuts have a tendency to stimulate economic activity by placing more spending power in the hands of consumers and corporations. Public policy can also be used to create benefits such as investment tax credits that will, in turn, stimulate further economic activity.

BUDGETS AND DEFICITS

Government budgets and budget deficits affect economic conditions, influence the money supply, and affect monetary policy. A country's need for borrowed funds due to deficits will usually affect overall interest rates and create competition with private industry for expansion funds. This can certainly slow economic growth.

NATIONAL INCOME

Government reports provide a great source of information that the procurement professional can use to better understand broad trends that affect overall business conditions in the economy. These trends, in turn, can help you develop estimates for how individual industries may perform.

National income is an important indicator of the resources available for spending, and its growth or contraction can signal major turning points in economic cycles. It is defined as the sum of the incomes of all the individuals in the country in the form of wages, interest, rents, dividends, and profits. It is calculated prior to any deductions for income taxes.

Figure 16.2 shows how the key economic measures in an economy (the United States in this case) relate to one another. Working from the bottom up, you

Line		2003
1	Gross domestic product	11,004.0
2	Plus: Income receipts from the rest of the world	329.0
3	Less: Income payments to the rest of the world	273.9
4	**Equals: Gross national product**	**11,059.2**
5	Less: Consumption of fixed capital	1,353.9
6	Private	1,135.9
7	Domestic business	942.6
8	Capital consumption allowances	1,225.6
9	Less: Capital consumption adjustment	283.0
10	Households and institutions	193.3
11	Government	218.1
12	General government	183.6
13	Government enterprises	34.5
14	**Equals: Net national product**	**9,705.2**
15	**Less: Statistical discrepancy**	**25.6**
16	**Equals: National income**	**9,679.6**
17	Less: Corporate profits with inventory valuation and capital consumption adjustments	1,021.1
18	Taxes on production and imports less subsidies [1]	751.3
19	Contributions for government social insurance	773.2
20	Net interest and miscellaneous payments on assets	543.0
21	Business current transfer payments (net)	77.7
22	Current surplus of government enterprises [1]	9.5
23	Wage accruals less disbursements	0.0
24	Plus: Personal income receipts on assets	1,322.7
25	Personal current transfer receipts	1,335.4
26	**Equals: Personal income**	**9,161.8**
	Addenda:	
27	Gross domestic income	10,978.5
28	Gross national income	11,033.6
29	Gross national factor income [2]	10,195.1
30	Net domestic product	9,650.1
31	Net domestic income	9,624.5
32	Net national factor income [3]	8,841.1

FIGURE 16.2   RELATION OF GROSS DOMESTIC PRODUCT, GROSS NATIONAL PRODUCT, NET NATIONAL PRODUCT, NATIONAL INCOME, AND PERSONAL INCOME (BILLIONS OF DOLLARS)

Source: U.S. Department of Commerce, Bureau of Economic Analysis

can see that national income is a derivative of **personal income** and rolls up to **net national product (NNP)**, **gross national product (GNP)**, and, finally, GDP.

POLITICS

Economic conditions are closely related to the political climate in virtually all economies and, depending on the specific area of the world, can be characterized as stable or unstable. Obviously, for the purchaser, risk increases dramatically during periods of political instability due to its effect on government services. In turn, this can significantly impact the availability of material, labor, and capital resources and can lead to escalating prices or unreliable supply. It is important, therefore, that the procurement professional pay particularly close attention to conditions in countries where the organization is purchasing strategic materials or conducting outsourced manufacturing.

(v) Import and Export Considerations. Market trends are also influenced by conditions affecting international trade, but because these conditions are typically governed by political considerations, they can be difficult to forecast. Some of the key areas to consider from this perspective include free trade, trade deficit and surplus, and countertrade.

FREE TRADE

Free trade means the flow of goods and services across national borders without restrictions or tariffs. This rarely exists because most countries adopt some form of protectionist stance in order to favor internal resources. Despite this, however, there have been numerous attempts to reduce trade barriers in some international circles and limited success on a regional basis. For example, in 1993, the United States, Canada, and Mexico entered into a trilateral free trade agreement, the North American Free Trade Agreement (NAFTA), designed to encourage trade between the partners as a means of providing long-term economic benefit to the region.

TRADE DEFICIT AND SURPLUS

A **trade deficit** is created when a country's imports exceeds its exports. It is considered to be a good measure of a country's economic condition because it is a calculation of the investment flows between other countries, as well as the balance of goods and services exchange. It is likely that the U.S. trade deficit—which reached its historical high of more than $500 billion in 2003—is the result of a net inflow of capital to the United States from the rest of the world because domestic investment has not kept pace with the opportunities. This is largely reflected in the lowered value of the U.S. dollar in relation to other currencies as a result of investors' fears that the trade and budget deficits will create higher investment risk.

COUNTERTRADE

Countertrade is a form of barter where goods are exchanged for financial credits that can only be used to buy other goods from the originating country or the trading partner. Countertrade also refers to reciprocal and compensatory trade agreements, whereby the seller assists the buyer in reducing the amount of net cost of the purchase through some form of compensatory financing or bartering. This form of business was favored by developing nations with abundant resources but limited liquid capital but has fallen into disfavor to a large extent in more recent time because of the burdensome administration associated with governing it and the often slow rate of receiving compensation.

(vi) Ongoing Monitoring of Data. Forecasts require frequent updating simply because economic conditions are continually changing. New technology, government policies, natural disasters, and a variety of related issues cause market-specific directions to alter in ways that often significantly affect the organization's planning horizon. Some of the more significant areas you will want to monitor to ensure that your forecasts are updated are discussed next.

FINANCIAL MARKETS

Financial markets that include stock exchanges, commodity exchanges, and money markets worldwide reflect the climate of business in their particular marketplace segments. They should be monitored for changes that may impact your procurement and economic forecasts. Money supply also affects economic conditions, influencing interest rates and the level of new investment. These, in turn, can have significant impact on market pricing and the pace of new product development investment.

LABOR MARKETS

The stability of labor conditions is critical to the long-range planning of organizations that purchase goods or services from labor-intensive sources. Obviously, increases in labor costs can have a direct impact on pricing, but you should also be concerned with the potential for strikes and work slowdowns resulting from organized labor movements or political unrest. While such events are difficult to forecast, they should nevertheless be monitored to validate the continued availability of supply at your projected levels of production and pricing requirements.

CAPACITY AND LEAD TIMES

Material shortages, plant shutdowns, financial crises, and adverse natural conditions can all directly impact delivery schedules and lead times. Spikes in demand can also strain production capacity and result in extended lead times. As you know, supply constraints usually lead to price increases and can significantly disrupt your planning assumptions. They should be continually monitored for trend changes.

POLITICAL CLIMATE

Although it would be impossible for you to become an expert in the politics of each nation your organization does business with, it is important that you remain sensitive to major changes in governmental policies that might affect the items you purchase. Despite the relatively stable political systems in many countries, including the United States, changes in government can bring changes in fiscal policy. Policy shifts can alter economic conditions, favoring certain industries over others, changing tariffs and quotas, adding or removing taxes, and altering the investment and monetary policies prevailing in the country. Consequently, it is important that you include these factors in any continuing risk assessments you perform for critical suppliers. They should be closely monitored for changes and addressed in your planning forecasts.

TECHNOLOGY

Shifts in technology are typically accompanied by shifts in economic conditions. Sometimes these shifts are global, such as in the telecommunications industry, and sometimes they are localized to the development of entirely new products to meet evolving technical standards. New technologies often give rise to new centers of innovative excellence, and attention shifts from one geographical region to another.

Technology also affects the methods of production and delivery for the goods and service you buy. Improved productivity as a result of automation is certainly one clear trend in many industries, and it can have a profound effect on output and prices. By leveraging this process, many organizations plan for declining prices by setting clear production learning-curve goals with their suppliers to deliver built-in price reductions.

To the extent that changes in technology can affect the products and services your organization markets, it is important that you monitor their potential impact on a regular basis and account for them as alternate scenarios in your planning forecasts.

ENVIRONMENTAL CONDITIONS

Changes in environmental conditions such as weather and natural disasters are difficult, if not impossible, to predict, and you will not be expected to do so. However, once such an event occurs, you must react quickly, assessing its impact on the goods and services you plan to purchase. Forecasts of the availability of supply and pricing trends should be evaluated in terms of their effect on your business and communicated to those in your organization who are most critically affected.

As part of their risk mitigation plans, most organizations look to their suppliers to have in place documented disaster recovery plans and backup sources of production.

16.4 SUMMARY

As you already know, developing effective procurement strategies is one of the most critical procurement professional responsibilities. Effective strategies reduce risk by ensuring continued supplies of favorably priced materials and services when they are needed. In this chapter, we examined the elements of various strategies and how they are best implemented and monitored. We also reviewed the most common methods for developing planning forecasts and coordinating them with suppliers, leveraging information gained from market analysis.

Demand- and forecast-based procurement strategies determine the method and timing of your purchases. Commonly used strategies include spot buying, procurement for current requirements only, JIT, long-term contracts, forward procurement, product life-cycle procurement, and commodity-based procurement. They also include strategies involving close supplier collaboration such as supplier-managed inventory and consignment methods. Implementing these strategies involves a number of specialized techniques such as hedging, speculative buying, dollar averaging, decision tree analysis, and supply chain management. Demand- and forecast-based planning also requires employing processes to estimate future demand requirements including the development of metrics, establishing collaboration with customers and suppliers for timely feedback, and creating internal accountability for timely forecast generation.

Market analysis examines economic and technology trends that might impact the organization's supply management planning. In areas such as new product introduction, market analysis assists with source development and pricing strategies. Typically, information is garnered from government and commercial databases, as well as publications and government reports, as a basis for analysis. You can apply a number of techniques to develop your projections, such as correlation analysis, regression analysis, trend analysis, time series analysis, measures of central tendency and dispersion, and the Delphi method. You should also examine current and projected economic conditions for the markets you are analyzing using specific economic indicators, price indexes, and government policies to assist your projections. Be sure to continually monitor these elements to ensure that your strategies address changing marketplace conditions.

KEY TERMS

Demand-based strategies

Forecast-based strategies

Requirements

Spot buying

Volume Purchasing Agreement
  (VPA)

Forward purchasing

Product Life-Cycle purchasing

Just-in-Time purchasing

Commodities

Commodity Exchange

Spot Price

Futures Options
Supplier-managed inventory (SMI)
Consignment
Options
Product mix
Changes indexes
Consumer Price Index (CPI)
ISM's Report on Business
Actionable
Constraint-based planning
Market analysis
New product introduction (NPI)
Correlation analysis
Regression analysis
Trend analysis
Time series analysis
Measures of central tendency
Measures of dispersion
Macroeconomics trends
Elasticity
Law of diminishing marginal utility
Perfect competition
Imperfect competition
Seasonal cycles
Expansion (increase in GDP)

Contraction (decrease in GDP)
Leading indicators
Coincident indicators
Lagging indicators
Price index
Consumer Price Index (CPI)
Producer Price Index (PPI)
Implicit Price Deflator
Interest rates
Gross domestic product (GDP)
Money supply
Rate of exchange
Balance of trade
Balance of payments
Deflation
Capacity utilization
Federal Reserve System
National income
Personal income
Net national product (NNP)
Gross national product (GNP)
Free trade
Trade deficit
Countertrade

CHAPTER 17

THE PROCUREMENT ORGANIZATION

LEARNING OBJECTIVES

1. Define the acronym "*SWOTS*" analysis. How is this used in effective strategic planning?
2. Compare and describe the difference between "Centralized" and "Decentralized" Procurement structures. What are the advantages of a "Centralized" organization and when it is used?
3. List the six functions of a budget described in the chapter.
4. Describe the definition off a "CAR", and explain how the Procurement Manager needs to respond.

The internal operation of the Procurement Department achieves focus through the development of procurement strategies and objectives. These are wide-ranging strategies and objectives created primarily to ensure that the department is in alignment with, and can support, the goals of its internal customers as well as the overall goals of the organization. To ensure alignment and, consequently, to effectively implement strategy, requires that you formulate specific and measurable goals for achieving the objectives of your strategy and establish a detailed plan so that your implementation can stay on track. These activities should also align with your operational policies and procedures so that they can be clearly and effectively put into practice.

The Procurement Department must continually inform its internal customers and the organization's senior management of the department's contributions and progress toward goal completion, so it is important that you understand what activities are relevant to their needs and how best to report on the status of these activities. Reporting typically requires the close management of large amounts of data. This data, along with the ongoing documentation of key activities, helps your group prepare timely reports as they are needed. It also helps when it is necessary to respond to financial or quality audits and when you are required to prepare corrective action reports to ensure compliance.

In addition to these activities, you will also find it necessary to develop and manage the departmental budget. You will be required to continually measure the department's performance in relation to the budget and in relation to several other key areas of metrics we will discuss in this chapter. These measures will not only determine your effectiveness as a professional, but they will also point out areas for needed improvement so that you can incorporate continuous improvement processes into your operational activities.

17.1 PLANNING PROCUREMENT STRATEGIES AND OBJECTIVES

Strategic planning is the process of defining the organization's long-term objectives and identifying the best methods to reach them. It is a disciplined technique of developing fundamental decisions and actions that will guide an organization's activities and provide structure for each of its individual functions. Effective strategic planning requires gathering a wide range of relevant information, exploring various alternative courses of action, and attempting to assess the future implications of current decisions. For successful implementation, strategic plans require clear communication and the ability to absorb divergent values and interests for the common organizational good.

We explore these concepts in further detail in the following section.

(a) SUPPORTING THE ORGANIZATION.   Procurement supports the organization primarily through the acquisition process and the department's management of the supplier community. To carry out these functions effectively, the department management needs to clearly understand the organization's strategy and plans so that it can develop a complementary supply strategy.

(i) Aligning with Organizational Strategy.   In general terms, Procurement typically supports its organization through activities focused on sourcing, cost reduction, developing supplier alliances, finding sources for collaboration in new technology development, financial audit compliance, and implementing process improvements. When these activities are performed exceptionally well, they can provide the organization with a clear competitive advantage. Sourcing strategy can be leveraged to ensure supply in times of strong demand. Cost reduction activities that examine the benefits of long-term contracts and collaborative product development with suppliers can add savings dollars directly to the bottom line and create a significant competitive edge. Effectively implemented strategies in areas that are consumer focused (such as price and technology) clearly aids the organization's ability to increase market share and revenue. Simplifying or eliminating tactical procurement processes and reducing parts and the number of suppliers, as well as employing a process improvement approach to all activities, adds even more value to the procurement process.

Can these activities lead the organization's efforts to implement its strategic vision? You bet—especially when they are executed superbly.

(ii) Strategic Planning Methods.   Planning should begin with an assessment of the organization's current and future supply needs. This usually requires gathering a detailed knowledge of your overall spending trends—by industry, supplier, customer or function, and transactional volume—as well as the priorities of your customers. You will generally want to focus your external efforts in areas that account for significant spending or encompass high risk, while directing your internal efforts to processes and constraints, workload, and customer satisfaction. This information will assist you in narrowing the scope to areas where you will be able to add maximum value.

Once you have identified potential areas for added value, you will want to determine the objectives and metrics that will produce a successful outcome and the resources that may be required to achieve it. It serves little purpose developing unachievable objectives or objectives outside the practical reach of available or potentially available resources.

Organizations often use a process known as **SWOT analysis** to assist them in developing strategic plans. SWOT is an acronym for strengths, weaknesses, opportunities, and threats.

- **Strengths.** Internal resources such as key personnel, supplier partnerships, distribution channels, patents, branding, funding, low cost profiles, and any other competitive differentiators.
- **Weaknesses.** Internal shortcomings that can open the door to competitions including poor cash flow, high cost structure and, in general, the absence of any of those strengths just listed.
- **Opportunities.** External factors that can provide additional revenue, profit, and growth. Opportunities are found in new markets, new products, and the development of new technologies.
- **Threats.** External factors that can work to the detriment of the organization such as rising interest rates that affect funding, a declining customer base, increased competition, international trade barriers, and new regulations.

(iii) Contingency Planning.   Contingency plans are usually associated with a specific project or situation and set out a series of actions to take in case of unanticipated circumstances that threaten to produce a negative outcome. Contingency planning addresses both strategic and tactical elements of the organization's operations. In routine procurement operations, for example, a commonly employed contingency plan provides for alternative sourcing in the event that a primary source is unable to meet its commitments.

Since developing contingency plans can become a time-wasting activity—there's little payback because you won't use the plan unless something goes wrong—the strategic aspect lies in the development of risk analysis and risk mitigation criteria so that contingency plans are restricted to high-risk, high-impact areas only.

NOTE

Refer to the decision tree model covered in Chapter 16 for what-if scenarios with different probabilities of outcomes.

Typically, risk mitigation strategies involve developing alternative sources of supply or production capacity, holding safety inventory, forming partnerships and joint ventures, and closely monitoring market conditions for important trend signal analysis.

(iv) Decision Making.   As part of the strategic planning process, you will want to make or coordinate a number of decisions relating to the overall plan. You will need to determine specific individual or team responsibilities for specific actions

that will evolve from the plan, what resources are available and where others will come from; time frames for completing actions, metrics, and reporting; and who has authority to approve the plan or deviate from the plan.

(v) Planning Horizons.   Strategic plans have traditional horizons, with time frames for short-term plans in the range of 1 to 2 years and long-term planning covering 3 to 10 years. This contrasts with tactical or operational planning, which covers periods from 30 days to one year.

(b) SUPPLY MANAGEMENT STRATEGIES.   Supply planning and supply management strategies primarily evolve from the long-term needs of the organization as it responds to external factors. These strategies often focus on how best to manage suppliers and the various elements in the supply base and how to formulate a consistent approach to managing inventories. In developing supply management strategies, you should evaluate a number of specific conditions at various levels, including:

- Capacity, technology, market dispersion, and business trends affecting the industry.
- Materials, complexity, and supply issues affecting the commodity.
- Procurement trends, supply base flexibility, and the level of standardization affecting the buying organization.

You should then look at the likely strategies you may want to use in developing your supply base. These could include, for example:

- Supplier consolidation
- Requirements consolidation
- Contracts
- Alliances and partnerships
- Competitive bidding
- Supplier development
- Supplier-managed inventory (SMI)
- Consignment
- Negotiations

One methodology for developing strategies from these elements is to link your approach to individual suppliers with the supply conditions observed in the industry, commodity, or your organization. One method of analyzing this is through a supply positioning matrix such as the one discussed next.

(i) Supply Positioning Strategies.   **Supply positioning analysis** is a commonly used tool for categorizing the key areas of spending by cost and associated risk, dividing them into categories, and formulating an approach to each of them. While there are many ways to look at purchases within the context of this approach, as shown in Figure 17.1, there are four common categories of spending: strategic,

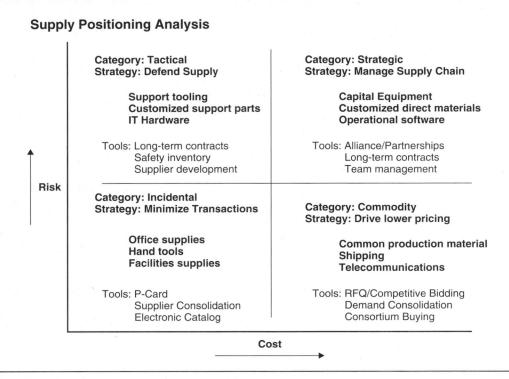

Supply Positioning Analysis

FIGURE 17.1   SUPPLY POSITIONING ANALYSIS MATRIX

tactical, commodity, and incidental. The matrix also shows typical items each category contains and a brief synopsis of the kind of strategy that might be employed.

By way of an explanation of terms, let's define low-risk items as those commonly capable of substitution including off-the-shelf items such as copy paper or interchangeable parts and tools such as capacitors or screwdrivers and pliers. High-risk items are those in limited supply, those with critical quality or technology features, or those requiring high levels of customization. From a cost perspective, high-cost categories are goods and services that account for a certain percentage of spending (for example, above 5 percent), whereas low-cost categories fall below that level.

The strategic category represents the highest cost, highest risk items such as capital equipment, customized direct materials, and operational software (to cite a few examples). The strategy can be characterized as requiring the organization to closely manage the supply chain by actions such as forming alliances and partnerships with suppliers, developing long-term contracts, and managing the products and services through teams and with cross-functional input.

The commodity category represents goods and services that, in aggregate, account for large amounts of spending but because of their interchangeable, off-the-shelf nature represent low risk. This category includes items such as common production material, freight and product shipping, and telecommunications. The tools commonly used for this category include, for example, competitive bidding, consolidation of demand, and consortium buying.

For the tactical category, composed of elements such as support tooling, customized support parts, and IT hardware, the primary strategy is to ensure (or defend) supply using long-term contracts and safety inventory and developing supplier capabilities (as well as alternative suppliers).

The incidental category represents low-cost, low-risk items such as office supplies, hand tools, and facilities supplies that can be purchased virtually anywhere. The strategy here might be to minimize the transactions associated with such purchases, removing the workload and associated overhead costs from the Procurement Department. This might be accomplished by using purchasing cards or electronic catalogs or by supplier consolidation or complete outsourcing.

TIPS AND TECHNIQUES

Keep in mind that no single strategy can be applied universally to all situations and under all circumstances, so a strategy that is effectively employed in a particular procurement segment may be ineffective in another.

(ii) Commodity Strategies.   Categorizing purchases by their respective commodities often helps develop a uniform strategy to manage multiple products that have closely related commodity attributes. This can enable the Procurement Department to employ an individual with specific expertise in the commodity (also known as a subject matter expert [SME]) who can focus primarily on managing a strategy for that specific group of suppliers. The added value of this approach is that the organization's management is given the opportunity to recognize the discipline required to establish specific commodity excellence in the procurement operation.

17.2 DEVELOPING DEPARTMENTAL GOALS AND OBJECTIVES

How the Procurement Department intends to support organizational procurement needs (and its goals) is often expressed in the form of a mission or charter statement. This statement, to a large extent, reflects the approach the Procurement Department takes in helping to meet organizational objectives and is fundamentally reflected in its choice of goals cited.

In this section, we look at how the department's mission or charter is typically defined and how it is used to formulate procurement goals and objectives:

(a) DEFINING THE DEPARTMENT'S MISSION.   The department's mission is generally expressed as an adjunct to a vision statement and is often written in the present tense to indicate a condition of being. The vision statement serves as the guiding principle for answering questions such as, "How are we different from other organizations?" or "What value do we add?" The department's mission statement then flows from its vision and guides the development of its goals and objectives.

In the following simplified examples, observe how the mission statement evolves from the organization's vision and how it applies that vision:

Vision: Our organization focuses on supporting organizational strategies that maximize value to our customers.

Mission: Our organization's mission is to obtain the greatest value in the acquisition of goods and services while ensuring the integrity and accountability of our processes.

(b) FORMULATING GOALS AND OBJECTIVES.   To carry the progression further, the department's specific objectives are linked to its mission statement, ensuring that the purpose and intent of the vision is translated into action. The Procurement Department's objective can then be expressed in terms of general activity statements. Following are some examples of possible objectives:

(i) Objectives.

- Reduce the overall cost of purchases by selecting the most qualified suppliers.
- Achieve maximum value in each acquisition.
- Support corporate directives to provide accountability.
- Minimize risk by ensuring alternative sources of supply for critical items.
- Hire and train staff to develop a world-class procurement practice.
- Actively promote strong supplier relationships.
- Encourage the use of small, minority-owned, and disadvantaged businesses.

Objectives can be translated into quantifiable and measurable goals as part of an annual plan. The preceding objectives might appear as specific goals, as listed next.

(ii) Goals.

- Reduce the average unit cost of direct materials by 6 percent.
- Develop a consignment program for spare parts that will eliminate 90 percent of current inventory.
- Report all take or pay purchases.
- Develop secondary sources for all "A" category supplies.
- Establish a training program to qualify 10 members of the staff as certified procurement professionals.
- Hold quarterly business reviews with all key suppliers on the approved supplier list.
- Increase the use of small, minority-owned, and disadvantaged businesses by 50 percent.

(c) KEYS TO SUCCESSFUL PLANNING.   Several aspects related to the development of objectives and goals must be considered to ensure successful outcomes. Some of those commonly noted include measurability, priority, and alignment:

- **Measurability.** Metrics need to be established so that the value of each goal to the organization can be clearly shown. By quantifying goals, you will be more able to demonstrate your department's effectiveness and measure the effectiveness of individual team members. Remember, too, the adage, "What gets measured gets done." Notice how the goals in the preceding section were developed with built-in measures that are quantified.
- **Priority.** Competing priorities can defeat accomplishment; that is, they can interfere with one another to the extent that none are completely successful. Therefore, it is critical that you establish priorities for the goals based on their potential impact for the organization, with goals that produce the most value receiving the greatest organizational resources.
- **Alignment.** It is important that the process for developing the Procurement Department's goals considers integration with the organization's overall goals. The importance of aligning with the goals and objectives of other departments is obvious, and you will want to avoid the appearance of "pulling the cart" in the wrong direction. This means that the priorities established by the organization should also be reflected in the priorities established by your department.

TIPS AND TECHNIQUES

When establishing goals, it is also important to consider potential conflict between them. Conflicting goals can lead to counter-productive internal competition for available resources. This is an excellent way to ensure that nothing gets accomplished.

17.3 FORMULATING OPERATIONAL POLICIES AND PROCEDURES

Operational policies and procedures are developed within the organization to ensure that standard methods are employed across the enterprise to accomplish goals and objectives. By using standard methods, communicating policies and procedures becomes much easier, and better control of the organization's resources is achieved. This helps safeguard the effectiveness of the organization's efforts to achieve success.

In this section, we will review the elements of formulating operational policies and procedures and how they are effectively structured.

(a) MANAGEMENT CONTROL. Management control is a mechanism used by the organization to achieve stated goals and objectives. Controls can be categorized according to the timing of their occurrence:

- **Preoperational controls.** These controls are established in advance of the specific operational activity. They include organizational policies, standard operating procedures (SOPs), strategic plans, budgets, and a variety of operational and contingency plans. **Preoperational controls** govern the tactical manner in which activities are intended to be conducted.

- **Operational controls. Operational control mechanisms** are intended to manage activities as they occur. Typically, they will include quality and inventory control, status reports, **Environmental, Health and Safety (EHS)** monitoring, and security.
- **Postoperational controls.** Audits are the most common *postoperational control* mechanism. Designed to measure how activities were actually conducted, they provide a variance feedback mechanism to assist in root cause analysis and foster continuous improvement. Postoperational controls also include performance reports and periodic reviews of processes and are used for providing input to management to help determine areas for further process improvement.

(b) WORKLOAD DISTRIBUTION.   The structure and distribution of procurement workload and responsibilities, while varying from organization to organization, typically responds to the nature of the working environment. You will find one type of structure prevalent in large manufacturing organizations, another in small to midsized service organizations, and still others in governmental organizations of various sizes.

Commonly used organizational work structures fall into a number of categories:

- **Rotational.** A rotational method generally assigns work to buyers on a random basis to provide active cross-training and achieve greater commodity and domain expertise across the staff. Its goal, typically, is to provide workload flexibility within the buying organization.
- **User department.** Buyers are often assigned to specific departments within the organization to focus commodity expertise in servicing a specific set of customer needs. While this often requires redundant skills development within the Procurement Department, the method can be an important key to proactive servicing of internal customers such as sales and marketing.
- **Supplier.** Duties are sometimes divided by suppliers to enhance supplier management and overall control objectives.
- **Commodity or Category.** Commonly used in larger manufacturing environments, this workload division focuses individual responsibilities according to commodity, industry, or category of goods and services, such as capital equipment or maintenance, repair, and operations (MRO). The intended result is to leverage commodity and domain expertise in specific areas to gain efficient use of talent.
- **Type.** Work can often be divided by the nature of the procurement process itself, with contracts going to a specific group, inventory items to another, and incidental purchases to still another.
- **Transactional volume.** In some environments, the tactical transaction workload created by purchase orders and inventory account adjustments

becomes an issue. To maintain departmental efficiency, work is assigned to balance individual workloads and thereby reduce cycle time.

(c) WORKLOAD TRACKING.   Most organizations today rely on computerized systems such as enterprise resource planning (ERP) to determine the electronic routing of requisitions to specific buyers, the status of individual orders, cycle times, and buyer transactional productivity. While in the past requisition approval was recorded on paper forms and PO activity was recorded on individual buyers' logs, today the level of tracking sophistication in computerized applications generally dispenses with the need to manually record and monitor these activities.

(d) ORGANIZATIONAL STRUCTURE.   When procurement departments span multiple geographical sites or divisions, questions regarding the degree to which control should be centralized generally arise. While each organization views its issues separately, there are a number of considerations that may be taken into account universally.

(i) Centralized versus Decentralized.   In the centralized organization, all major procurement is controlled from one central location. In the decentralized organization, the major procurement decisions are made at the divisional or business unit level. Many hybrid versions are also common, where responsibilities are shared to one extent or another or where broad policy is developed centrally but implemented locally.

In general, centralized procurement is more commonly used when the need for control is stringent or when the purchased products or services are used by many groups within the organization. Conversely, decentralized procurement occurs most often when divisions are engaged in dissimilar operations and purchase widely divergent goods and services. Each method has advantages in specific situations. The advantages of centralization include the following:

- **Pricing.** Leverages larger volumes for price improvements.
- **Expertise.** Volume enables the development of specialized areas of commodity and domain expertise.
- **Operational cost.** Greater procurement efficiencies can be gained through automation in a centralized operation. There is also less likelihood that tactical tasks such as reporting and filing will be duplicated.
- **Supplier consolidation.** Fewer suppliers are required when purchasing from central locations and when purchases from several locations can be consolidated.
- **Terms.** In addition to lower prices, centralized procurement can leverage increased volumes to gain more advantageous terms and conditions such as consignment inventory, freight discounts, or supplier payment terms.

The advantages of decentralization include the following:

- **Timing.** Purchases can be better timed when made closer to the source of the requirement.
- **Communication.** Improved contact with the internal customer generally results in improved support and responsiveness.
- **Control.** Local management of procurement generally improves control and supplier performance.
- **Ownership.** Local procurement results in greater buyer ownership of problems and issues.

(ii) Reengineering.   Reengineering is the broad process of examining and altering an existing business process and reconstituting it in an improved form. In procurement, reengineering efforts generally focus on automating the requisitioning system and ordering process as a means of improving responsiveness and reducing ordering cycle time. As a result, there are significant reductions in inventory levels and greater support for just-in-time operations.

Process mapping is employed to reduce total cycle time by tracking and recording each step in the ordering process. This provides a detailed analysis of each step in the work flow and systems, defining the relationships between each of their elements. Once mapped, the opportunities to eliminate tasks that add no value or waste time become apparent. Mapping also reveals steps that are currently sequential but that can often be performed in parallel, thus further reducing cycle time.

Reengineering also allows more detailed analysis of spending patterns, which, in turn, enables greater supplier consolidation and reduced pricing. It has also led to a more disciplined approach to continuous process improvement, eliminating activities that do not add value.

17.4 PREPARING DEPARTMENTAL REPORTS

Reports are an essential means of communication in most organizations. In a variety of formats—written, oral, or a combination, as in a PowerPoint presentation—reports inform management of the department's progress toward its goals and the status of current tactical and strategic activities. The reporting process is also an important tool that can call attention to the department's contributions to the overall objectives of the organization. Significant achievements, especially those that can be measured and that add value to the organization's bottom line, can be a powerful tool for obtaining resources when they are needed, so it is important that you communicate your department's success with management. You can view this communication not so much as a matter of tooting your own horn as sharing the added value of the procurement organization.

(a) IDENTIFYING RELEVANT ACTIVITIES.   Most often, activities that are relevant to reporting are those closely linked to the department's current goals and objectives. While these, of course, vary from organization to organization, there are several areas that are of common interest.

(i) Spending and Savings. Negotiated savings and cost avoidance are key areas of interest to most senior managers, especially to the extent that they apply to their own operating budgets. Your report structure should always acknowledge this fact by highlighting both accomplishments and areas that have not been as productive as planned.

As you report spending and savings, you will want to keep in mind some of the following points:

- Metrics are vital. Be certain your numbers are meaningful, timely, and correct.
- The Finance Department is generally charged with the responsibility for reporting budget performance. Coordinate your spending reports with its staff as a means of substantiating your numbers.
- Savings are usually generated by a cross-functional team's effort and not just your department.
- In most cases, the savings belongs to your internal customer through the budgeting process. Allow your customer the option of reporting it first.
- Distinguish between actual savings and cost avoidance. The former may affect budget performance while the latter may not.
- Easing of specifications that result in savings should be credited to the group doing the specification review.
- Consider savings from internal productivity improvements as *soft dollars* that typically do not impact the bottom line unless there is some accompanying reduction in head count.

To provide additional perspective, consider grouping your savings and spending reports according to the category of spending: strategic, commodity, tactical, and incidental. You might also want to highlight more specific areas of savings such as indirect or MRO, direct materials, capital equipment, or inventoried materials or services. Be careful to keep your audience in mind and provide detail according to individual needs and interests. Chances are, for example, that the chief financial officer will already know the extent of the savings and may have only a casual interest in how it was accomplished.

(ii) Acquisition Plans. As part of reporting on future activities, you should consider highlighting significant planned acquisitions and noting their current status. Specifically, cover any important concerns you might have regarding constraints or challenges that may affect the outcome of major acquisitions.

(iii) Supplier Relationships. Continuous improvement is the hallmark of a successfully managed supply base. Key measures for reporting include quality

performance, delivery performance (cycle time), service levels, and cost. These should be reported graphically, showing relevant trends for easy comprehension. Figure 17.2 provides an example of a trend analysis chart for the quality performance of a supplier.

In addition to statistical data, you will want to present information from the supply community that will impact the performance of internal users, such as planned technology releases, mergers and acquisitions, change of key personnel, and benchmarks of your competition. This information is often not readily available to internal customers when they have little contact with the supplier.

(b) SELECTING AND MANAGING DATA.   In selecting information to report, you must also consider how you will gather data and manage the systems that provide it. While there are no specific criteria available universally to define a set of measures and no best way to measure performance, you should consider some basic criteria for selecting data:

- Make it easily accessible—you won't want to invest huge amounts of time gathering basic information.
- It should be well maintained so that you can be confident it is accurate and up to date.

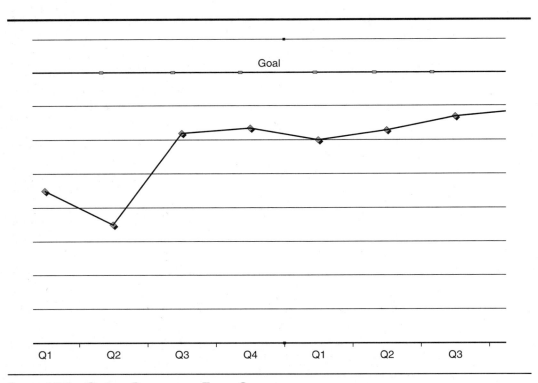

FIGURE 17.2   QUALITY PERFORMANCE TREND CHART

- It should be used by others in the organization to avoid lengthy discussions on its meaning.
- Make sure you can quantify value by using metrics to describe performance.
- Benchmark with other similar organizations to select goals and provide performance comparisons between your organization and others in the same sector.
- It should relate to goals and objectives—show how performance supports the organization's goals.
- You should highlight key accomplishments to avoid overwhelming the audience with minutia.

(c) METHODS OF PRESENTATION. Having excellent material available is of little value unless you can present it properly. From this perspective, there are two considerations: (1) the method you will use to convey the information and (2) the type and level of detail of the information you will present. The guiding principle to selecting both is to understand your audience and know where their interests lie.

Presentations can be written or oral or a combination of both. Following are some of the basic principles you should keep in mind when preparing them.

(i) Written Presentations. Written presentations can take many forms—statis-tical reports, PowerPoint presentations, charts, graphs, e-mails, memos, or formal letters. Your choice depends upon organizational preference and the nature of your audience. Some points to keep in mind while preparing a written presentation include the following:

- The written document must be well organized. This will likely depend upon the material being presented. An executive summary is a common way to present summarized information about a specific subject or project. (See Figure 17.3 for more details.) Ideally, the summary provides a brief synopsis in a structured format that guides a reader to the major elements of review.
- The written document should be clear and easy to understand. Simplicity can be accomplished by limiting the subject matter to one or two key points and by introducing these at the beginning of the presentation. Everything that follows should readily tie back to the introductory points. Obviously, you will want to avoid the use of unfamiliar technical terms or acronyms— or at least define them as they are introduced.
- Written documents may contain large amounts of technical information as in the case of a statement of work used in an RFP. In such documents, it may be advisable to include a glossary of terms or definitions section so that your readers will have a common reference point.

There are some basic elements that should be included in every written summary so that you can ensure the majority of the reader's questions will be addressed:

Background

Briefly describe the history related to this project or contract and explain what led to the determination of its need or why it is under consideration at this time.

Known Risks and Threats

Outline specific elements that require special care or attention.

Prior Experience

Reference other similar projects or contracts, how they were handled, and their current status or outcome.

Key Facts

List key facts describing the current situation. Possible questions you may want to answer:

What is generating the need?

What is the scope/spend of the project?

Who is involved and what are their roles?

Who are the suppliers and what are their market positions?

Are there competing proposals?

Who are the internal customers and what are their issues?

What are the critical dates? Milestones?

Opportunities

Describe the program's objectives and outline what might be accomplished by the successful completion of the contract or project. Some examples include:

Cost savings

Improved quality

Greater capacity

Strategic competitive advantage

Better service or customer satisfaction

Faster time to market

Ensured supply

Alternative Courses of Actions

Alternative courses of action outline the different options available to achieve the objectives. For example:

Develop new source of supply

Competitive bidding event

Revisit specifications to reduce cost

FIGURE 17.3   ELEMENTS OF AN EXECUTIVE SUMMARY

Under each potential alternative, list the following:

The known risks

Pros and cons

Cost estimates

Recommendation

Submit the alternative you believe provides the greatest opportunity to achieve the objective. Briefly describe why this alternative is best. For example:

"The first option outlined has a greater possibility of success because it leverages the competitive marketplace to provide the lowest possible price for the existing statement of work."

Anticipated Outcome

In a brief narrative, describe the results your recommendation will achieve. For example: "This project will result in savings of approximately $240,000 against the budget. It will help mitigate our risk by combining several existing purchase orders into a single contract."

Threats and Potential Negative Outcomes

Outline potential conditions or events that could negatively impact your desired results. For example:

A change in market conditions

Schedule slippage

Material shortages

Unproven technology

Quality issues

Defense

Describe what steps can be taken to minimize these threats and reduce the risk of potential negative impacts. For example:

Dual sourcing

Penalty clause in contract

Liquidated damages

FIGURE 17.3   (*continued*)

(ii) Oral Presentations.   Oral presentations can be extremely demanding since you must deal with the presentation format and your manner of presenting as well as the material itself. However, there are a number of methods you can use to help make the presentation successful:

- Begin the presentation by stating your objectives. Are you asking for approval of a project proposal? Are you conducting a review or briefing to update those in attendance?
- Build your presentation by clearly linking your purpose with organizational goals and objectives. State the objective you are addressing and the solution you propose. Demonstrate the efficacy of your proposed solution with solid reasoning.
- Thoroughly understand your material. Questions will arise during any presentation, and you must be prepared to answer them. Avoid getting flustered if you can't answer; simply offer to follow up later with the information requested.
- Thoroughly understand your audience and how the information you are presenting might be received. How much do they know about your subject?
- If you are presenting new ideas or concepts, clearly establish the background without being overly detailed. Try to relate the new ideas to specific problems faced by the organization.
- Pay attention to your appearance and demeanor. Dress appropriately and deliver your presentation with confidence, avoiding poor posture and mumbled speech. If you are uncomfortable speaking in public, consider taking a class or joining an organization that will provide experience and feedback such as Toastmasters. Above all, demonstrate your enthusiasm for the topic.
- Use appropriate and easy-to-understand language and avoid the use of acronyms. Be concrete and deliver solid facts. Tie accomplishments to backup data without overreliance on unimportant details. Use the present tense and include action verbs as much as possible.
- When presenting PowerPoint or other graphical information, be sure to keep your slides simple and uncluttered. One rule of thumb suggests no more than five bullets on each slide, but even two can be excessive if they are totally unrelated to one another. Similarly, do not try to cram graphs and charts together in a way that could confuse your audience. It might be best to limit each slide to one main point and use more slides if you are in doubt. Try to supplement the slides with additional data and commentary. Reading slides verbatim is a sure way to put your audience to sleep.

17.5 RESPONDING TO AUDITS

An audit is usually an independent review and examination of records and activities to assess the adequacy of Procurement Department controls. It determines if purchases have been properly authorized and if awards to suppliers have been made correctly and fairly. Audits also seek to verify that procedures are being followed correctly and that organizational policy is being observed in the acquisition of goods and services. Some audits look at the performance of the Procurement Department in relation to others in the industry—for example, are prices being paid for common goods in line with what would normally be expected—as well as the performance of its staff. Audits are conducted by financial organizations, government agencies, and international quality certification bodies (such as the ISO).

Audits are best prepared for in advance by routinely following established processes and procedures (not at the last minute when the auditors are in the lobby). In all cases, the Procurement professional is responsible to ensure compliance from the Procurement staff.

(a) VALIDATING CURRENT PROCESSES. Planning for the audit requires specific knowledge of the standard used in the process being audited and how that process will be evaluated. Aside from the specific focus of the audit—financial, quality, or process control—most audits are geared to determining how well existing activities conform to written documentation established by the organization and legal requirements established by legislation and regulatory agencies.

Depending on their general purpose, audits are conducted by internal or external resources.

- An **internal audit** is an appraisal activity within the organization using internal staff that is used to verify the reliability of accounting records, determine the proper expenditure of funds and the safeguarding of company assets, and determine that management's policies are being carried out.
- An **external audit** is an appraisal conducted by a third party, usually for the same purposes as internal audits. In the case of a financial audit, the third party may be the organization's accounting firm; in the case of ISO 9000:2000, QS-9000, and ISO/TS 16949, there are specially trained and designated auditors for hire. Recent legislation such as Sarbanes-Oxley will likely create additional audit requirements, too. Some of the more common processes that will be observed include:
  - Proper authorization and approval processes for contracts, purchases, and payments.
  - Documentation of competitive bids and awards.
  - Effective monitoring of supplier selection and performance.
  - Planning and forecasting activities.
  - Inventory management.
  - Adherence to proper receiving and inspection processes.
  - Effective selection of transportation methods.
  - Audit trails for invoices.
  - Internal customer satisfaction.
  - Tax coding of POs.
  - Proper training of the procurement staff.

Audits themselves generally progress according to a recognized routine. There is typically an initial meeting between the auditors and the managers in the department to review the process. The auditor will expect that a specific process owner will be assigned to the audit team to collect documentation as it is requested and to find the correct staff member to answer specific process questions. Following the audit, there is usually a closing meeting during which some of the preliminary findings may be disclosed and dates established for area(s) cited for corrective action. This is followed some time later by an official audit finding report to the organization's management.

(b) RESPONDING TO CORRECTIVE ACTIONS.   In its final report, the auditors will point out areas where significant deficiencies exist and other areas where improvements may be needed. When auditors find instances of significant nonconformance to processes, typically a **corrective action request (CAR)** will be issued. The CAR will require a response that outlines what actions are being taken to immediately contain the nonconformance and what actions will be taken to ensure that it will not reoccur. Generally, these issues have previously been discussed in the closing meeting with the auditors, so you will likely be prepared to take action immediately.

At the basic level, corrective actions should resolve the immediate problem and prevent the problem from recurring within the organization. The process should also define the individuals responsible for the actions and the timetable for completion. Typically, the corrective action process includes the following steps:

1. Identify the problem.
2. Investigate to identify the root cause.
3. Define the solution.
4. Implement the solution.
5. Document the solution.
6. Communicate the solution.
7. Evaluate the effectiveness of the solution.

(c) CONFLICT RESOLUTION.   Audits often uncover internal conflicts that have gone previously unnoticed by management but can seriously hamper the organization's tactical performance. They may develop from a failure to clearly assign responsibility for performing a specific function when one party feels that another party should be doing the job or one group feels another group has not provided sufficient information to ensure the process completes properly. Regardless of the circumstances, as a professional, you will be responsible for resolving such conflicts.

There is no widely established method for resolving conflicts, but certainly whatever process you establish will require a fact-finding initiative and an opportunity for each individual involved to be heard. Once the facts and points of view are established, a logical approach can be proposed in order to obtain buy-in from all of those concerned. If this process doesn't produce results, it may be possible to benchmark how other organizations handle similar issues and from that analysis draw a course of action.

Having established an initial resolution, you will want to follow up at regular intervals to ensure that it is working as intended. Make corrections as though the process were one of continuous improvement.

17.6 EVALUATING PROCUREMENT DEPARTMENT PERFORMANCE

Effective performance requires continuous evaluation and improvement to ensure that the department is meeting organizational objectives and expectations. While many objectives are formalized by departmental goals, new expectations will arise as conditions change. As a result, you will need to develop relevant assessments of your department's performance in terms of how well you are achieving established goals *and* how well you are able to respond to evolving situations.

(a) PURPOSE OF THE PERFORMANCE EVALUATION.   Evaluating procurement performance on a regular basis serves to assess the department's effectiveness. It helps determine if the department is contributing as planned to the goals and objectives of the organization and to validate that it is on track to reach its own planned objectives. It also evaluates the professional's performance in leading the department and deploying its talent.

Regular performance evaluation also identifies areas for improvement and provides a framework for continuous improvement activities.

(b) PERFORMING THE EVALUATION.   While there does not appear to be a standard method for evaluating the Procurement Department's performance specifically, the following several actions are important elements that apply to most organizations in general.

(i) Analyze Objectives.   As an initial point of departure, the department's key objectives need to be clearly identified so that functional activities can be specifically tied back to them. Activities and accomplishments can thus be evaluated in terms of how well they serve the department's primary objectives. For example, if the organization's stated goal is performance quality and technical leadership, the Procurement Department needs to find and measure suppliers who lead their commodity peers in high quality and advanced technology.

(ii) Determine Adequacy of Metrics.   How well do the measures chosen for the department's goals actually demonstrate its performance? Naturally, measures must reflect the true performance of the department in relation to its goals and in relation to the goals of the organization. For example, reporting cost savings alone does not demonstrate added value when the organization is committed to technological leadership.

(iii) Validate Evaluation Criteria.   As part of the evaluation, the criteria you are using should be vetted for its applicability to the department's goals. The next section describes this in more detail.

(c) EVALUATION AND APPRAISAL CRITERIA.   The primary criterion for evaluating any department's performance is the degree to which that department adds value to the organization. Looking at it another way, this can mean determining how effective your group is in relation to the assets being deployed—staff, training, systems, and support—and how effective it *could* be in comparison to similar operations elsewhere.

The following sections discuss some of the key factors that are likely to be addressed in performance measures.

(i) Cost Reduction and Cost Containment.   Cost reduction and cost containment are measures of overall savings and include the following:

- Savings due to negotiated contracts or procurement initiatives.
- Value of additional benefits that are negotiated such as longer payment terms, extended warranties, or consignment inventory.
- Cost reductions due to competitive bidding or use of alternative products.
- Savings developed from improved supplier quality and lower loss rates.
- Savings as a contribution to the bottom line.

(ii) Supplier Performance.   Supplier performance measures supplier support by assessing the following:

- Quality improvement and performance relative to goals.
- On-time delivery performance.
- Responsiveness to service requests.
- Flexibility to accommodate late scheduling.
- Favorable return policy.
- Overall reliability.

(iii) Supplier Development.   Supplier development measures how effectively the supply community is leveraged by looking at the following:

- Formation of supplier alliances for competitive advantage.
- Identification of new sources for key goods and services.
- Supplier consolidation.
- Increased use of small, minority, and female-owned or disadvantaged businesses.

(iv) Internal Procurement Systems and Processes.   Internal procurement systems and processes measure the efficiency of the Procurement Department by determining:

- The volume of procurement transactions conducted electronically.
- The volume of procurement transactions conducted through other transaction methods such as the purchasing card.
- The volume of transactions conducted through aggregated contracts.
- The reduction in transaction and inventory management costs.

(v) Internal Customer Satisfaction.   Internal customer satisfaction is usually determined through customer surveys that measure the following:

- Degree of satisfaction with service levels and response times.
- Level of satisfaction with procurement processes.
- Perceived value of purchased goods and services for the money spent.
- Perceived degree of effectiveness of procurement decision making and authority lines.
- Overall satisfaction with procurement systems and processes.

(d) BENCHMARKING PERFORMANCE.   Taken in isolation, there is no way to substantiate the adequacy of any department's goals. To better assess the validity of your goals (and their accompanying metrics), you should consider developing benchmarks with other organizations in your industry. Benchmarking is the process of comparing the performance of other organizations with that of your own. It is often accomplished using data from industry organizations or by engaging consultants to gather the information independently.

17.7 ADMINISTERING DEPARTMENTAL BUDGETS

In most cases, procurement professionals are held responsible for the fiscal budgets of their departments. A budget is simply a financial plan outlining anticipated expenditures for a specified period of time, typically one fiscal or calendar year. It is detailed by the nature of the expenditure—salaries, office supplies, subscriptions, and so on—usually broken down by an accounting *cost code*.

The Procurement Department is also often held responsible for the part of the budgets affecting other departments that it may manage such as inventory, direct material, and some outside services such as travel services. These expenditures, while perhaps not directly charged to the Procurement Department, will be included in its goals and objectives and in evaluations of its performance.

(a) BUDGET FUNCTIONS.   Budgets serve a number of specific functions. Let's look briefly at just a few of them:

- A budget creates a financial baseline that can be used to measure actual results as a way of evaluating performance.
- It forces an organization to carefully consider the expected resources that will be required to meet the business plan goals.

- It keeps managers informed and fosters improved coordination within the organization.
- It can be used to reflect priorities for the organization and convert them into the appropriate resources required to achieve those priorities.
- It can be used to preapprove specific spending and monitor certain types of spending (such as capital equipment) that are not aggregated into operational departments or sections.
- As an operational tool, budgets can highlight potential funding allocation problems in sufficient time to take corrective actions.

17.8 BUDGETING PROCESSES

Budgeting processes vary a great deal from one organization to another, but there are a number of common elements that will likely be found in all of them. Budgets in some organizations are developed from the top down; that is, funding is allocated to each department or section based on anticipated revenue and a preestablished formula for dividing up funding allocation. In other organizations, budgets are developed from the bottom up; that is, the budget is initially established at the departmental level and then reviewed, adjusted, and approved by senior management.

(a) GENERAL BUDGET TYPES.   There are numerous types of budgets commonly used by organizations. However, in general, these can be described in terms of two major categories, operating budgets and capital expenditure budgets.

(i) Operating Budgets.   This type of budget presents the financial plan for each cost center during the budget period and reflects day-to-day operating activities involving both revenues and expenses. In the case of the Procurement Department, revenues are not applicable, so only expenses will be listed, although at some point a relationship between cost savings or cost avoidance (or volumes) and operational activities can be used for evaluation.

(ii) Capital Expenditures Budgets.   These budgets present plans for the acquisition (or disposal) of major fixed capital assets. Typically, the Procurement Department will be concerned with equipment rather than real estate or other financial holdings.

(iii) Other Budget Types.   As adjuncts to these general categories, budgets can also be developed for a number of other purposes:

- **Cash flow budgets** are used for determining the availability of cash so that the timing of major expenditures can be coordinated.
- **Project budgets** track expenditures by specific project so that profit (or loss) can be attributed to a particular contract. These are commonly used in construction or in the military contracting areas.

- **Zero-based budgets** do not rely on prior years' expenditures or budgets; instead they start fresh from a zero base. As a result, each item must be justified separately, usually in terms of the organization's current goals. Zero-based budgets are often tied to a bottom-up budgeting approach so that they are generated at the operational level.
- **Flexible budgets** are based on a set of revenue and expense projections at various volume levels. The cost allowances for each expense item are thus able to vary as income or production varies.
- **Open-to-buy budgets** are used primarily in retail operations to control inventory restocking. Funds are allocated to each budgeting period and released based on a planned investment schedule.

(iv) Budgets versus Forecasts.   Budgets invariably change. They are commonly derailed for a number of reasons; for example, often customer demand changes or technology becomes obsolete and needs to be replaced. Sometimes unexpected changes in the economy or the global political situation cause prices to rise or fall.

It is virtually impossible to accurately predict the future, regardless of what systems, tools, or models are employed. For this reason, many organizations also develop forecasts throughout the budget execution period. The purpose of a forecast is to continually update the expected results for the period based upon the latest information available. Forecasts then get tied back to an adjusted budget, and a new profit/loss expectation is established. This is why publicly traded companies (and the analysts that follow them) so often focus on quarterly results—they are based on updated forecasts and are therefore more accurate.

17.9 WORKING WITH OPERATIONAL FORMS

Forms are used extensively within the procurement function, and they will often play a key role in the processes and systems that you use. Traditionally, forms were designed to be completed by hand, but they are increasingly being automated, and it is just a matter of time before paper is no longer used at all. However, you must continue to be prepared to design, use, file, and store a great variety of forms as part of routine operations. It is perhaps symbolic that your very life both begins with a form—the birth certificate—and ends with a form—the death certificate.

(a) FUNCTIONAL PURPOSE OF FORMS.   The use of forms helps standardize information and provide a framework for communication. Forms function as records of activities or the status of a set of conditions, such as inventory reconciliations, and so generally demand a uniform approach. This uniformity aids in reducing the time it takes to report routine actions and provides a basis for summarizing data that can be used in consolidated reports. Forms also serve as written documentation for audit trails and are often used as legal records.

(b) COMMONLY USED FORMS.   Procurement organizations employ a number of processes that are documented through the use of forms. Varying in design from organization to organization, they apply, nevertheless, to a fairly standard set of functions. Listed here are those you might find commonly assigned to your department (in either paper or electronic formats):

- **Purchase requisition (PR) or material requisition (MR).** Completed by the user to request materials and services ordered from suppliers through the Procurement Department. They are also traditionally used to document approval authority by recording the signatures of those authorizing the purchase.
- **Purchase order (PO).** A contract used to convey requirements and authorization to the supplier. POs usually contain a standard set of terms and conditions, as well as description of the goods or services and quantity ordered, the price paid, and how and when the goods or services should be shipped or completed.
- **Receiver or receiving form.** Used to document the receipt of goods and notify users of their receipt. Receiving documents are typically submitted with the shipment (as a **packing slip** and/or **bill of lading**) and include information directly from the original purchase order. Receiving documents may also be used to record the condition of the shipment when it arrives. Receiving documents are also used as part of the traditional three-way match to authorize invoice payment.
- **Inspection documents.** Used by the Quality Control Department (when it exists) to record the quality of the material being received and to note any nonconformity or rejection. These documents supplement the receiving document in most cases when they are used.
- **Traveling requisitions.** Contain standard information (such as descriptions and part numbers) and are used to request repetitive purchases or the release of production materials under a blanket order from the supplier. They are also used to request material from storeroom stock.
- **Change orders.** Similar to purchase requisitions but used only for changes to (or cancellations) existing orders.
- **Return authorization (RA) or material return form.** Used to document the required return of materials to the supplier. Typically, a supplier will issue an RA number that is recorded internally as the supplier's authorization to ship back the product.
- **Check request.** A form used by many organizations to request payment by the Accounting Department to a supplier when no purchase order exists.
- **Contracts.** Often exist in standardized format but vary widely in their nature and use from organization to organization. The nondisclosure agreement (NDA) is one of the more frequently used contract forms in most environments.

(c) DESIGNING AND MANAGING FORMS.   Despite the fact that forms are increasingly becoming automated as elements in computerized systems, you'll still find the need to design the occasional form to customize it to your organization's needs.

For those instances, here is a set of guidelines for well-designed forms you may want to consider:

- Decide what information you want to capture.
- Lay out the form so that it can be completed in logical order and it is easy for the user to fill out.
- Ensure that instructions are written in clear, precise language.
- Use white space as much as possible to balance the look and feel of the form.
- Use as few methods as possible for collecting the information. For example, try not to mix check boxes with other information you want circled.
- Clearly define the data fields to encourage correctly formatted information.
- Allow enough space in the data fields to properly complete the form without running outside the field.
- Choose a font style that is easy to use and that can be later scanned for optical character recognition (OCR). Courier, Arial, and Times Roman are the more commonly used fonts.

Forms should be numbered and titled. Keep them consistent with your organization's policy and indicate if they are subject to any specific record retention program.

17.10 SUMMARY

The Procurement Department establishes its strategic plans in alignment with those of the organization as a means of providing maximum support. Planning usually begins with an assessment of the organization's needs and an analysis of where value can be added. SWOT analysis can be used as a tool to aid this process. In selecting strategies, the Procurement professional reviews specific conditions related to capacity, market conditions, business trends, and numerous other factors affecting the materials and services being purchased. Supply positioning analysis is one method of developing strategy.

Similarly, departmental goals are developed in alignment with organizational goals so that they can provide maximum support. Goals and objectives are formulated in alignment with the department's vision and mission statement. When planning goals, the Procurement professional should ensure that they are measurable and attainable.

The Procurement professional also leads the department in formulating operational policies and procedures. These are designed as a means of developing management control to help ensure the attainment of its goals. They are often translated into organizational structure and workload distribution as methods of control that assist in securing positive outcomes. As a part of standard procedure in most organizations, periodic reports are essential to monitoring departmental progress. Identifying relevant reports and determining the most appropriate format for presenting them thus becomes essential.

Typically, reports on cost savings and supplier relationships are fundamental to the procurement function.

Responding to internal and external audits as a means of validating current processes is another Procurement professional responsibility. Integral to this is handling corrective actions in a systematic manner. Similarly, evaluating Procurement Department performance is a way of determining the department's effectiveness in managing cost and supplier performance and validating the efficacy of internal systems and processes. Customer satisfaction is always a key factor in this evaluation.

The Procurement professional is also responsible for managing the department's budget effectively. To do this, you will need to understand the budget function and its purpose, as well as the various elements of the budgeting process.

We also reviewed the elements of working with operational forms, including their function and design. There are several common forms that are relevant to procurement activities, and the Procurement professional is generally their owner.

KEY TERMS

SWOT analysis
Supply positioning analysis
Preoperational controls
Operational control mechanisms
Environmental, Health and Safety
    (EHS)
Internal audit
External audit

Corrective Action Request (CAR)
Cash flow budgets
Zero-based budgets
Project budgets
Flexible budgets
Open-to-buy budgets
Packing slip
Bill of lading

HUMAN RESOURCES FOR PROCUREMENT

LEARNING OBJECTIVES

1. Define "leadership" and "management" and compare them.
2. Describe the pros and cons of promoting from within the organization.
3. Name the five parts of a performance review as described in the chapter.
4. List the basic principles of the "Americans with Disabilities Act." Whom is it intended to protect?

In addition to supply management responsibilities, the Procurement professional, in the role as a manager, has the responsibility for leading and managing the Procurement Department's staff. This role includes a number of important organizational responsibilities such as recruiting and hiring new team members to replace or complement existing team members and strengthen the entire procurement group. It also includes training the staff for new or improved skills and in new methods that enhance the department's competency level.

Managing the department also involves appraising job performance on a regular basis and providing employees with feedback and coaching that helps improve their performance. Feedback is relevant in the assessment of both positive and negative performance: It involves recognizing and rewarding outstanding contributions and promoting employees when merited. It similarly includes correcting performance issues and taking disciplinary action when required.

In leading the department, it is also the procurement manager's responsibility to ensure compliance with internal and external audit requirements, applicable statutory workplace regulations, and policies regarding environment, health, and safety. Compliance also means preventing workplace discrimination and sexual harassment.

In this, the final chapter of this book, we cover the important aspects of managing personnel and leading the supply management team in an effective and rewarding manner.

18.1 LEADING THE SUPPLY MANAGEMENT TEAM

While leadership is a very difficult characteristic to define, it is generally recognized as the ability to influence others in a way that guides and directs their activities toward some specific goal(s). Implied in this concept is that leadership combines the efforts of many individuals into a team that performs operations in a manner the leader determines as most effective. Teamwork also involves the ability of a group of individuals to work together toward a common mission or vision, and so, to this extent, leadership incorporates the ability to direct individual accomplishments toward organizational objectives.

Nothing in the concept of leadership, however, implies control. Management, on the other hand, specifically requires the exercise of control. That is essentially the difference between leading and managing. Management is a function that requires an individual—the manager or supervisor—to control resources and processes within a specific span of responsibility. As an administrator, the manager's function encompasses providing technical and administrative direction to individuals to ensure the accomplishment of specific organizational goals. The traditional functions of a manager thus include functions such as planning, organizing, directing, and controlling work within a given area of authority.

(a) UNDERSTANDING MANAGEMENT THEORY.   In the course of collective human endeavors, a variety of theories have developed to describe how best to manage and motivate individuals and teams engaged in work activities. Many of these focus on the key aspects of leadership, while others focus on the planning and administrative roles of management. Let's review some of the more commonly referenced theories.

(i) Bureaucracy.   Max Weber (1864–1920), one of the pioneers of modern sociology, observed that **bureaucracy** was the most rational structure for the newly emerging large organization. Bureaucratic management theory provides guidelines in the form of policy and procedures, clearly defined hierarchy, and a systematic division of labor. The basic elements of this structure have been in existence since humans began forming into goal-directed groups:

- Organizations operate on the basis of rules and regulations.
- Behavior is governed by these formal rules.
- Authority is delegated through an organizational hierarchy.
- Uniform operations and continuity are maintained despite changes in personnel.
- Authority is based on position rather than on an individual.
- Authority is limited by the scope of the position.
- Tasks are allocated according to some logical method.
- Division of labor is based on functional specialties.
- Promotion is based on demonstrated competence and merit.
- Officers have limited discretion.
- Employment is based on tenure.

(ii) Scientific Management and Operational Theory.   Historically, much of today's management theory begins with Frederick Taylor (1856–1915), considered the father of scientific management. Taylor theorized that management failed to provide the correct motivational incentives to its workers. He took the approach that work should be broken down into its individual components and that workers should focus on the core components of their tasks and receive compensation based on their ability to perform these tasks. From Taylor's bottom-up approach developed the practice of work specialization designed to increase worker productivity by removing the planning and discretionary control from job duties. This, in turn, gave rise to the assembly line and, eventually, the **time-in-motion work standardization** method. This also led to the centralization of the planning and control

functions in the hands of managers, allowing for the additional specialization of the management function.

(iii) Administrative Management.   At about the same time as scientific management gained popularity, **administrative theory** was also introduced. Its key proponent, Henri Fayol (1841–1925), opted to view management in broad administrative terms, looking at organizational structure from the top down, in contrast to Taylor's bottom-up approach. Advocates viewed the job as precursor to the employee and developed guidelines to formalize organizational structures and internal relationships. This theory emphasized the manager and the functions of management, developing the concept of the manager's five functions:

1. Planning
2. Organizing
3. Commanding
4. Coordinating
5. Controlling

(iv) Behavioral or Human Relations Theories.   Behavioral or human relations management originated in the 1920s and placed the emphasis on the human aspects of organizations. This approach gained influence as a result of the Hawthorne Studies that demonstrated that people tend to perform better when they know they are being studied (or, in effect, considered important).

TIPS AND TECHNIQUES

THE HAWTHORNE EFFECT

During the period from 1927 to 1932, a team of Harvard Business School researchers conducted a series of experiments at the Hawthorne Plant of Western Electric in Cicero, Illinois. The most notable of these were the illumination experiments that intended to determine the effect of better lighting on workers' productivity. The surprising results were that both the experimental group (those receiving improved lighting) and the control group (those with the original lighting) achieved higher productivity rates during the period. The landmark conclusion was that the improvement was based on the attention the workers were given and not the improved lighting. There was no causal relationship between productivity and working conditions; it was the attitude of the workers that determined their productivity.

Adherents thus emphasized motivation and leadership as the key drivers of worker incentive. The human relations school held that much of employees' creativity and competencies remain untapped by employers due to inadequate recognition systems. Employees, they held, want meaningful assignments where they can participate in decision making and can contribute to the organization's overall well-being.

(v) System Theory. By definition, a system is a combination of related parts organized into a complex whole. The **systems theory of management**, therefore, views the organization as an interrelated, interdependent group of elements that functions as a single entity. An open system—one that interacts with its environment—consists of external inputs such as customer requirements, materials, and personnel and outputs such as final products that are put back into the environment. External feedback from the environment then completes the cyclical loop. Included in the systems view are functional subsystems such as manufacturing, finance, and supply management.

The systems approach holds that a synergy develops from these interdependent functional elements that create a greater whole than the theoretical sum of its parts. The combined and synchronized activities of the system are held to create more value than the individual parts could achieve independently.

(vi) Contingency Theory. **Contingency theory** allows that management and decision-making styles should flow from the particular situation based on the best possible analysis at the time. In a highly creative environment, for example, the framework of a collaborative style might be most appropriate, whereas in a military environment the style would be autocratic. To be effective, however, the manager's actions must clearly communicate expectations to subordinates.

(vii) Chaos Theory. **Chaos theory** recognizes that events can rarely be completely controlled in an organization, and to survive, their systems must adapt and evolve. Organizational systems, by their very nature, tend toward increasing complexity. As this occurs, the systems become unstable, and more effort is required to maintain their complexity. As systems expend more energy, they seek more structure to maintain stability. This trend continues until the system divides, combines with another system, or completely disintegrates.

(b) PRINCIPLES OF ORGANIZATIONAL MANAGEMENT. In addition to the broad concepts of organizational theory, you might also want to consider a number of common principles that define how the actual management structure operates and how work is distributed. The following are some of the more commonly referenced of these principles:

- The **Scalar Principle** describes an essentially hierarchical system of work distribution, where authority and accountability move directly from the highest levels in the organization to the lowest level of competency.
- The **Unity or Chain of Command Principle** suggests that each individual report to only one supervisor or manager. Responsibility and accountability are therefore clearly defined, and work can be effectively delegated. This concept commonly also includes the Scalar Principle.
- The **Line-Staff Principle** distinguishes production (or operational) functions from support functions.

- The **Span of Control Principle** describes the number of subordinates that reports to a specific manager. There are no particular metrics indicating what this number should be, but the general principle appears to specify that individuals should have no more subordinates than they can effectively supervise. Of course, this number depends upon the situation and the individual's ability.
- The **Exception Management Principle** suggests that routine duties are handled by subordinates and that the manager responds only to issues outside the normal course of events.
- The **Departmentalization** *Principle* maintains that similar activities should be grouped within the same administrative section. Activities can be related by similarities in process, product lines, location, or purpose.
- **Management by objective (MBO)** is a widely used method of goal setting in which performance objectives are agreed upon by subordinates and managers. In this process, periodic reviews of progress toward objectives take place, and rewards are allocated on the basis of this progress. Other important considerations of MBO include:
  - Objectives are properly identified and defined.
  - Organizational goals and objectives flow from the top down.
  - Goals and objectives are realistic and achievable, as well as challenging.
  - Plans for goal achievement are detailed and milestones identified.
  - Measurements and time tables are well defined and agreed upon in advance.
  - Performance monitoring and feedback systems are in place.

- The **flat organization** attempts to reduce the levels of management hierarchy in the organizational structure. It is a decentralized approach to management that encourages high employee involvement in decisions. The purpose of this structure is to create independent small businesses or enterprises that can rapidly respond to customers' needs or changes in the business environment. In this organizational structure, managers tend to have a more personal relationship with their employees.

(c) MANAGEMENT STYLES.   Management styles vary widely and often depend significantly upon the individual and the organization's personality. Indeed, very few managers exhibit consistent and predictable managerial behavior all the time. Nevertheless, there appears to be some general patterns that can be used as a source of categorization. In his book *The Human Side of Enterprise*, Douglas McGregor defined ways that managers typically view subordinates as **Theory X** and **Theory Y**.[1]

---

1.   McGregor, Douglas. *The Human Side of Enterprise*. New York: McGraw-Hill, 1960.

(i) Traditional or Manager Controlled.   The traditional view of managerial direction and control is termed Theory X. Its central tenets are as follows:

- Most employees dislike work and will avoid it whenever possible.
- Because of the inherent dislike of work, most people must be controlled and threatened with punishment to get them to demonstrate adequate effort toward the achievement of organizational objectives.
- The average person prefers to be directed and has no desire for responsibility and relatively little ambition.
- Employees are motivated mainly by money.

The organization and manager following the traditional approach rely primarily on control tactics such as using procedures and techniques for directing employees, measuring compliance, and administering rewards and punishment.

(ii) Employee Focused.   McGregor's Theory Y holds the view that organizational goals and individual goals can be mutually compatible. Theory Y managers believe that employees are capable of hard work and have cooperative, positive attitudes. In practice this means:

- Physical and mental work efforts are no different than play or rest.
- Commitment is directly related to the reward associated with the achievement of a goal.
- The average person learns to accept and even seek responsibility.
- Individuals have the ability to exercise a relatively high degree of imagination and creativity in the workplace.
- Creativity, imagination, and ingenuity are not limited to the exceptional few; rather, they are widely distributed in the general population.
- Under typical conditions, the average person's intellectual potential is only partially utilized.

The organization and manager following this approach tend to create an environment in which the employee's goals and the organization's goals can be achieved together. Overall, the style in this environment is participative, collaborative, and nurturing.

(iii) Group Dynamics.   People learn social skills from one another when they begin socializing as children. As adults, most people work in a group environment. In this context, the term "group dynamics" refers to the observation that an individual's behavior tends to differ in relation to current connections to a particular group. Urges to belong to a particular group may result in different behaviors, and the influence of a group may override an individual's natural tendencies and actions.

Organizational development theory recognizes that groups go through four main phases:

1. Forming: Individuals are introduced to one another.
2. Storming: Competition between the interests of members emerges.
3. Norming: Team members learn to work together.
4. Performing: The team produces results and meets objectives.

Work groups also tend to follow formal and informal organization patterns. The formal work group is generally the officially sanctioned team or department, functioning within the scope of a specific task or responsibility. The informal work group is usually a subset of the formal group that develops around special interests or social needs.

(iv) Managing Change.   An additional consideration closely related to group dynamics is the **management of change**. Change, of course, is an important part of the organizational process, and it has to be managed so that employees embrace new processes positively. Creating successful change often depends on your ability to implement a number of key processes:

- Initiating the change as early as possible.
- Developing strong and effective executive sponsorship.
- Reducing employee resistance (at all levels, including management).
- Providing aligned communications, with the same message delivered across all organizational boundaries.
- Eliminating fear of the unknown or of losing control.
- Avoiding work overload during change implementation.

18.2 RECRUITING, HIRING, PROMOTING, AND TERMINATING EMPLOYEES

As a manager, few aspects of your career will carry more importance than your ability to facilitate the work of others. Regardless of the management style or methodology you might use, the results you produce through the direction of others will be the true measure of your effectiveness. In this section, we'll examine some of the fundamental tasks inherent in this managerial process.

(a) RECRUITING AND HIRING STAFF.   Managers are generally responsible for selecting and hiring competent individual professionals for their team. Working with the Human Resources representative in your organization, you may use a variety of methods to recruit candidates when a position is open in your department, including newspaper ads, solicitations through professional organizations, and your own personal network. Depending upon the experience level and specificity of the position, you may be recruiting from regional, national, or international labor markets.

(i) Specifying Position Requirements.   To begin the recruitment process, you will be required to specify the scope of the job duties and the level of skill required. In general, you will want to develop these specifications carefully so that you and your recruiter can select only the most qualified people applying for the position.

Creating a job analysis essentially involves describing a list of duties or work that must be performed by the individual being hired. This often means beginning with a basic categorization of the job level such as manager, buyer, senior buyer, and so on. This title can then be cross-referenced to standard job descriptions for your industry or geographical region, which can be obtained through your HR Department, as a means of ensuring that you have captured sufficient detail.

In preparing the job description, keep in mind not only your present requirements but also possible future needs. You will also want to include a description of the typical decisions that the individual will be making in the normal course of work, as well as levels and types of communications necessary and any specific supervisory responsibilities. It is a good idea to rank the importance of each of the functions once you get the list compiled and the frequency or percentage of the job that it will encompass.

A typical job description will most likely include:

- Position title.
- A description of each major duty function.
- The relative importance of the job function.
- The approximate time spent performing each duty function.
- The expected performance level of each functional duty.
- The level (or amount) of supervision required.
- Educational requirements.
- Competencies (such as facility with specific software programs).
- Professional certifications desired or required.
- Amount of time spent traveling.
- Citizenship requirements.
- Expected working hours.

(ii) Determining the Required Level of Skills.   Following the preparation of the job description, you will want to list the knowledge, skills, and abilities it takes to perform each of the most important tasks of the job as well. Include in this list specific industry or product knowledge, financial level of negotiations, acquisition amounts, supplier development and management abilities, analytical skills, project management expertise, presentation and communication skills, and specific computer-based knowledge.

This information can help form the basis for determining the education, accreditation, and experience qualifications. Consider expected outcomes, level of responsibility, and criticality of performing appropriately when applying the knowledge or skill or using a given skill set ability. Determine the degree of experience, training, and education needed to gain this knowledge, skill, or ability. The highest level of performance in any of the critical tasks should determine the minimum level of experience you will require.

(iii) Evaluating Previous Experience.   How do you determine if the individual meets your basic requirements? Most commonly, candidates' resumes are reviewed, and those that are most promising are selected for a telephone interview to screen for skills and experience and to determine personal compatibility. The top two or three candidates are then interviewed in person by you and key internal customers, along with other interested managers and HR. (See the next section for more detail on the interviewing process.)

Following the interview, you will likely require some form of written documentation such as a college transcript to verify education. Your HR department can perform most of these routine checks to ensure veracity. However, to evaluate years of experience and level of experience, *you* should always conduct a reference check. It is a good idea to prepare for this process ahead of time. Know exactly what you need to find out before you start the process. Be sure to get the permission of the candidate before conducting a reference check so you do not jeopardize the individual's current employment. Speak with several previous managers who actually reviewed the individual's work performance. You can ask questions regarding the level of performance and how the individual was ranked in relations to peers. However, be aware that some organizations have specific policies regarding disclosure, and you may not always get the information you request.

(iv) Interviewing.   The interview, like other selection processes, should be structured to measure important knowledge, skills, and abilities. A *structured interview* process is designed to assess past behaviors and accomplishments. Focus your questions on some well-defined, important areas of knowledge, which will be needed to perform the key job duties.

- Ask candidates to indicate how and in what way they perform specific duties that require the knowledge you want to assess.
- Ask all candidates the same questions.
- Probe each candidate's answers with further questions structured to find out the individual's level of knowledge and ability.
- Select a few questions that can be covered in detail rather than many questions that produce inconclusive results.
- Consider asking candidates about their experience with one or two projects they worked on that are closely associated with the work you will assign.

It is usually a good idea to ask each of the interviewers to cover specific areas (such as communication skills or analytical ability) so that you can put together a more complete picture at the end of the process. A rating sheet is often helpful so that you can standardize the feedback and use it to help make a final decision.

(v) Making the Selection.   In the final selection process, you should be certain to follow organizational hiring policies and procedures. These are typically established to ensure fairness and meet regulatory obligations.

From your evaluation, select the candidate whose abilities are most closely associated with solving your department and organization's problems or challenges. Evaluate skills that complement and balance those in the present work group team and are most likely to be needed in the future. It is often recommended that you list the strengths and weaknesses as discovered in the selection process and to consider each as objectively as possible. Remember to base your evaluation on the needs of the job and always refer back to your original job specification.

(b) PROMOTING EMPLOYEES.   Promoting existing employees can be a motivational tool of encouragement to the team and can serve as an example of the results of improved effort. But it can also have its downside. As a manager, you should assess the pros and cons of promoting from within for each particular situation and then consider them in relation to the overall goals of the organization, as well as the needs of the individual employees.

(i) Pros.   In addition to their motivational aspects, internal promotions can also improve retention rates since employees are encouraged to feel that the organization provides future value to their careers. Higher retention rates in turn mean lower hiring and training costs for the department and the organization. Promoting from within can also provide a somewhat greater depth of experience for the position since the internal candidate is already familiar with other areas of the organization and knows its history.

(ii) Cons.   Promoting from within does not necessarily reduce the hiring process since it invariably creates another opening. One promotion can often lead to a cascade of promotions, creating several sets of training requirement in the department that can seriously affect productivity. Promoting internal candidates can also affect the budget because typically external candidates will have less seniority and therefore earn less for the same work. Similarly, external hiring promotes new ideas and new ways of looking at problems; conversely, internal promotions tend to produce inbreeding using the same methods and processes as those currently in place.

18.3 TRAINING FOR PROFESSIONAL COMPETENCE

Training is the key to individual job performance improvement. In the working environment, training generally consists of expanding knowledge, developing and improving skill sets, and providing opportunities for professional development.

Training is also used when new processes or procedures are introduced into the workplace.

This section outlines some of the more important characteristics that the manager must keep in mind when analyzing training needs and implementing related programs.

(a) TRAINING REQUIREMENTS.   It is advisable to begin your assessment of training needs by starting with an analysis of any anticipated organizational changes and developments to determine which skills will be needed in the future and to what degree. A side-by-side comparison of these needs with current skill levels can help you estimate training requirements and accompanying budgets. Analysis should also identify the elements of current or future tasks to be done so that you can identify broad requirements. Performing a gap analysis between future requirements and current skill sets is often helpful. Typically, you will be required to do this on an annual or quarterly basis.

In addition, training requirements are often developed through a personal needs analysis. This involves an assessment of each individual's developmental requirements and interests and an agreed plan for accomplishment. Clear and measurable objectives should be developed before training begins and after you have identified the employees' training needs. You might consider developing goals and objectives for specific training by using the tools of collaborative planning and jointly determining an acceptable level of overall performance.

Having clearly defined objectives will enable you and the employee to evaluate when (and if) the objectives have been reached. For a training objective to be effective, it should identify as precisely as possible what the employees will do to demonstrate that the objective has been reached. Using specific, action-oriented language, training objectives should describe the desired knowledge, practice, or skill and its observable behavior. Objectives should also describe the important conditions under which the individual will demonstrate competence and define what constitutes acceptable performance. Objectives are most effective when worded in sufficient detail so that others can recognize when the desired knowledge or behavior is exhibited.

(b) TRAINING METHODS.   For training to be effective, employees should be convinced that it is important to them. To ensure this, explain the goals of the training and provide training that is clearly relevant to the individual's work environment. Training should be simple but, at the same time, carefully thorough.

Commonly employed training methods include:

- On-the-job training (OJT), where individuals learn from actually performing job duties.
- Job rotation, where individuals are cross-trained to enhance the department's staffing flexibility.

- Instructor-led classroom training, for a more formal approach to learning new skills and the reinforcement of the learning developed from peer groups.
- Lecture, demonstration, and hands-on training—the "see/do" approach—to enable a combination of instruction and OJT in a controlled environment.
- Computer-based training (or online distance learning), for self-paced learning using a multimedia approach that reinforces written instruction with audio and visual aids.
- Blended learning, a combination of instructor-led and self-paced training that provides the benefits of both systems.
- Self-study, through reading and other individualized learning tools.

Physical training environments often include training on the job; at a corporate training center or conference facility, community college or university site, hotel meeting room; or at workshops, seminars, and professional conferences. Materials can include handouts, posters, operations manuals, magazine articles, slides and photographs, film, instructional manuals, books, outlines, and diagrams.

Periodic evaluation of the training is a key element in developing a successful and effective training program. Training should be reevaluated whenever new processes or techniques are introduced into the workplace. As the manager, you should evaluate the training to ensure that it continues to be effective and to determine if any further training is needed given current circumstances. Evaluations should consider the complexity of the job for which the training is conducted since more complex tasks may require more frequent training. Evaluation of the training's effectiveness should be conducted periodically—at least annually—for ongoing training.

It is also a good idea to involve employees in the training evaluation. Feedback from each class will help ensure that future groups gain the benefit of those preceding them. You will specifically want to measure how effectively the objectives of the training are being reached.

(c) TRAINING.   The manager or training instructor should combine domain expertise and the ability to effectively transfer knowledge to those being instructed. Some of the typical steps in the training cycle include:

- Providing an oral and written overview of the training objective.
- Illustrating the material with examples of the task.
- Enabling employees to apply the training on the job.
- Monitoring employees' progress and offering additional coaching.
- Evaluating employees' success rate and adjusting the training as required.
- Retraining where improvement is needed.
- Reviewing training objectives.
- Employing methods to continually evaluate training effectiveness during future job performance.

Trainers sometimes use a simple principle: "Tell the students what they are about to learn, teach the material, and then reinforce the lesson by summarizing what the students just learned."

(d) PROFESSIONAL DEVELOPMENT. Professional development generally refers to the ongoing process of improving personal skill sets, knowledge, and abilities in order to improve job performance and, ostensibly, further one's career.

Professional development usually takes the form of advanced education and formal training. This is encouraged by many organizations that reimburse their employees for such expenses if they demonstrate a relation to their jobs. In addition, professional certification as a **Certified Purchasing Manager (CPM)** through the Institute for Supply Management (ISM) or similar certifications offered by other professional groups should be formally encouraged.

Other procurement and supply management–related certifications include:

- Certified Federal Contracts Manager (CFCM), Certified Commercial Contracts Manager (CCCM), and Certified Professional Contracts Manager (CPCM), offered by the National Contract Management Association (NCMA), *www.ncmahq.org/*.
- Certified Public Purchasing Officer (CPPO) and Certified Professional Public Buyer (CPPB), administered by the National Institute for Governmental Purchasing (NIGP), *www.nigp.org*.
- Certified in Production and Inventory Management (CPIM), Certified Fellow in Production and Inventory Management (CFPIM), and Certified in Integrated Resource Management (CIRM), designations awarded by APICS (the Association for Operations Management, formerly APICS (*www.apics.org*)

18.4 JOB PERFORMANCE

Job **performance appraisal** and employee evaluations are processes that take place—formally and informally—in the organization on a daily and an annual basis. In fact, the continuing evaluation of individual work performance is a method of control, tying ongoing performance to rewards or corrective actions. However, in most organizations the performance appraisal process is a formal, structured system that compares employee performance to established standards and agreed-upon goals. The manager's assessment of the employee's job performance is presented to the employees being appraised through one of several traditional methods of formal reviews.

(a) APPRAISAL FACTORS. Performance appraisals should include objective criteria for measuring employee performance and ratings that summarize how well the employee is doing against stated objectives. Successful appraisal methods have clearly defined and explicitly communicated standards or expectations of employee performance on the job.

(i) Performance Appraisal Methods.   While it is important that an organization (and department) maintains a uniform method of approach to ensure fairness, appraisals can be structured in a number of different ways. Some of the more commonly used methods are discussed next:

- **Traditional form-based approach.** Goals are listed on a standardized review document and performance is evaluated by the manager on a sliding numerical scale. Scores are then calculated arithmetically according to a predetermined weighting method.
- **Graphic rating scale system.** In a similar process to the form-based approach, the **graphic rating scale** is a set of performance factors such as job knowledge, work quality, and cooperation that the reviewing manager uses to rate employee performance on an incremental scale.
- **Written narrative appraisal.** This assesses an employee's strengths, weaknesses, past performance, and potential, along with recommendations for improvement.
- **Comparative standards or multiperson comparison.** Rather than an absolute method of the traditional form-based approach, the **comparative standards** or **multiperson comparison** is a relative system that compares one employee's job performance with that of others in the same function or at the same level of compensation.
- **Individual rank ordering system.** This system requires the reviewing manager to list employees from highest to lowest in performance rating.
- **Group rank ordering system.** This system requires the reviewing manager to place employees into a particular classification such as the top 25 percent or the bottom 25 percent. This forces a ranking according to group levels.
- **Paired comparison method.** In this method, the reviewing manager compares each employee with every other employee in the group and rates each as either the superior or weaker of the pair. After all comparisons are made, each employee is assigned a summary or ranking based on the number of superior scores received.
- **Critical incidents review process.** During this process, the manager reviews specific or key performance factors that separate effective from ineffective performance.
- **Behaviorally anchored rating scales (BARS).** This system combines elements from critical incident and graphic rating scale approaches. The manager thus evaluates employees according to items on a numerical scale.
- **Management by objective (MBO).** This method evaluates how well an employee has accomplished goals agreed upon at the beginning of the reviewing period. It also attempts to align objectives with quantitative performance measures such as cost savings or completed contracts.

- **360-degree feedback process.** This process provides a comprehensive perspective of employee performance by utilizing feedback from the full circle of people with whom the employee interacts: supervisors, subordinates, and coworkers. It is effective for career coaching and identifying strengths and weaknesses.

(ii) Forming Appraisal Judgments. Appraisal judgments can be either objective or subjective, that is, quantitative or qualitative. Objective factors are observable and measurable results that can be readily documented. They include such factors as errors and missed deadlines. Subjective factors, on the other hand, are simply opinions. They can be difficult or impossible to quantify and often open the door to charges of bias. Examples of subjective factors include such elements as personality traits, dependability, initiative, and perseverance. To remain objective, managers should double-check ratings to be sure they don't favor one employee or make unsupported judgments. Supported judgments will have documented incidents of employee performance to illustrate the ratings.

The halo effect is a rating error that occurs when the evaluator tends to base overall judgments or evaluations on selected pieces of information rather than on all available relevant information. This usually occurs as the result of specific knowledge of an employee's performance on one favorable or unfavorable incident that affects the ratings on all others. The halo effect can be reduced by rating and comparing all employees' performance on a single factor before going on to another factor.

(iii) Leveraging Performance Appraisals. Performance appraisals can be employed in a number of important management functions, both evaluative and developmental. In addition to assessing the progress of the employee's efforts toward reaching objectives and providing the framework in which to develop improvements, the appraisal process often helps determine future compensation. Typically, organizations budget annual salary increases based upon merit, and it is the manager's job to divide the dollar amount set aside for the department equitably among the staff. As such, it is an important tool in providing recognition and reward that fosters individual motivation and talent retention.

The appraisal also can be a tool to recommend individuals for promotion. A strong record of documented achievements can provide the basis for evaluating an employee for future assignments. On the other hand, inadequate performance can also be documented, and the review process can be used to develop ways in which to improve. In both of these cases, the review becomes part of the employee's official record and can help guide the employee's future managers in setting goals in a way that provides objective continuity.

(iv) Conducting the Review. Because the review can be critical to an employee's career, it is important that you conduct the appraisal conference in a consistent and professional manner. While techniques for conducting the review vary

widely from organization to organization, there are a number of elements you should consider:

- **Communicate.** Begin your meeting with a summary of your evaluation, touching upon the major accomplishments during the period, as well as areas of potential improvement.
- **Develop consensus.** Ask for input and listen to the employee's comments, being certain to take notes and acknowledge your understanding. Resolve any significant differences of opinion using as many examples as you can.
- **Gain acceptance.** While full agreement may not be possible, it is important that the employee accepts the rating.
- **Review areas for improvement.** Go over specific areas for improvement and the reasons it is needed. Cover how these might work into future goals.
- **Agree.** Develop targets to consider in the next period, and gain the employee's commitment to them. Determine what you can do to help. Consider setting a date to discuss goals and objectives for the next period.

18.5 HANDLING EMPLOYEE PERFORMANCE ISSUES

The manager's goal is to continually improve employee performance. However, a manager should also be able to identify situations and behavior patterns that may require immediate corrective action and understand what steps should be taken to resolve them.

(a) IDENTIFYING PROBLEMS AND PERFORMANCE ISSUES.   Managers need to be able to recognize early signs that an employee may be heading for difficulties. These commonly include:

- Sudden change of behavior
- Poor attendance
- Negative attitude
- Stress
- Reduced productivity
- Carelessness
- Irritability
- Insubordination
- Signs of fatigue
- Missed deadlines
- Difficulty following instructions

In addition, there are some situations that may call for additional intervention by security or Human Resources, such as signs of substance abuse, theft, sexual harassment, threats of physical violence, and ethical or legal violations.

(b) IMPLEMENTING CORRECTIVE ACTION.   Corrective action generally takes one of two forms, counseling or formal discipline. Because of potential legal implications, most organizations have established specific guideline policies and procedures for conducting such activities, and you should be sure you understand them before engaging in corrective action. Here are some general processes you might want to cover.

(i) Counseling.   Counseling is a behavioral control technique that you can use to help resolve performance problems. It is often a process where the manager assists an employee through purposeful conversation in a collaborative and understanding atmosphere. It has as a goal the clarification of issues and guidance in resolving them. As a counselor, the manager seeks to assist the employee by discussing the problems that are preventing adequate job performance with the specific intent of resolving them.

Effective counseling requires active listening and reflection. Listening is reassuring and helps the employee feel more valued. During the counseling session, the employee should be encouraged to talk and actively explore ways to better understand the particular performance issues. By providing support, the manager will help the individual focus on the underlying causes of the performance issue and examine a corrective course of action that might provide effective resolution.

Counseling techniques cover a fairly broad range from directive to nondirective and are usually dependent upon the specific situation. **Nondirective counseling** simply summarizes what has been said. Using the nondirective approach you might say, "You feel stressed because you have not had enough team support in conducting the project." **Directive counseling**, on the other hand, provides direct advice. Using the directive approach you could say, "I want you to assign a specific responsibility to each team member." **Interactive counseling** is a combination of both nondirective and directive techniques.

Following are some of the steps you should consider when the situation calls for counseling:

- **Identify the problem behavior.** Let the employee know that work performance has faltered. Explain in very specific terms what the issues appear to be and what needs to be done so the employee can perform to the organization's performance expectations.
- **Ask for comments.** Let the employee describe what might be causing the change in unacceptable behavior. Listen and protect confidentiality.
- **Help develop a solution.** Emphasize positive and affirmative actions. Allow the employee the time to demonstrate positive improvement and reinforce any visible efforts.
- **Gain commitment.** Seek ways to establish the employee's course of action and direct special attention to correcting the problem.

- **Follow up.** Continue to monitor the situation, even after it has been seemingly resolved. Consider providing additional skills training, if appropriate, as a way of ensuring that the problem does not resurface.

(ii) Disciplining.   Discipline is a form of corrective action and behavioral control taken when an employee is unable to correct performance issues. Effective discipline helps eliminate misconduct and inappropriate behavior such as rules violations or an unwillingness to meet established performance criteria.

Discipline processes generally involve progressive escalation from a verbal reprimand through termination. Two of the steps to consider for disciplinary actions prior to termination are a written reprimand and suspension.

A reprimand follows the procedure just outlined for the counseling process (when appropriate), and after documenting the verbal warnings, the manager may escalate the process by issuing a formal letter of reprimand. The letter should outline previous informal efforts and the current problem. It should also state the required actions to be taken by the individual to correct the problem.

Since this procedure may have further legal implications, it is important that organizational policy and procedures are followed precisely. Prior to issuing the letter, it's wise to consider involving your HR and Legal Departments.

Suspension is done through a formal letter summarizing the prior progressive discipline and the current problem. It should specify the time frame for suspension and identify further discipline and possible termination as a potential consequence for not meeting and maintaining standards for improvement outlined in the previous warning letters.

As with the written reprimand, this serious action should involve your HR Department.

(iii) Terminating Employees.   Termination may be necessary when discipline measures are not successful in improving performance. It is usually a very difficult and somewhat emotional process that requires both structure and sensitivity. In general, since most employment is based on mutual consent, both the employee and the organization have the right to terminate employment at will, with or without cause, at any time. However, it is extremely important that you follow proper procedure to legally protect your organization from actions for *wrongful termination*.

Once the decision to terminate an employee has been made, you should schedule the formal action as soon as possible. Identify and contact your internal resources such as HR and Legal for assistance and advice on moving through the process in conformance to legal practice and organizational policy. Some of the typical steps you will take are listed here:

1. **Prepare a summary and termination letter.** Clearly cite the reasons for the termination. List any actions that have preceded termination. In addition

to performance issues, reasons for the termination might include a reorganization, new technology, or change in strategic direction.

2. **Establish a security procedure.** Prepare for the individual to collect personal effects from the organization's property. Personal effects can also be forwarded later, after a qualified security person has had the opportunity to evaluate their contents. If the individual has access to confidential material, take whatever precautions are possible to ensure their safekeeping. For example, change computer passwords and secure documents.

3. **Determine the time and location.** Establish a specific time for the action, keeping disruption to other team members at a minimum. Have ready whatever documents need to be signed and the individual's final paycheck prepared.

4. **Plan official announcements.** Establish who needs to be informed of the departure, both internally and externally, and what form the announcement should take.

An outline of the steps in a termination plan might look something like this:

Step 1. Communicate the decision to the individual.
Step 2. Explain the reasons for the decision and events leading up to it.
Step 3. Explain severance terms in the case of a layoff.
Step 4. If appropriate, offer the option to resign.
Step 5. Review outplacement assistance, if applicable.
Step 6. Review procedures for references.
Step 7. Make arrangements to gather personal belongings.
Step 8. Collect company property and security badges.
Step 9. Obtain signatures on required documents.
Step 10. Ensure that the individual exits the premises.

18.6 PREVENTING WORKPLACE DISCRIMINATION AND HARASSMENT

What constitutes discrimination in the workplace? The precise definition of discrimination in the workplace and what is illegal discrimination varies somewhat from state to state. However, discrimination can be defined as treating one person unfairly over another according to factors unrelated to their ability or potential, such as age, race, disability, sex, sexual orientation, religion, or national origin. There are numerous laws and regulations that attempt to eliminate unfair discrimination, and many organizations have established policies and procedures to align with them. In this section, we'll outline some of the regulations you are most likely to encounter.

(a) ADMINISTERING EQUAL OPPORTUNITY PROCESSES.   While it would be hard for you as a manager to be completely up to date on all the specifics of existing laws, it is nevertheless your responsibility to ensure that discrimination and harassment are never present in your workplace. To accomplish this, you will need to be familiar with some of the key laws and regulations and how they operate to provide equal opportunity for all employees.

(i) Laws and Regulations. The U.S. **Equal Employment Opportunity Commission (EEOC)** (*www.eeoc.gov*) is charged with the enforcement of the body of federal laws governing equal employment opportunity.

The key federal laws prohibiting job discrimination are discussed next:

- **Title VII of the Civil Rights Act of 1964, 1972, 1991).** Prohibits employment discrimination based on race, color, religion, sex, or national origin. It also allows for employers to use a Bona Fide Occupational Qualification (BFOQ) to establish employment requirements where a need legitimately exists. (For example, an advertising director can require a female model for a bathing suit ad.)
- **Equal Pay Act of 1963 (EPA).** Protects men and women who perform substantially equal work in the same establishment from sex-based wage discrimination.
- **Age Discrimination in Employment Act of 1967, 1978, 1986 (ADEA).** Protects individuals who are 40 years of age or older.
- **Title I and Title V of the Americans with Disabilities Act of 1990 (ADA).** Prohibits employment discrimination against qualified individuals with disabilities in the private sector and in state and local governments.
- **Sections 501 and 505 of the Rehabilitation Act of 1973.** Prohibits discrimination against qualified individuals with disabilities who work in the federal government.
- **Civil Rights Act of 1991.** Provides, among other things, monetary damages in cases of intentional employment discrimination.

In general, the presence of a specific set of conditions can confirm the existence of illegal discrimination. Unfair treatment does not necessarily equal unlawful discrimination. Treating a person differently from others violates Equal Employment Opportunity (EEO) laws only when the treatment is based on the presence of a protected characteristic rather than on job performance or even on something as arbitrary as an employee's personality. Keep in mind, however, that discrimination claims can be highly subjective when reviewed by an arbitrator or a jury.

To avoid discrimination, you do not have to extend preferential treatment to any employee. The law requires only that you extend the same employment opportunities and enforce the same policies for all employees.

(ii) Affirmative Action. Affirmative Action became law with the passage of the Equal Employment Opportunity Act of 1972, whereby employers, labor unions, employment agencies, and labor management apprenticeship programs must actively seek to increase the employment opportunities for protected groups such as racial minorities and the disabled. Although Title VII of the Civil Rights Act of 1964 outlawed

future discriminations in employment practices, it did nothing to redress already existing imbalances. The 1972 law, later strengthened by Executive Order 11246, required employers to draw up a detailed written plan for equalizing economic salaries, training programs, fringe benefits, and other conditions of employment. These plans included numerical goals and timetables for achieving such changes.

In recent decisions, however, the U.S. Supreme Court has significantly reduced the scope of federal affirmative action programs requiring that such actions serve a compelling interest and be narrowly defined. In 1994, the Fourth U.S. Circuit Court of Appeals rejected a University of Maryland scholarship program restricted to African-American students. In 2004, the Fifth Circuit rejected an admissions procedure at the University of Texas Law School that divided applicants into two groups—first, blacks and Mexican-Americans, and second, all others—and then applied different admissions quotas to each group. The Court held that the law school's interest in diversity did not constitute a compelling state interest and that the school could not take race into account in any form in its admissions process. The Supreme Court let both decisions stand without further review. While as a matter of law other states are not absolutely debarred from continuing race-restricted scholarships or preferential admissions policies, the consensus is that these programs are unlikely to survive the all-but-certain legal challenges they will face.

Some areas of affirmative action are still being enforced, though. Title 5, Section 503 of the Rehabilitation Act, does require that affirmative action be taken in employment of persons with disabilities by federal contractors.

(iii) Americans with Disabilities Act (ADA).   The EEOC provides an outline of the basic principles of the Americans with Disabilities Act (ADA). We will discuss those principles next.

The ADA prohibits discrimination on the basis of disability in all employment practices. It is necessary to understand several important ADA definitions to know who is protected by the law and what constitutes illegal discrimination:

- **Individual with a disability.** An individual with a disability under the ADA is a person who has a physical or mental impairment that substantially limits one or more major life activities, has a record of such impairment, or is regarded as having such impairment. Major life activities are activities that an average person can perform with little or no difficulty such as walking, breathing, seeing, hearing, speaking, learning, and working.
- **Qualified individual with a disability.** A qualified employee or applicant with a disability is someone who satisfies skill, experience, education, and other job-related requirements of the position held or desired, and who, with or without reasonable accommodation, can perform the essential functions of that position.
- **Reasonable accommodation.** Reasonable accommodation may include, but is not limited to, making existing employee facilities readily accessible

to and usable by persons with disabilities; job restructuring; modification of work schedules; providing additional unpaid leave; reassignment to a vacant position; acquiring or modifying equipment or devices; adjusting or modifying examinations, training materials, or policies; and providing qualified readers or interpreters. Reasonable accommodation may be necessary to apply for a job, to perform job functions, or to enjoy the benefits and privileges of employment that are enjoyed by people without disabilities. An employer is not required to lower production standards to make an accommodation. An employer generally is not obligated to provide personal use items such as eyeglasses or hearing aids.

- **Undue hardship.** An employer is required to make a reasonable accommodation to a qualified individual with a disability unless doing so would impose an undue hardship on the operation of the employer's business. Undue hardship means an action that involves significant difficulty or expense when considered in relation to factors such as a business's size, financial resources, and the nature and structure of its operation.
- **Prohibited inquiries and examination.** Before making an offer of employment, an employer may not ask job applicants about the existence, nature, or severity of a disability. Applicants may be asked about their ability to perform job functions. A job offer may be conditioned on the results of a medical examination, but only if the examination is required for all entering employees in the same job category. Medical examinations of employees must be job-related and consistent with business necessity.
- **Drug and alcohol use.** Employees and applicants currently engaging in the illegal use of drugs are not protected by the ADA when an employer acts on the basis of such use. Tests for illegal use of drugs are not considered medical examinations and, therefore, are not subject to the ADA's restrictions on medical examinations. Employers may hold individuals who are illegally using drugs and individuals with alcoholism to the same standards of performance as other employees.

(b) ELIMINATING SEXUAL HARASSMENT. Sexual harassment in employment is any kind of sexual behavior that is unwelcome and/or inappropriate for the workplace. The EEOC has defined sexual harassment as "unwelcome sexual advances, requests for sexual favors, and other verbal or physical conduct of a sexual nature … when … submission to or rejection of such conduct is used as the basis for employment decisions … or such conduct has the purpose or effect of … creating an intimidating, hostile, or offensive working environment."

Sexual harassment is also defined as unwelcome sexual advances or conduct. Sexual harassment can include verbal harassment (derogatory comments or dirty jokes), visual harassment (sexually explicit posters, cartoons, or drawings), physical harassment, and outright sexual advances or confrontation with sexual demands. Sexual harassment also includes animosity that is gender-based and a sexually charged work environment. In the workplace, sexual harassment can come from the owner, supervisor, manager, lead person, foreperson, coworker, and/or customer.

In a series of major decisions in 1998, the U.S. Supreme Court clarified and broadened the law. In a unanimous decision in March 1998, the Court ruled that when the workplace is permeated with discriminatory intimidation, ridicule, and insults that are sufficiently severe or pervasive to alter the conditions of the victim's employment and create an abusive working environment, Title VII is violated.

To prevent sexual harassment, organizations typically develop a written policy concerning sexual harassment that clearly states that it is not only against the law, but against company policy, and will not be tolerated. Organizations also create an effective complaint or grievance procedure for employees who feel they have been victims of sexual harassment. The procedure should make it easy and comfortable for an employee to file a complaint, especially if the harasser is a direct supervisor. The procedure should also be such that a solution to the problem can be arrived at quickly and effectively.

As a manager, you should ensure that your staff is aware of the organization's policy and that they value treatment of others in a professional manner.

18.7 SUMMARY

Managing the Procurement Department requires specific knowledge and skills focused on leadership and team management. Various systems of management and management theory have been applied in contemporary organizations, including bureaucracy, scientific management, administrative management, behavioral and human relations theory, systems theory, contingency theory, and chaos theory. Invariably, no one management concept applies to all situations.

Similarly, a number of common principles have been identified to define how management structures operate and how work is distributed. These principles include the scalar, unity or chain of command, line-staff, span of control, exception management, departmentalization, management by objective (MBO), and the principles of flat organization. In conjunction, management styles take the form of traditional or manager-controlled and its opposite counterpart, employee- focused (Theory X and Theory Y).

Recruiting, hiring, training, promoting, and terminating staff is another set of the key responsibilities of the manager. Recruiting and hiring require the ability to specify job requirements and skill levels and to evaluate the experience of candidates for employment. Managers are also required to conduct interviews with candidates and to make the final hiring decision.

During the course of employment, virtually all employees will require some degree of training, depending on changes within the organization and the organization's environment. This means the manager will need to understand the methods commonly used in the training process and how to employ them. The manager should also be aware of professional development opportunities and encourage staff participation.

Another key responsibility of the manager is developing and conducting the job performance appraisal in a manner that reinforces continuous improvement. Managers will also be required to identify and resolve problems and performance issues, taking appropriate corrective and disciplinary action up to and including termination of employment.

As the management representative for the department, the procurement manager is also responsible for ensuring that applicable laws and organizational policies regarding workplace discrimination and sexual harassment are uniformly enforced. To perform effectively, the manager should be familiar with Federal Equal Employment Opportunity legislation and what constitutes sexual harassment so that all employees value the fair treatment of others.

KEY TERMS

Bureaucracy
Time-in-motion work standardization
Administrative theory
Systems theory of management
Contingency theory
Chaos theory
The Scalar Principle
Unity or Chain of Command Principle
Line-Staff Principle
Span of Control Principle
Exception Management Principle
Departmentalization Principle
Management by Objective (MBO)
Flat Organization

Theory X
Theory Y
Management of change
Certified Purchasing Manager (CPM)
Performance appraisal
Graphic rating scale
Comparative standards
Multiperson comparison
Nondirective counseling
Directive counseling
Interactive counseling
Equal Employment Opportunity
    Commission (EEOC)

SAMPLE PURCHASE REQUISITION FORM

	PURCHASE REQUISITION
	No. 464881

1) DATE: 11/10/2005

ENCUMBRANCE

2) ACCOUNT 102418	3) CHAR. OBJECT 7340	4) AMOUNT $5718.00	5) ORDER TYPE ( ) Supplies and Expense (X) Equipment ( ) Confirming Order	6) IDENTIFY IF APPLICABLE: ( ) Radioactive Materials ( ) Radiation-Producing Agent (X) Laser
7) DATE REQUIRED 10/26/00	8) SPECIAL ATTACHMENTS/DOCUMENTS QUOTES			

ITEM(S)

IMPORTANT: Information must be typed or printed neatly. Instructions for completion are on reverse.

9) DESCRIPTION	QUANTITY	UNIT	UNIT PRICE	UNIT TOTAL
Auxiliary Generator Model Jm41 General 410cc 3600 RPM, Air Cooled	1	ea.	$4619.00	$4619.00
Auto Laser 900 Stock#55060	1	ea.	$1099.00	$1099.00

VENDOR(S)

NINE DIGIT FEDERAL ID# IS REQUIRED

10) FED. ID# 123456789	11) FED. ID# 101112131	12) FED. ID# 415161718
13) NAME AND ADDRESS Joe's Hardware 1313 Hollow Way East Blackford, NJ 01239-1234	14) NAME AND ADDRESS $6300.00 Bill's Hardware, Supply Co. 360 Main Street Pleasant, OH 44774-8888	15) NAME AND ADDRESS $6100.00 Best Value Hardware North 59th East Street Viking, New Hampshire 60789
16) PHONE (616) 689-2121 FAX # (616) 689-1919	17) PHONE (777) 298-2345 FAX # (777) 299-6789	18) PHONE 1800-234-9999 FAX # (716) 555-4521
19) DELIVER ITEMS TO (NAME/BLDG/ROOM): John Smith/SBA	20) DEPT PHONE: 434-0000	21) _____ AUTHORIZED SIGNATURE (REQUIRED)

PURCHASING

To be completed by the Purchasing Office:

22) PURCHASE ORDER #	23) PO DATE	24) COMMODITY GROUP # 39000	25) STATE CONTRACT P	26) CHECK ALL THAT APPLY: ( ) MBE ( ) WBE ( ) Recycled/Remanufactured	27) BUYER PURREQST 3RD 10/97

RETURN REQUISITION TO

KEEP PINK COPY FOR YOUR FILES

28) Name Jane Doe   29) Department Equipment Management   30) Bldg/Room MSC 302

SAMPLE PURCHASE ORDER FORM

| PURCHASE ORDER and CLAIM VOUCHER ① | (LOGO) | ② YOUR USD #123 456 Your Street, Box 789 Anytown, KS 12345 785-555-9987 | **NO. 001001** ③ Show this Purchase Order No. on invoice and on outside of each Package and Carton. |

VENDOR: ⌐   ⌐ DELIVER TO: ⌐

⌊   ⌊ ⌊

BILL TO: YOUR USD #
④   456 Your Sreet, Box 789
Anytown, KS 12345

| DATE ISSUED: | DELIVERY DATE: | FUND: | PAID BY WARRANT: NO.   DATE: |

QUANTITY AND UNIT	CATALOG NUMBER	DESCRIPTION	UNIT COST	TOTAL ESTIMATED COST	TOTAL ACTUAL COST

⑤ This purchase order is in compliance with K.S.A. 44-1030-44-1033

INSTRUCTIONS TO VENDORS ⑥
1. Submit two copies of your itemized invoice to this office.
2. Invoice of the correct amount due, must reach our business office not later than the 25th day of the month to receive payment in the following month.
3. Federal Excise Tax exemption certificates will be furnished on request.
4. Each shipment must be covered by separate invoice.
5. If shipment cannot be made as requested, notify us at once.
6. All transportation charges, if any, are prepaid and added to the invoice.
7. Show person's name to whom package is being delivered, on each package and carton.

FEDERAL TAX ID NO. ▓▓▓▓▓▓ ⑦

STATE SALES TAX	EXEMPT	EXEMPT
FEDERAL EXCISE TAX	EXEMPT	EXEMPT
TRANSPORTATION CHARGES IF ADDED		
TOTAL CHARGES		

I hereby certify that within itemized account is true and correct, and remains due and unpaid in the amount shown hereon. ⑧

I certify that there is sufficient money available in the within named fund and for the purpose of this purchase. ⑩

ADMINISTRATOR ⑨   DATE

AUTHORIZED SIGNATURE ⑪

ELECTRONIC CATALOG EXAMPLE

1. Initial Search Page and Catalog Listing
Test Equipment Selected – Sorted by Manufacturer

Search

Antennas
A/V Interconnects
Audio
Batteries
Caps & Resistors
CATV
CCTV
Chemicals
Computer
Connectors
Datacom Install Tools
Datacom Test Tools
DSS – Home Theatre
Fuses
Leviton
Premise Wiring/Ethernet
Racks
Relays & Switches
Residential Structured Wiring
Security Systems
Semiconductors
Soldering & Desoldering
Sound
Surge/UPS/Power Strip
Telephone
Test Equipment
Tools
Tool Cases
Transformers
Video
Wire & Cable
Wire Management

Tech Notes

FLUKE networks.

CableIQ Residential Qualifier

IntelliTone 200 Toner and Probe Kit

TS90 Cable Fault Finder

TS100 Cable Fault Finde

FLUKE.

73-3 DMM

110 Compact True-RMS Multimeter - No Amps

112 Compact True-RMS Multimeter

175 Digital Multimeter

177 Digital Multimeter - with Backlight

179 Digital Multimeter - with Backlight & Temperature

189 High Performance Multimeter - True RMS - with Data Logging

322 400A AC Clamp Meter

333 400A AC Clamp Meter

335 600A AC Clamp Meter - True RMS

336 600A AC/DC Clamp Meter - True RMS

62 Mini infrared Thermometer

1AC-A1 II VoltAlert

API AVEX PROBES INC.

500 Series Modular Oscilloscope Probes

510 Series Monolithic Oscilloscope Probes

BK PRECISION

330B 1000A AC Current Clamp

2. General Search
Search for Specific Item
Select Results for Display

eCatalog / order online

Safety Test Leads

Search

Antennas
A/V Interconnects
Audio
Batteries
Caps & Resistors
CATV
CCTV
Chemicals
Computer
Connectors
Datacom Install Tools
Datacom Test Tools
DSS - Home Theatre
Fuses
Leviton
Premise Wiring/Ethernet
Racks
Relays & Switches
Residential Structured Wiring
Security Systems
Semiconductors
Soldering & Desoldering
Sound
Surge/UPS/Power Strip
Telephone
Test Equipment
Tools
Tool Cases
Transformers
Video
Wire & Cable
Wire Management

Results 1 to 5 of 5 (estimated)

Oldaker Standard **Safety Test Leads** / With Clips
... Oldaker Standard **Safety Test Leads** / With Clips: This **safety test** lead set features
4" flame retardant ABS plastic probe handles with **safety** ring.; The tip is ...

Oldaker Adjustable Tip Series **Safety Test Leads**
... Oldaker Adjustable Tip Series **Safety Test Leads**: This **safety test** lead set features
5" Probe with a 3.5" adjustable tip, Fully Insulated; The tip is .025" dia ...

Xcelite Heavy Duty Shearcutter
... Surge/UPS/Power Strip Telephone **Test** Equipment Tools Tool Cases ... and harnesses. Maximum
durability. **Safety** clip on 2178D and 2178M models prevents flying **leads**. ...

Xcelite General Purpose Shearcutter
... Surge/UPS/Power Strip Telephone **Test** Equipment Tools Tool Cases Transformers ... with
half the effort. **Safety** clip on 175M and 175D models prevents flying **leads**. ...

Pomona Banana Plugs, Jacks and Binding Posts
... UPS/Power Strip Telephone **Test** Equipment Tools Tool Cases ... Set screw secures wire;
Safety collar insulates exposed wire **leads**; Accepts standard banana ...

3. Displayed Results
Standard Safety Test Leads
Detail for Company

Standard Safety Test Leads / With Clips

- This safety test lead set features 4" flame retardant ABS plastic probe handles with safety ring,
- The tip is .080" dia. with 8-32 threads for attachments, material brass, nickel plated
- The wire is a heavy duty, 18 ga. 65 × 36 tinned copper stranding with EDPM rubber insulation .145" O.D.
- The lead length is 4 foot, sold as sets 1 red 1 black

Part Number	Description	Plug	Price	Buy
582	Standard Banana Plug		$12.42	Buy
581	Slotted Jack Fits Simpson 260 Meters		$12.42	Buy
486-6	Recessed Standard Banana Plug .312" O.D		$12.42	Buy
486-5	Standard Banana Plug		$12.42	Buy
486-3	Standard Banana Jack		$12.42	Buy
486-18	Retractable Standard Plug		$14.43	Buy
486-2	Recessed Standard Banana Plug		$12.42	Buy

COMMON AUCTION TYPES

THE ENGLISH AUCTION

The most common of the auction formats, goods are sold to the highest bidder with bids taking place in ascending order. Frequently, a reserve price must be met. The reserve price is the lowest price at which the auctioneer will sell the goods. This price is sometimes disclosed to the bidders and sometimes not.

THE DUTCH AUCTION

In a Dutch auction, bidding starts at an extremely high price and is progressively lowered until a buyer claims an item by calling "mine," or by pressing a button that stops an automatic clock. When multiple units are auctioned, normally more takers press the button as price declines. In other words, the first winner takes his prize and pays his price and later winners pay less. When the goods are exhausted, the bidding is over.

THE VICKREY AUCTION

Named for William Vickrey, winner of the 1996 Nobel Prize in Economics, it is also known as the second-price auction. Bids are sealed and the item is awarded to the highest bidder but at a price equal to the second highest bidder's price. If, for example, three bids are received, one for $100, one for $90 and one for $75, the winner will be the $100 bidder. However, the winner will only have to pay $90, the second highest bidder's price.

THE SEALED BID AUCTION

As the name implies, this auction uses a sealed bid, where each bidder is allowed to bid only once. Generally, there are two steps to the process. First, the requirements are established by the buyer and, second, the sealed bids are opened. The highest qualified bidder receives the goods or, in the case of a service, the lowest qualified bid wins.

THE YANKEE AUCTION

A Yankee Auction is a variation of the Dutch Auction where successful bidders pay what they bid as opposed to paying the price determined by the lowest qualified bidder (as in a Dutch Auction).

In this format, when the auction closes, the highest bidders win the available merchandise at their bid price. Bids are ranked in order of price, then time of initial bid. If the reserve price is not met, neither the seller nor the high bidder is under any further obligation.

THE REVERSE AUCTION

In a Reverse Auction, the seller provides bids for a seller's requirements. At the end of an allotted period of time, the bid is awarded to the lowest priced, qualified supplier.

COMMONLY USED FINANCIAL RATIOS

E.1 CURRENT RATIO: LIQUIDITY

The current ratio tells you whether an organization is able to meet its current obligations. It measures an organization's ability to meet short-term debt obligations; the higher the ratio, the more liquid the organization.

The current ratio is calculated by dividing current assets by current liabilities. Current assets are those that can be converted to cash within a year; typically, cash, marketable securities, inventory, and accounts receivable. Current liabilities are those that are due within a year; typically, accounts payable, accrued salaries and wages, outstanding lines of credit, and the principle of long-term loans.

The standard current ratio for a healthy business is two, meaning it has twice as many assets as liabilities.

E.2 QUICK RATIO: LIQUIDITY

Very closely related to current ratio, the quick ratio measures an organization's ability to fund its short-term financial obligations through its most liquid assets. It is also called the acid test.

The quick ratio is calculated by taking current assets *less inventories*, divided by current liabilities.

A low quick ratio indicates an organization may be slow in paying its obligations.

E.3 RECEIVABLES TURNOVER RATIO: LIQUIDITY

This ratio calculates how many days it takes the organization to receive payment from its customers.

Receivables turnover is calculated by dividing net sales (in dollars) by receivables.

The faster accounts receivable are converted to cash the greater the ability of the organization to meet its current liabilities.

E.4 PAYABLES TURNOVER RATIO: LIQUIDITY

This ratio indicates how long it takes, on average, for an organization to pay its bills. It is a calculation of how often payables turn over during the year.

It is calculated by dividing the cost of goods sold by payables.

A high ratio means there is a relatively short time between purchase of goods and services and payment for them. A low ratio may be a sign that the company has chronic cash shortages.

E.5 DEBT-TO-EQUITY RATIO: LIQUIDITY

This ratio indicates how much the company is leveraged (in debt) by comparing what is owed to what is owned. Equity and debt are two key figures on a financial statement, so lenders or investors often use the relationship of these two figures to evaluate risk. The ratio of an organization's equity to its long-term debt provides a window into how strong its finances are.

Equity will include goods and property, plus any claims it has against other entities. Debts will include both current and long-term liabilities.

Debt-to-equity is calculated by dividing total liabilities by total equity.

A high debt-to-equity ratio could indicate that the company may be over-leveraged.

E.6 INVENTORY TURNOVER RATIO: EFFICIENCY

This ratio calculates how many times a business's inventory turns over—that is, was sold and replaced—during the year. Generally, a higher number indicates that inventory is moving quickly and being minimally stocked.

Inventory turnover is calculated by dividing the cost of goods sold by the average value of inventory.

E.7 GROSS PROFIT MARGIN RATIO: PROFITABILITY

The gross profit margin ratio indicates how efficiently a business is using its materials and labor in the production process. It shows the percentage of net sales remaining after subtracting cost of goods sold. A high gross profit margin indicates that a business can make a reasonable profit on sales, as long as it keeps overhead costs in control.

It is calculated by dividing gross profit by total sales.

E.8 RETURN ON ASSETS (ROA) RATIO: PROFITABILITY

This calculation shows how effective an organization is at using its assets. The ROA is a test of capital utilization—how much profit (before interest and income tax) a business earned on the total capital used to make that profit.

- Return on assets is an indicator of an organization's profitability.
- It is calculated by dividing earnings before interest and taxes (EBIT) by net operating assets.

REQUEST FOR PROPOSAL (RFP) EXAMPLE

RFP No: _____

REQUEST FOR PROPOSAL

FOR

[Name of Project]

ON BEHALF OF

COMPANY, Inc.

[RFP Date]

Deadline: [Proposal Due Date]

THE INSTRUCTIONS CONTAINED HEREIN ARE IMPORTANT.
READ THEM CAREFULLY.

These instructions ("Instructions") are a part of Company' Request for Proposal ("RFP") and must be followed in the preparation of any proposal ("Proposal").

This RFP is Company confidential and proprietary information subject to restrictions stated herein.

[Obtain an executed Non-Disclosure Agreement protecting Company's information prior to releasing the RFP to a potential supplier. At the RFP stage, only a unilateral Non-Disclosure Agreement in favor of Company should be used.]

TABLE OF CONTENTS

1.   Introduction

1.1   Corporate Overview

1.2   Statement of Purpose

Company is issuing this RFP to solicit proposals from one or more potential suppliers ("Supplier") for cost, delivery, and product/service information for Company's **[Describe the product or service and, if applicable, markets]**. Company makes no representations, warranties or agreements with respect to this RFP. In addition, Company makes no commitment to purchase any products or services or take any other action, including but not limited to, awarding a contract to the Supplier submitting the lowest cost proposal.

Material contained in this RFP is to be considered Company confidential and proprietary information, subject to restrictions outlined in Section 2.1.1, below.

Company reserves the right to amend or cancel this RFP at any time for any or no reason. All amendments to this RFP shall be in writing.

1.3   Description of Product or Services

[Provide a detailed description of the products and/or services required.]

[Insert detailed description here]

1.4   Critical Proposal Dates

[Complete chart below.]

Date*	Day of Week	Description
		Intent to Respond Letter Due
		Final date for Questions or Comments from Supplier Due (if applicable)
		Company Responses to Questions or Comments Due (if applicable)
		Proposals Due

* Company reserves the right to revise these dates.

1.5   RFP Coordinator

Upon Supplier receipt of this RFP, all communications concerning the RFP must be directed to Company' RFP Coordinator (the "RFP Coordinator") listed below. Thereafter, contact regarding the RFP with other Company employees may result in Supplier being disqualified from further participation in this solicitation or from further business with Company. Oral communications between Company and Supplier regarding this RFP are unauthorized and non-binding.

[Name], RFP Coordinator
Company, Inc.
[Address]
[City, State Zip]

        Telephone Number: **[Telephone Number]**
        Facsimile Number: **[Fax Number]**
        E-Mail: **[E-Mail]**

---

2.   RFP Response Guidelines & Information

2.1   Confidential Information

2.1.1   This RFP, including any information provided by Company in connection with it, is to be treated by the Supplier as Company confidential and proprietary information and subject to the restrictions stated in a non-disclosure agreement ("NDA") entered into by the Supplier and Company in contemplation of this RFP. In addition, and notwithstanding the foregoing, as a condition to the receipt of such information, Supplier agrees that all information provided by Company to Supplier in connection with this RFP shall be treated confidentially and used by the Supplier for the sole purpose of preparing its proposal. Furthermore, the Supplier shall restrict the distribution of this RFP, including any related Company communications, only to Supplier employees who have a need to use it for preparing Supplier's proposal. No access, use or disclosure of Company confidential and proprietary information provided in connection with this RFP shall be made to any other person or entity without Company' prior written approval and execution of an NDA by the intended recipient, which contains equivalent or greater protections for Company' confidential and proprietary information.

2.1.2   If Supplier is not selected to provide products or services in connection with this RFP, upon request by Company, Supplier will immediately return all Company-provided RFP information and documentation to Company.

2.1.3 All proposals and materials submitted by the Supplier in connection with this RFP become the property of Company. In the event of Supplier non-selection, Company may retain same.

2.1.4 Unless otherwise permitted by Company (e.g., through a mutual non-disclosure agreement entered in contemplation of this RFP), Supplier shall not submit its own confidential information in response to this RFP, and Supplier's marking of a proposal as confidential, proprietary or with other similar legend will not be honored. In addition, such submission may disqualify Supplier from further participation in the RFP.

2.2 Errors and Omissions

Company shall not be responsible for or liable to any party for any errors or omissions that may exist in this RFP or may occur during the RFP process. However, in the event of such an error or omission, Company may elect to amend this RFP.

2.3 Submittal Requirements and Delivery

2.3.1 Suppliers are responsible for errors or omissions contained in their proposals.

A Proposal may be withdrawn or amended prior to the Proposal Due Date. To withdraw or amend a Proposal, the Supplier Contact Person identified in Section 3.2.1 must submit a written request to the RFP Coordinator. After withdrawing a Proposal, Supplier may submit another Proposal at any time up to the Proposal Due Date. Suppliers are referred to Section 3.1, below, for additional proposal submission instructions.

Supplier shall not be permitted to alter its Proposal after the Proposal Due Date.

2.3.2 **[Indicate what means of transmission – e.g., by facsimile, U.S. Mail, and/or other electronic means.]**

2.4 Proposal Preparation

2.4.1 Proposal Costs

Any resources and costs expended by Supplier in responding to this RFP are the sole responsibility of the Supplier.

2.4.2   Intent to Respond

The Supplier is required to notify the RFP Coordinator in writing, using the form attached hereto as Attachment A (the "Intent to Respond Form"), by **[Date and Time]** of its intention to submit a Proposal.

The Intent to Respond Form must provide the name and title of the single point of contact within Supplier's organization ("Supplier Contact Person") who should be contacted in the event Company has questions or other communications regarding Supplier's Proposal.

Suppliers declining to submit a proposal must return the Company RFP package to the RFP Coordinator, at the address specified in Section 1.6.

2.4.3   Proposal Format

Suppliers shall furnish all the information required by this RFP in the format set forth in Section 3.   Failure to do so may be grounds for rejection of Supplier's Proposal.

2.5   Exceptions, Variances and Alternate Proposals

Any exceptions, variances or alternative proposals to the requirements of this RFP, including but not limited to terms, delivery dates and provisions, must be specifically identified in Supplier's Proposal.   Such submissions must comply with Section 3.4, below.   Exceptions and variances may be a basis for Proposal rejection.

Unless otherwise indicated by Supplier, signature on its Proposal will indicate unqualified acceptance of all the terms and provisions of this RFP, including all attachments hereto.

2.6   RFP Communications

2.6.1   Supplier Questions or Requests for Clarification

(a)   It is Supplier's obligation to become fully acquainted with all aspects of this RFP.

(b)   Supplier questions or requests for clarification must be submitted by **[Indicate how]** to the RFP Coordinator.

(c)   Inquiries must be made in writing and shall make reference to the applicable RFP requirement section and page number.   Company may communicate a question and its response or clarification to other participating suppliers.

(d)   All questions or requests for clarification are due NO LATER THAN **[Time & Date]**.

(e)   Questions directed to anyone other than the RFP Coordinator will not be answered.

2.6.2   Contact with Company Personnel

(a)   All communications regarding this RFP must be submitted as provided in Sections 1.6 and 2.6.1.

(b)   <u>No communications or inquiries may be made by Supplier to any other individual within Company unless specifically instructed to do so by the RFP Coordinator.</u> Unauthorized communications regarding this RFP with any other Company employee, even those employees associated with current supplier relationships and existing agreements with Company, may result in the disqualification of Supplier from further consideration for this RFP and even future Company business.

2.7   Terms of Negotiation

Supplier's response to this RFP indicates its understanding and agreement that the RFP is not an offer to contract by Company with Supplier. Company reserves the right, in its sole discretion, to withdraw or amend the RFP, to reject or disqualify proposals; to select or not select suppliers, including, without limitation, participants in this RFP process; and/or to identify one or more RFP participants with whom Company wants to solicit additional or supplemental offers (e.g., "best and final" offers) and/or to whom Company may want to issue a modified RFP. The foregoing is without limitation of Company's further right, in its sole discretion, to award any or all of its business to one or more supplier or potential supplier, within the context of this RFP or independently of it, or to discuss matters related to such business with any of the foregoing.

2.8   Validity Period

Supplier must guarantee that its pricing and other terms provided in its Proposal shall remain valid for a period of at least **[Insert time period]** following submission of its Proposal.

2.9   Proposal Evaluation

On receipt of proposals from potential Suppliers, Company will conduct an evaluation process using requirements and criteria set forth in this RFP. Responses to this RFP will be evaluated on the basis of net program cost, the completeness of the response, and the ability of a Supplier to meet all requirements set forth in this RFP. Evaluation criteria will generally include financial stability; Supplier management; billing procedures; warranty, maintenance and other technical support; and Supplier quality controls, including compliance with Company' quality and service standards. Company may also consider its prior experience with the Supplier as well as information obtained from references, public resources, or other parties for whom the supplier has provided products or services. [Change as appropriate]

The selection of the Supplier may be made without discussion and/or negotiation on price or other terms; therefore, the proposal should be submitted complete and should include the most favorable terms that the Supplier is prepared to offer to Company.

2.10   Notification of Award

In the event of a selection, Company will give notice to the selected Supplier regarding the award. However, Company will not provide information concerning any selection, if any, to non-selected Suppliers nor will Company provide the basis for any non-selection to non-selected Suppliers.

2.11   Agreement Terms and Conditions

2.11.1 Agreement Provisions

(a)   Nothing in this RFP nor any Supplier Proposal shall create any contractual relationship between Company and Supplier.   The entering into of any agreement to provide services and/or products hereunder shall be subject to Company' internal review and approvals, including approval by Company' senior management.

(b)   Supplier's response to this RFP shall constitute its agreement to accept the terms and conditions set forth in this RFP as the basis for a contract, if one should be offered by Company to Supplier. Any award made pursuant to this RFP is expressly conditioned upon the execution of a final agreement between the parties substantially in the form attached to this RFP as Attachment C. Unless Supplier specifically objects in writing to a term of the attached agreement in the submission of its Proposal, Supplier shall be deemed to have accepted each term of the attached agreement. [Company contract should be attached to this RFP. Standard form template contracts, previously approved by the Legal Department, may need to be further modified prior to RFP release. In addition, a non-standard contract may need to be prepared for a particular RFP. These modifications or additions can be made when the RFP is reviewed by the Legal Department.]

2.11.2 Subcontracting Requirements

Company **[will/may/will not]** accept proposals which include the use of subcontractors. **[Add the following if subcontractors will/may be used: However, Company will consider proposals which contemplate the use of subcontractors only if Supplier agrees to take responsibility for all actions of subcontractors. Full details regarding the use of any subcontractor, including the name and the capabilities of proposed subcontractors, must be provided with the Proposal. The Supplier is responsible for obtaining any applicable non-disclosure agreements with subcontractors prior to sharing this RFP as further set forth in Section 2.1.1.]**

2.12 New Agreement to Supersede Existing Agreement

Company may already have agreements in place with Supplier for **[Insert Project Name]** ("Existing Agreements"). Company, at its sole option, may choose to supplant any Existing Agreements, at the earliest possible convenience, with the agreement that may result from this RFP.

Therefore, in the event that Supplier is a party to one or more Existing Agreements, by submitting a Proposal in response to this RFP, Supplier hereby agrees to offer Company the option of terminating those Existing Agreements upon thirty (30) days' notice.

In addition, Supplier agrees to allow such early termination without any termination liability or increased prices on the remaining portion of the Existing Agreements. Supplier agrees to refund any prepayments or credits on a prorated basis if terminated.

If Supplier is party to any Existing Agreement(s), a copy of each Existing Agreement shall be provided by Supplier to the RFP Coordinator.

3.   Proposal Content and Format

3.1   Proposal Instructions

3.1.1   General Instructions

Supplier's Proposal must contain all the information set forth below. Non-conforming Proposals may be disqualified.

3.1.2   Proposal Format

This section describes the format of the Proposal. Proposals should be presented on 8 1/2" x 11" single-sided paper, placed in a binder with tabs separating major sections. All pages should be numbered. **[If anything else is required -- *i.e.*, floppy disks -- indicate that here.]** The proposal package ("Proposal Package") shall contain the following:

(a)   <u>Proposal Cover Letter</u>

Supplier shall submit a cover letter transmitting its Proposal Package to the Company. The cover letter shall be signed and dated by an individual authorized to contract with Company on behalf of Supplier.

(b)   <u>Executive Summary</u>

This section shall include a summary of the technical, management and pricing proposals; Supplier's qualifications; and any other information Supplier believes is relevant to the Proposal.

(c)   <u>Statement of Qualifications</u>

The statement of qualifications is a presentation of the qualifications and experience of the Supplier and the staff that will be participating in the contract.

(d)   <u>Detailed Proposal Requirements</u>

This portion of Supplier's Proposal addresses the Proposal requirements in detail. Technical specifications, product support, maintenance, warranties, pricing and other relevant product and service requirements will be addressed.

3.2   Executive Summary

Supplier shall summarize Supplier's business, *e.g.*, its corporate history, identity, and experience in the marketplace so that Company may better understand the Supplier's ability to provide products and services that will be compliant with this

RFP and meet Company' business needs. The summary should be in a form appropriate for executive management review.

3.2.1   General

Enter the information requested in the spreadsheet provided below:

Contact Person:	
Title:	
Phone:	
Fax:	
E-mail:	
Company Name:	
Address:	
Phone:	
Fax:	

3.2.2   Company Profile

Provide a background of Supplier's company, including size, lines of business, technical resources, manufacturing capabilities, manufacturing facilities, research and development labs, date established, ownership type, total number of employees and number of employees engaged in providing supporting products and services which are the subject of this RFP.

3.2.3   Company Experience

Summarize past and present experience in development, manufacturing and support of the products and services called for in this RFP. Highlight any technological leadership, awards, innovative products, product support and customer care programs. Include any experience that Supplier has in developing and manufacturing other telecommunications or similar products and services.

3.2.4   Executive Summary

Provide a description of the product and/or service that Supplier is proposing noting any distinguishing or differentiating characteristics of the product(s) and/or service.   Future evolution plans may also be summarized.

3.3   **Statement of Qualifications**

3.3.1   Corporate Revenues

Enter responses in the spreadsheet provided. **[Provide information in the chart as needed.]**

	Year	Year	Explanation
Other (in $MM)			
Total Revenues (in $MM)			

3.3.2   References

Provide the names, telephone numbers and addresses of three (3) current customer references.   These references shall be organizations of comparable size and complexity with needs similar to those of Company. The list shall provide the appropriate person at this site who can be independently contacted by Company.

3.3.3   Financial Statements

Provide audited financial statements for the past three (3) years.

3.3.4   Complaints and Lawsuits

Indicate whether Supplier has been involved as a defendant in, or the subject of, any administrative complaint, investigation, or civil or criminal actions in the past six (6) years. Supplier should attach a separate sheet furnishing details, including the name of plaintiffs, investigatory body or regulatory agency, action number or other reference number, style of complaint and the current status.

3.4   **Scope of Work**

All numbered paragraphs shall be addressed.

3.4.1 General

Detail Supplier's participation in the development, manufacturing, sales and/or support of **[Fill in description of product/service]**.

3.4.2 Technical Specifications

Provide a point-by-point response to each requirement of this Section.

A table summary of Supplier's point-by-point response must be provided in the beginning of this section in the following format:

Sub Section	Compliance Code	Comments

[Create/Design the format in which you want the response to come back.]

As previously stated, if Supplier takes an exception or variance (and/or proposes an alternative) to an RFP requirement, it should clearly state the exception or variance and the reasons why it cannot comply with the RFP requirement. If a requirement can be satisfied at a future date, Supplier must provide a date when the requirement will be satisfied. If no exceptions or variances are explicitly stated, Supplier shall meet all requirements.

For each subsection listed below, Supplier must indicate in the table summary above if the requirement is met by indicating Compliance (C), Partial Compliance (PC), Compliance at a Later Date (LC), or Non Compliance (NC).

(a) **Standards and Specifications**

Company is committed to the principal of zero defects, and will insist on that same commitment on the part of Supplier. **[If appropriate, fill in the standard or provide a requirement (like the ISO 9000) by which you expect the supplier to comply with.]** The Supplier is required to meet the following standards and specifications, including general physical, electrical and environmental requirements. **[List if appropriate]**

(b)   Product Description and Delivery Schedule

The Supplier is required to provide a detailed description of the proposed products and services.   Supplier must include, as applicable, technical specifications, diagrams, test results or any other relevant material.

(1)   If Supplier's Proposal is for more than one model, Supplier should provide a product description that covers all models. It should address any features that distinguish one model from another.   Indicate commercial availability for each product and lifecycle.

(2)   The Supplier's delivery schedule, including any requisite lead times, should also be addressed in detail.   Highlight any milestones or phases, including availability of pre-production units, commercial units and upgrades.

(c)   Production Management Capabilities

[If applicable, include a table.]

(d)   Documentation

Supplier shall provide sufficient documentation and literature for the product or service. **[If applicable state how many hard and soft copies will be needed.]**

(e)   Installation

[Complete if installation will be required.   If applicable, describe what the Supplier will need to do.]

3.4.3   Detailed Warranty Description

The Supplier must provide details of its warranty policies and procedures including, but not limited to a clear statement of the duration and conditions of warranties, and the warranties of Supplier's suppliers. At a minimum, the Supplier must warrant that products and services must be free of defects in materials and workmanship for a period of ___ **[Fill in as appropriate]** from **[Indicate when the warranty period begins, e.g., date of acceptance, installation, etc.] [Consider repair or return warranties.]**

3.4.4   Support and Maintenance Requirements

The Supplier is required to provide the following additional product and service support:

[Consider such support as on-site installation and repair, training and/or telephone support and spare parts, etc.]

(a)   **Test Equipment and Fixtures** [Include if required]

Supplier shall provide a list of all the test equipment and test fixtures that will be made available to Company for product support.

(b)   **Training** [Include if required]

Company will require training on all products provided by Supplier, including any accessories that are supported by Supplier. Training course must include topics such as **[Indicate topics]**. Therefore, a training plan must be included in the Proposal. **[Specify if Train the Trainer approach is preferred. What about right to copy and distribute internally training materials at no charge?]**

(c)   **Hardware and Software Upgrades**

Supplier shall provide a detailed description of hardware and/or software upgrade programs. Using the format provided in the following table, Supplier must list all hardware and software that will be used by Company to support this program: **[Design the format in which you want the response to come back.]**

3.4.5   Price and Billing Proposal

(a)   **General Information**

The Supplier shall provide pricing based on **[Indicate which is appropriate: hardware, software, training, service pricing and delivery schedules.]**

The Supplier must guarantee that its proposed pricing and delivery schedules shall remain firm for a period of at least **[Indicate time frame, e.g. 90 days]** following the submission of its Proposal. The Supplier is required to provide Company with Most Favored Customer Status.

(b)   **Pricing**

[Describe below as appropriate]

**Price per Unit for
Quantities of**

Model   _____   _____

Model   _____   _____

Model   _____   _____

**[Possible issues to consider: firm pricing vs. time and materials
pricing, volume discounts, maintenance charges, time frames
etc.]**

(c)   Billing

The Supplier shall invoice Company in a format acceptable to
Company. The Supplier's invoice for billing should include those
fields, as determined by Company, which are necessary for proper
accounting at Company. **[Indicate if a monthly report is
required and what information is needed]**

3.4.6   Company Quality Control Program

Provide a description of Supplier's quality control measures, including
how they have improved Supplier's performance over time.

Provide customer satisfaction data that supports Supplier's commitment to
quality and improving results.

3.4.7   Disaster Recovery Plan

Supplier must submit a copy of its Disaster Recovery Program with its
Proposal and how it would apply to Company.

3.4.8   Implementation Plan

The Supplier shall provide a complete implementation plan that it will
utilize to ensure that no delays are experienced following contract award.
Include details of the level of involvement, if any, expected from
Company, e.g., staff, facilities, etc. This should also include the timeline
for conducting all required research for implementation or installation, for
training, and for meeting all other Company requirements.

3.4.9   Foreign-Based Services

In its Proposal, Supplier shall be required to represent and identify any
service performed by Supplier pursuant to this RFP that shall be provided,
directed, controlled, supervised, or managed through a site located outside

of the United States., and any Company data communication (voice or data) relating to any such service that shall be stored or transmitted, at, in, or through a site located outside of the United States. **[If appropriate]**

3.4.10 M/W/DV BE Questionnaire

Supplier shall complete the M/W/DV/BE questionnaire attached hereto as Attachment B.

3.4.11 Environmental, Health and Safety Requirements

Supplier shall be cognizant of and in compliant with Company' EH&S requirements as contained in Exhibit B to the Proposed Agreement attached hereto as Attachment C.

3.4.12 Code of Conduct Policy

Supplier shall be cognizant of and in compliant with Company' Code of Conduct Policy while providing services on Company' facilities. The Code of Conduct as contained in Exhibit D to the Proposed Agreement, and attached hereto as Attachment D.

4.   Attachments

Attachment A
Intent to Respond Form

INTENT TO RESPOND FORM
FOR
REQUEST FOR PROPOSAL

RFP Name:_____

In response to the Request for Proposal (RFP) dated **[Date]** the undersigned provides notice to Company of its intent to submit a proposal in response thereto.   The undersigned also acknowledges that it has examined the RFP, including without limitation, Sections 1.2 and 2.5 thereof.

Supplier: _____

Address: _____

Authorized
Signature: _____

Printed Name   _____

Title: _____

Date: _____

RETURN TO: [Fill in name and address information that also appears in Section 1.5]

RFP COORDINATOR

ADDRESS:

Attachment B
M/W/DV BE Questionnaire

Company is firmly committed to utilizing qualified minority, women and service-disabled veteran-owned business enterprises and certified small business concerns (M/W/DV BEs) to provide products and services. Company will seek to utilize M/W/DV BEs to the maximum extent practicable, consistent with its procurement policy, to seek out and acquire products and services, which best fit its business needs and requirements, regardless of source. To this end, Company has implemented a strong internal process designed to increase dollars spent directly with diversified suppliers as well as tier 2/subcontracting activities with M/W/DV BEs by its primary suppliers.

M/W/DV BEs are business enterprises that are 51% owned, operated and controlled by a Minority, Woman, Service Disabled or Vietnam-era Veteran. These enterprises must be certified by a recognized third party agency. These agencies may include: NMSDC, WBENC, Office of Small and Minority Business (OSMB), California Utilities Clearinghouse, State Governing Bodies, SBA, Association for Service Disabled Veterans, Native American Business Alliance, US Pan Asian Chamber of Commerce, etc.

Our intent is to give primary suppliers recognition for increasing their expenditures with certified minority- and women-owned businesses. We accept minority- and women-owned certification from all city, state, or federal governmental agencies, Minority Purchasing Councils (MPC's), and other generally recognized certifying agencies.

Note that prospective suppliers responding to this RFP are required to submit to Company a "Tier 2/Subcontracting Utilization Plan" which includes their projected goals and utilization of minority-, women- and disabled veteran-owned business enterprises. The Plan of Action submitted by the Supplier will be an evaluation criterion considered by Company in awarding contracts for its products and services.

Goals:

Company has a corporate-wide goal to increase procurement dollars from Diversified Suppliers and this goal is recommended for inclusion in the tier 2/subcontracting plans of all prospective suppliers. Continuous improvement in the percentage of diversified supplier participation/utilization is expected in every multi-year agreement.

Please complete the following information request and submit it along with any other items you wish to have considered as part of your Diversified Utilization Plan.

   1. Are you a M/W/DV BE? If so, please include a copy of your certification. If you are a M/W/DV BE, but have not been certified or are in the process of being certified, to which agency or advocacy group have you submitted your application?

   Check One: ☐ Yes   ☐ No

   Certifying Agencies:

2.   Who is your designated Supplier Diversity Coordinator?

Name: _____

Title: _____

Telephone Number: _____

Fax Number: _____

Address: _____

State and Zip Code _____

E-Mail Address _____

3. What are your projected M/W/DV BE purchases in direct support of this product or service line? In other words, what are your projections for the utilization of M/W/DV BE business entities in subcontracting activities directly linked to this potential contract?

A.   Specify the product or service to be subcontracted to the M/W/DV BE.

B.   Specify the M/W/DV BE suppliers to be used for this subcontracting activity, include the following: Name, address, telephone number, contact person, and e-mail address.

C.   Estimate the annual percentage of utilization from each M/W/DV BE.

D.   Estimate the annual dollar value from each M/W/DV BE.

A.   _____

B.   _____

C.   _____

D.   _____

4.　　Describe in detail any new or creative solutions that you may offer to utilize M/W/DV BEs.

_____

_____

_____

_____

5.　　Do you agree that as a Primary Supplier to Company you will complete our quarterly Prime Supplier Diversity Performance Report that is due fifteen (15) days after the close of each quarter?

Check One:　☐　Yes　　☐ No

Attachment C
Proposed Agreement

[Purchasing Representative to work with the Company Legal Department to identify the appropriate contract to be provided to Suppliers with this RFP.]

REQUEST FOR QUOTATION EXAMPLE

REQUEST FOR QUOTATION **(THIS IS NOT AN ORDER)**		THIS RFQ ☐ IS ☐ IS NOT A SMALL BUSINESS SET-ASIDE		PAGE OF PAGES
1. REQUEST NO.	2. DATE ISSUED	3. REQUISITION/PURCHASE REQUEST NO.	4. CERT. FOR NAT. DEF. UNDER BDSA REG. 2 AND/OR DMS REG. 1 ▶	RATING
5a. ISSUED BY			6. DELIVER BY (Date)	

5b. FOR INFORMATION CALL (NO COLLECT CALLS)			7. DELIVERY	
NAME	TELEPHONE NUMBER		☐ FOB DESTINATION ☐ OTHER (See Schedule)	
	AREA CODE	NUMBER	9. DESTINATION	
			a. NAME OF CONSIGNEE	

8. TO:

a. NAME	b. COMPANY	b. STREET ADDRESS
c. STREET ADDRESS		c. CITY
d. CITY	e. STATE f. ZIP CODE	d. STATE e. ZIP CODE

10. PLEASE FURNISH QUOTATIONS TO THE ISSUING OFICE IN BLOCK 5a ON OR BEFORE CLOSE OF BUSINESS (Date)

IMPORTANT: This is a request for information, and quotations furnished are not offers. If you are unable to quote, please so indicate on this form and return it to the address in Block 5a. This request does not commit the Government to pay any costs incurred in the preparation of the submission of this quotation or to contract for supplies or service. Supplies are of domestic origin unless otherwise indicated by quoter. Any representations and/or certifications attached to this Request for Quotation must be completed by the quoter.

11. SCHEDULE (Include applicable Federal, State and local taxes)

ITEM NO. (a)	SUPPLIES/ SERVICES (b)	QUANTITY (c)	UNIT (d)	UNIT PRICE (e)	AMOUNT (f)

12. DISCOUNT FOR PROMPT PAYMENT ▶	a. 10 CALENDAR DAYS (%)	b. 20 CALENDAR DAYS (%)	c. 30 CALENDAR DAYS (%)	d. CALENDAR DAYS NUMBER PERCENTAGE

NOTE: Additional provisions and representations ☐ are ☐ are not attached.

13. NAME AND ADDRESS OF QUOTER	14. SIGNATURE OF PERSON AUTHORIZED TO SIGN QUOTATION	15. DATE OF QUOTATION
a. NAME OF QUOTER		
b. STREET ADDRESS	16. SIGNER	
c. COUNTY	a. NAME (Type or print)	b. TELEPHONE AREA CODE
d. CITY e. STATE f. ZIP CODE	c. TITLE (Type or print)	NUMBER

OUTLINE OF UNIFORM COMMERCIAL CODE AND ARTICLE 2

UNIFORM COMMERCIAL CODE

http://www.law.cornell.edu/ucc/
http://en.wikipedia.org/wiki/Uniform_Commercial_Code

Table of Contents
Article 1. General Provisions [Search]
Article 2. Sales [Search]
Article 2A. Leases [Search]
Article 3. Negotiable Instruments [Search]
Article 4. Bank Deposit [Search]
Article 4A. Funds Transfers [Search]
Article 5. Letters of Credit [Search]
Article 6. Bulk Transfers and [Revised] - Bulk Sales [Search]
Article 7. Warehouse Receipts, Bills of Lading and Other Documents of Title
    [Search]
Article 8. Investment Securities [Search]
Article 9. Secured Transactions

Uniform Commercial Code - Article 2

PART 1. SHORT TITLE, GENERAL CONSTRUCTION AND SUBJECT MATTER

- §2-101. Short Title.
- §2-102. Scope; Certain Security and Other Transactions Excluded From This Article.

PART 2. FORM, FORMATION AND READJUSTMENT OF CONTRACT

PART 3. GENERAL OBLIGATION AND CONSTRUCTION OF CONTRACT

PART 7. REMEDIES

- §2-723. Proof of Market Price: Time and Place.
- §2-724. Admissibility of Market Quotations.
- §2-725. Statute of Limitations in Contracts for Sale.

IMPORTANT U.S. IMPORT/EXPORT REGULATIONS

- **Export Administration Regulations Database**
  U.S. Dept of Commerce—Bureau of Industry & Security
  http://www.access.gpo.gov/bis/ear/ear_data.html

- **Arms Export Control Act (AECA)**
- **International Trafficking in Arms Regulations (ITAR)**
  U.S. Dept. of State—Defense Trade Controls
  http://www.pmdtc.org

- **International Emergency Economic Powers Act (IEEPA)**
- **Money Laundering—18 USC Section 1956**
  U.S. Treasury Dept—Office of Foreign Assets Control
  http://www.treas.gov/offices/enforcement/publications/

- **Customs-Trade Partnership Against Terrorism (C-TPAT)**
  U.S. Customs & Border Protection
  http://www.customs.gov/xp/cgov/import/commercial_enforcement/ctpat/

- **Export Licensing**
- Introduction to Commerce Department Export Controls
  http://www.bis.doc.gov/Licensing/exportingbasics.htm

- **Foreign Trade Zones Act**
  http://ia.ita.doc.gov/ftzpage/19uscftz/ch1a.html

- **Trade Compliance Center**
  http://tcc.export.gov/Trade_Agreements/index.asp

SAMPLE TERMS AND CONDITIONS

PURCHASE ORDER TERMS AND CONDITIONS

1. CONTRACT. This Purchase Order includes these Purchase Order Terms and Conditions, the purchase order form (the "Form") and any exhibits thereto. The Contract Documents consist of this Purchase Order, and all of the following supplied by Purchaser; the General Conditions, Supplementary Conditions and the Specifications (where applicable), and all addenda issued before, and all Modifications issued after execution of this Purchase Order. These form the Contract, and all are as fully a part of the Contract as if attached to this Purchase Order or fully set forth herein. Commencing performance of or accepting this Purchase Order shall indicate Supplier's intent to be bound by the terms and conditions of the Contract Documents (the "PO Terms"), shall constitute an acceptance by Supplier of each of the PO Terms, and shall form a contract under the laws of the Commonwealth of Pennsylvania. The Contract Documents shall constitute the entire agreement between the parties with respect to the subject matter of this Contract and may not be modified, added to or rescinded except by a subsequent writing signed by Purchaser. Notice of objection is hereby given to any different or additional terms in Supplier's quotations, acknowledgments, invoices, or in any other communication from Supplier unless Purchaser expressly agrees to such terms in writing. Payment, acceptance of goods, or inaction by Purchaser shall not constitute Purchaser's consent to or acceptance of any such terms.

2. PARTIES. a. Purchaser or Owner (terms are interchangeable): ——————— - Of ————————

b. Supplier or Contractor (terms are interchangeable): As set forth on the Form.

3. TERMS. a. The term "goods" includes goods, material, chattels, equipment, machinery, manufactured articles, merchandise, fixtures, products, appliances, plant and any other items to be supplied pursuant to this Purchase Order. b. The term "warranty" includes warranties, guarantees, representations and promises.

4. DELIVERY. The goods shall be tendered by delivery to Purchaser at the time and place specified in the ASHIP TO@ Section on the Form. The times set forth for delivery are of the essence. Supplier is responsible for maintaining and providing proof of delivery. Packing lists must accompany each case or parcel, showing this POs number and a complete description of contents. Supplier shall prepay all transportation charges. If transportation of the goods is undertaken by an entity other than Supplier, Supplier shall be responsible for and handle all claims against such entity for shortages, damages, theft and other such occurrences.

5. IDENTIFICATION/RISK OF LOSS/TITLE. Identification of the goods shall occur as soon as the Purchase Offer is received by Supplier. Risk of loss of and clear title to the goods shall pass to Purchaser at the time that conforming goods are received and accepted by Purchaser.

6. PURCHASE PRICE. The Purchase Order Total Price (also referred to as the Contract Sum) and Unit Prices shall be as specified on the Form, subject to Section 9 hereof. They shall not include sales and use taxes for which an exemption is applicable. Purchaser shall have no responsibility for payment of over shipments, goods not delivered due to shortages, theft, etc., or otherwise non-conforming shipments. Purchaser's count shall be accepted as final and conclusive for all shipments. If Purchase Price is omitted and is not covered by a blanket order or agreement, this order is to be filled at the lower of (i) the price last quoted or charged or (ii) the lowest prevailing market price. All prices are FOB Purchaser's on-Site receiving area unless otherwise specified. If shipment is indicated as FOB Supplier's plant, Supplier will arrange for shipping, prepay the freight charges and add them to the invoice. Collect shipments will be returned at Supplier's expense.

7. PAYMENT. a. Payment shall be processed generally as follows except that in the event of a conflict with the terms of the General Conditions, the terms of the General Conditions shall prevail. b. For contracts not requiring on-Site Work, payment shall be processed generally as follows subject to the General Conditions. One invoice shall be submitted for the Purchase Order. No invoices will be processed for payment until Purchaser has received goods, has inspected them and has determined that they are conforming. Invoices shall be considered as dated the later of the day the invoice is received or the day the goods are received and accepted by Purchaser. Payment for conforming goods shall be paid within fifty (50) days of the later of the date of Final Completion or the date of the invoice. With respect to invoices covering mechanical equipment and similar goods which cannot immediately be put into operation, Purchaser reserves the right to withhold from payment of such invoice retainage of 10% of the amount thereof pending approval of the operation of such equipment and/or goods. Purchaser shall pay for the goods by check. Payments on cash discount items will be rendered less any applicable cash discount.

8. WARRANTIES. a. Supplier warrants to Purchaser that all items covered by this Purchase Order conform to the samples, drawings, specifications, plans, or other descriptions provided by Purchaser (collectively, "Specifications"). Suppliers are not authorized to substitute. All goods shall be merchantable; fit for Purchaser's intended purpose; of good material, workmanship and design; and free from defect. Supplier also guarantees that the goods are of sufficient size or capacity to perform as specified.

b. Supplier agrees that Purchaser and any representative designated by Purchaser, for itself and on behalf of Purchaser ("Purchaser's Representative"), shall have the benefit of all manufacturers warranties, express or implied, issued on or applicable to the goods and Supplier authorizes Purchaser and/or Purchaser's Representative to obtain the customary services furnished in connection with such warranties and guaranties. Supplier hereby assigns such warranties to Purchaser.

c. This Purchase Order incorporates by reference any and all warranties (express, implied, oral or written) made by Supplier prior to or at the time this Purchase Order is accepted, including those contained in brochures, catalogues, advertisements, owner's manuals, etc., provided that in the event of a conflict, the warranty providing the most protection to Purchaser shall prevail.

d. All warranties shall survive inspection, acceptance and payment.

e. Supplier agrees to repair or replace free of charge any goods or parts of goods which prove defective or which operate unsatisfactorily. This warranty does not apply to normal effects of corrosion or wear and tear. Such remedies shall be available to Purchaser in addition to all others afforded to it by this Contract or at law or equity.

9. RIGHT OF INSPECTION. Within a reasonable time after delivery of the goods in accordance with Section 4 Purchaser shall have the right to inspect the goods to determine their conformity with the Specifications. Thirty (30) days from the date of delivery or installation is deemed to be the reasonable time for Purchaser to inspect the goods. If all or any part of the goods are found to be non-conforming, Purchaser may reject such non-conforming goods, whereupon such rejected goods promptly shall be removed by Supplier at Supplier's cost, and the Purchase Price with respect to such rejected goods either shall be refunded by Supplier if already paid, or shall be reduced if still owing. In either case, if Purchaser so directs in writing, Supplier shall promptly replace such non-conforming goods with goods conforming to the Specifications. All direct and incidental costs of rejecting and removing such non-conforming goods shall be borne by Supplier.

10. REMEDIES. In addition to remedies provided in the Contract Documents, Purchaser shall have all other rights and remedies available under applicable law. NOTWITHSTANDING ANYTHING TO THE CONTRARY CONTAINED IN THE CONTRACT DOCUMENTS, IN NO EVENT SHALL SUPPLIER BE ENTITLED TO ANY PAYMENT ON ACCOUNT OF LOST PROFITS OR CONSEQUENTIAL DAMAGES IN CONNECTION WITH ANY TERMINATION OF

THE CONTRACT, OR OTHERWISE IN CONNECTION WITH THE CONTRACT.

11. INDEMNIFICATION. To the fullest extent permitted by law, Supplier shall indemnify and hold harmless Purchaser, the Commonwealth of Pennsylvania and any Purchaser's Representative and all of their respective trustees, directors, officers, employees and agents (collectively, "Goods Indemnities") from and against all claims, liabilities, damages, losses, costs (including, without limitation, reasonable legal fees) and expenses (collectively, "Claims"), arising from or relating to the undertaking of Supplier hereunder or any defect(s) in the goods supplied, provided such Claims are caused in whole or in part by any negligent act, omission, recklessness or willful misconduct of Supplier or anyone for whose acts Supplier may be liable, or provided Supplier may be held responsible for same under products liability law or under other applicable legal or equitable principles. Supplier further agrees to assume the defense of any suit brought against Goods Indemnities and to protect Goods Indemnities from all Claims arising out of claims for infringement of any patent, invention, design, trademark or copyright in connection with the goods.

12. REGULATORY COMPLIANCE AND NONDISCRIMINATION. The Supplier must comply with all applicable laws, ordinances, rules, regulations and orders of any public authority having jurisdiction ("Laws") including, without limitation the applicable provisions of the following and any Laws referenced in the General Conditions, all as amended and in effect as of the date of this order: the Anti-Kickback Act (41 U.S.C. Sections 51 *et seq*), the Civil Rights Act of 1964 (42 U.S.C. Section 2000a *et seq.*), Executive Orders 11246 and 11375, the Age Discrimination in Employment Act of 1967 (29 U.S.C. Section 621 *et seq.*), the Rehabilitation Act of 1973 (29 U.S.C. Sections 701 *et seq.*), the Americans With Disabilities Act of 1990 (42 U.S.C. Section 12101 *et seq.*), and of all other applicable Laws dealing with labor and wages, workmen's compensation, employer liability, unemployment compensation, old age benefits, safety, antitrust and anti-collusion, fair trade, the environment, equal employment opportunity and discrimination on the basis of race, color, religion, gender, national origin, veteran's status or disability.

13. WAIVER OF LIENS

a. Supplier, for itself and for all its Subcontractors, agrees that no mechanic's or materialman's lien or other claim shall be filed or maintained by Supplier or by any Subcontractor, laborer or any other person, whatsoever, for or on account of any work done on goods furnished under this Contract. This agreement shall be an independent contract.

b. In every subcontract entered into by Supplier after the execution and delivery of the Contract or in connection herewith, Supplier shall incorporate a provision similar to the foregoing subsection to the effect that neither the Subcontractor nor any party acting through or under it shall file or maintain any mechanic's lien or other claim against Purchaser in connection with the work.

14. WAIVER OF BREACH. Waiver, forbearance or inaction by Purchaser of a breach by Supplier of any PO Term shall not be deemed a waiver of future compliance with all PO Terms, and all such PO Terms shall remain in full force and effect as to future performances.

15. CANCELLATION. If the subject matter of this Purchase Order (or any design, prototype, drawing, or other sample) is subject to prior review and approval by Purchaser, Purchaser may cancel this Purchase Order upon its determination that such design, prototype, drawing or sample does not conform to any applicable project specifications; and Purchaser shall have no further obligations or liability hereunder.

16. ASSIGNMENT/DELEGATION. Supplier shall neither assign any right or interest in this contract, nor delegate any obligation owed by it hereunder without the prior written consent of Purchaser. Any attempted assignment or delegation absent Purchaser's consent shall be wholly void and totally ineffective for all purposes.

17. COMMUNICATIONS. With the exception of invoices and monthly statements of account, which are to be directed to————— Accounts Payable, all communications and acknowledgments from Supplier concerning this Purchase Order must be directed to————— Purchasing Department.

18. TAXES. Purchaser's tax exemption certificate will be supplied upon request. Supplier shall provide Purchaser with an executed IRS form W-9 prior to submission of the initial invoice.

19. NON-COLLUSIVE BIDDING. Supplier certifies that the Purchase Price has been determined independently without collusion with Purchaser's employees or any other supplier.

20. RIGHT TO AUDIT. Supplier shall provide Purchaser reasonable access to its books, documents and records as necessary to ensure Supplier's compliance with the provisions of the Contract Documents.

21. MISCELLANEOUS. a. No agreement or other understanding in any way modifying the Contract Documents shall be binding upon Purchaser unless made or accepted by Purchaser in writing. This Purchase Order shall be subject to modification, amendment and/or cancellation by Purchaser in event of fire, accident, strike, Government acts or other conditions beyond Purchaser's control. Purchaser shall promptly provide to Supplier written notice of the occurrence of such events requiring such modification, amendment and/or cancellation. b. This writing and the other Contract Documents is intended by the parties as a final expression of their agreement with respect to the subject matter hereof. c. Any provision in the Contract Documents that is held to be inoperative, unenforceable, voidable or invalid in any jurisdiction shall as to that jurisdiction, be ineffective, unenforceable, void or invalid without affecting the remaining provisions, or the enforce ability of all provisions in any other jurisdiction and to this end, the provisions hereof are declared to be severable. The contract resulting from the acceptance of this Purchase Order is to be governed by and construed in

accordance with the laws of the Commonwealth of Pennsylvania without regard to the choice of laws provisions thereof. The Supplier agrees to bring any federal or state legal proceeding arising under this Contract in which the Commonwealth of Pennsylvania or Purchaser is a party, in a court of competent jurisdiction within the City of Philadelphia and Commonwealth of Pennsylvania. This Section shall not be construed to limit any rights a party may have to intervene in any action, wherever pending, in which one of the others is a party. e. All indemnification, payment, warranty, lien waiver, title and remedies provisions shall survive the termination of expiration of this Purchase Order.

ADDITIONAL TERMS AND CONDITIONS

(IF APPLICABLE)   1. Approved Equal: Wherever the term "or approved equal" is used herein, it is to be understood that reference to the specified trade name, brand name, manufacturer's name, model number and/or catalog number has been made solely for the purpose of indicating the minimum standard of quality required in material, workmanship and service. Any alternate item quoted on shall be clearly identified and will be subject to review prior to acceptance by————— .

2. Damage To————— Property: The contractor shall be totally responsible for any damages done to————— property during delivery, assembly, installation/placement of the materials and/or the furnishing of the services described herein and shall repair or cause to be repaired at his expense any such damages in a manner satisfactory to————— .

3. Removal of Debris: The contractor shall be totally responsible for the daily removal of debris (empty cartons, crates, packing material, etc.) Resulting from delivery, assembly and/or installation/placement of material or the furnishing of services described herein, from————— property, as required by fire code regulations. Rubbish must not remain overnight. FAILURE TO COMPLY WITH THIS PROVISION WILL RESULT IN CONTRACTOR PAYING————— , AS LIQUIDATED DAMAGES AND NOT AS A PENALTY FOR SUCH FAILURE, THE SUM OF $100.00 (ONE HUNDRED DOLLARS) PER DAY, FOR EACH DAY THAT DEBRIS REMAINS ON————— PROPERTY, CORRESPONDING AMOUNT SHALL AUTOMATICALLY BE DEDUCTED FROM CONTRACTOR'S INVOICE.

GENERAL TERMS & CONDITIONS OF THIS REQUEST

(IF APPLICABLE)   1. Appropriate Trade Labor: All companies shall indicate how they would attempt to avoid and/or resolve work stoppages or labor unrest on the project and provide a satisfactory explanation of any work stoppages or labor unrest which occurred on projects they have worked during the preceding five-year period. Companies may be required to provide sufficient evidence of an established satisfactory grievance procedure for the resolution of disputes between the bidder and employees. Such procedure shall continue to be followed by the contractor for the duration of the project. All Companies shall provide sufficient evidence of an active and satisfactory federally or state approved apprenticeship program or equivalent. The contractor shall comply with such program for the duration of the project. Contractor shall maintain on-site work forces compatible with those of other on -site contractors for the duration of the contract

2. Insurance agrees to maintain, at its expense, for the full term of this contract and extension thereof, insurance coverage, protecting itself and———————— from losses incurred and/or all claims, directly or indirectly, arising out of, relating to, or resulting from the furnishing of the services described herein. The Contractor must have coverage, which includes commercial general liability with limits of not less than $2,000,000 per occurrence and general aggregate. In addition, the Contractor must provide———————— with a Certificate of Insurance which names———————— of the Commonwealth System of Higher Education as an "additional insured" solely with respect to Contractor's liability hereunder, and include the additional insured endorsement. Coverage must also include Automobile Liability of no less than $1,000,000. Worker's Compensation coverage with at least statutory limits.

Contractor and the University shall agree to carry their own fire insurance coverage. The University will assume no responsibility for Contractors equipment on University premises in the event of a fire. Contractor shall be totally liable for payment of all costs and expenses that the Contractor and the University incur as a result of or in any way related to fire attributable to the equipment or services being provided by the Contractor.

Contractor shall be totally responsible for and "deductible" on its insurance policy.

Thirty days notice is to be provided to———————— in the event of any amendment to or cancellation of insurance coverage. In the event of expiration of Contractor insurance policy during the term of this contract or any extension thereof, Contractor shall provide———————— with a current certificate of insurance.

LINKS TO RELATED PROFESSIONAL ORGANIZATIONS

3PL Central Inc   http://www.3plcentral.com
A.T. Kearney Procurement Solutions   http://www.atkearneyprocurement-solutions.com
ADR International   http://www.adr-international.com
APCO International   http://www.apcointl.org
APICS Online   http://www.apics.org
ATM Forum   http://www.atmforum.com
AccountantsWorld.com   http://www.accountantsworld.com
American Arbitration Association   http://www.adr.org
American Association of Exporters & Importers   http://www.aaei.org/index.asp
American Boiler and Manufacturers Association   http://www.abma.com
American Electronics Association   http://www.aeanet.org
American Farm Bureau Federation   http://www.fb.com
American India Foundation [The]   http://www.aifoundation.org
American Institute of Certified Public Accountants   http://www.aicpa.org
American Institute of Graphic Arts   http://www.aiga.org
American Management Association   http://www.amanet.org
American Mobile Telecommunications Association   http://www.amtausa.org
American National Standards Institute   http://www.ansi.org
American Psychological Association   http://www.apa.org
American Purchasing Society (The)   http://www.american-purchasing.com
American Society for Testing and Materials   http://www.astm.org
American Society of Engineering & Education   http://www.asee.org
American Society of Heating Refrigeration & Air   http://www.ashrae.org
American Society of Mechanical Engineers   http://www.asme.org
American Society of Transportation & Logistics (The)   http://www.astl.org
American Staffing Association   http://www.natss.org
Association of Professional Material Handling Consultants

http://www.mhia.org/PS/PS_APMHC_WhatIsAPMHC.cfm
Association for Computing Machinery, San Francisco   http://www.sfbayacm.
   org/#
Association for Corporate Growth   http://www.acg.org
Association for High Technology Distribution   http://www.ahtd.org
Association for Interactive Marketing   http://www.interactivehq.org
Association for Local Telecommunications Services   http://www.alts.org
Association for Manufacturing Technology   http://www.mfgtech.org
   http://www.globalservicesmedia.com
Association for Operations Management (The)   http://www.apics.org
Association for Standards and Practices   http://www.e-centre.org.uk
Association for Women in Computing   http://www.awc-hq.org
Association of Communications Enterprises   http://www.ascent.org
Business Software Alliance   http://www.bsa.org
CA Association of Public Purchasing Officers Inc   http://www.cappo.org
CDMA Development Group   http://www.cdg.org
Canadian Association of Supply Chain & Logistics Management
   http://www.infochain.org
Canadian Wireless Telecommunications Association   http://www.cwta.ca
Cellular Telecommunications Industry Assoc.   http://www.wow-com.com
Chartered Institute of Purchasing & Supply (The)   http://www.cips.org
Churchill Club of Silicon Valley   http://www.churchillclub.com
Comergent Inc   http://www.comergent.com
Commonwealth Club of California   http://www.commonwealthclub.org
CompactFlash Association   http://www.compactflash.org
Competitive Telecommunications Association   http://www.comptel.org
Computer Law Association [The]   http://cla.org
Computing Technology Industry Association   http://www.comptia.com
Computing Technology Industry Association Inc (The)   http://www.comptia.org
Consultant-News.com   http://www.consultant-news.com
Consumer Electronics Association   http://www.ce.org
Council of Logistics Management   http://www.clm1.org
Council of Supply Chain Management Professionals   http://www.cscmp.org
Counselors to America's Small Business - SF, CA   http://www.sfscore.com
Counselors to America's Small Business - San Jose   #http://www.svscore.org
Data Interchange Standards Association [The]   http://www.disa.org
Demand Management Inc   http://www.demandsolutions.com
Dun & Bradstreet   http://www.dnb.com/us
E-Certa   http://www.e-certa.com
EAN Intl / Uniform Code Council, Inc   http://www.ean-ucc.org/home.htm
EC Sourcing Group   http://www.ecsourcinggroup.com
Electronic Commerce Code Management Assoc   http://www.eccma.org
Electronic Design Automation Consortium   http://www.edac.org/

Electronic Industries Alliance   http://www.eia.org
Electronic Representatives Association   http://www.era.org/
Electronics Industry Data Exchange Association   http://www.eidx.org/index.html
Employment Policy Foundation   http://www.epf.org
Emptoris Inc   http://www.emptoris.com
Enterprise Content Management Association (The)   http://www.aiim.org
Equipment Leasing Association   http://www.elaonline.com
Equipment Leasing Association of America   http://elaonline.com
Expense Management Solutions Inc   http://www.expensemanagement.com
Fabless Semiconductor Association   http://www.fsa.or
Global Academy Online Inc   http://www.globalacademyonline.com
Global Business Network   #http://www.gbn.org
Global Services   http://www.globalservicesmedia.com
Global Wireless Education Consortium   http://www.gwec.org
Hispanic Association on Corporate Responsibility   http://www.hacr.org
IBX   http://www.ibxeurope.com
ICG Commerce   http://www.icgcommerce.com
Iasta.com Inc   http://www.iasta.com
Industrial Distribution Association   http://www.ida-assoc.org
Industrial Telecommunications Association   http://www.ita-relay.com
Insight Inc   http://www.insight-mss.com
Institute for Supply Management   http://www.ism.ws
Institute of Electrical and Electronic Engineers   http://www.ieee.org
Institute of Logistical Management   http://www.logistics-edu.com
Institute of Packaging Professionals (The)   http://www.iopp.org
Instrument Society of America   http://www.isa.org
Insurance Information Institute   http://www.iii.org
International Network of Women in Technology   http://www.witi.com
International Society for Six Sigma Certifications   http://www.isssc3.com
International Society of Logistics (The)   http://www.sole.org
International Warehouse Logistics Association (The)   http://www.iwla.com
International Federation of Purchasing and Materials Management   http://www.svme.ch/ifpmm/english/index.html
Irish Institute of Purchasing and Materials Management   http://www.iipmm.ie
MIT Stanford Venture Laboratory   #http://www.vlab.org
Massachusetts Software Council Inc   http://www.swcouncil.org
Material Handling Industry of America   http://www.mhia.org
Materials Information Society   http://www.asm-intl.org
Mechanical Contractors Association of America   http://www.mcaa.org
Mobile Wireless Internet Forum   http://www.mwif.org
National Association of Computer Consultant Businesses   http://www.naccb.org
National Association of Purchasing Card Professionals   http://www.napcp.org

National Association of Broadcasters [The]   http://www.nab.org
National Association of Procurement Professionals
    http://www.nappconference.com
National Association of Purchasing & Payables
    http://www.nappconference.com
National Association of Purchasing Card Professionals (The)
    http://www.napcp.org
National Business & Disability Council   http://www.business-disability.com
National Business Incubation Association   http://www.nbia.org
National Center for Manufacturing Sciences   http://www.ncms.or
National Computer Security Association   http://www.icsa.net
National Education Association   http://www.nea.org#
National Electrical Manufacturers Association   http://www.nema.org
National Electronics Manufacturing Initiative   http://www.nemi.org
National Fluid Power Association   http://www.nfpa.com
National Institute of Governmental Purchasing   http://www.nigp.org
National Tooling & Machining Association   http://www.ntma.org
National Vehicle Leasing Association   http://www.nvla.org
New Monterey Business Association   http://www.newmonterey.org
Next Level Purchasing   http://www.nextlevelpurchasing.com
Northern CA Electronics Rep Association   http://www.ncalera.org
PCI Industrial Computer Manufacturers Group   http://www.picmg.com
PDA Industry Association   http://www.pdaia.org
Pacific Industrial and Business Association   http://www.piba.org
Portable Computer and Communications Association   http://www.pcca.org
Power Transmission Distributors Association   http://www.ptda.org
Product Development & Management Association   http://www.pdma.org
Professional and Technical Consultants Association   http://www.patca.org/main
Promotion Marketing Association Inc   http://www.pmalink.org
Robotics Industries Association   #http://www.robotics.org
SCSI Trade Association   http://www.scsita.org
SDForum   #http://www.sdforum.org
Silicon Valley Help Desk Institute [The]   http://www.svhdi.com
Silicon Valley Manufacturing Group   http://www.svmg.org
Singapore Institute of Purchasing & Materials Management
    http://www.sipmm.org.sg
Society of Incentive & Travel Executives   http://www.site-intl.org
Society of Manufacturing Engineers   http://www.sme.org
Society of Professional Consultants [The]   http://www.spconsultants.org
Society of Women Engineers   http://www.swe.org
Software & Information Industry Association   http://www.spa.org/
Software Development Forum   http://www.sdforum.org
Source One Management Services LLC   http://www.sourceoneinc.com

Special Libraries Association   http://www.sla.org
Supplier Excellence Alliance   http://www.seaonline.org
Supply & Demand Chain Executive   http://www.sdcexec.com
Supply Chain Consultants Inc   http://www.supplychain.com
Supply Management.com   http://www.supplymanagement.co.uk
SupplyChainBrain.com   http://www.supplychainbrain.com
Technology Forecasters Inc   http://www.techforecasters.com
Tek-Tips Forums   http://www.tek-tips.com
The Conference Board   http://www.conference-board.org
The Institute of Operations Management   http://www.iomnet.org.uk
The Open Group Messaging Forum   http://www.opengroup.org/messaging
Trade Show Exhibitors Association   http://www.tsea.org
UCCnet Inc   http://knowledgebase.uccnet.org
United States Internet Service Provider Association   http://www.cix.org/

BIBLIOGRAPHY

CHAPTER 1 PROCUREMENT AND BEST BUSINESS PRACTICES

Benton, W. C. *Purchasing and Supply Management*, 2nd ed. McGraw-Hill/Irwin, 2009.

Burt, David, et al. *World Class Supply Management: The Key to Supply Chain Management*, 8th ed. New York: McGraw-Hill, 2009.

Cavinato, Joseph, et al. *The Purchasing Handbook: A Guide for the Purchasing and Supply Professional*, 6th ed. New York: McGraw-Hill, 2000.

Leenders, Michiel, et al. *Purchasing & Supply Management*, 14th ed. New York: McGraw-Hill, 2010.

Ostring, Pirkko. *Profit-Focused Supplier Management: How to Identify Risks and Recognize Opportunities*. New York: AMACOM, 2004.

CHAPTER 2 SOURCING

Benton, W. C. *Purchasing and Supply Management*, 2nd ed. McGraw-Hill/Irwin, 2009.

Burt, David, et al. *World Class Supply Management: The Key to Supply Chain Management*, 8th ed. New York: McGraw-Hill, 2009.

Leenders, Michiel, et al. *Purchasing & Supply Management*, 14th ed. New York: McGraw-Hill, 2010.

Ostring, Pirkko. *Profit-Focused Supplier Management: How to Identify Risks and Recognize Opportunities*. New York: AMACOM, 2004.

CHAPTER 3 SELECTING SUPPLIERS AND MEASURING PERFORMANCE

Benton, W. C. *Purchasing and Supply Management*, 2nd ed. McGraw-Hill/Irwin, 2009.

Burt, David, et al. *World Class Supply Management: The Key to Supply Chain Management*, 8th ed. New York: McGraw-Hill, 2009.

Leenders, Michiel, et al. *Purchasing & Supply Management*, 14th ed. New York: McGraw-Hill, 2010.

Ostring, Pirkko. *Profit-Focused Supplier Management: How to Identify Risks and Recognize Opportunities*. New York: AMACOM, 2004.

CHAPTER 4 FORMING CONTRACTS

Benton, W. C. *Purchasing and Supply Management*, 2nd ed. McGraw-Hill/Irwin, 2009.

Burt, David, et al. *World Class Supply Management: The Key to Supply Chain Management*, 8th ed. New York: McGraw-Hill, 2009.

Cavinato, Joseph, et al. *The Purchasing Handbook: A Guide for the Purchasing and Supply Professional*, 6th ed. New York: McGraw-Hill, 2000.

Leenders, Michiel, et al. *Purchasing & Supply Management*, 14th ed. New York: McGraw-Hill, 2010.

CHAPTER 5 ADMINISTERING CONTRACTS

Burt, David, et al. *World Class Supply Management: The Key to Supply Chain Management*, 8th ed. New York: McGraw-Hill, 2009.

Cavinato, Joseph, et al. *The Purchasing Handbook: A Guide for the Purchasing and Supply Professional*, 6th ed. New York: McGraw-Hill, 2000.

Christopher, Martin. *Logistics & Supply Chain Management: Creating Value-Adding Networks*, 4th ed. *Financial Times*, Prentice Hall, 2011.

CHAPTER 6 MANAGING PROJECTS

Bolstorff, Peter. *Supply Chain Excellence: A Handbook for Dramatic Improvement Using the SCOR Model*, 3rd ed. American Management Association, 2011.

Chase, Richard. *Operations Management for Competitive Advantage*, 12th ed. New York: McGraw-Hill/Irwin, 2008.

Gray, Clifford, et al. *Project Management: The Managerial Process*, 4th ed. New York: McGrawHill/Irwin, 2008.

Kerzner, Harold. *Project Management: A Systems Approach to Planning, Scheduling, and Controlling*, 10th ed. Hoboken, NJ: John Wiley & Sons, 2009.

Stevenson, William, J. *Operations Management*, 11th ed. New York: McGraw-Hill/Irwin, 2011.

CHAPTER 7 MANAGING NEGOTIATIONS

Benton, W. C. *Purchasing and Supply Management*, 2nd ed. McGraw-Hill/Irwin, 2009.

Brett, Jeanne. *Negotiating Globally: How to Negotiate Deals, Resolve Disputes, and Make Decisions Across Cultural Boundaries*, 2nd ed. New York: Jossey Bass, 2007.

Cavinato, Joseph, et al. *The Purchasing Handbook: A Guide for the Purchasing and Supply Professional*, 6th ed. New York: McGraw-Hill, 2000.

Geraghty, Michael. *Anybody Can Negotiate—Even You!: How to Become a Master Negotiator*. iUniverse, Inc., 2006.

Stark, Peter, et al. *The Only Negotiating Guide You'll Ever Need: 101 Ways to Win Every Time in Any Situation*. New York: First Broadway Books, 2003.

CHAPTER 8 USING COMPUTER-BASED SYSTEMS

Arnold, Tony, et al. *Introduction to Materials Management*, 7th ed. Columbus: Prentice Hall, 2011.

Benton, W. C. *Purchasing and Supply Management*, 2nd ed. McGraw-Hill/Irwin, 2009.

Burt, David, et al. *World Class Supply Management: The Key to Supply Chain Management*, 8th ed. New York: McGraw-Hill, 2009.

Chase, Richard. *Operations Management for Competitive Advantage*, 12th ed. New York: McGraw-Hill/Irwin, 2008.

Handfield, Robert, et al. *Supply Chain Redesign: Transforming Supply Chains into Integrated Value Systems*, 1st ed. *Financial Times*, Prentice Hall, 2002.

Leenders, Michiel, et al. *Purchasing & Supply Management*, 14th ed. New York: McGraw-Hill, 2010.

Nelson, Dave, et al. *The Purchasing Machine: How the Top Ten Companies Use Best Practices to Manage Their Supply Chains*. New York: Free Press, 2001.

Simchi-Levi, David, et al. *Managing the Supply Chain: The Definitive Guide for the Business Professional*. New York: McGraw-Hill, 2004.

Walker, William. *Supply Chain Architecture: A Blueprint for Networking the Flow of Material, Information and Cash*. Boca Raton: CRC Press, 2005.

CHAPTER 9 MANAGING QUALITY

Benton, W. C. *Purchasing and Supply Management*, 2nd ed. McGraw-Hill/Irwin, 2009.

Burt, David, et al. *World Class Supply Management: The Key to Supply Chain Management*, 8th ed. New York: McGraw-Hill, 2009.

Cachon, Gerard. *Matching Supply with Demand: An Introduction to Operations Management*, 3rd ed. New York: McGraw-Hill/Irwin, 2012.

Cavinato, Joseph, et al. T*he Purchasing Handbook: A Guide for the Purchasing and Supply Professional*, 6th ed. New York: McGraw-Hill, 2000.

Chase, Richard. *Operations Management for Competitive Advantage*, 12th ed. New York: McGraw-Hill/Irwin, 2008.

Leenders, Michiel, et al. *Purchasing & Supply Management*, 14th ed. New York: McGraw-Hill, 2010.

Stevenson, William, J. *Operations Management*, 11th ed. New York: McGraw-Hill/Irwin, 2011.

CHAPTER 10 MAINTAINING INTERNAL RELATIONS

Benton, W. C. *Purchasing and Supply Management*, 2nd ed. McGraw-Hill/Irwin, 2009.

Burt, David, et al. *World Class Supply Management: The Key to Supply Chain Management*, 8th ed. New York: McGraw-Hill, 2009.

Greenhalgh, Leonard. *Managing Strategic Relationships: The Key to Business Success*. New York: Free Press, 2001.

Handfield, Robert, et al. *Supply Chain Redesign: Transforming Supply Chains into Integrated Value Systems*,1st ed. *Financial Times*, Prentice Hall, 2002.

Leenders, Michiel, et al. *Purchasing & Supply Management*, 14th ed. New York: McGraw-Hill, 2010.

CHAPTER 11 SUPPLIER RELATIONSHIP MANAGEMENT

Benton, W. C. *Purchasing and Supply Management*, 2nd ed. McGraw-Hill/Irwin, 2009.

Cavinato, Joseph, et al. *The Purchasing Handbook: A Guide for the Purchasing and Supply Professional*, 6th ed. New York: McGraw-Hill, 2000.

Christopher, Martin. *Logistics & Supply Chain Management: Creating Value-Adding Networks*, 4th ed. *Financial Times*, Prentice Hall, 2011.

Handfield, Robert, et al. *Supply Chain Redesign: Transforming Supply Chains into Integrated Value Systems*,1st ed. *Financial Times*, Prentice Hall, 2002.

Neef, Dale. *The Supply Chain Imperative: How to Ensure Ethical Behavior in Your Global Suppliers*. New York: AMACOM, 2004.

Nelson, Dave, et al. *The Purchasing Machine: How the Top Ten Companies Use Best Practices to Manage Their Supply Chains*. New York: Free Press, 2001.

Simchi-Levi, David. *Designing and Managing the Supply Chain*, 3rd ed. New York: McGrawHill/Irwin, 2008.

Simchi-Levi, David, et al. *Managing the Supply Chain: The Definitive Guide for the Business Professional*. New York: McGraw-Hill, 2004.

CHAPTER 12 MAKING SOUND SOURCING DECISIONS

Benton, W. C. *Purchasing and Supply Management*, 2nd ed. McGraw-Hill/Irwin, 2009.

Brown, Douglas, et al. *The Black Book of Outsourcing: How to Manage the Changes, Challenges, and Opportunities*. New York: John Wiley & Sons, 2005.

Burt, David, et al. *World Class Supply Management: The Key to Supply Chain Management*, 8th ed. New York: McGraw-Hill, 2009.

Leenders, Michiel, et al. Purchasing & Supply Management, 14th ed. New York: McGraw-Hill, 2010.

Mayer, David. *Business Leasing for Dummies.* New York: Hungry Minds Inc., 2001.

Nevitt, Peter, et al. *Equipment Leasing*, 4th ed. New Hope, PA: Frank J, Fabozzi Assoc., 2000.

Ostring, Pirkko. *Profit-Focused Supplier Management: How to Identify Risks and Recognize Opportunities.* New York: AMACOM, 2004.

Simchi-Levi, David *Designing and Managing the Supply Chain*, 3rd ed. McGrawHill/Irwin, 2008.

Stevenson, William, J. *Operations Management*, 11th ed. New York: McGraw-Hill/Irwin, 2011.

CHAPTER 13 MANAGING MATERIAL AND SUPPLY OPERATIONS

Arnold, Tony, et al. *Introduction to Materials Management*, 7th ed. Columbus, OH: Prentice Hall, 2011.

Benton, W. C. *Purchasing and Supply Management*, 2nd ed. New York: McGraw-Hill/Irwin, 2009.

Cachon, Gerard. *Matching Supply with Demand: An Introduction to Operations Management*, 3rd ed. New York: McGraw-Hill/Irwin, 2012.

Chase, Richard. *Operations Management for Competitive Advantage*, 12th ed. New York: McGraw-Hill/Irwin, 2008.

Leenders, Michiel, et al. *Purchasing & Supply Management*, 14th ed. New York: McGraw-Hill, 2010.

Simchi-Levi, David. *Designing and Managing the Supply Chain*, 3rd ed. McGrawHill/Irwin, 2008.

Simchi-Levi, David, et al. *Managing the Supply Chain: The Definitive Guide for the Business Professional.* New York: McGraw-Hill, 2004.

Stevenson, William, J. *Operations Management*, 11th ed. New York: McGraw-Hill/Irwin, 2011.

CHAPTER 14 LOGISTICS

Benton, W. C. *Purchasing and Supply Management*, 2nd ed. New York: McGraw-Hill/Irwin, 2009.

Christopher, Martin. *Logistics & Supply Chain Management: Creating Value-Adding Networks*, 4th ed. *Financial Times*, Prentice Hall, 2011.

Handfield, Robert, et al. *Supply Chain Redesign: Transforming Supply Chains into Integrated Value Systems*,1st ed. *Financial Times*, Prentice Hall, 2002.

Simchi-Levi, David. *Designing and Managing the Supply Chain*, 3rd ed. McGrawHill/Irwin, 2008.

CHAPTER 15 ADDING VALUE TO THE ORGANIZATION

Benton, W. C. *Purchasing and Supply Management*, 2nd ed. New York: McGraw-Hill/Irwin, 2009.

Burt, David, et al. *World Class Supply Management: The Key to Supply Chain Management*, 8th ed. New York: McGraw-Hill, 2009.

Leenders, Michiel, et al. *Purchasing & Supply Management*, 14th ed. New York: McGraw-Hill, 2010.

Nelson, Dave, et al. *The Purchasing Machine: How the Top Ten Companies Use Best Practices to Manage Their Supply Chains*. New York: Free Press, 2001.

CHAPTER 16 STRATEGIC PROCUREMENT PLANNING

Boone, Tonya, et al. *New Directions in Supply-Chain Management: Technology, Strategy and Implementation*. New York: AMACOM, 2002.

Cachon, Gerard. *Matching Supply with Demand: An Introduction to Operations Management*, 3rd ed. New York: McGraw-Hill/Irwin, 2012.

Chase, Richard. *Operations Management for Competitive Advantage*, 12th ed. New York: McGraw-Hill/Irwin, 2008.

Handfield, Robert, et al. *Supply Chain Redesign: Transforming Supply Chains into Integrated Value Systems*,1st ed. *Financial Times*, Prentice Hall, 2002.

Leenders, Michiel, et al. *Purchasing & Supply Management*, 14th ed. New York: McGraw-Hill, 2010.

Walker, William. *Supply Chain Architecture: A Blueprint for Networking the Flow of Material, Information and Cash*. Boca Raton: CRC Press, 2005.

CHAPTER 17 MANAGING THE PROCUREMENT ORGANIZATION

Benton, W. C. *Purchasing and Supply Management*, 2nd ed. New York: McGraw-Hill/Irwin, 2009.

Burt, David, et al. *World Class Supply Management: The Key to Supply Chain Management*, 8th ed. New York: McGraw-Hill, 2009.

Cavinato, Joseph, et al. T*he Purchasing Handbook: A Guide for the Purchasing and Supply Professional*, 6th ed. New York: McGraw-Hill, 2000.

Nelson, Dave, et al. *The Purchasing Machine: How the Top Ten Companies Use Best Practices to Manage Their Supply Chains*. New York: Free Press, 2001.

CHAPTER 18 MANAGING THE PROCUREMENT TEAM

Benton, W. C. *Purchasing and Supply Management*, 2nd ed. New York: McGraw-Hill/Irwin, 2009.

Cavinato, Joseph, et al. *The Purchasing Handbook: A Guide for the Purchasing and Supply Professional*, 6th ed. New York: McGraw-Hill, 2000.

Dessler, Gary. *Human Resource Management*, 12th ed. Upper Saddle River, NJ: Prentice Hall, 2010.

Leenders, Michiel, et al. *Purchasing & Supply Management*, 14th ed. New York: McGraw-Hill, 2010.

INDEX

NOTES

7/14/12 : what is project management?

- Process:
  - initiating
  - planning
  - executing
  - monitoring and controlling it
  - closing

- Knowledge areas:
  - integration
  - scope
  - cost
  - time
  - quality
  - procurement
  - human resource
  - communication
  - risk management

- what is project risk?
- process of risk management
  - what is likely to happen (or could happen)?
  - what can be done about it?
  - what are the warning signs? what are the likely outcomes?
- project risk
  - any possible event that can negatively affect
- project risk = (~~profitability~~ probability of event) (consequences of event)
  - Comprehensive Report Approach
    - risk management planning
    - risk identification

- Systematic Stages
  - Risk identification
- financial risk
  - financial exposure
  - technical Risk
    - unproven technology
  - Commercial Risk
    - market conditions
    - commercial success of product

- execution risk
  - poorly trained team manager

- contractual or legal Risk
  - cost plus terms, fixed cost, liquidated damages

NOTES

- Common types of Risk
  - resignation
  - staff pulled away
  - skills unavailable
  - ineffective training
  - initial specifications incomplete
  - time overruns
  - absenteeism
  - work or change orders multiply due to various problems

- Expert Opinion
  - Delphi Approach: collects and consolidates the judgement of isolated anonymous respondents
  - Experience Counts: simply identify and consult with people who have had similar experiences in running projects in the past

- Risk Mitigation Strategies
  - accept
  - minimize
  - share
  - transfer
  - mentoring
  - cross training
  - contingency reserves
    - task contingency
    - managerial contingency

NOTES

NOTES

NOTES

NOTES

NOTES

NOTES